VERY SPECIAL ADMIRAL

PATRICK BEESLY was born in 1913
and educated at Oundle School and Trinity
College, Cambridge. He joined the RNVR
in June 1939 and served in the Naval
Intelligence Division as deputy head of
the Submarine Tracking Room. Married
with two daughters, he is now retired and
lives in Lymington. His first book, *Very
Special Intelligence*, was widely acclaimed
and has also been published in the USA and
Germany. It is due to appear in the Soviet
Union in 1981.

By the same author

VERY SPECIAL INTELLIGENCE

PATRICK BEESLY

VERY SPECIAL
ADMIRAL

The Life of Admiral J. H. Godfrey, CB

WITH A FOREWORD BY
Captain S. W. Roskill
CBE, DSC, LITT.D, FBA, RN

HAMISH HAMILTON
North Pomfret, Vermont 05053

First published in Great Britain 1980
by Hamish Hamilton Ltd
Garden House, 57/59 Long Acre, London WC2E 9JZ

Copyright © 1980 by Patrick Beesly

British Library Cataloguing in Publication Data
Beesly, Patrick
Very special Admiral.
1. Godfrey, John
2. Admirals - Great Britain - Biography
1. Title
359.3'3'20924   DA89 . 1 G/
ISBN 0-241-10383-5

Printed in Great Britain by
WESTERN PRINTING SERVICES LTD
Bristol

CONTENTS

ILLUSTRATIONS

Between pages 166 and 167

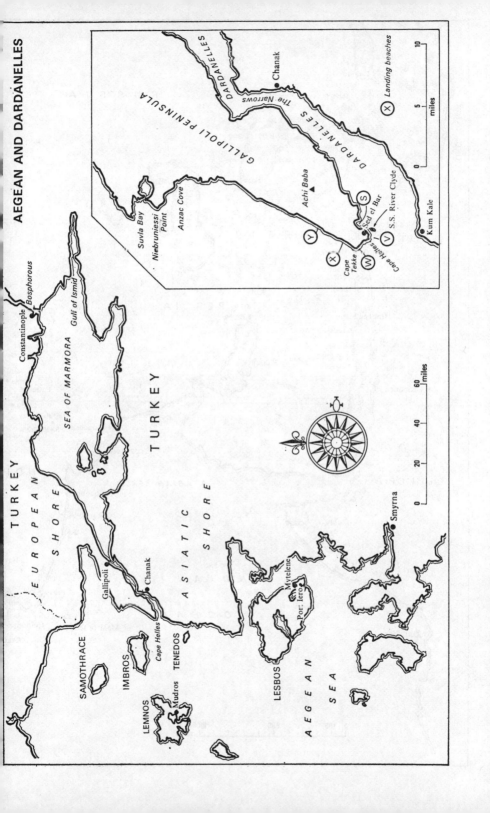

AEGEAN AND DARDANELLES

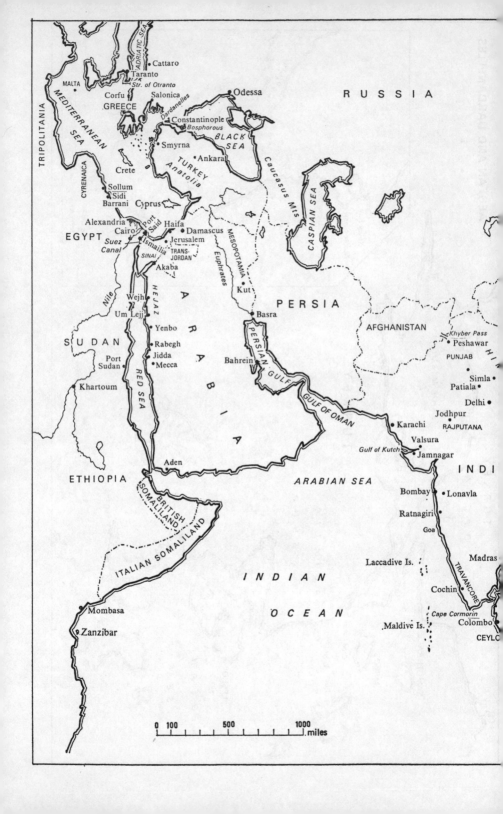

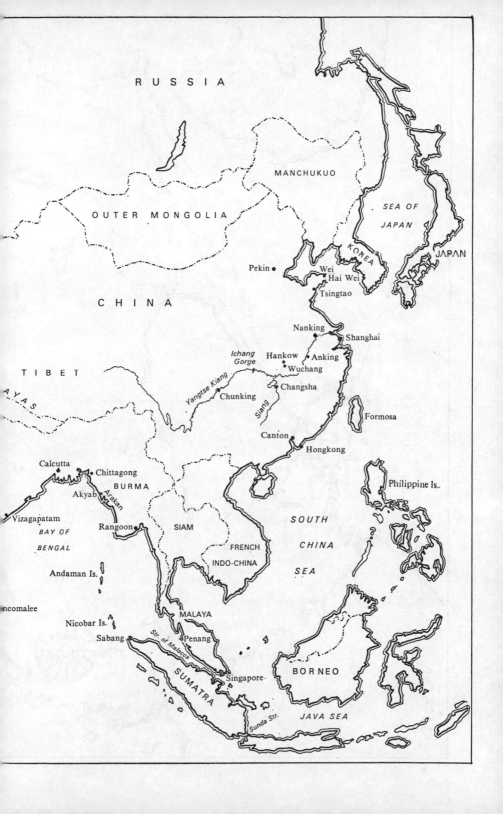

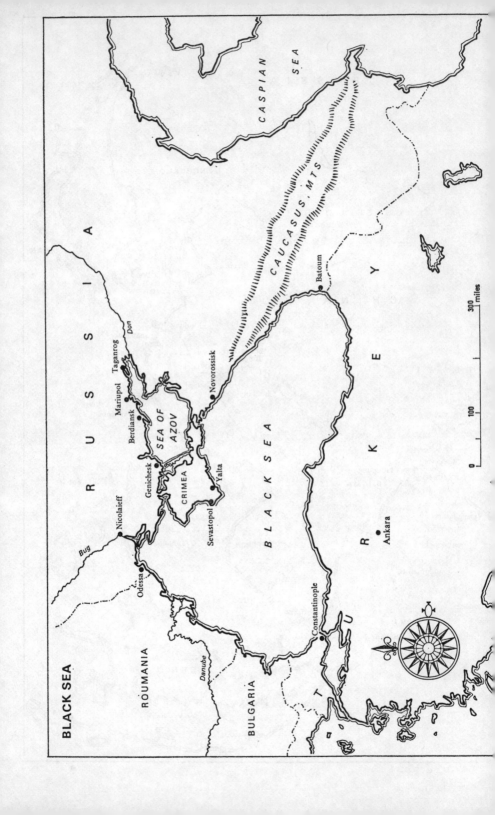

LIST OF ABBREVIATIONS

ADC	Aide de Camp
ADNI	Assistant Director of Naval Intelligence
ANA	Assistant Naval Attaché
APES	Advanced Planning (Enemy) Section
ARP	Air Raid Precautions
BAD	British Admiralty Delegation (Washington)
BBC	British Broadcasting Corporation
B.Dienst	German Naval Intelligence. *See also* xB Dienst
'C'	Head of the Secret Intelligence Service
Captain (D)	Captain of a Destroyer Flotilla
CB	Companion of the Order of the Bath
CGS	Chief of General Staff
CIA	Central Intelligence Agency
CIE	Commander of the Order of the Indian Empire
CIGS	Chief of Imperial General Staff
C-in-C	Commander-in-Chief
CO	Commanding Officer
DCNS	Deputy Chief of Naval Staff (title changed in 1940 to Vice-Chief of Naval Staff)
D-DAY	6 June 1944, Invasion of Normandy
DDNI	Deputy Director of Naval Intelligence
D/F	Direction Finding
DMI	Director of Military Intelligence
DNI	Director of Naval Intelligence
DSD	Director of Signal Division
EF	Eastern Fleet
EI	East Indies
FANY	First Aid Nursing Yeomanry
FECB	Far East Combined Bureau
FOCRIN	Flag Officer Commanding Royal Indian Navy
FOES	Future Operations (Enemy) Section
GC & CS	Government Code and Cypher School
GHQ	General Headquarters
GOC	General Officer Commanding
GSO	General Staff Officer

HMAS	His Majesty's Australian Ship
HMS	His (or Her) Majesty's Ship
HO	Hostilities Only
HQ	Headquarters
IAF	Indian Air Force
ISTD	Inter Service Topographical Department
JIC	Joint Intelligence Committee
JIS	Joint Intelligence Staff
KBE	Knight Commander of the Order of the British Empire
KCB	Knight Commander of the Bath
KCIE	Knight Commander of the Order of the Indian Empire
KCSI	Knight Commander of the Star of India
KI and II	Kitchener's First and Second Volunteer Armies in World War I
MEW	Ministry of Economic Warfare
MI5	Department 5, Military Intelligence, dealing with security and counter-intelligence
MI6	Secret Intelligence Service
NA	Naval Attaché
NAAFI	Navy, Army and Air Force Institute
NHQ	Naval Headquarters
NID	Naval Intelligence Division
OBE	Order of the British Empire
OIC	Operational Intelligence Centre, Section 8 of Naval Intelligence Division
ONI	Office of Naval Intelligence
OSS	Office of Strategic Services
OUP	Oxford University Press
PA	Personal Assistant
PMO	Principal Medical Officer of a warship
PRU	Photographic Reconnaissance Unit (of RAF)
PSC	Passed Staff Course
PSV	Private Secretary to the Viceroy
PWE	Political Warfare Executive
RAF	Royal Air Force
RIAF	Royal Indian Air Force
RIASC	Royal Indian Army Service Corps
RIM	Royal Indian Marine
RIN	Royal Indian Navy

RINR	Royal Indian Naval Reserve
RINVR	Royal Indian Naval Volunteer Reserve
RM	Royal Marines
RN	Royal Navy
RNR	Royal Naval Reserve
RNVR	Royal Naval Volunteer Reserve
RNVR(A)	Royal Naval Volunteer Reserve (Air)
SIS	Secret Intelligence Service
SNO	Senior Naval Officer
SNPE	Summary of Naval and Political Events
SOE	Special Operations Executive
UK	United Kingdom
USN	United States Navy
VCNS	Vice Chief of Naval Staff (*see* DCNS)
VCO	Viceroy's Indian Commissioned Officer
WAAF	Womens' Auxiliary Air Force
WAC(I)	Womens' Auxiliary Corps (India)
WIR	Weekly Intelligence Report
WRINS	Womens' Royal Indian Naval Service
WRNS	Womens' Royal Naval Service
WSC	Winston Spencer Churchill
W/T	Wireless Telegraphy
WVS	Women's Voluntary Service
xB Dienst	Cryptanalysis Section of German Naval Intelligence
'Y'	Interception of enemy wireless signals

FOREWORD

by Captain Stephen Roskill,

CBE, DSC, LITT.D, FBA, RN

IT WAS in 1936 that, as Patrick Beesly here records, I first met
the future Admiral John Godfrey, then Captain of the battlecruiser *Repulse*. But he does not tell how that encounter came
about, and as it is revealing about Godfrey's character and
tastes I take this opportunity to recount it. My wife and I had
been supping on board the yacht which that delightful and
piratical character Mike Cumberlege and his enchanting young
wife Nan had just brought into Grand Harbour, Malta. After
the meal, Mike suddenly said, 'Let's go and visit John Godfrey.'
I was a little alarmed because most Post Captains of those times
did not take kindly to visits by uninvited and unknown junior
officers. However, Mike persisted, and so I found myself in the
presence of a very impressive, slightly daunting but obviously
highly intelligent officer. That visit taught me two things about
John. The first was that, as the furnishing and fittings of his big
day cabin made plain, he had excellent and unusual taste and
was a very cultured man, while the second was that his friendship with Mike demonstrated his liking for unorthodox and
original characters. Though I kept in touch with Mike and Nan
until shortly before Mike was captured by the Germans in a
madcap attempt to block the Corinth Canal after the fall of
Greece in 1941, and was I believe tortured to death by the
Gestapo, I did not see much of Godfrey until early 1939 when
I joined the Naval Staff as a very junior Commander and he
was Director of Intelligence. His office and those of many of his
Sections were in the same part of the building as mine, so if we
were enjoying a quiet spell late at night (which was unusual
while Churchill was First Lord) I used sometimes to drop in and
discuss current problems with the brilliant band whom Godfrey
had recruited from a vast and disparate number of sources.
Later on many of those contacts proved very valuable to me. It
was then that I gradually became aware of the scope and scale
of Godfrey's achievements as DNI, and also of his occasional

exhibition of regrettably bad temper—some instances of which Beesly mentions. Of course we were all working under very severe strain in those early months of the war, when the consequences of the deficiencies from which the navy suffered in every field came home to roost. No one probably suffered worse from that state of affairs than Godfrey, and I hold that one of the most unhappy results of Churchill's long period of exile in the political wilderness was that when he returned to the Admiralty he simply did not understand what the effects of twenty years of cheese paring had been. Thus he often demanded the impossible, and if one tried to explain why that was so a torrent of abuse and accusations of 'obstructionism' usually descended on one's head. Some quite senior members of the staff quickly found themselves, quite unjustly 'Stellenbosched' —to use a metaphor from an earlier war. I am sure that Godfrey came in for more than his share of such encounters, since Intelligence had been one of the Cinderellas of the naval service in peace time, and he had to make bricks with little or no straw to bind together the clay of his requirements. Beesly makes all these troubles admirably clear, though my own view is that Godfrey was a more highly-strung and complex character than he makes out, and his nerves were sometimes stretched beyond breaking point—which made him unnecessarily combative and so created enemies.

I was at sea from the autumn of 1941 to early in 1944 so did not learn of Godfrey's dismissal from NID in September 1942 until much later, by which time the dust had subsided and victory was in prospect—which of course made the work of his successor vastly easier. That it was largely Godfrey who was responsible for the successes accomplished by NID after 1942 is now as plain as the fact that the treatment meted out to him, was as harsh as the repudiation of the promise of a sea command made to him earlier was regrettable.

In 1946 I led the British Joint Services team to the atomic bomb trials at Bikini in the Pacific, and when I returned home and settled down to get our report to the Chiefs of Staff dealing with the effects of nuclear fission on all aspects of maritime war ready for printing, I found myself working in a basement room in the Admiralty's 'citadel' next door to that in which Godfrey was writing the Monographs dealing with the wartime work of NID—to which Beesly has, quite incomprehensibly, been denied access. Though I was trying to gaze into the crystal ball of the future and Godfrey was recording the lessons of the past, we often exchanged thoughts and ideas. That process developed further when Admiral W. E. Parry invited me to leave my basement room and become one of his two Deputies in NID; and when in 1948 the first serious trouble with the USSR arose and we had to reconstruct and re-orientate the NID's organisation (which had been almost wholly demolished as soon as the guns stopped firing), it was natural that we should turn to Godfrey and his former colleagues and associates for help and advice—which was given unstintingly. It was then that Godfrey invited me to join the 'Number 36 Club' (named after his wartime flat in Curzon Street) where I could meet his former staff and exploit their experience freely.

I knew very little about Godfrey's final naval appointment as Flag Officer Commanding the Royal Indian Navy, except that it ended tragically in the mutiny of 1946, until I read Beesly's account of how he tackled a most difficult assignment; but I thought at the time and still think that the fact that he was the only Admiral who received absolutely no recognition for his wartime service was a disgraceful act of prejudice.

Beesly's book is in fact much more than a straightforward biography of John Godfrey; for it is virtually two histories within one cover. The first is that of the wartime Naval Intelligence Division, of its early trials and failures, and of the men and women who made its ultimate remarkable successes possible; while the second is that of the Royal Indian Navy from its remote beginnings through its fine contribution to the victory of 1945 to its dissolution with the partition of the subcontinent.

Finally I would say that it was in my view entirely typical of the man whose life-work Beesly here describes, that not only did he never make any complaint about the harsh way he was treated but that in his retirement he should have devoted most of his gifts and energy to work as Chairman of the Management Committee of the Chelsea Group of Hospitals and to founding the renowned Cheyne Centre for spastic children.

Though some well-informed readers will probably disagree with Beesly on certain controversial points, to me it is clear that he has produced a valuable contribution to two of the less well-known aspects of the history of the Second World War, as well as an absorbing study of a most unusual naval officer.

PREFACE

THIS IS the story of a very unusual sailor; of an intellectual in a Service which, in Captain Roskill's words, 'has by no means always regarded such men favourably'; of an officer from a family with no naval connections who rose to the rank of full Admiral but was nevertheless the only officer of that rank to receive no official recognition of his wartime services; of a fine seaman who longed to 'fly his flag' at sea but never did so; of a Director of Naval Intelligence who was as great as, if not greater than, the legendary Blinker Hall, but was 'sacked' by Sir Dudley Pound just when all his work was beginning to bear fruit; of one of the earliest and most ardent advocates of inter-Service co-operation in the Intelligence field whose Army and Air Force colleagues finally declared that they could not work with him; of the head of the Royal Indian Navy who, devoid of racial prejudice and full of admiration for India and the Indians, could not prevent the post-war mutiny of the Service whose expansion and well-being he had done more than any other man to foster.

The paradoxes and contradictions of John Godfrey's career were only equalled by the quirks and complexities of his character; ambitious, extremely able, physically and mentally resilient, he was shy and suffered from an inferiority complex; liberal minded, forward looking and capable of many acts of personal kindness and thoughtfulness, he was also ruthless and sometimes selfish; inspiring general admiration, much loyalty and often affection, he could equally arouse antagonism, jealousy, even dislike; a charming host and a good listener, he did not suffer fools gladly and made little attempt to conceal his contempt for colleagues of lesser mental calibre; an excellent chooser of men, fiercely loyal to his subordinates, he was sometimes naïve about his superiors; a superb organiser of the devious and unscrupulous art of Intelligence, he was a man of great moral courage, who refused to depart from the very high standards he had set himself and his Division and so fell foul of Churchill, Pound and Alanbrooke; a man with a marked talent for securing help from important and influential people for any project he had in hand, he was unable or unwilling to use that talent for his own personal advantage.

His greatest achievement was undoubtedly to revive the Naval Intelligence Division between 1939 and 1943; to adapt Pitt's phrase, he saved Naval Intelligence by his exertions and Allied Intelligence as a whole by his example.

I must disclose an 'interest'. I was a small boy when, shortly after his marriage to my cousin Margaret Hope, I first met John Godfrey. From that time onwards he showed me much kindness. He encouraged my childish ambition to join the Royal Navy and, when that came to nothing because of short sight, subsequently did all he could to help me gain a commission in the RNVR. I served under him for three years in the Naval Intelligence Division and although, as a very junior officer, I was aware of only a fraction of his tremendous work, I was very conscious of the splendid spirit and feeling of pride with which he imbued us all and of the universal sense of loss we experienced when he departed. His kindness to me did not cease then and, after the war, when the difference in our ages grew less important, I like to think that I became a friend. Certainly my small daughters regarded him as one; 'Oh, you mean our friend John' they proudly said when someone referred to the Admiral. I may therefore be accused of partiality. I have however tried to bring to life, warts and all, a man to whom his countrymen owe an immense and hitherto largely unrecognised debt.

I have wanted to write this book for a long time, but it was only after the publication in 1977 of my account of the Admiralty's Operational Intelligence Centre, *Very Special Intelligence*, that I summoned up the courage to ask Margaret Godfrey to allow me to do so. I must thank her not only for agreeing but for giving me so much help and full access to all her husband's papers. She has imposed no conditions and I must make it clear that neither she nor any of the many other people I have consulted should be held responsible, unless opinions are specifically attributed to them, for any of the views expressed, which are mine alone.

It would not be quite true to say that Godfrey is entirely unknown to the general public. The late Donald McLachlan's classic book, *Room 39*, gives a splendid account of Naval

Intelligence in action and has much to say about the DNI.
But McLachlan was writing about the Division as a whole,
about its achievements not only during but also after Godfrey's
tenure of office, about an organisation rather than an individual.
Moreover, although he too had access to Godfrey's papers and
was able to discuss each chapter as he wrote it with Godfrey,
this was a mixed blessing. Godfrey was a most modest man,
totally opposed to anything which might savour of self-
glorification. McLachlan had to omit much that I have felt
free to include. McLachlan in fact saw papers which I did not;
he had access to the secret Monographs on Naval Intelligence
which Godfrey, at official request, wrote after the war. These I
have not been permitted to examine, although I understand
that they are likely to be declassified in the near future. However, when McLachlan wrote security restrictions had not been
relaxed so that the privilege accorded him was of doubtful
value. Nearly half my book is devoted to Godfrey's period as
DNI, but that period occupied only four of the forty-three
years of his naval service and it must be studied in the light of
his career before and after, a career which I hope the reader will
find as fascinating as I have done.

In 1963, in response to many requests, Godfrey began to
write his 'Naval Memoirs'. He did so for the benefit of his
friends and family and in the hopes that they might provide, as
he said, "heaps of constructional material for which some
builder-historian may find a use". Although he refused to
consider general publication he did send copies of the eight
volumes of typescript to selected friends, to the editor of *The
Naval Review*, of which he was a member for nearly sixty years,
to the Admiralty Library and to the National Maritime
Museum at Greenwich. The author and critic William Plomer,
who had served in NID under Godfrey, wrote an Epilogue to
them in which he said: 'Among other traits one notices especially a decent reticence, and a complete freedom from the vanity,
peevishness and self-justification which mar certain books by
men who, like himself, held important posts during the War.
His equilibrium is reflected in the uncommon clarity, accuracy
and sobriety of his way of writing, which seems exactly to
convey his thoughts. They are the thoughts of a man who
knows what he is talking about, and whose professionalism has
never been narrow.' On the other hand the Memoirs are very

long and although I have quoted extensively from them there is much I have had to omit. Moreoever they are sometimes a little discursive and disjointed, occasionally repeating in slightly different words an account of an episode already given earlier. I have, therefore, had to do a certain amount of 'editing', combining excerpts from them with quotations from his private and official correspondence in the interests of clarity and chronology. I have never knowingly distorted his meaning and have never attributed words to him which he did not write.

Because few of the Naval Intelligence records containing secret information (apart from the highly valuable German Naval decrypts), have so far been released to the Public Record Office, Godfrey's own papers have been my main written source, but he was a scrupulously truthful and accurate man whose excellent memory had been refreshed when he wrote the Monographs after the war. I do not think, therefore, that the official records, when they are declassified, will contradict his account in any major respect, although they will no doubt add to it. The first volume of Professor Hinsley's great work, *British Intelligence in the Second World War* (ending in mid 1941), appeared just as I was completing this typescript. It deliberately eschews personalities and neither Godfrey's name nor that of any other leading figure in the wartime Intelligence world even appears in the index. This, I feel, is a pity since history, after all, is made by people, people whose human strengths and weaknesses shape events. The written records sometimes conceal as much as they reveal. Reading between the lines, however, I think that the official history does not invalidate the account I have given.

Practically nothing, so far as I know, has been published about the Royal Indian Navy, but fortunately for me Godfrey's surviving official and private papers are voluminous. Here, too, I have had to omit much that I would like to have included. The RIN was a very fine service, whose achievements, like those of the Admiral who commanded it, deserve much wider recognition.

I have endeavoured to check and expand Godfrey's own account of his life by interviews and correspondence with as many of those who knew him as I have been able to trace. Sadly, but inevitably, most of his contemporaries are now dead or understandably reluctant to wrack their memories for details of events which happened forty or more years ago. Fortunately there are still a number of people who, in one capacity or another, knew Godfrey and who have replied with great courtesy and patience to my questions. Without their help I could not have written this book or have formed a balanced picture of the man himself. I hope they will accept my very sincere thanks and will forgive me if, in a few cases, I have not felt able to agree with the views they expressed. It would be invidious to single out any one person but I should like to record my debt to:

P. G. Alexiades, Esq
Mrs Philip Astley
Captain A. J. Baker Cresswell, DSO, RN
Commander Patrick Barrow-Green, RN
Captain S. Barry, RN
Rear-Admiral Stuart Bateson, CB, CBE
Lord William Bentinck, CMG
Rear-Admiral R. S. Braine, CB
Vice-Admiral Sir Ronald Brockman, KCB, CSI
Sir George Bull, Bart
W. Mayne Butcher, Esq
Vice-Admiral Sir Ian Campbell, KBE, CB, DSO
Sir Christopher Chancellor, KCMG
Lady Chancellor
Admiral A. L. Chattergi, Indian Navy
M. Davenport, Esq
Captain Henry Denham, CMG, RN
The late Vice-Admiral Sir Norman Denning, KBE, CB
Captain Charles Drake, RN
Commander W. A. Dunderdale, CMG, CBE, RNVR
Admiral Sir Robert Durnford-Slater, KCB
Vice-Admiral Sir Robert Elkins, KCB
Charles Fletcher-Cooke, Esq, QC, MP
The Lord Gladwyn, GCMG, GCVO, CB
Captain K. L. Harkness, CBE, DSC, RN
Robert Harling, Esq
Dan. G. Harris, Esq
Michael Hope, Esq
Lt General Sir Ian Jacob, GBE, CB, DC
Sir Clifford Jarrett, KBE

Lt Commander Peter Kemp, OBE, RN
Professor John Kinmonth, MS, FRCS
Sir Gilbert Laithwaite, GCMG, KCB, KCIE, CSI
Major General C. R. W. Lamplough, CBE, DSC, JP, RM
Sir John Lang, GCB
The late Commodore John Lawrence, CBE, RIN
Lt Colonel W. W. Leary, BEM, Intelligence Corps
Commander Sir Clive Loehnis, KCMG, RN
Rt Hon Lord Longford, KG, PC
Professor Arthur J. Marder
Philip Mason, Esq, CIE, OBE
Admiral Sir Geoffrey Miles, KCB, KCSI
G. H. Millis, Esq, DSO, MC
The Hon Ewen Montagu, CBE, QC, DC
The late Admiral of the Fleet the Earl Mountbatten of Burma,
    KG, PC, GCB, OM, GCSIE, GCVO, DSO
Commander R. W. Pearce, RN
Mrs Mary Pearce
The late Admiral Sir Arthur Peters, KCB, DSO
Colonel Humphrey Quill, CBE, DSO, MVO, RM
Captain Stephen Roskill, CBE, DSC, LITT.D, FBA, RN
Mrs J. St G. Saunders
Lt Commander Tom Sheppard, RIN
Captain W. W. Sheppard, OBE, RN
Mrs Charles Simms
Mrs Peggy Skipwith
Sir Peter Smithers, VRD, D.PHIL
David Sweet-Escott, Esq
Captain S. J. Thomson, CIE, RIN
Captain D. A. Wilson, CBE, RN
The late Captain F. J. Wylie, CBE, RN

I am also grateful to David Higham Associates Ltd for permission to quote from David Dilks' *The Cadogan Diaries* and Sir Kenneth Strong's *Men of Intelligence*; to William Collins & Co. Ltd for quotations from S. Roskill's *Churchill and the Admirals*; to Peter Davies Ltd for quotations from Ewen Montagu's *Beyond Top Secret U*; to Her Majesty's Stationery Office for quotations from *The Strategic Air Offensive Against Germany* and from S. W. Roskill's *War at Sea*; to The Oxford University Press for quotations from A. J. Marder's *From the Dreadnought* to *Scapa Flow*; and to Weidenfeld & Nicolson for quotations from Donald McLachlan's *Room 39*.

Once again I am most grateful to Mrs Mary Pain for her skill in tracking down documents in the Public Record Office. I owe very special thanks to Annaliese Hamilton, who, with unfailing charm, has somehow managed to transform my appalling typescript into a text which I could submit to my publishers.

CHAPTER ONE

Edwardian Cadet

WHEN JOHN GODFREY was born in 1888 there were, in his words, "many people living who had seen and even talked to Napoleon, Nelson, Talleyrand and Wellington". When he died in 1971 man had already landed on the moon, "a period which historians writing in the year 2000 are almost bound to single out as one of the most remarkable in the recorded history of mankind". In his youth the British Empire covered one-third of the globe. The great powers were Britain, Imperial Germany, Czarist Russia, and France with a colonial empire second only to Britain's. Japan had only just emerged from medievalism and the United States, still relying on the Monroe doctrine and the Royal Navy, remained preoccupied with its own internal affairs. By the time he was thirty Godfrey had seen the collapse of five ancient Empires, the Chinese, Russian, Austro-Hungarian, Turkish and German. Before he reached sixty the Third Reich and the Japanese Empire had mushroomed up and disintegrated, Britain and France had become second-class powers and the world scene was dominated by the two giants, Russia and America. For eleven of the forty-three years of his Service career Great Britain was fighting for her existence and the magnitude of the political, social and technological changes which occurred during that time is now strangely hard to comprehend.

The Royal Navy which he joined as a cadet in 1903 had not fought a major action since the Battle of Navarino in 1827, when a combined Anglo-French-Russian fleet destroyed the Turkish-Egyptian forces. There had been the Crimean War and many scares of war with France, but in general Britannia's supremacy had been unchallenged, and the Navy's tasks had consisted in 'showing the Flag', suppressing piracy and the slave trade, assisting the British Army in colonial wars and in giving help to all and sundry in cases of natural disaster. Its ships were the last word in smartness, its seamen the best in the world, its size formidable, and its traditions and reputation without equal. It was, nevertheless, something of a whited sepulchre. Professor Marder describes it as 'having run in a rut for nearly a century. Though numerically a very imposing force, it was in certain respects a drowsy, inefficient, moth-eaten organization.' In 1903 all this was beginning to change, and to change with dramatic speed. On Trafalgar Day that year Admiral 'Jacky' Fisher hoisted his flag as Commander-in-Chief Portsmouth and a year later he became First Sea Lord. When he himself had joined the Navy in 1854, his Commander-in-Chief at Plymouth had been Sir Peter Parker, one of the last of Nelson's captains. Fisher, like all of his contemporaries and, indeed, most of the captains and commanders in the Edwardian Navy, had been brought up in sail. But Fisher, unlike many who considered that what had been 'good enough for Nelson was good enough for them', saw the pressing need for far-reaching, radical and immediate change. A new and highly efficient enemy could now be discerned across the North Sea, or German Ocean as it was not inappropriately called. The Kaiser's Hoch See Flotte, unhampered by out-of-date and largely misunderstood tradition, was becoming a threat which could not be ignored. In six years Fisher transformed the Navy. He acted 'Ruthlessly, Relentlessly and Remorselessly'. Old ships, which could neither fight nor run away, were scrapped; the new all big gun *Dreadnought* was built, rendering at a stroke all previous battleships obsolete; gunnery was improved out of all recognition and effective ranges went up from 2000 to 16,000 yards. The Fleet was concentrated in Home waters; a new scheme of entry for officers was introduced and the old *Britannia* replaced by colleges ashore at Osborne and Dartmouth; pay and conditions of the Lower Deck were improved; the infant submarine and aircraft branches of the Service were developed; wireless telegraphy was introduced. When the acid test came in 1914 the Royal Navy, despite some continuing weaknesses, notably the lack of any proper Naval Staff, was ready to play a decisive part in the total defeat of Imperial Germany. The abject surrender of the Hoch See Flotte at Scapa Flow in 1918 could not have been achieved without Fisher. He had been, in Marder's words, 'A tornado of energy, enthusiasm, and persuasive power, a man of originality, vision, and courage, a sworn foe of all outworn traditions and customs, the greatest of British naval administrators since St Vincent'.

This tremendous revolution was not accomplished without casualties. Fisher made many enemies and has frequently been accused of splitting the Navy into two camps, of destroying Nelson's concept of a 'band of brothers'. But Fisher knew what had to be done and how little time there was in which to do it. He was convinced that the forces of prejudice, conservatism, indolence and ignorance would not be overcome by compromise and kindness. The Navy was sick and only drastic methods could cure it. The medicine may have been unpleasant but it was both necessary and effective.

In 1903, however, most of this was still to come and life for Edwardian naval cadets and midshipmen would not have seemed so very strange to their forbears one hundred years earlier. Officers were still drawn from a very restricted social class. Although never a very snobbish Service in the way that fashionable Army regiments were, naval officers mostly came from upper-middle-class homes. A few were the younger sons of the aristocracy, but the majority were the offsprings, as they had been in Nelson's day, of country squires, parsons and professional men, or of officers of the Army or Navy. They considered themselves 'gentlemen' and 'gentlemen' looked down on 'trade' or 'industry', an attitude which was to linger on for many years to come. John Godfrey did not have this conventional background. He had been born in Handsworth, at that time a pleasant and expanding suburb of Joseph and Arthur Chamberlains' bustling, booming Birmingham. His father was Secretary of a small company, Mapplebecks and Wilkes, and seems to have been a rather colourless character. His mother, by contrast, was a very strong personality, an ardent Anglo-Catholic and a passionate imperialist. Their youngest child was christened John Henry, after Cardinal Newman, and much of the Godfrey parents' spare time was taken up with Church matters and the discussion of such esoteric subjects as whether the Blessing should be pronounced with three or only two fingers extended. The family was, however, a highly intelligent and cultured one. Charlie, the eldest son and fifteen years older than John, was a brilliant mathematician. A Wrangler of Trinity College, Cambridge, he became senior maths master at Winchester and revolutionised the teaching of the subject, producing, in co-operation with his fellow master Bell and Siddons of Harrow, text books which were to remain the standard ones in universal use for forty years. He subsequently became headmaster of Osborne and then Professor of Higher Mathematics at the Naval College, Greenwich. Harold, eight years John's senior, was a talented musician and studied the organ under Parrott at Windsor. He died of enteric fever contracted while serving with Kitchener's Horse in the Boer War. Marjorie, the third child, was artistic and much influenced by William Morris. During World War I she studied at Queen Charlotte's Hospital and took up maternity nursing as a qualified midwife. John himself shared to a greater or lesser extent all these interests. He too was good at maths, had a love of music and art and in his retirement was to devote himself with great success to hospital administration and the founding of the pioneering Cheyne Spastic Centre. At the age of ten, he tells us, he had already read *Comparative Religion* by Rhys Davies which opened his eyes "to the oneness of Buddhism, Christianity and the doctrine of Mohammed", a view which he sensibly kept to himself so as not to grieve his devout parents.

Like his brothers before him he went as a day boy to King Edward's Grammar School, an institution almost as renowned as that in Manchester. In 1901, presumably at Charlie's instigation, he sat for a scholarship to Winchester, but, although he did well in Maths and Latin, he failed rather ignominiously because, surprisingly, he had not been taught English or English Literature at King Edward's. Some time previously Harold had become very interested in everything to do with the sea as a result of a trip to New Zealand and had fired his mother with his own enthusiasm. She and Charlie now decided that John should become a naval officer. He himself was not consulted. Had he been asked if the idea of a life on the ocean wave would appeal to him he tells us he would probably have replied "No", but the die was cast and he was sent for two terms as boarder to Bradfield, which specialised in preparing a few boys for the Navy. He sat the examination for a Naval Cadetship in November 1902 and much to everyone's surprise passed fifteenth out of two hundred-odd applicants.

The January 1903 term was one of the last to join *Britannia* rather than go to Osborne and then Dartmouth. The establishment consisted of two old wooden three-deckers, *Britannia* and *Hindustan*, moored bow to stern in the Dart opposite where the new college was being built. Although conditions were in some respects fairly primitive (*Britannia*'s 'heads' discharged over her bows from where the water was drawn for the communal bathroom in *Hindustan*'s stern, which resulted in constant impetigo epidemics among the cadets), the regime was on the whole an enlightened one and compared favourably with that of most boys' public schools of the time. Only a few of the cadets came from Bradfield, the majority having attended the two famous naval crammers, Stubbingtons and Littlejohns. John therefore had few ready-made friends and his Birmingham background and natural shyness cannot have made the first few weeks easy. He had little taste for competitive games, but these were not compulsory and he enjoyed the pulling whalers and sailing cutters, beagling, walking and the gymnasium. Above all he found the new subjects with which he was confronted, seamanship, spherical trigonometry, elementary navigation and the sciences "absorbingly interesting". He also liked singing in the choir. Although no extrovert he obviously soon began to enjoy his new life and formed friendships with youngsters whose names were later to become household words, for many of his generation were to hold high commands in World War II. Bobbie Harwood, victor of the River Plate, and Tom Phillips, lost with *Prince of Wales*, were among his friends.

The year in *Britannia* passed quickly and was followed by three months, still as a cadet, in a training cruiser, with trips to Vigo and Arosa Bay in the north of Spain, to Gibraltar and Madeira and to the West Indies. On 15 May 1904 he joined the battleship *Prince George* and at the end of that month, six weeks before his sixteenth birthday, received his promotion to midshipman. He spent the next three years in the battleships *Majestic*, *Ceasar* and *Exmouth*. Life in their gunrooms was less supervised and regulated than it had been in *Britannia* and much depended on the sub-lieutenant or senior midshipman. In *Majestic* John suffered under a sadistic sub-lieutenant who rewarded the slightest real or imaginary peccadillo with up to twenty-four cuts with a piece of flexible rhinoceros hide and terrorised all his juniors. He must have been an extraordinary as well as a very unpleasant character. He could never resist a bet and, on being challenged to cut off his finger, and a meat chopper being handy, he promptly did so on the gunroom table and thereafter wore a silver thimble. He deserted in New

York a little later and was last seen driving a taxi! No wonder Godfrey always maintained that Charles Morgan's controversial book, *The Gunroom*, was in no respect exaggerated. In 1906 one junior midshipman became so enraged by this sort of treatment that he got hold of a pistol and shot his tormentor in the leg. There was a great scandal and finally an Admiralty instruction was issued to the effect that a senior executive officer was to be detailed in every ship to look after the midshipmen. They very soon became known as the 'Snotties' nurse' and there was a general improvement all round. On the whole, however, midshipmen enjoyed themselves in the same carefree way that Mr Midshipman Easy had done one hundred years before, and John was no exception. The emphasis was all on seamanship, gained by taking charge of one of the ship's boats, which under sail or oar maintained communications with the shore in harbour and provided the duty sea boats, ready to rescue a man overboard, when at sea. When cruising off the north of Spain the Fleet was supplied with fresh meat from cattle on the hoof, driven down to the nearest jetty, slaughtered there, and then shipped off in the ships' cutters and whalers, as had been done for the past two hundred years. The use of steam picket boats was frowned on and the rougher the sea the better the training for the 'young gentlemen'. Their education and instruction in technical subjects varied greatly from ship to ship, but in some, *Majestic* for one, it was largely neglected and at the best haphazard. Godfrey records that when the yearly examinations came along the "first subject was gunnery. A glance at the paper showed that it dealt with a variety of subjects with which we were unfamiliar, but a copy of the exam paper had in the meantime been smuggled out to the gunnery lieutenant and a quarter of an hour later a paper giving the correct answers fluttered down through the skylight. When the results came out *Majestic*'s midshipmen did very well. Cribbing in such a wholehearted way, with the acquiescence and indeed the active collaboration of the invigilator, ceased to be wrong, but the end result of all this neglect was that we attained the rank of sub-lieutenant ill equipped to perform our duties. No one seemed to mind."

John was appointed acting Sub-Lieutenant in July 1907 and promoted Sub-Lieutenant on 1 May 1908 after the usual courses at Portsmouth and Greenwich in gunnery, torpedoes, pilotage and navigation. In February 1909 he joined the destroyer *Welland* as her Executive Officer. *Welland* was one of 1st Flotilla of the Home Fleet, based on Harwich and Felixstowe. Although only four years old, she was a small ship, 225 feet in length and of 550 tons displacement. Her coal-fired reciprocating engines gave her a top speed of just over twenty-five knots and she carried four small guns and two torpedo tubes. Into her were crammed a crew of seventy-five men with two officers, Lieutenant 'Snatcher' Stirling in command, the Sub, Godfrey, and two Warrant Officers as Gunner and Engineer. Tension with Germany was mounting and both Admiralties were obsessed with the fear of a surprise pre-emptive attack by the other on the lines of the British at Copenhagen in 1808 or the Japanese more recently at Port Arthur in 1904. The Eastern Destroyer Group, of which the 1st Flotilla formed a part, was virtually on a war footing pointing, in its senior officer's words, like a pistol at the heart of Germany. "Life", according to Godfrey, "was very strenuous, two or three weeks of continual seatime from Monday morning to Thursday evening, patrolling all night and in all weathers between the Sunk and the Outer Gabbard lightships across the mouth of the Thames, followed by a week in harbour devoted to harbour drills". It was magnificent experience and Godfrey was fortunate that from the outset his captain frequently left him on his own in full control on the bridge to take whatever action was necessary. It was very far removed from the carefree existence of a battleship's snotty.

After six months as 'number one' of a destroyer in which one could get to know every member of the crew individually, Godfrey found that "there was a strong temptation to accept this way of life with its associations in preference to the more academic and technical career of a specialist". Nevertheless, specialisation was the way to advancement and he decided that he would specialise in navigation, which he considered as an "extension of seamanship and an introduction to staff work", rather than in the more material fields of gunnery, torpedo-electrics, or submarines which attracted the majority of his contemporaries. He had been promoted Lieutenant in July with seniority backdated to October the previous year as a result of obtaining five first class certificates in the qualifying examination, and despite the fact that he only got a second class in the sixth subject, navigation, was accepted for the five month course in the Navigation School, HMS *Dryad*, at the beginning of August 1909. He completed this and six months' seatime successfully and was then asked what appointment he would prefer. He tells us that "in 1909 war with Germany, although imminent, did not seem so close as to preclude the possibility of a light-hearted commission on some far distant station. For many years I had followed in the papers the progress of events in China and India and had conceived a strong desire to visit those countries and penetrate as far as possible into their interiors." He therefore applied for an appointment as navigating officer of one of the fleet of gunboats which Britain, in common with most of the major naval powers, maintained in China. In June 1910 he was duly appointed to HMS *Bramble*, a twelve-year-old first class sea-going gunboat of 710 tons on the China Station.

China in 1910 was on the eve of revolution. Although the vast country had been pacified after the anti-European Boxer revolt ten years previously, the ancient, ramshackle Manchu Empire was tottering and was in fact only held together by foreign loans. The sole security for these loans was provided by the Chinese Imperial Maritime Customs Service, under Sir Robert Hart, who held the post from 1863 until his death in 1911. This highly efficient service, largely British staffed, collected revenue at the thirty-two so-called Treaty Ports and was responsible for posts and telegraphs, lighthouses, buoyage, pilotage and river conservancy on the many thousands of miles of China's coastline and up and down her mighty rivers. European, American and Japanese firms carried out their trading operations from 'Concessions' in the ports and big cities, enjoying extra-territorial rights with their own courts presided over by their consuls. It was largely to protect these interests and to support the Customs Service that the Great Powers maintained their China Fleets and squadrons of gunboats.

The biggest of all China's rivers is the Yangtse Kiang, navigable for more than two and a half thousand miles from Shanghai to Nanking, Hankow and then through the Ichang gorges on to Chunking and beyond, right into the very heart of China. The gunboats were commanded by lieutenants with one or at the most three other commissioned officers and mixed

British and locally recruited Chinese crews of thirty to sixty. Until 1911 none of them was fitted with wireless, so, once away from the Commander-in-Chief at Shanghai or Hankow (the highest point which cruisers could reach), the young officers were entirely on their own. They represented law and order not only for the foreign communities up and down the river and its tributaries but also for tens of thousands of Chinese villagers along the banks and for the crews of innumerable junks and steamers which plied on it, so much so that they were frequently called upon to settle, on an entirely unofficial basis, civil disputes which those concerned preferred not to take to their own Chinese courts.

The officer Godfrey relieved as Navigator of *Bramble* was Lieutenant Henry Moore. As Vice-Chief of Naval Staff in 1942, he was to play an unfortunate role in a crucial episode in the career of the future Director of Naval Intelligence. Moore was "in a hurry to get away to catch the down river steamer so we didn't waste much time in turning over. The three essentials were to see that the money and the rum were right and the charts up to date." The Lieutenant and commander (for the rank of Lieutenant-Commander had not then been copied from the Germans) was Basil George Washington and the first lieutenant Godfrey's friend Bobbie Harwood, who, without great success, tried to teach him the arts of snipe shooting and bridge, the two main relaxations in their isolated existence.

To the uninitiated the difficulties of navigating a gunboat on a river which in places rose or fell one hundred feet according to the melting of the Tibetan snows, whose current ran at times at ten knots and whose channels changed constantly might seem daunting, but Godfrey had no "hesitation in taking charge of the ship all the 600-odd miles to Hankow after doing it once going down. Night passages were different; not to take a pilot would have been unwise." For this he received a specialist navigating allowance of half-a-crown a day and special pilotage fees which might add up to £100 a year. His basic pay was ten shillings a day and he also received an allowance of one shilling a day for acting as paymaster and being in charge of stores. Living was cheap and out of his four hundred a year he managed to pay off his creditors and have quite a balance in the bank at the end of his two-year commission.

Godfrey's two years in China were, he said, "neatly divided

into two equal halves, old China as it was under its age-old
civilisation and ritual, and revolutionary China determined to
get rid of everything that reminded them of their conquerors,
including the pigtail which had been imposed on them as an
emblem of subservience by the Manchus. Sometime early in a
Yangtse commission it was encumbent on the captain of a
gunboat to call on the great Chinese dignitaries with capitals
on the banks of the river—the viceroy of Nanking, the governors
of Anking and Wuchang. At Anking the Governor, a mandarin
of the old school, asked our captain and two officers to lunch.
On the day before an emissary of the Governor came on board
to arrange the protocol. We must have Chinese visiting cards.
I forget what Washington's or Harwood's names were in
Chinese, but mine was Gau Fu Li. It was written with bold
strokes of the brush in Indian ink on a strip of scarlet card-
board about eighteen inches long and six inches wide—from
top to bottom. The wardroom messman Ling po, a most
endearing old fellow with wives in Hankow, Shanghai and
Hong Kong, had, in the meantime, got in touch with the
Governor's chef so that the menu might be agreed beforehand.
This is what Ling po committed us to:

Oxtail and pigeon egg soup
Boiled shark's fin
Frozen goose liver
Mandarin fish
Shrimps
Crab
Boiled asparagus
Pigeon
'Tomato Duck'
Boiled Beef
'Pudding with English dates'

The status of a person in old China was indicated by the
colour of his sedan chair. The chef de protocol explained—a
blue chair for Washington and two green chairs for Harwood
and myself. These would be at the landing steps at noon and
would convey us up through the city and then up the innumerable steps beyond to the Yamen where His Excellency would
receive us. The doctor prescribed eighteen hours' semi-starvation
and some bicarbonate of soda about 11 a.m.

The day arrives. Up through the city's crowded streets, steps all the way, and the coolie bearers, four to each chair, keeping up that sing song shouting cry to everyone to get out of our way. No, not every one. The coolie with a yoke and two almost overflowing tubs of liquid manure quite rightly has absolute priority and his own particular shouting noise to which all give heed. Clear of the city, the impressive Yamen and a long flight of steps looms ahead. The chef de protocol is there with our three visiting cards, fanned out and held at arms length above his head. He has become a herald and advances up the steps, we three following in our chairs. At the top we see our host, a dear old man in a beautiful but simple robe, with the long thin beard and moustache which has been the fashion in old China for thousands of years. With him are his staff, courteous and urbane. He shakes hands and welcomes us to an ample repast and through an interpreter gives an unconscious and perfect demonstration of hostmanship and how to put one's guests at their ease, an experience the memory of which I have always treasured. It was never to happen again for, within a fortnight, the revolution was to shake the world. Nothing would ever be the same again. Our charming host and his staff were rounded up and massacred while trying to escape over the city walls. We had been present not only at a gastronomic marathon but had witnessed the end of an era."

By the end of 1911 the revolution had engulfed the whole of the Yangtse valley. Hankow had been sacked and telegraphic communication with the outside world cut. The gunboats, which had recently been fitted with wireless (with a range of two hundred miles or less depending on conditions), were stationed at strategic points to fill the communications gap and to provide protection for the Concessions, although the revolutionaries were not, on the whole, anti-European. In January 1912 Godfrey saw the arrival in Nanking of Sun Yat Sen, the father of the revolution. "He was a very small man and sat in the back of a car sandwiched between and indeed almost hidden by two enormously fat Chinamen. As an additional precaution the car was surrounded by police mounted on little Manchu ponies, each fingering the trigger of a Mauser pistol. This incongruous cavalcade—big car, fat men and little horses —formed a tight little bunch which moved surprisingly rapidly and provided simple but effective security."

Conditions returned to normal fairly quickly, and as early as the autumn of 1911 Godfrey was able to take a short holiday trip in one of Butterfield and Swire's river steamers to visit Changsa, a fine city on the Siang River. Among the other passengers was the head of Butterfield and Swire's Hankow branch, Neilage Brown. It was typical of Godfrey not only that he should wish to see as much of the country as possible but that he immediately struck up a friendship, which was to endure until Brown's death, with this older and already important civilian. When he returned again to China in 1931 Neilage Brown had become the 'Number One' or Taipan of all the vast Butterfield Holt enterprises in the Far East.

Godfrey was fascinated with China, but by the end of 1912 his time was up and he took passage home to England. He was now an expert in coastal and river pilotage, but he still lacked experience in "deep sea navigation and fleet work which could only be gained by serving in a cruiser in the Home Fleet, where I should learn something about the shoals and tides, currents, fogs and mists of the North Sea, Channel and Western Approaches, and about fleet work and tactics". He was therefore delighted to be appointed, on 23 January 1913, as Lieutenant (N) of the brand new light cruiser *Blanche*. She was the flotilla leader of the Fourth Destroyer Flotilla whose senior officer was Captain Wilfred Henderson, "one of Fisher's men, and reputed to be brainy, impatient and formidable. He worked everyone very hard and thrust a lot of interesting staff work onto me. He was a humourless, loud-laughing, earnest, hard-working man. He put all he had into modernising the Navy. He suffered from some gastric trouble which triggered off his quick temper and was apt to make him unpredictable, unreasonable, petulant and, at times, very angry. After these fits he would become quite exhausted and wisely retired to his cabin and lay down. On one occasion he foamed at the mouth. On another occasion, I having successfully navigated our flotilla of twenty-four destroyers through the Needles Channel on their way to an anchorage off Gosport, Henderson took it into his head that we should go *over* the middle ground instead of to the north or south of it. He insisted, I said no. There was, in fact, sufficient water for us to go over, but not much to spare. I got stubborn and walked off the bridge which was, of course, an insubordinate and quite wrong thing to do. He ordered me back to the upper bridge, and fortunately there was time for me to set a course that took us clear of the middle ground and headed us for our pre-arranged anchorage in Stokes Bay. I had acted impetuously and laid myself open to the charge of insubordination. Had I been a different person, with more tact, discrimination and experience, I should have acted in a different and more considerate way and saved my Captain the frustration and even humiliation which incidents of this sort are liable to create. As far as I was concerned the incident seemed to be closed and I did not seem to have suffered any diminution in Captain Henderson's confidence. 'Wilf' was a tough customer and perhaps he did not mind. He had the reputation of having himself behaved in a rather similar manner on many occasions. Such a close disciple of Fisher must have had many encounters with insubordination at the top. He was the only experienced naval officer with a first class brain with whom I had so far worked in close contact and my own experience must have been greatly enriched by the association."

Godfrey left *Blanche* in April 1914 after a "most useful and enjoyable fifteen months" which had given him an insight into light cruiser and flotilla work with a large fleet. He was then appointed to the Navigation School at Portsmouth for a three months 'first class ship' course, successful completion of which entitled him to navigate a ship of any draught and size. At the end of the course the Captain of the Navigation School asked Godfrey if he would "like an appointment to *Arethusa*, a light cruiser just completing. Had I accepted the rest of my life would have been different as within a few months she became flagship of Commodore Tyrwhitt commanding the Harwich Force" which was to see more action in the North Sea during World War I than almost any other unit of the Navy in Home waters. However, she was smaller than *Blanche* and in the hopes of something better Godfrey turned the offer down. It so happened that nothing else was immediately available and Godfrey had to be content, for the time being, with a 'war appointment' as Lieutenant (N) of the twenty-year-old light cruiser *Charybdis* in the event of war or mobilisation. *Charybdis* formed part of the Reserve Fleet and Godfrey confessed to feeling a twinge of disappointment at the idea of going to war in "such an inadequate and rusty old ship" but consoled himself with the thought that something more 'first class' would soon turn up. Like millions of others that August he was to be rudely undeceived.

"We all knew that war was in the air, but none of us thought that it would come so suddenly or so soon. Contrary to the general belief, by no means all the Reserve Fleet was kept in commission after the three weeks' mobilisation manoeuvres in the summer of 1914, and our little group all paid off and commissioned again with different ships' companies less than a fortnight later. The 'warning telegram' addressed *Charybdis* as Flagship of G Cruiser Group—the 12th Cruiser Squadron—the other ships being *Diana*, *Eclipse* and *Talbot* [also cruisers of similar size and vintage]. The officer commanding our little squadron was Rear-Admiral Wemyss, his flag captain Rudolf Burmester who, together with Dick Bevan the flag lieutenant and signal officer joined on 2 August. Commander Jack Marriott joined us later as second in command. We were at sea before dusk on 4 August, and at midnight a telegram was received directing all ships to 'commence hostilities at once against Germany'."

CHAPTER TWO

The Dardanelles

GODFREY'S APPOINTMENT to *Charybdis*, which he had hoped would be no more than a stop-gap until something better turned up, was in fact to have a decisive influence on his life and career. One of the results which flowed from it was that he spent practically the whole of the war in the Mediterranean rather than in the North Sea. Although the Mediterranean was a secondary theatre, it provided him with a wealth of experience and responsibility which no junior officer in the Grand Fleet could have hoped to enjoy. Secondly it brought him into contact with a number of senior officers with ideas far removed from the rigid autocracy which was then almost universal in the higher ranks of the Service.

"Rear-Admiral Sir Rosslyn Wemyss was a great-grandson [on the wrong side of the blanket] of King William IV. He had always been known to the Navy as 'Rosy', a name which somehow suited him very well. He was a gay, robust and amusing person and one of the few 'naval statesmen' that have emerged from either of the two World Wars. He did not know much about the technical side of the Navy but he thrived on responsibility, and the more he had the happier he became. He was fearless and outspoken and fully made up for his lack of technical knowledge by his statesmanlike qualities, a capacity to decentralize, when autocracy and one-man rule was all the rage in the Navy, by a natural capacity to handle situations and people and to get the best out of subordinates. He did not expect to be employed and was pleasantly surprised when he was 'offered' Cruiser Force G. I am sure that it never occurred to him in those early days that within four years he would be First Sea Lord.

"I was equally lucky to serve continuously under such a splendid chief as Rudolf Burmester, and it was entirely due to him that I got involved in such interesting work at the age of twenty-six, which nowadays would be carried out by much more senior officers. In days when staff work and decentralization were words that conveyed only a very vague impression, he seemed to know instinctively how to organize and run a large staff and a complicated and scattered command. His method, probably unconscious, was to take his staff and subordinates into his confidence beforehand and then throw on them full power and responsibility, avoiding any appearance of interference. I became convinced that this was the only method likely to achieve success under modern conditions, but realised it was diametrically opposed to the traditions prevailing in my earlier ships where senior officers tended to usurp the functions of their subordinates. Twenty-four years later, as Director of Naval Intelligence, I decided to adopt the Burmester technique in my dealings with all NID sectional heads.

"What I most remember about Burmester was his complete informality and friendliness to all. These qualities, combined with a very real modesty and impressive quietness put him in a strong position when dealing with bombastic and loudspeaking contemporaries and seniors. To subordinates down to the latest joined boy he was invariably courteous and kind. He was certainly as clever as Wilfred Henderson and many of the men who stood round Fisher. Though not a great initiator, he was extremely receptive to new ideas from others and knew how to exploit them and speed them on their way. His judgement was rarely at fault. Slightly built, with a quick active walk and an equally active mind, when once he had decided what to do he did not let the grass grow under his feet."

Charybdis's Commander, Jack Marriott, was another very able and charming character. "His sympathy and sincerity", wrote Godfrey, "endeared him no less to his ship-mates of the lower-deck than to his messmates in the ward-room. I was proud of his enduring friendship. His untimely death in 1938 left a great hole in many people's lives." Dick Bevan, the flag lieutenant and signal officer was another with whom Godfrey was to form a life-long friendship.

The first task of the 12th Cruiser Squadron, in co-operation with a French armoured cruiser squadron, was to cover, from the west, the passage of the British Expeditionary Force to the Channel ports and St Nazaire. Liaison officers were exchanged and Godfrey had his first experience of working with allies. All went off very smoothly and the squadron was then employed on patrolling in the Chops of the Channel, searching for non-existent U-boats and intercepting homeward-bound German merchant ships unaware of the outbreak of war. This monotonous and largely unrewarding work continued until 10 September, when the little cruiser squadron was ordered to proceed with all despatch to Halifax, to escort the first Canadian troops to England. The convoy was, by any standards, a large one, consisting of thirty-one transports, with nearly 33,000 troops on board. With women and children and the crews of the passenger ships and the cruisers the total reached just under 41,000. "In 1914 no naval officer had ever seen a convoy, or had met anyone who had ever seen one. No merchant ship captain had ever sailed in convoy or met anyone who had steamed in formation close to other merchant ships. We had literally nothing to guide us. When we assembled in Gaspe Bay at the mouth of the St Lawrence opinion among the captains of the transports was about equally divided as to the feasibility (as distinct from the desirability) of convoy. But when, fourteen days later, we dispersed off the coast of Cornwall everyone, even the most apprehensive, was converted to the idea. In spite of this experience, we had to learn all over again in 1917 that merchant ships can steam in escorted formation and a good deal closer than the four cables (800 yards) adopted by Admiral Wemyss." Godfrey, as navigating lieutenant of the flagship, had been largely responsible for working out the formation and for drafting all the instructions. It was an early example of his talent for staff work.

After this interlude the Squadron returned to its old patrols in the south-western approaches, the only major change being that the Admiral shifted his flag to *Euryalus*, a larger, more commodious and slightly less obsolete cruiser. He took with him his staff, including Godfrey. Then, at the end of January 1915 came rumours of an assault on the Dardanelles, and *Euryalus* received orders to proceed to Port Said.

The Dardanelles is now chiefly remembered as a magnificent failure, the brilliant brain-child of the First Lord, Winston Churchill, which, if only it had been better planned and more resolutely executed, would have changed the whole course of the war, cut short the holocaust on the Western Front and left a Europe very different from that which emerged in 1919. An epic tragedy indeed, but one which in fact should never have been necessary.

The decaying Ottoman Empire, 'the sick man of Europe' for nearly one hundred years, was still extensive, including not only its heartland, modern Turkey, but all the Levant and Arabia, that is present-day Syria, Lebanon, Israel, Palestine, Sinai, Iraq, Jordan and Saudi-Arabia. Egypt, though nominally a part of its dominions, was in practice under British control, while Cyrenaica and Tripolitania had recently been lost to Italy. The holy city of Mecca lay within its territories and Constantinople was the leader of the Muslim world. The British had for long regarded Turkey as a barrier, if a somewhat ramshackle one, against the advance of Russian Imperialism and British influence in and support for Turkey was strong. A British Naval Mission was actually reorganising the Turkish Navy in 1914, although the Army looked to Germany. One would have thought that the need to keep Turkey in the Allied camp, to ensure free communication with Russia through the Black Sea and with India through the Suez Canal would have been given the highest priority, but immediately on the outbreak of war two events took place which drove this potential ally into the arms of the Germans; the Admiralty commandeered two Turkish dreadnoughts, building in British yards, and then, by a combination of muddle and ineptitude, the powerful German battlecruiser *Goeben* and her accompanying cruiser *Breslau* were permitted to escape from the Mediterranean and take refuge in Constantinople. On 31 October hostilities started.

With the concentration of the Royal Navy's most modern ships in the North Sea, the main responsibility for the Mediterranean had been placed in the hands of the French. Italy, despite a defensive alliance with Germany and Austro-Hungary, was sitting on the fence, as was Greece under its German King, Constantine. There were, however, a number of older British battleships and cruisers available, and on Winston Churchill's instructions a combined Anglo-French squadron proceeded on 3 November to bombard the outer forts on the European and Asiatic shores of the Dardanelles. The Turks were taken by surprise and considerable success was achieved. Content with this the Allies then steamed off, leaving the Turks, galvanised into activity by their German advisers, not only to repair the damage but to reinforce their troops and improve their defences.

In the meantime the Turks launched a violent offensive against the Russians in the Caucasus, and almost broke through. The Grand Duke Nicholas, Commander-in-Chief of the Russian Armies, appealed in the most urgent terms for the British to do something to relieve the pressure on his southern front, and the decision was taken to renew the attack on the Dardanelles. Kitchener refused to release any troops for the purpose, and Churchill, convinced that the Navy could do the job on its own and ignorant as was everyone else that the Russians had won a decisive victory over the Turks and no longer needed immediate help, gave orders for an attempt to force the Dardanelles. By 19 February 1915 sufficient ships had been assembled and the bombardment of the forts was resumed. Once again initial success was achieved and the outer forts silenced. Marines and bluejackets were landed and the enemy guns blown up. Had the Fleet pressed on it would almost certainly have been able to reach Constantinople with only modest losses, although what it would then have been able to achieve without troops to occupy the city is a matter of debate. Unfortunately over a month elapsed before the inner forts were attacked. Even then success was almost within sight and the Turks were in despair, when several ships were mined and it was decided to withdraw to await the arrival of the troops, which had at last been promised.

On 25 April landings were made by British, Australian, New Zealand and French troops at Cape Helles on the southern tip of Gallipoli, at Anzac Cove on its western side and at Kum Kale on the Asiatic shore. Despite the greatest gallantry on the part of the troops, the difficulties of the terrain, the stubborn defence of the Turks and the poor leadership of the British generals soon produced a stalemate. The invaders were pinned to within a few hundred yards of the shore and casualties both from enemy action and disease mounted alarmingly.

Towards the end of May German U-boats arrived on the scene, which greatly increased the difficulties of the Navy in its tasks of supplying the Army with all its stores and ammunition and of providing continuous artillery support. The deadlock was complete, and it was decided to attempt to break it by another landing further up the western side at Suvla Bay. Fresh troops were sent out but Kitchener refused to release any seasoned men and the enthusiastic volunteers of his K1 army

were given no time to acclimatise themselves or get even a taste
of active service before they were thrown ashore on an unknown,
unmapped coast. The corps and divisional commanders were
old and incompetent, and although the landings were not, at
first, seriously contested, and a half company of Ghurkas
actually reached the crest of the heights and looked down on
the Dardanelles on the other side, the command faltered and
the attack again bogged down, a remarkable foretaste of Anzio
in 1944.

Once again it was a choice of reinforce or retreat. Lord
Kitchener was despatched to sum up the situation on the spot.
He opted for evacuation, and as on so many occasions before
and since, from Corunna to Dunkirk, the British somehow
managed to ward off total disaster. Suvla and Anzac were
evacuated on 18 and 19 December 1915 with the loss of hardly
a man. Incredibly, the exercise was repeated with equal success
at Cape Helles on 8 and 9 January. The gamble had failed and
World War I was to continue for nearly another three years
with all its appalling loss of life and destruction. This, briefly,
was the background to the first twelve months of Godfrey's
time in the Mediterranean.

Admiral Wemyss had departed in January 1915 to take up
the post of Governor of Lemnos which, although a possession of
neutral Greece, was to be the base for the descent on the
Dardanelles. When *Euryalus* reached Suez she became the
flagship of Admiral Peirce, the Commander-in-Chief East
Indies and Egypt. Almost at once he was ordered to take the
battleships *Triumph* and *Swiftsure* under command and bombard the defences of Smyrna, and Godfrey had his first experience of being under fire. He noted in his diary, "On the whole
I can't say I enjoy being fired at. At first the temptation to get
behind even the flimsiest cover is irresistible but that soon
wears off, and the feeling becomes instinctive that one's best
protection is an accurate and suitable reply in kind." *Triumph*
and *Euryalus* were both hit by the shore batteries and suffered
some casualties, but although the attack was maintained for
four days the results were not encouraging. Godfrey wrote,
"One can't help feeling disappointed in the result of the last
two days' operations. There being no means of spotting the fall
of shot either by reconnaissance aircraft, kite balloon or flank
spotting ship, we do not know if we have knocked out any of

their batteries except some field guns on the beach. The seaplanes on which we were building such great hopes have failed us, and the minesweeping has been far from successful. In fact, even assuming that a channel is swept, what is to happen then? Their concealed batteries could give us a bad time if we attempted to approach nearer than 6000 yards and we have no means of gauging the effect of our replies." After an abortive attempt to negotiate with the Vali, or Turkish governor, the operation was abandoned and *Euryalus* returned to Port Said. It was an ominous preliminary to the Navy's attempt to reduce the forts in the Narrows of the Dardanelles which was to take place a week later.

The Cabinet having decided that an attempt should be made to capture the Gallipoli peninsula by a combined operation, Admiral Peirse was ordered to send *Euryalus* to Mudros, the harbour of the island of Lemnos, where the great armada of transports and warships was gathering. She arrived on 12 April and Godfrey found the harbour "a wonderful sight. There must be at least 80 ships assembled. Admiral Wemyss is in command of the base and the Captain went over to see him as soon as we arrived, and returned with the good news that he is going to hoist his flag in *Euryalus* again, in command of the big landing at Cape Helles. The Captain has asked if I may go over to Tenedos and the Dardanelles, if an opportunity occurs, and reconnoitre landing places." This duly took place and on 21 April Godfrey noted that he had been "at work until 1 a.m. helping to draft the final orders for our part of the business". In his Memoirs he remarks, "The naval operations staff was certainly very small compared with what was considered necessary during World War II. It consisted of the Flag Captain, Burmester, Lieutenant Bevan (signals), and myself working in collaboration with the Naval Transport Officer's staff. It was my job to deal with navigational matters, buoyage and so on, and among other things I had to produce and duplicate the plan showing where *River Clyde** should be run ashore and the position and area of fire of the five bombarding battleships.

"We left Mudros today [23 April] with Admiral Wemyss on

---

* *River Clyde* was the old merchantman hastily converted to a landingship which was run ashore on V Beach, Cape Helles, and from which the Munsters and Hampshires were to disembark with such appalling casualties.

board again, full of smiles and looking much better than he ever did on the Western Patrol. For twelve days we have been practising all the various details of this undertaking—embarking and disembarking men, horses and munitions, getting them on shore, getting them off again, testing towing gear—and at last I really think we are as ready as we shall ever be. The one doubtful element is the weather. It takes very little imagination to see the chaos that would ensue if one tried to land these soldiers and maintain communications in a rough sea. We have General Hunter-Weston and the divisional staff on board and until the troops are firmly established ashore, *Euryalus* will be the Divisional Headquarters. The 29th Division are a splendid lot of men—all from foreign stations and averaging six years' service.

"The problem of the navigators of *Euryalus*,* *Cornwallis* and *Implacable* (myself, Clayton and Bell) was to lead the tows of boats and small craft in the right direction during the night, and deliver them accurately off W, X and V beaches an hour before dawn, 25 April. As we were approaching Cape Tekke I was soon able to get a rough fix by bearings of the right and left extremities of the land at Sed el Bahr and the cliffs to the west of Achi Baba. It was a still, dark night and final adjustments of course and speed were made that enabled us to reach our stopping points about 1500 yards from land with reasonable accuracy, and well up to time.† The dip in the hills over W beach, which I had noted during the reconnaissance on 15 April, was visible well before dawn. It was immediately behind W beach over which a blinding sun was to rise half an hour later.

"The bridge at sea is the nerve centre of the ship and the best place for seeing what is going on all round. Naturally it became General Hunter-Weston's headquarters as long as he was on board, my chartroom being the office of his Chief Staff Officer, Colonel Street. The 9·2 inch forward gun was firing about every five minutes and whenever it went off it made chaos of the

---

* *Euraylus*'s boats were to land the Lancashire Fusiliers on W beach.

† Godfrey notes that the navigational problem at Anzac was much greater and the landing there was made well to the left of the intended position. His friend Lieutenant Tom Phillips had suggested that a submarine should be used as a marker, as was done on D-Day in 1944, but the suggestion was not adopted.

divisional signals and reports which had been laid out in neat rows on the chart table. The confined space on the raised compass platform on the upper bridge is usually only used by the Captain, navigating officer and officer of the watch. During the landings we were joined by the Admiral and the General and I was in a good position to note their reactions to the stirring events we were witnessing. After disappearing for about a quarter of an hour, our boats were seen to be emerging from the mist and smoke that obscured the beaches. The General's and the Admiral's first reaction was 'My God, they haven't got ashore', but they had and what we saw was the boats pulling off, some of them with only two sailors at the oars.

"The plan had been that the wounded should be given first aid and left on the beach to be collected afterwards by ambulance trawlers, but the sailors could not bear to leave the Fusiliers in this manner. They landed and, carrying the wounded through the surf into the boats, brought them on board *Euryalus*, whose upper deck very soon resembled a casualty clearing station. To add to the discomfort of the wounded, *Euryalus* was carrying out a continuous bombardment with her foremost 9·2 and 6 inch guns, but they were very grateful for being brought off and infinitely preferred lying on the upper deck than on the beach.

"From the first I thought that something might go wrong and was never impressed by the soldiers' optimistic 'Achi Baba* tonight'. Something was going radically wrong, just round the corner, at V, S and Y beaches, but we could not see what was happening. The Admiral and the General had five landings to control. They should have been together in a sloop, destroyer or small cruiser so that they could move rapidly from one beach to another, go close in shore if necessary and see what was going on. To tie them to one ship, *Euryalus* drawing 28 feet, unable to leave the vicinity of W beach or to go close in due to her draft, was a mistake. Naval tradition tempts the senior officer to over-ride, in emergency, the powers delegated to a junior. The expression 'the Senior Officer is always right' may sound ridiculous, but it nevertheless contains an element of truth. In an Army, the chain of command, down and up, seemed to me, as I watched the divisional general and his staff at work on the bridge, to be fragile and at times almost impal-

* Achi Baba, more properly Alchi Tepe, was the ridge dominating the southern tip of Gallipoli.

pable. My instinct, following naval tradition, would have been to go and look and, if necessary, intervene. But this would have been contrary to military ethics and so we continued to pour troops into V beach where the resistance was strongest and failed to exploit the soft spots at Y and S. After an almost unopposed seizure of two flanking positions, they were evacuated due to a flaw in the chain of command, hesitation of senior officers to alter previous arrangements or interfere with their juniors in spite of the receipt of new and good intelligence, lack of mobility and some unaccountable difficulty of communications."

Euryalus was not only flagship of Admiral Wemyss and, for a time, Hunter-Weston's divisional headquarters, but also an 'attendant ship' and a 'bombarding ship'. As attendant ship she had to look after the naval beach parties, transport crews, boats and boats' crews, the evacuation of the wounded, repairs to boats and lighters, to buoyage and so on. The days and weeks which followed the Helles landings were therefore ones of intense activity for Godfrey and he was frequently ashore. On 6 May, for example, he was ashore when the French, in their bright blue coats and red trousers, with their drums and bugles sounding the charge, attempted to capture Achi Baba. "I watched the battle from the crest of Hill 114 behind W beach. The French started well and under a splendid barrage of ·75's advanced about half a mile with great gallantry, taking trench after trench. Then the shrapnel began to fall around them and they stopped advancing, took cover and started to drift back in two's and three's till very soon the whole right flank was thick with Frenchmen running in all directions, apparently quite disorganized. Eventually they got back to some sort of cover, a trench, banks, a nullah, and rallied. There followed a pause, devoted to violent altercation, and then out they were again, with bayonets fixed, charging up the slopes and almost regaining their former line.

"The torpedoing and sinking of the battleship *Goliath* [on the night of 12 May] by a Turkish destroyer commanded by a German made the impending arrival of U-boats seem more menacing than ever. It was a pitch dark night and *Goliath* was anchored about 800 yards from *Euryalus*. She heeled over and sank quite silently in two minutes and the first we knew about it was the arrival alongside of a picket boat with the navigating

officer and a few survivors aboard. Just after I got on the bridge
we began to hear the noise of the men in the water, a most
distressing eerie sound. I was told later that it was singing, but
to us it sounded like anything but that. The combination of
darkness, silence and the instantaneous loss of 600 men made
us feel rather uncomfortable."

On 17 May Admiral Wemyss shifted his flag to the old gunboat *Hussar* and *Euryalus* again became a private ship. The
following extracts from Godfrey's diary give some indication of
his activities for the next few months.

"26 May. Got orders early in the morning to proceed to Port
Iero, Mytelene, and relieve *Minerva* as SNO [Senior Naval
Officer] of the Smyrna and other Aegean patrols. The job
sounds interesting. Port Iero is a large land-locked harbour
approached through a narrow and tortuous channel. There are
shoals at the head of this channel where it opens out into a
completely land-locked basin about five miles long and three
miles wide. As the survey was made in 1830 I have my doubts
about the accuracy of the chart and shall have to buoy the
entrance before we go in."

The arrival of the German U-boats meant that Port Iero had
to be made into a secure base for the Smyrna patrols and
searchlights and guns were landed and observation posts
established. At the same time steps had to be taken to prevent
the U-boats using the Gulf of Smyrna.

"2 June. Went over to the Gulf of Smyrna yesterday in the
Kennet [destroyer] to make a reconnaissance of the new works
between Smyrna and Vourish. A Greek deserter from the
Turkish Army accompanied me. We went up to our old bombarding positions and my Greek showed me the batteries that
gave us such a hot time in March.

"The minelayer *Gazelle* has arrived from Mudros, also the
French minelayer *Casabianca*. Tonight *Casabianca* is going to lay
74 mines and *Gazelle* 48 across the entrance to the Gulf. The
mines are French and are supposed to be rather unsafe to
handle. The Captain [Burmester] will be in charge, with
myself, the young doctor and Sandford, late torpedo officer of
Irresistible and an expert on mines, on board *Gazelle*."

"3 June. . . . All went well until *Casabianca* had laid her 56th
mine. This exploded on striking the water and raised a huge
column of water under her stern, without doing any material

damage to the ship or stopping the laying of the mines. We hadn't got further than the third mine when exactly the same thing occurred again. From the bridge the explosion seemed enormous but was nothing compared with what happened half a minute later. Apparently the mines on the port side got out of control and as there is no 'stop' that allows only one mine to go out at a time, the whole twenty slid into the sea at intervals of about five yards. Two of them went over practically on top of one another and exploded only about four yards from *Gazelle*'s stern. There was a tremendous upheaval—it looked as if the whole after part of the ship would be blown off—sparks, steam and water mixed with splinters from the mine flew in all directions and came down all over us rather like a dense cloud of rain. That four yards saved us; any nearer would have been fatal but as it was all that happened to the ship was the slight throwing out of the starboard engine. The Captain dashed aft and found Sandford covered with splinter wounds and bleeding like a pig; one of the splinters had entered his eye. Notwithstanding all this he had cut the wires that connected the starboard mines and was prepared to carry on with the laying. However the Captain thought it wasn't good enough and we returned to Port Iero. Sandford has had quite his fair share of narrow escapes. To start with he was in charge of the demolition party that was landed to blow up the Seddul Bahr and Kum Kale guns. He placed and fired every charge himself and was very nearly killed by debris. His left ear drum was broken. Then followed the Naval assault on 18 March when he was on board first *Irresistible* and then *Ocean* when they blew up and what was almost worse in the destroyer on the 14th when the shells were falling all round."

In spite of these mishaps the operation was resumed on the next night. This time *Casabianca* blew up and sank with the very first mine she laid. Seventy of her crew were lost. Godfrey's remark that "these French mines seem to be a great danger to any ship which lays them" seems rather an understatement. To conclude the story of the mine-laying, three weeks later further mines of the same type were received and were duly laid by *Gazelle*, with Burmester and Godfrey on board. This time the operation went off without a hitch. A final lay was carried out on 26 July. Godfrey's diary for the next day records, "Left harbour at 7 p.m. last night and laid a second line of mines quite successfully, getting back at 2 a.m. The Fleet Surgeon came with us and we took the precaution of taking deck chairs with us. The trip there and back seemed quite like a Channel crossing, the illusion being made all the more realistic by the fact that *Gazelle* in her palmier days plied from Weymouth to Jersey."

Reverting to June we get the following glimpses of the Smyrna Patrol.

"13 June. The navigator of *Vengeance* and I have decided that the narrow entrance to this wonderful harbour needs surveying and have just completed a fairly accurate plotting sheet."

"16 June. The *Vengeance* people had a most unfortunate accident. It was intended to blow up a small rock that obstructed the view of the 3-pounder gun on Square Island. Their steam pinnace was down there with about eight of their officers. As it happened, I was just close, in the whaler, waiting for them to fire the guncotton charge, when a great flame leaped up in the stern of the steam pinnace and everyone proceeded to jump overboard. We rescued them all, but they were frightfully badly burned about the arms, legs and face. Of course the salt water gave them agony. One or two had their clothes burned to a cinder. One of them has since died of shock, but the remainder are getting on all right. It was only by the merest fluke that I was not in the steamboat at the time."

"27 June. There have been several little affairs in the Gulf of Smyrna and the neighbourhood but they have mostly ended disastrously for us. Two seaplane accidents and an abortive cutting out expedition. This was carried out by the auxiliary *Heroic* and resulted in 12 casualties and no result. Unfortunately the captain of *Heroic* didn't do what he was told or all might have been well.

"It has been very hot, temperatures ranging from 87 during the day to 78 at night, but by no means unpleasant as the air is quite dry.

"I have been much too busy to get pessimistic about things, but there's plenty of scope for those that like to take a gloomy view of Russia's extraordinary set-back,* our own internal dissensions† at home and the apparent dead-lock out here."

* The Germans had overwhelmed the Russians in Galicia and Poland.

† Churchill and Fisher had left the Admiralty and Asquith's Liberal Government had been replaced by the Coalition under Lloyd George.

"4 July. I have nearly finished the fair chart of my survey—it looks very nice, and I really think it is a reliable piece of work."

"17 July. An uneventful two days—all days are uneventful here, but some are less uneventful than others by the arrival of news from Gallipoli or elsewhere."

By the end of July preparations were being made to try to break the deadlock at Gallipoli by the landing at Suvla Bay. Godfrey noted in his diary:

"1 August. Transports containing about a Brigade have arrived at Port Iero and further large reinforcements are reaching Mudros daily. Captain Burmester has been placed in command of the transports starting from Port Iero, and told me all about it a week ago, as I am to accompany him in *Honeysuckle* [a new sloop]. The transports all contain Irish units of Kitchener's first army. A very great proportion of K1 are fellows who have every qualification for being officers; the result is that a platoon commander, after training his men for about six months, suddenly finds himself deprived of the best ones to make officers for K2."

Subsequently, in his Memoirs, Godfrey wrote, "The troops were very young and unseasoned. The only regular officers were the Brigadier (a retired Colonel) and the Brigade Major. The Brigadier had not met General Stopford [the Corps Commander in charge of the landings, who was at Mudros], neither had there been any conference prior to landing. The Brigade did not know where they were going and the only map of Suvla Bay was one lent to the Brigadier by Captain Burmester. As part of a deception plan they had been issued with maps of the Asiatic side. Our doctors warned the Brigade of the dangers of bathing in the heat of the day and drinking unboiled water, but they were either sceptical about this advice or unable to impose the necessary hygenic discipline. To endemic dysentery was added severe sunburn and on the day they left Mytelene over 600 men were on the sick list. The command structure seemed to me weak, and there appeared to be a lack of aggressive leadership. The atmosphere and talk on board the transports was placid, indolent and fatuously wishful. I had grave forebodings that they would be unable to achieve their limited objectives (of which they were ignorant before the landing) much less overcome the resistance of the seasoned Turkish Armies."

"6 August. The actual place where these troops would be landed was kept secret, and I really believe that up to the day before not more than two dozen people outside the GOC's staff knew where it would be.

"Having embarked the troops at Port Iero the troop carriers sailed at intervals during the afternoon [5 August] with orders to be off the southern end of Suvla Bay at 4.30 a.m. [6 August]. At 2.30 a.m. we passed eight hospital ships slowly steaming north. They looked very pretty with their rows of green lights and illuminated red crosses, but it seems rather a mistaken policy to herald an attack by such a very conspicuous row of beacons.

"As it got light it was possible to make out the forms of a great many ships all converging on Suvla Bay. It seems that the landing was commenced at 10.30 last night, and went on practically without any interruption till at daylight 14,000 men had been put ashore. There was a little sniping and a few outposts were encountered, but these at once fell back.

"The troops from *Honeysuckle* and the remainder of the transports were landed in motor lighters on the south side of Niebruniessi Point and marched round to the cover afforded by some sandhills. At about 3 p.m. they began to advance by battalions in open order across the perfectly bare piece of ground to northward of Salt Lake. It seemed to us on board that shrapnel was falling among them the whole time, but I hear since that their casualties were small."

"14 August. The situation ashore is disappointing. They have absolutely failed to get straddled across the two main roads, and they have failed even to reach either of the Anaferta villages. Their line is exactly as it was on the second day after the landing. In passing judgement on this somewhat negative result of a week's operations one must bear in mind that these are new troops, so far quite untried in even the subsidiary parts of modern warfare and also that, contrary to the usual practice, they are not even stiffened with a small percentage of regular soldiers. Contrast the work these men have to perform with the fighting in Flanders. There the country is easy, every inch has been carefully reconnoitred scores of times, transport and supply is as perfect as ingenuity, money and modern machinery can make it. Here the men are landed after three weeks in a transport on a practically unknown shore, the country is one maze of gullies and clefts which have been made almost impregnable by means of barbed wire and redoubts and carefully concealed machine guns. There, after three weeks of breaking in, they are only called upon to hold a line of well-prepared trenches: here they have to attack, attack and always attack, contesting every inch of the ground and being continually sniped at by invisible enemies. Can one wonder that for the first few days they, poor fellows, are rather dazed and fail to perform the task that the staff demand. The Brigadier in command of the troops that sailed from Port Iero had no military orders of *any sort* till within twenty minutes of going ashore. He hadn't even got the maps, and he only knew the place of the landing through having been shown the naval orders by Captain Burmester."

The troops in Flanders might not have entirely agreed with Godfrey's assessment of their lot, but it is interesting to see his early realisation of the need for first class topographical information. When he became Director of Naval Intelligence he was determined that Allied forces should not again be thrown ashore on a 'practically unknown' terrain.

"15 August. We were shelled again this morning and had to shift berth during which we nearly got foul of the nets. A submarine was seen outside yesterday, and fired a torpedo at *Monica*, which passed underneath, so altogether plenty of small excitements. Situation ashore is unsatisfactory. General advance ordered this morning only resulted in the gain of a few yards on our left, and the taking of the first ridge as seen from the ships. Advance on right and in centre is insignificant. Shelled again this evening."

"16 August. General Stopford (Commanding 9th Army Corps) and General Mahon (11th Division) have been relieved and left for Mudros this morning.

"I have been asked to survey, buoy and mark the approaches to the Northern or A beaches. This ought to be rather an interesting job, and will give me a chance of getting ashore.

"The Turks counter-attacked heavily all day, and with the help of bombs and shrapnel succeeded in driving back our advanced line over most of the ground gained yesterday. This is rapidly becoming trench warfare of the most hackneyed description."

"21 August. Have been living in khaki most of the last three days and spending my time on and about the beaches. Interesting work, occasionally given additional spice when one comes under shellfire. Situation ashore practically unchanged. Our Army has so far been unable to make any decisive headway against a numerically inferior foe in a strong defensive position.

"Later. A big attack is to take place this afternoon on the right, a fact which has been gratuitously presented to the Turks by the presence of three hospital ships in the offing. At 2.30 p.m. we commenced a general bombardment of the Turkish trenches and batteries. This continued until 3.10 p.m., the last five minutes being very rapid fire.

"During the night our troops were subjected to several counter-attacks but managed to hold their own. Our casualties were about 3,000 wounded and 500 or so killed.

"The original scheme which was planned and carried out with secrecy failed at once; now the stereotyped attack with tremendous artillery preparation has also failed."

"23 August. The failure of the attack on the night before last has made the GOC [General Officer Commanding] and his staff do some furious thinking. I gather that they had practically decided to give up the Suvla Bay operation and were only dissuaded by the Army Corps General on the spot."

"1 September. Hit by a small shell on Saturday; it entered the mess deck through a scuttle, blew scuttle and deadlight to atoms and killed an unfortunate stoker.

"I have been surveying the northern beaches most of the time and have just got round Suvla Point where there is a small bay I am anxious to see exploited. It is protected from the southwest and I am sure would be useful during the southerly winds we get later in the year."

"5 September. A busy five days for me, and now the survey is completed. We have light-heartedly spattered the chart with the names of the officers doing the survey—Capes Campbell and Godfrey, Taylor Island and Berridge Bay, Albion Beach and Talbot Shoal."

To Godfrey's surprise he discovered, forty-eight years later, that the names had found their way onto the Admiralty charts. "Posterity may wonder," he remarked, "who were these obscure individuals and why their names should be inscribed on the chart when such famous names as de Robeck, Mustapha

Kemel, Wemyss, Keyes, Hamilton and Birdwood were available."

Euryalus spent October and November back at Port Iero, Mytelene, and Godfrey had his first taste of flying.

"5 October. Our seaplane did a reconnaissance over Aivali this morning but as usual saw nothing of the submarine that people are continually reporting there. Wright, the pilot, took me up for a spin round the harbour at about 1000 feet. A most exhilarating experience. Tomorrow he is reconnoitring Dikili and Ali Agha and the Captain has asked me to go as an observer."

"7 October. The reconnaissance yesterday didn't come off. After circling round the harbour at 1200 feet one of the engines began 'missing'. When this happens the speed is affected at once, this causes fluctuations in the lifting power of the machine and a curious up and down motion ensues. Accordingly Wright brought the seaplane down close to the ship, and after fiddling about for an hour or two decided to give the works a good overhauling.

"It's extraordinary what a lot of apparatus an observer has to take and work. Binoculars, camera, notebook, wireless set, four 20 pound bombs, two bottles attached to chunks of wood for dropping messages, a rifle and 50 rounds of ammunition in case we meet anything hostile."

"8 October. After one or two unsuccessful starts we got away by 9 a.m. Forty minutes later we were flying over Ali Agha at a height of 5000 feet. We tried to bomb the pier first and missed it, and then got one fair and square on the road outside Ali Agha. We couldn't stay very long as we hadn't much petrol, so skirted round the coast over Ajanos and after dropping another bomb among some trenches on the beach reconnoitred Dikili. Nothing to see here so we shaped course back to Mytelene. All well until we were about a mile from the land when the engine started 'fluffing' and then stopped dead. We started dropping at once and I was told to 'lean well back', and after three circles we took the water very nicely about 1000 yards outside the harbour where *Gazelle* was lying. Ignorance is bliss on these occasions. A 5000 feet drop in four minutes gives one's rate of approaching the earth at about 1200 feet per minute or 20 feet per second. When Wright sang out 'lean well back' I was only aware of a rather swift but quite even volplaning movement, and all the time he was fairly wrestling with the elevators to prevent her nose diving. He was quite done up when we reached the water. We were towed back by *Gazelle*, rather an ignominious ending to the most exhilarating two hours I have ever spent."

Life continued much as before for several weeks, but on 14 November the diary records "Kitchener has arrived at Mudros so we are in the state of standing by for the next move".

By 3 December *Euryalus* was back at Mudros. "The first thing we learn is that we are not going to Malta just yet. The reason being that *anything* might happen during the next week. One hears the most extravagant yarns, but the most probable is that there is some idea afoot of partially evacuating the peninsula."

"4 December. Just had a most interesting talk with Bevan, who says that Admiral Wemyss is very taken with being Vice-Admiral Eastern Mediterranean Squadron, and determined not to go back to the humdrum duties of SNO Mudros.

"I'm told Kitchener came out here with the idea of hanging on to Gallipoli but became convinced that a partial evacuation would be necessary. Helles, it appears, is to remain occupied and Suvla and Anzac abandoned."

"11 December. A week of rumours of the most sensational description has culminated in our being sent to Kephalo (on the island of Imbros). This is significant, as it entailed the cancellation of our previous orders to go to Malta, to refit. The ostensible reason for this delay is that *Terrible* is to be taken in hand and the dockyard cannot compete with more than one ship at a time. The real reason I think is that it has been decided to evacuate Suvla Bay and Anzac, which is what I thought would happen all along."

"20 December. Ten days ago the evacuation was a mere rumour, a possibility that one preferred not to dwell on. Its danger seemed considerable. One put the casualties inflicted in what seemed the inevitable rearguard action at anything up to 10,000.

"Now it is accomplished, all the strain and suspense is over and our total casualties are two slightly wounded; it sounds incredible. The order to evacuate came on the 8th and the removal of guns and men started immediately, small numbers being removed every night so as not to excite attention. We had two days' strong northerly blow but for the most part the weather was perfect and the sea almost flat calm. Captain Burmester had been appointed Senior Naval Officer, Kephalo, the kicking off place for all Gallipoli operations, irrespective of the presence of more senior officers. By the 18th only 20,000 men remained at Anzac, about the same at Suvla and about 20 guns. Rifle fire had purposely been slackened away each night, so that by the 18th it had almost ceased. The final evacuation was to take place on the nights of 18th and 19th, 10,000 men being removed from each place each night. Arrangements were made to leave medical staff to attend to casualties if these proved to be heavy, but this step was not necessary as the evacuation on both nights took place without the Turks having an inkling of what was going on. The whole affair was most ordinary and humdrum, and was not even accompanied by the usual shelling of the beaches which is almost part of the daily routine. It appears the Turks got it into their heads that we were landing men instead of removing them and were moving up large bodies of troops in anticipation of a general attack. I believe there was serious trouble at Anzac as to who should form the rearguard. The original 'Anzacs' said that they saw the show in and ought to see it out, while the younger ones said that the old chaps had had their turn and ought to give the freshers a chance. The last man left Suvla at 4 a.m. and at 4.30 a.m. a slow match having burnt its appointed length there was an enormous conflagration of fodder and stores which was clearly visible fifteen miles away at Kephalo."

So ended Godfrey's participation in the Dardanelles Campaign. If his experiences had not been so horrific as those of the troops, he had had his fair share of excitements and a great deal of novel, interesting and rewarding work. Now an entirely new chapter was about to begin. On 23 December he noted "Admiralty very pleased with Admiral Wemyss and have made him Commander-in-Chief Indies and Egypt. He is taking the Commander with him as Flag Commander and has asked that *Euryalus* may be his flagship."

CHAPTER THREE

Mediterranean Staff Officer

ADMIRAL WEMYSS hoisted his flag as Commander-in-Chief Egypt and East Indies on 22 January 1916. The geographical area of his command was large and his responsibilities wide and varied. The command covered the whole of the eastern Mediterranean, the Canal Zone and the Red Sea, the Arabian Sea and Persian Gulf, and the western Indian Ocean as far as Colombo. It was responsible for the defence of the Canal (in co-operation with the Army who had only recently moved five miles out into the Sinai Desert); the seaborne aspect of the defence of Egypt's western frontier (where the Senussi, aided by the Turks, were in revolt against the Italians and British and in occupation of Sollum); anti-submarine operations south of Crete and as far west as Corfu (where the German and Austrian U-Boats were becoming ever more active); co-operation with the Arab leaders (who were about to throw off the Turkish yoke) in the Red Sea and coasts of Arabia; co-operation with the Army in Mesopotamia (where General Townsend was soon to be besieged in Kut); and protection and control of shipping from the Red Sea as far east as the east coast of Ceylon (where there was, as yet, no threat). The staff remained small; Burmester was Chief of Staff; Marriott the flag commander; Godfrey's friend Dick Bevan was signal officer, his place as flag lieutenant having been taken by Lieutenant Neville; Paymaster Commander Miller was the Admiral's secretary; Godfrey was appointed assistant to the Chief of Staff in addition to his duties as squadron navigating officer. Ashore, there were two Royal Marine officers—one dealing with politico-military affairs and co-operation with GHQ Cairo, the other with Mediterranean and shipping problems. A third Marine was stationed at Colombo.

Godfrey, as Burmester's assistant, was at once involved in many interesting staff problems, accompanying his chief to meetings in Cairo, Alexandria and Ismailia. The first incident of note, however, was a further brief taste of active service: a

combined operation to recapture Sollum. It was also hoped to
rescue the crew, largely merchant navy men, of the armed
boarding steamer *Tara*, which had been torpedoed and sunk
some months earlier, who were being held prisoner by the
Senussi. Burmester was placed in charge of the naval side and
Godfrey accompanied him. Sidi Barrani was captured by what
Godfrey, in his diary, described as "a brisk and dashing piece
of work, the co-ordination of artillery and infantry being perfect
and the final sweep of the cavalry exceptionally brilliant. Their
only regret is that the latter were not armed with lances and
pistols, but only with swords with which they were often unable
to reach the Arabs who threw themselves flat on the ground."
There were virtually no facilities at Sidi Barrani and stores had
to be landed in ships' cutters on the open beach, much as they
had been done in Nelson's day. The Senussi, however, rapidly
became dispirited and the Navy, at least, had more trouble
from north-westerly gales than from the enemy. However, when
the General proposed that a battalion should be landed at
Sollum under the cover of the ships' guns, Godfrey records that
"the Captain, after our experience at Helles and elsewhere felt
amply justified in putting the veto on this unless he could
guarantee no opposition. A couple of machine-guns, well
placed, could account for half the landing force and turn the
affair into a shambles." In the event the Senussi evacuated
Sollum and the Army marched in virtually without opposition.
Godfrey's first job was to buoy the channel and to arrange for
the landing of supplies. It was all a little tame compared with
events which took place on the same stretch of coast twenty-five
years later, but Godfrey remarked, "we walked through the
camel lines to a broken-down building that for the time was
GHQ. All the buildings, including the coast guard offices have
from time to time been severely battered by our patrol craft
and are naturally in a deplorable condition. The bay is backed
by a 500-foot plateau, whose sides are for the most part very
steep and much cut up by deep ravines. It would have been a
difficult place to take in the face of much opposition but one
cannot but regret that they did not put up some sort of fight."
There was a happy sequel. Armoured cars, commanded by the
Duke of Westminster, set off to rescue the *Tara*'s prisoners. They
encountered about 300 Bedouin "encamped to the left of the
road, and during the approach over some bumpy ground came

under fire from two 10-pounders that the Senussi had either captured from the Italians or got from a submarine. Anyhow the going improved and the cars, which must have been magnificently handled, charged the guns at about 40 miles an hour, mowing down the gun teams as they advanced." Shades of the Eighth Army! Two days later *Tara's* crew were found and rescued from their many months of uncomfortable captivity.

Burmester and Godfrey now returned to *Euryalus* at Ismailia and Wemyss decided to visit the eastern part of his command. On 27 March *Euryalus* left Suez for Aden, the Persian Gulf, Bombay, Colombo and Penang.

"British policy in Arabia on the outbreak of war with Turkey had two main objects, to keep open and undisturbed communications through the Suez Canal and Red Sea; to nullify by all possible means the Turkish attempt to raise the Mohammedan world against the Allies by the proclamation of Jihad, a Holy War. As to the former, Turkey was not in a position to make any serious attacks upon British shipping from the Arabian coast, but it was possible for the Hejaz railway to bring mines and even supplies for German submarines to within easy reach of the shore of the Red Sea. [Godfrey does not explain how U-boats were to reach the Red Sea.] The attitude of the chiefs of Western Arabia and above all the Sherif Hussein was a matter of deep concern. The Hejaz, both from its geographical position and because it contained the shrines of Islam might serve either as a conduit, or barrier to Turkish propaganda according to the temper and actions of Sherif Hussein. A Jihad endorsed by Mecca would have to Islam an appeal more powerful than one dependent on Turkish religious authority alone." Hussein and his two sons, Feisal, later to be King of Syria and Iraq, and Abdulla, Emir and later King of Jordan, therefore occupied key roles. Abdulla had made contact with Kitchener before the war to let him know of Hussein's ambition to secure the autonomy of the Hejaz, and when Turkey declared war encouraging messages had been sent back by the British authorities in Egypt. In January 1915 the new High Commissioner, Sir Henry McMahon, and Sir Reginald Wingate, the Governor-General of the Sudan, renewed British overtures, but neither the British nor the Arabs were, at that time, able or willing to take very positive action. The Turks, preoccupied with Gallipoli, the Russians and the situation in Mesopotamia, were equally quiescent. By early 1916, however, all parties were prepared to try to advance their own interests more actively, and the British as a first step established the Arab Bureau to work for an Arab revolt. The role of the Indian Government (India was, at this time, the largest Mohammedan power in the world) complicated matters, as Delhi was responsible for Aden, Arab questions in the Red Sea and the annual pilgrimage to Mecca. Admiral Wemyss played a large part in removing these anomalies and in getting political control centred in Sir Henry McMahon in Cairo. In the spring of 1916 the Arab Revolt broke out and T. E. Lawrence began to make his name. Lawrence wrote in *Revolt in the Desert*, 'I found that Admiral Wemyss's active mind and broad intelligence had engaged his interest in the Arab Revolt from the beginning. He had come down again and again in his flagship, *Euryalus*, to lend a hand when things were critical, and had gone out of his way twenty times to help the shore, which properly was Army business. He had given the Arabs guns and machine guns, landing parties and technical help, with unlimited transport and naval co-operation always making a real pleasure of requests and fulfilling them in overflowing measure.'

On the way to Colombo in March *Euryalus* had cruised down the Red Sea and called at various ports in the Persian Gulf, and the inadequacy of the existing charts for inshore operations by the ships of the Red Sea Patrol under Captain Boyle (later Admiral of the Fleet the Earl of Cork and Orrery) in co-operation with the Arabs became very apparent. The squadron consisted of two old cruisers, some sloops, monitors and a seaplane carrier of the Royal Navy, one Australian ship and four armed transports of the Royal Indian Marine. "With dozens of ships operating on a hostile coast very much encumbered with uncharted, or only roughly charted coral reefs it was not surprising that there were frequent groundings. The number of these, two dozen during the last year, was disturbing and we were lucky that some of these did not become total wrecks, or necessitate prolonged salvage operations. The Arab pilots whom I consulted gave the position of many detached shoals in relation to villages which were not marked on the chart, and such maps as existed were very sketchy, and attributed names which bore no relation to anything known and understood by the pilots. The only solution was a properly triangulated survey of the approaches to harbours and inshore channels most frequented by HM ships with easily distinguished topographical features on islands, and mainland, if such existed. Concurrently with such a survey an examination was needed into the matter of place names. The names of all capes, harbours, villages and so on should be those used by the Arabs, with whom we were co-operating, and should be spelt in a way that we should find easy to pronounce, and the Arabs to understand, and which could be written in English or Arabic without risk of ambiguity. It was in pursuit of a solution to the question of place names that I met T. E. Lawrence. I remember walking up and down *Euryalus*'s quarter-deck with him one evening between Jidda and Port Sudan while, for an hour, he explained how and why there were over twenty ways of spelling and pronouncing the word Cairo.

"When we returned to the Suez Canal at the end of July, I at once set in motion the measures needed to survey in detail certain dangerous areas through which ships were constantly passing and where most of the groundings occurred. Both the C-in-C and Captain Boyle welcomed the idea which also had the backing of the Hydrographer. E. M. Dowson, the Director of the Survey of Egypt, undertook the production of the charts, and later a surveying officer was attached to Dowson's department to take charge of this work which to them was entirely new. Within three months the new charts were being issued to the ships.

"A great deal of rubbish has been written about Lawrence who was almost an exact contemporary of mine having been born in August 1888. Now the films have taken him up, glamourising him and trying to create a character utterly different from the man I knew in 1916. Ninety per cent of him was practical, logical, hard working and amazingly knowledgeable about Middle East archaeology, topography and Arabic roots. He loathed publicity like a great many other people, and when it was thrust upon him he developed his own sort of protective covering. It so happened that the soldiers at GHQ did not at first appreciate his ideas and unconventional behaviour, and towards them he adopted a puckishly disdainful manner which they naturally found hard to bear. The general staff attitude at Cairo irritated him and he liked having a dig at them. He cared nothing for uniform and at that time GHQ was very booted, spurred and red tabbed and remote from the fighting soldier. Dowson, Trelawney, Clayton and all the people in the topographical world in Egypt and in the geodetic survey admired him tremendously and it was unfortunate that he had a chip on his shoulder about military staff officers who swarmed at the Continental Hotel and did not try to understand this badly dressed little man who cared nothing for clothes or rank, and annoyed them by his unconscious mannerisms and indifference to appearances. For example, he would go about wearing only one red tab, or lieutenant colonel's pips on one shoulder, with his coat unbuttoned and no tie, until both were very sensibly abolished. If he didn't like anybody he did not try to hide it, and in this and in some other respects he resembled Wingate, whom I met in Palestine in 1938, raising Jewish commandos and ambushing Arabs, and again in India in 1944. Both Lawrence's and Wingate's methods and conception of irregular strategy and tactics were abhorrent to the traditionally minded soldier but against this one should remember that Lawrence had the support of a really great soldier, Allenby, and Wavell was Wingate's patron. Certainly the Lawrence I knew bore little resemblance to the Alec Guiness version with its long and dismal soliloquies and clever-clever conversation. The Lawrence revealed by himself in *The Seven Pillars of Wisdom* and *Revolt in the Desert* is a very practical down-to-earth person.

"1916 was the great year of collaboration between the Royal Navy and the Arab princes, sons of Hussein. Led by Lawrence, the Arabs and the Red Sea patrol successively occupied Yenbo, Rabegh, Um Lejj, Wejh and Akaba after which operations, culminating in the occupation of Damascus, moved inland. The unique combination of three such exceptional men, Wemyss, Boyle and Lawrence, came about quite by chance and worked extremely well. The collaboration of the Navy, a group of Arab chiefs and a handful of specially selected Army officers succeeded because men of such dissimilar temperament as Wemyss, Allenby, Wingate, Clayton, Boyle, Burmester, Ronald Storrs and T. E. Lawrence were able to work in harmony, to appreciate each other's outstanding qualities and to inspire confidence in the Emirs Feisal, Abdulla and other Arab leaders.

"In September we found ourselves in Jidda, the port of Mecca, attending the ceremonial landing of the Holy Carpet. Although

Jidda was technically in enemy territory *Euryalus* anchored inside the reefs, dressed ship, and fired a salute. The Holy Carpet was brought in a ship from Egypt escorted while afloat by the Royal Navy, and after it was landed by a considerable force of Egyptian soldiery commanded by a Brigadier, and all clad in white garments similar to bath towels, and sandals. The officers wore Sam Brown belts. According to custom they wore no head covering, but as the sun was very hot umbrellas were allowed. The Carpet was in several pieces, each carried by a white she-camel. The Official History gives the episode a mention: 'The total number of pilgrims was 26,000 . . . enthusiasm and gratitude for British aid was so great that the local Sheik, after being shown over *Euryalus*, officially invited the Admiral to ride at the head of the procession through the town; an offer which was prudently if reluctantly declined.' However, Wemyss, although as a non-Muslim debarred from visiting Mecca, was thrilled to be able, and allowed to telephone Mecca, and speak to the Grand Sherif who was soon to adopt the title of King Hussein."

Godfrey was, from mid 1916, increasingly occupied with pure staff work. When Wemyss visited the East Indies in June 1916 a conference had been held with the Commander-in-Chief China, Admiral Grant, to concert all measures needed to meet the threat which would be posed to British trade if a German raider should appear in the Indian Ocean, which had been free of such marauders since the destruction of the light cruiser *Emden* by HMAS *Sydney* in 1914. "Briefly these measures consisted of dispersion, patrol of focal points, and convoy of transports. The principle in devising this routing system was to scatter shipping as much as possible and to do away with the continuous and congested traffic streams round the coasts of India and Ceylon, by providing ships with several alternative tracks. Merchant ships, with the exception of those under Government charter, were not 'controlled' by the Government, but were generally content to obey orders where they might have ignored advice. Sailing orders were therefore printed and issued by order of the Vice-Admiral, Commander-in-Chief, whose name appeared at the bottom and, of course, carried great weight. To bring into force the decisions of the Penang Conference, I plotted all the routes on a chart of the Indian Ocean. From three to seven routes emanated from the Cape and from Mombassa, the Gulf of Aden, the Persian Gulf, Bombay, Colombo, Calcutta, the Malacca Straits, the Sunda Straits, and Western Australia, with a different set for transports. The completed picture looked rather complicated until redrawn by the skilled draftsmen of the Survey of Egypt. On the final charts that were issued to all men of war, five colours were used, an expensive process which, however, made the charts easy to interpret. We were back in Ismailia in early August and all this work, which needed a great deal of checking and rechecking, proof correcting and many visits to the Survey of Egypt and Government Press in Cairo, took the best part of two months to complete. It was finished, all the forms, charts, routes, etc., distributed and the scattering of shipping carried out by mid November 1916. The raider *Wolf* was then fitting out in Germany. On 3 January 1917 the Admiralty [doubtless as the result of the work of Room 40 in decrypting German signals] warned Wemyss and Grant that a raider might be about to attack trade in the Indian Ocean. They were able to report that all the measures needed for the spreading of traffic were in force and that available ships were stationed ready to patrol off the Straits of Malacca, Sunda Straits, Colombo and Aden. *Wolf* entered the Indian Ocean in January and from then until her return in February 1918, she and her auxiliaries accounted for only a dozen Allied merchantships." This was not exactly an epoch-making British success, but it was another example of Godfrey's ability to enlist the help of non-naval organisations and to demand and obtain the very highest standards of service and workmanship which he was not to forget when he came, in World War II, to organise, with the help of Oxford University and the Oxford University Press, the Inter Service Topographical Department.

In January 1917 Godfrey, who had been promoted Lt Commander in the previous October, when just twenty-eight, left *Euryalus* to concentrate on his duties as Assistant to the Chief of Staff, Burmester. In the last quarter of 1916 Wemyss's attention had been focussed more and more on the Mediterranean. The command situation was highly complicated. The post of British Commander-in-Chief, Mediterranean Fleet, formerly one of, if not the most important in the naval hierarchy, had been abolished in 1914 when all the Navy's most modern ships were concentrated in the North Sea and the Atlantic.

There were, in addition to Wemyss's own command, Flag Officers at Gibraltar, Malta, in the Aegean and at Taranto, the latter working under supreme Italian command.*

The Mediterranean as a whole was "under the shadowy suzerainty of a French Allied Commander-in-Chief (Admiral Gauchet) with the French battlefleet at Corfu. The French were naturally very interested in the safety of their base at Corfu from landward as well as seaborne attack, and of their lines of communication with Algeria which they used to call the granary of France. They also had political aspirations in Athens, Salonica and what is now Syria and the Lebanon. The Italians, who never appeared to recognize the Allied C-in-C, had their own spheres of influence, which they guarded most jealously, in the Adriatic, on the coasts of Cyrenaica, Tunis, in Rhodes and the Dodecanes and on the adjacent coast of Anatolia."

So far as the Central Powers were concerned, the Austro-Hungarian Fleet was bottled up in the Adriatic, but as it included four modern, powerful dreadnoughts as well as a number of older battleships, the threat of a breakout against the Western Allies' communications could not be ignored. A similar threat was posed by the battlecruiser *Goeben* and the light cruiser *Breslau* at Constantinople. Although nominally flying the Turkish flag they were still manned by their German crews, and, under effective German control, exercised a quite disproportionate influence on events in just the same way that the battleship *Tirpitz* was to do from Norway in World War II. The real danger, however, came from the U-boats, German and Austrian. By the end of 1916 the Germans alone had some twenty boats operating in the Mediterranean, based mostly on the Austrian port of Cattaro (now Kotor) but some on Constantinople.

"The various British naval authorities worked directly under the Admiralty. Their intelligence centres exchanged information, but apart from this there was little need for collaboration until the German submarines started operating against Allied merchant ships. These intelligence centres were in charge of Marine officers, Lampen at Malta, Temple at Mudros, Trant Luard at Alexandria and Caulfeild at Colombo. It was natural

---

* Italy had entered the war on the Allied side as a result of the territorial promises made to her under the secret Treaty of London.

that these extremely able officers should not only give information to merchantmen about the position and possible intentions of German submarines and surface raiders, but should advise them regarding the best route to follow to keep them out of trouble, and to issue instructions about how to avoid minefields laid in the approaches to Allied and neutral harbours. When escorts were available two or three ships would be gathered together and sailed in company with small escorts, and so gradually a tentative system of convoy came into being. Trant Luard, in urging on his own Senior Naval Officer at Alexandria and on the Commander-in-Chief at Ismailia, the development of a system of convoy and escort was in every sense a pioneer and ahead of Admiralty policy, which adopted convoy unwillingly. He had the enthusiastic backing of Admiral Wemyss. It was quite a complicated business to introduce a system of routing, dispersion and ultimately convoy involving much detailed work not only at the ports—Alexandria and Port Said—but on the staff of the Commander-in-Chief. Special charts had to be produced and instructions printed by the thousand, and here we were again fortunate in finding such willing collaborators in the Survey of Egypt and the Egyptian Government Press. They gave the Navy a very high priority and were quick to appreciate our needs and to brush aside difficulties. All the staff work in connection with this new activity fell to my lot, and involved many visits to Cairo to see Dowson and Trelawney, and to Alexandria to collaborate with Trant Luard.

"Admiral Wemyss's non-technical mind was already ranging far ahead and, leaving all the details to Rudolph Burmester and me, he quickly saw that nothing less than the complete control of shipping throughout the Mediterranean was involved, and that this could only be done by a centralized Command with authority similar to that of the Admiralty in the North Atlantic to move men of war and resources from one part of the Mediterranean to another and to establish routing and convoy assembly authorities wherever they were needed. He also saw that such a step might meet with opposition from the Allied Commander-in-Chief at Corfu, and from our own 'petty rajahs' in the Aegean and elsewhere whose status would be reduced by the interposition of a British Commander-in-Chief between them and the Admiralty. The fact that so much was actually achieved during 1917 must be attributed to Wemyss's prestige, powers of persuasion, and to his willingness to shoulder responsibility and to take risks. He was wise but impulsive, and wildly optimistic. He realised this and used to say that he needed a chief of staff who would trample on his wildcat schemes, and this was exactly what Burmester used, very tactfully and gently, to do. They both realised that the idea of a British co-ordinator or Commander-in-Chief would be more acceptable to the Admiralty if it reached Whitehall as a unanimous proposal from all five flag officers—Gibraltar, Malta, Taranto, Aegean and Egypt. Wemyss, therefore, proposed a conference at Malta to go into the whole question of anti-submarine measures. Rear-Admiral Ballard (Rear-Admiral, Malta) was known to have aspirations in this direction and agreed to preside. Wemyss was represented by Trant Luard and myself—not even by his Chief of Staff, Burmester. We produced a strong recommendation for unified command of all anti-submarine measures under a British Flag Officer subordinate to the Allied Commander-in-Chief. That was as far as we could go, and was an essential preliminary to an Allied conference at Corfu.

"It duly met on board the French flagship, Admiral Wemyss being represented this time by Burmester and myself. Admiral Gauchet, a stout little Breton peasant, presided at the first meeting and sub-committees were formed to study individual aspects of the problem—patrol, convoy, the Otranto barrage* and actual names and number of craft available. The all-important question of high command was hardly mentioned, but the rumour gradually got around that, so long as the integrity of French Supreme Command was preserved, the French would be reasonable and delegate the conduct of the anti-submarine operations and all that implied to the British who, it was clear, would have to provide most of the ships. The French conception of this new organization was a sort of committee consisting of French, British, Italian and Japanese Admirals with the British Commander-in-Chief as Chairman, and this was roughly the idea which Burmester took back with

---

* The Otranto Barrage was a system of nets, minefields and patrols across the Straits of Otranto designed to bottle up the German and Austrian U-boats in the Adriatic. Due largely to technical difficulties it was almost completely ineffective.

him to Egypt. Shipping would be 'controlled' and routes allotted by officers stationed at all important ports such as Marseilles, Genoa, Bizerta and Algiers. An outline and very sketchy plan was produced but details were left to the new British command and the committee, for which the French had already found a name, the 'Commission de Malte'.

"There followed a lull, and then the welcome and not altogether unexpected news that Vice-Admiral Wemyss had been offered the job and invited to come to London before taking up his new command. Wemyss had always wanted to be Commander-in-Chief Mediterranean which, in the form it was offered to him, would put him in operational control of the Flag Officers Gibraltar, Aegean, Malta, Egypt, and Italy (but not of Commodore Kelly with his cruiser squadron and destroyers based on Brindisi), in addition to the organization under British and French Admirals of anti-submarine patrols that had to be set up all over the Mediterranean. What had been four months ago a vague and ill-defined idea was now well on the way to becoming a plan with all its administrative and operational implications. A voluminous bundle of papers arrived on my desk. I was encouraged by Burmester to apply myself to the problem without delay. I still have the paper I submitted to him on 15 June 1917 called 'General remarks and suggestions regarding the organization of the Mediterranean command' which bears a strong resemblance to the organization that was finally adopted.

"It was apparent that we had a lot to learn about the control of merchant shipping and that the only place to learn it was the Admiralty. Admiral Wemyss had decided to go home during July and it was suggested that I should go to the Admiralty a fortnight or so in advance to make personal contact with all concerned and pick up as much information as possible about the new command. I travelled home via Malta and Taranto, receiving a rather frosty reception from Admiral Ballard, and reaching London early in July. I sought out Paymaster Commander Manisty, with whom I had been staff mates at the beginning of the war when he was Wemyss's secretary in Cruiser Force G. He, Commander Reggie Henderson and Mr Leslie, a shipping man, had started the new convoy section in the Admiralty House dining room and it was from them that I learnt that Wemyss was not after all to have the

Mediterranean command, and had been summoned home to be vetted by Geddes (the new First Lord) and Lloyd George for the post of First Sea Lord. This was supposed to be very secret but, as everyone I met was gossiping about it I felt justified in breaking the news to Jack Marriott who happened to be in England. We decided that, at all costs, Wemyss must be told of this development before he reached Paris, where he would be attending the Supreme Allied Council in a few days and where he would meet Jellicoe, Geddes and Lloyd George, as well as Admiral de Bon, the French Chief of Naval Staff and an old friend of Wemyss. Until Jack Marriott met Wemyss at the Gare de Lyon the Admiral had no idea that an intrigue to displace Jellicoe was afoot. The Paris Conference did confirm the Corfu recommendations and when it was finished Lloyd George asked Wemyss to come back to Calais with him in his special train. Admiral Wemyss made some excuse and refused, as he did not want to get involved in a political intrigue, and we all travelled home together.

"About a week later Wemyss sent for me to the Berkeley, where he was staying, and broke the sad news that his life's ambition, the Mediterranean command, had eluded him. He said I should be appointed to the staff of Vice-Admiral Gough-Calthorpe (who was to be the new Commander-in-Chief Mediterranean), as Assistant to the Chief of Staff, Rudolph Burmester. Dick Bevan became Signal Officer and Gerald Dickens Flag Commander, in place of Jack Marriott, who went with Wemyss, when the latter became Second Sea Lord and later Deputy First Sea Lord prior to assuming the office of First Sea Lord and Chief of Naval Staff."

By the end of August 1917 Gough-Calthorpe and his staff were installed in Malta. Other officers were soon added to the staff to cover specialised matters such as wireless, gunnery, intelligence and so forth, but the organization remained a much smaller one than would have been considered necessary in World War II. The hitherto independent flag officers at Malta, Gibraltar, the Aegean, Egypt and Italian bases came under the control of the Commander-in-Chief, and some of them resented the fact, and things took some time to settle down. Godfrey found Gough-Calthorpe "a most gentle, unassuming and modest man". In dealing with the many problems which at once confronted him he was, initially, "not sufficiently sure of himself,—he temporized and waited. He knew what to do but was too considerate to do it. He has been described as ninety per cent wisdom and ten per cent initiative. Later, however, when he got his second wind and was appointed High Commissioner Turkey and Black Sea, Admiral Gough-Calthorpe became tougher. He was a shrewd negotiator with the Turks and did not hesitate to order Maude and Allenby to halt their Armies in Mesopotamia and Syria.

"Our staff was very modest and on the operations side, working under Commodore Burmester, the Chief of Staff, consisted only of Gerald Dickens the Flag Commander, myself Assistant to the Chief of Staff, Eagar the Chief of Staff's Secretary and the necessary clerical help. Dickens and I divided the Mediterranean between us, he looking after matters connected with the French, Italian and Greek Navies, the Otranto Barrage, the Adriatic and Aegean, while I dealt with papers about anti-submarine operations, port organizations, Egypt, Red Sea, Levant, North Africa, Gibraltar, Spain and the Japanese squadron. One or other of us accompanied the C-in-C when he visited the various commands in the early part of 1918, so that I got a trip to Gibraltar, Oran, Algiers, Bone, Alexandria, Port Said and Ismailia.

"During my trip to London I had collected a dozen or so lady clerks and another dozen Writers, the former for secretarial and cipher duties and the latter to form the shipping intelligence centre, which enabled us to keep track of the position and movement of all merchantmen in the Mediterranean. Both the Commander-in-Chief and the Chief of Staff encouraged me to correspond with Captain Henderson and Paymaster Commander Manisty in the convoy department at the Admiralty, and with Jack Marriott now the First Sea Lord's Naval Assistant. Old-fashioned officers frowned on such a procedure and, of course, it could be abused. If these letters touched on anything controversial I always showed them to Commodore Burmester.

"What we had not anticipated was the spate of administrative problems that were created by the introduction of convoys not only about the merchant ships, aircraft and escorting men of war but in the organization and economy of ports. There were many matters that demanded the attention of Gerald Dickens and myself. Here are a few of the questions we had to attend to:

1. Action to be taken to counter an attack by the Austrian Fleet from the Adriatic, or the *Goeben* and *Breslau* from the Dardanelles, on Allied shipping or on the flank of our Army in Palestine or on the Suez Canal.
2. The political and largely anti-allied activities of the Italians in Libya, the Red Sea and the Dodecanese and neighbouring parts of the Turkish coast and Arabia.
3. Efforts to induce the Italians to take part in the war. We had not then realized that the Italian object was to keep their Navy intact as a post-war pawn in peace negotiations.
4. The building up of the Otranto mobile barrage organization.
5. Day to day liaison with Commander Sakano, the Japanese liaison officer, and Capitaine de Vaisseau Benoit D'Azy, the French resident naval officer, Capitaine de Corvette de Laurens Castelet, Admiral Gauchet's liaison officer on the C-in-C's staff, and Captain Como, Italian liaison officer.
6. Situation created by the appearance of scouting Zeppelins in the Eastern Mediterranean.
7. Abandonment of the Spanish coastal route, and the establishment of large Gibraltar-Genoa and Gibraltar-Bizerta convoys. (This obvious step encountered great opposition.)
8. Employment of kite balloons, brigs and submarine minelayers.
9. Laying of deep minefields in the Malta Channel.
10. A multitude of questions about port defences and organization.
11. Limits of the Mediterranean Command.
12. Operational aspects of intelligence.
13. Anti-submarine operations.

"Allied co-operation on the highest plane was achieved by the presence at Malta of French, Italian and Japanese Admirals and later Captain Leigh, USN, who, under the chairmanship of the British Commander-in-Chief, Vice-Admiral Gough-Calthorpe, formed the 'Commission de Malte'. For me, the interest in Allied liaison was centred in the persons of Commander Sakano and Capitaine de Vaisseau Benoit d'Azy. We all three lived in the Cecil Hotel and met constantly before, during and after meals. Sakano was one of that all too small band of internationally minded Japanese Naval Officers who disapproved of the expansionist policy of the military party to whom, in those days, the Navy was subservient. In 1917 Japan was still proud of being our ally and we were fortunate in finding in Sakano a man who could give practical expression to this feeling in terms of loyal co-operation by the Japanese destroyer flotilla, which was allotted the task of escorting all our troop convoys, mostly between Marseilles and Alexandria and, towards the end of the war, direct to Haifa and Beirut, although Japan did not actually declare war on Turkey. Sakano and I had very few secrets from each other and he was very outspoken about the personalities of Japanese destroyer captains, some of whom committed hara-kiri when a German submarine sank a ship they were escorting. In those days a Japanese gentleman would see nothing odd in ceremonial suicide. A Japanese when recounting such an event is inclined to laugh or rather giggle in a nervous self-conscious way as if apologising for the strange customs of his countrymen. "Very funny," said Sakano, and thereby relieved the tension and absolved one from the obligation of looking solemn. I valued Sakano's friendship. We met in London and afterwards in China in 1932 when he was the Japanese Rear-Admiral Yangtse.

"Benoit d'Azy was an aristocrat, Catholic and very friendly officer of the old school. He had a rough way of speaking of officers of his own service of humble origin and referred to them collectively as 'socialists'. In this category he included his own Commander-in-Chief, Admiral Gauchet. For General Sarrail, the Allied Military Commander-in-Chief at Salonika, admittedly a politician, he had no use at all. 'Socialist, Free Mason, Bolshevik, follower of Bolo Pasha'—no epithet was too bad. I saw a good deal of him and greatly enjoyed his company. He was actively pro-British without ceasing to be 100 per cent French. His assistant, Pichon, became so attached to the British Navy that he designed a new uniform based on the British model. De Laurens Castelet was a real charmer and very popular. All in all we became very fond of our French colleagues and I had an uneasy feeling that some of the British delegation at the French Headquarters had not been chosen so carefully.

"Captain Como, the Italian, had a difficult job in making the best of his Government's policy, which was roughly to do as little as possible and to preserve the Italian Navy to be used as a negotiating pawn in the peace conference. He was always two or three steps ahead of the Ministry of Marine at Rome. With such men representing their Navies liaison was easy, productive and pleasurable.

"Captain Leigh could not have been more co-operative. Admiral Grant paid a glowing tribute to the work of the American escorts based on Gibraltar. These and the American chasers on the Otranto barrage acted entirely under the orders of the local British authority and occupied positions nearly similar to those of British ships. Greek destroyers also performed excellent work in the eastern Mediterranean and the part which they, the Japanese and the Americans played in convoy escort work was in striking contrast to that of France and Italy. In terms of seakeeping, the Japanese spent 72 per cent of their total time at sea, the British 60 per cent, the French and Italians about 45 per cent."

By the middle of 1918 the new organisation was working well, although the Mediterranean always suffered from being a 'secondary' theatre and in consequence from shortages of ships, equipment and training facilities in comparison with Home waters. For various reasons, but principally due to their own passive attitude, the effective control passed from the French to the British, so that when the Central Powers began to collapse with overtures for peace, first from Bulgaria and then from Turkey, Gough-Calthorpe was instructed by the Admiralty to take sole charge of the negotiations with the latter, merely keeping the French Commander-in-Chief informed of what he was doing. Intelligence about the situation in Turkey was very meagre and fears were still felt about *Goeben*. In fact she had been severely damaged by mines during a brief raid into the Aegean in January 1918, when the cruiser *Breslau* had been sunk, and she was incapable of any further action. Moreover, in the previous December the Russians had concluded an armistice with the Germans and there was considerable anxiety that they would take over the Russian Black Sea Fleet, which included three dreadnoughts, as well as cruisers, destroyers and submarines.

"Gough-Calthorpe arrived at Mudros on 11 October accompanied by the Flag Commander Gerald Dickens, Lieutenant Commander Dicken and the Secretary Lynes. Burmester and I followed later. The Commander-in-Chief proved to be an astute and determined negotiator with the Turks, at the same time keeping the French at bay who were literally clamouring to be let in. He secured the acceptance of practically all the terms of the Armistice with Turkey which was signed on 30 October.

"While Burmester and Dickens were fully engaged in dealing with Armistice questions, Dickens also doing most of the inter-preting, I busied myself with drafting the orders for the passage of the Allied Fleet through the Dardanelles and Sea of Marmora and its berthing off Constantinople and in the Gulf of Ismid. This had to be preceded by the clearance of the minefields outside and inside the Dardanelles, the occupation of the forts at Sed el Bahr, Kum Kale and in the Narrows, and the establishment of anti-submarine and air patrols—the whole thing quite a complicated business. As we still did not know what had happened to *Goeben* and the German submarines in Turkish waters, precautions had to be taken. All that the Turkish delegation would tell us was that 'it would be all right'. Drafting the orders for the passage of the Allied Fleet from Mudros to Constantinople was rather like drawing up the instructions for a procession which has to overcome some obstacles, pass through a narrow defile, and is composed of units whose conduct is unpredictable. We did not know if the French, Italian, or Greek ships had ever steamed in close order or could take in or transmit signals, so, to be on the safe side, gaps were interposed between them. The combined Fleet consisted of four British, two French and one Italian battleship, one Greek armoured cruiser, six British armoured cruisers, eighteen destroyers, an aircraft carrier* and hundreds of auxiliary craft.

"The clearance of channels through the minefields was com-menced at once and completed by 11 November. To make doubly sure that it really was completed to the satisfaction of Captain Higginson, in charge of minesweepers, Burmester sent me up the Dardanelles in a destroyer on the 11th. Higginson was able to assure me that all was well and I carried this message back to Mudros but if anything had gone wrong I was quite conscious that, in giving the all clear, I should have been held responsible. However, all did go well, and on 12 November 1918 the Combined Fleets entered the Dardanelles. British and

* More strictly an aircraft transport. Aircraft carriers in the modern sense were still in the very early stage of development.

Indian soldiers manned the battlements of the Chanak forts and presented arms as the Fleet flagship passed. It was a stirring moment. The torpedo tube which had always been regarded as such a deterrent to a hostile ship passing through the Narrows turned out to be a tin-pot affair, wheeled out on a little iron jetty which could have been demolished by gunfire. *Goeben* we found completely out of action at a jetty half way up the Bosphorous. All the U-boats had fled. On 13 November the Fleet anchored off Constantinople. Thus ended the great enterprise that had commenced on 25 April 1915 when the Lancashire Fusiliers landed at W beach on Cape Helles.

"My Commander-in-Chief was appointed High Commissioner Constantinople and Black Sea, a role which combined the functions of what would be British Ambassador Turkey and Commissioner for winding up German activities in South Russia and Turkey, expediting the return to Germany of German personnel and the surrender of war material. After a stay of ten days in Constantinople he embarked in *Superb* and arrived at Sevastopol at the head of an Allied Fleet on 26 November. Some days before Commander Turle had been despatched to Yalta in the Crimea to get in touch with the Dowager Empress of Russia, who together with the Grand Duke Nicholas and a large number of relatives and courtiers was known to be there. The Dowager Empress, who was a staunch believer in the divine right of kings, could not believe that the Czar and Czarina had been murdered at Sverlovsk. In the course of a conversation with Turle she said it was only a matter of time and Great Britain would have a Bolshevik government. Turle ventured to disagree with her. As it was against protocol to disagree with royalty, and a novel experience for Her Majesty, Turle was instantly dismissed as *persona non grata*. All the royalties and grand dukes and duchesses were evacuated, but such was the bitterness of feeling between the Dowager Empress and the Grand Duke Nicholas that they and their entourages were transported in different ships.*

"The German Army and Navy, who were in control at Sevastopol when we arrived, behaved very correctly and gave us all the information we asked for about the state of the

---

* Godfrey was mistaken about this. Both the Dowager Empress and the Grand Duke were evacuated from Malta in April 1919 in HMS *Marlborough*.

Russian Navy and ports and were evidently only too anxious to get home. We found ourselves in control of a large naval arsenal and dockyard full of Russian men-of-war, some without crews, some sunk in harbour, one or two bottom up, and of vast underground depots containing every sort of mine and munition. The arrival of the Bolshevik forces in the Crimea was only a matter of weeks, and the sooner we destroyed the mines and ammunition the better. The Bolshevik forces were peasants from the heart of Russia and the Ukraine and knew nothing about ships or sea power. They made no attempt to impede the immobilisation of the old Russian Navy. The sterns of destroyers were blown off and submarines were towed to sea and sunk in deep water, explosives were placed inside the cylinders of battleships and cruisers and detonated and other large units towed away to Bizerta.

"In breaking through into south Russia we had literally burst our way into an unknown sea. There had been no information from this part of the world for four years except for the military mission with the White Russian General Denikin. In order to find out what was going on ships were despatched at the end of November to Odessa, Berdiansk and Ghenickhesk, to Mariupol and Taganrog, to Novorossisk and to Batoum. Contact was made with the Don and Kuban cossacks as yet untainted with bolshevism, and the ships were received with acclamation. The most important mission was reserved for Captain George Chetwode (Captain (D)), who arrived at Nicolaieff on 5 December, with two British and one French destroyers. On this mission I was lent to him as staff officer. As soon as our little flotilla secured alongside the jetty at Nicolaieff the White Russian General Augustoff in command of the local volunteer army, Admiral Rimsky-Korsakoff, Captain of the port, the governor of the City, the Mayor and several other leading officials came on board. These included Mr Dunderdale of the firm Peter Regier, trading in the Black Sea, and his son Bill, with whom I had much to do as DNI in World War II. A large crowd on the pier greeted us with the greatest enthusiasm. A conference was held in the ward room, Mr Dunderdale translating, and the officials explained the political situation. Nicolaieff being the port through which the German armies retiring from the Caucasus and the Black Sea ports had to pass, there was a considerable German base and transit organisation, and until recently the German Army acting in conjunction with the Russians had been in control of the town. It had been handed back to the Russians and was now run by a small Russian Naval force commanded by Admiral Rimsky-Korsakoff. A local brand of Bolshevist controlled the hinterland and was infiltrating into the city.

"Having got a rough idea of the situation Captain Chetwode, accompanied by me and the captain of the French destroyer, visited General von Gillhausen, commanding the German forces, at his headquarters. He was all that one expected a Prussian general to be, correct, courteous, immaculately dressed—pickelhaube helmet, stiff collar, monocle and all—and was supported by an extremely efficient staff. Chetwode explained our mission, which was to expedite by every possible means the evacuation of the German forces around the Black Sea; the General in turn explained that this was also their object, but that, to an increasing degree, it was being hampered by the state of lawlessness in Nicolaieff which was only kept in check by the presence of the German Army. However, the evacuation was progressing at the rate of one train-load a day and, the war being over, no one was more anxious to go home than the Germans in Russia. 'But,' he said, 'you must realise, gentlemen, that I am not my own master. The German Armies on the eastern front have been infected with the Bolshevist virus and any orders I give must be counter-signed by the Committee of Soldiers and Workmen who are actually in session in the next room.' Folding doors were then, rather dramatically, flung open and there they were, the Committee of Soldiers and Workmen, sitting around another table.

"We felt this was a problem for the Germans to solve but promised to assist them in maintaining the needful collaboration, on our side by myself, and on their side by Major Muller, who when the war started had been in the process of becoming an American citizen and spoke perfect English. We had all got used to working with Naval Allies during the war and my personal assessment as regards reliability and sea-keeping put them in the order Japanese, American, Greek, French and Italian. Now we could add the German Army and the White Russian Navy to our collection, which I placed in the following order: the German Army on an equality with the Japanese and the Americans, and the Russian Navy after the Italians.

We found the Germans very easy to work with, obedient, conscientious and resourceful and we never had cause to doubt their reliability.

"We liked the charming Russian Admiral, Rimsky-Korsakoff, especially his name. We assumed he was a relation of the great composer, but had no clue as to his reliability. Conclusive evidence of his duplicity was, however, available within ten days when he and his staff embarked in a small merchantman and sailed under cover of darkness down the river Bug, destination unknown. He had cleverly interposed the British between himself and the Germans, who used to keep a guard on all ships, and one must give him full marks for a well-executed deception plan and for the poker face he maintained at our frequent meetings which continued until a few hours before his flitting. By daylight he was well clear of the estuary of the Bug, the same River Bug down which Potemkin had sailed a hundred and thirty-one years before with Catherine the Great and successfully concealed from her the impoverishment of the country by planting imitation villages along the bank of the river."

Nor was it only in the Black Sea that the Royal Navy was active. A small force, whose second in command was Godfrey's former captain in *Bramble*, Basil George Washington, had crossed Persia to the Caspian, seized and armed some Russian oilers and was to have some spirited actions with the Bolshevik forces. In the Baltic cruisers and submarines under Admiral Walter Cowan (who in World War II and when in his seventies fought unofficially with the Long Range Desert Group) helped to establish the independence of Latvia, Lithuania and Estonia. In Murmansk, Archangel and Vladivostock naval forces also supported the army in the unsuccessful attempt at intervention. The British Empire, as it was still known, appeared to be larger and stronger than ever. It is something that is now difficult to visualise.

Godfrey was back in Constantinople before the end of the year. There "General Sir George Milne lately in command of British forces operating from Salonika and now holding the terrific title of Commander-in-Chief of the Black Sea, established his headquarters in a palatial villa on the Bosphorus. Our relations with his staff were close and cordial, my opposite numbers being Lt Colonel James Horlic, GSO Intelligence and

Lt Colonel Gayer Anderson, GSO Operations. I also had to keep in daily touch with the staff officers of the military Governor of Constantinople, Burt-Marshall and Gifford. Co-operation with such able and charming people presented no difficulties. The Navy, having no base nearer than Malta, demanded a hundred and one services which only the Army could provide and which were invariably settled on staff officer level. This was as it should be but was rather a new experience for the Navy which tends to overload its senior officers with too much detail.

"The C-in-C divided his time between the flagship, where Burmester continued to preside over the Naval Staff and dealt with a whole range of questions relating to the whole Mediterranean station, and the Embassy. Gerald Dickens and I continued to split the operation staff duties but later, after the fall of Sevastopol (to the Bolsheviks), affairs in the Black Sea cooled off a bit and Dickens returned to Malta. To cope with the High Commissioner and diplomatic work, Admiral Gough-Calthorpe was provided with an Assistant High Commissioner, Rear-Admiral Webb, a Minister, Hohler, a Naval Attaché and diplomatic staff. One very important activity was the detection and winding up of German activities in Turkey. To achieve this a new department was created and Mr Stanley Wyatt (afterwards Sir Stanley Wyatt and alternate President of the Ottoman Debt Council) was appointed as Controller of Enemy Banks. I saw a lot of Stanley Wyatt and, forty-five years later, we remain firm friends.

"Constantinople was starved, indescribably dirty, cold and almost coal-less. The exodus of the White Russians from the Ukraine and Caucusus had already assumed alarming proportions and neither the French nor the Americans were disposed to collaborate in dealing with the transport side of refugee problem. During the spring of 1919 the French were allotted a zone of influence in the Black Sea, which included Odessa and the estuary of the River Bug leading to Nicolaieff, where a few Russian submarines were said to be nearing completion. Opinion wavered between ignoring these submarines and bottling them up with nets, sunken ships and mines. The French did not possess the ships or material but would be quite willing to borrow them from the British. We knew, however, that any British resources 'lent' to the French would be a dead loss. In

the event a laisser-faire policy was adopted and as things turned
out the Reds, when they overran Nicolaieff had neither the
will nor the ability to operate the submarines. The Governor of
Taurida, a White Russian official of the old school, when he
called on our Commander-in-Chief, warned him laughingly,
'You be careful, Navies that come to Sevastopol invariably
mutiny.' He was thinking of his own White Russian Navy, and
then the same Navy when taken over by the Germans. How
right he was; within two months the morale of our French
Allies broke; the sailors massed on the forecastles of the French
battleships and destroyers and 'demonstrated' in a way that
was quite unmistakable. Their crews came from Toulon and
wanted to go home. Within a month the French Fleet sailed
away and that was the last we saw of them. The mutiny at
Sevastopol was led by a seaman-machinist André Marty, son
of a worker condemned to death for his part in the Paris
Commune (1871). He attracted Stalin's attention as the man
who refused to take up arms against the Soviet Union in 1919
and in 1936 he became the supreme 'Troika' of the International Brigade Volunteers who fought for the Spanish
Republic.

"The British did not want to fight Russia any more than the
French. 'Thrice armed is he who hath his quarrel just'. We
did not feel that ours *was* just and we did not agree with Mr
Churchill who seemed to be trying to propel the country into a
real war with Bolshevist Russia. The hundreds of trawlers,
drifters and other small craft that had been collected in the
Adriatic, Aegean and Black Sea were being sent home but
there was delay in sending out active service reliefs for the
crews of those that had to stay, and this led to much discontent.
Not only was intervention unpopular but the conviction was
growing that the White Russians were not militarily worth
supporting. I was suddenly confronted with the realities of life
by finding myself one of a board of enquiry into the state of
discipline on board our base ship at Constantinople. The futility
of our Russian and Turkish policy seemed obvious to me and
my colleagues, but evidently not to Whitehall. It set us against
Russia, an ally to whom we owed so much, and Turkey, who
never should have been an enemy. With Turkey relations could
have resumed their normal pattern had it not been for the
Smyrna Greek episode in 1919 and 1922. As a result British

men-of-war were not even allowed to pay courtesy visits to Turkish ports until 1937 when the ice was broken by *Repulse* during my term of command.

"As the summer of 1919 approached we realised that our period of service in the Mediterranean and Black Sea was drawing to a close. We returned to Malta late in August and shortly afterwards Admiral Gough-Calthorpe accompanied by Burmester, Lynes, Dicken and myself left Malta for Marseilles and home.

"Looking back on my nine months in the Black Sea I used to wonder what had been achieved. Mighty little. On the one hand our Prime Minister, Lloyd George, hypnotised by Venizelos, had launched a Greek Army into Asia Minor thereby exacerbating instead of abating the bad relations between Greece and Turkey. This was done during the temporary withdrawal from the Supreme War Council of the Italian representatives, who were naturally incensed. On the other hand, Winston Churchill, as Minister of War, was doing his best to propel the British Empire into war with Russia. Soviet Russia will never forget or forgive us for invading or trying to invade or menace Russia. The British Navy was a sort of maid of all work—sweeping mines, evacuating refugees, turning chaos into order, providing transport; common services which the French, Italians and Americans were only too glad to accept while they pursued personal and commercial ends.

"For me it was the end of a most interesting chapter, which had commenced with my appointment to *Charybdis* in August 1914."

John Godfrey had certainly had a rather unusual war, differing in most respects from that of the majority of his contemporaries. He had spent five years abroad, experiencing neither the boredom, enlivened by brief moments of excitement such as Jutland, of the Grand Fleet, nor the arduous life of the ships of the Dover Patrol or the convoy escorts. There had, nevertheless, been plenty of action and, during 1915 in particular, he had probably seen more shots fired in anger than most officers in Home Waters. Under Wemyss, Gough-Calthorpe and Burmester he had been given, for a young man still in his twenties, an extraordinary amount of responsibility and had been encouraged to use his own initiative and form his own judgements to a degree which fell to the lot of few

lieutenants or lieutenant-commanders in those days. He had
dealt with a very wide range of staff problems and had gained
quite invaluable experience of working harmoniously with
officers of other services, British, French, Italian, Arab, Greek,
Japanese, Russian and even German. He had seen Gallipoli
fail, the Arab Revolt succeed, British naval power in the
Mediterranean restored, Turkey in defeat and Russia in
disintegration. He had gained some insight into the manoeuvres
in the corridors of naval power during the reshaping of the
British naval commands in the Mediterranean and the appointment of his own Commander-in-Chief to the post of First Sea
Lord. Gough-Calthorpe reported that he 'has carried out the
duties of his appointment with great ability and success. He
shows remarkable aptitude for staff work.' Burmester's comments included the following: 'Ability considered to be exceptional. Lieutenant-Commander Godfrey has what may be
called a Staff mind, and possesses remarkable aptitude for
working out and expressing in orders the details of operations
involving the co-ordination of large forces, e.g. he had rendered
invaluable service in connection with the arrangements and
orders for the control and protection of Allied shipping in the
Mediterranean . . . I can only add to the above that this
Officer is an extraordinarily zealous, loyal and hardworking
staff officer who appears to me to be marked out for employment
on the War Staff. At the same time I have always found him
an extremely able and conscientious Navigating Officer.' This
was in an age when 'naval tradition was blame yes, praise no'.
Godfrey had every reason to feel pleased with the judgement
passed upon him.

CHAPTER FOUR

The Years Between

DESPITE THE excellent reports from Gough-Calthorpe and Burmester and the fact that he had twice been mentioned in Despatches and had been awarded the Legion of Honour by the French Government and also the Order of the Nile by the Egyptians, Godfrey, like many regular officers at the end of the war, was worried about his future prospects in the Navy. He had decided before the war to specialise in Staff work and had applied for the 1915 'War Staff' course. Such courses had of course been suspended for the duration, and although he had spent the last three years almost entirely on staff work, he did not have the specialist qualifications. Moreover, staff work, however interesting, did not in those days pave the way to promotion. Early in 1919 Godfrey had, at the suggestion of his great friend Sir Ernest Dowson, now Financial Adviser to the Egyptian Government, and with the support of his superiors, applied to join the administrative and political side of the Egyptian Civil Service. However for various reasons nothing came of this. Suffering, as he confesses, from an acute inferiority complex, Godfrey remained very anxious until he was notified of a fresh appointment as junior war staff officer on the Staff of Sir Charles Madden, Commander-in-Chief of the renamed Home Fleet.

Before taking up this appointment Godfrey took the five months' leave to which his five years' uninterrupted war service abroad had entitled him. Anxious to improve his French he characteristically spent three months of his leave at a course for foreigners at the Sorbonne in Paris. The only other paying guest in the French family with whom he stayed was an eighteen-year-old English girl, Margaret Hope, a fact which did little to help him master the French language. They were immediately attracted to one another and two years later were married. By a coincidence, Margaret also came from Birmingham, although they had never previously met. Her father, Donald Hope, was a dynamic and successful business man, the

Managing Director of his family firm, Henry Hope & Sons Ltd, one of the oldest and certainly finest manufacturers of bronze and steel window frames in the world. A collector of antique furniture, a connoisseur of good printing and lettering, a lover of good food and good clothes and a member of White's, he was far removed from the usual impression of a provincial manufacturer. Her mother was a Chamberlain, fourth daughter of Joe Chamberlain's brother Arthur. The Chamberlains, who were Unitarians, were a large and closely-knit clan. With the Kenricks, Nettlefolds, Cadburys and other Non-Conformists they were the leaders of Birmingham's civic, business and social life and were still represented at the centre of the national political scene by Austin Chamberlain, and, later, Neville.

It was, therefore, a powerful and influential family into which Godfrey was going to marry, albeit one with little interest in or knowledge of the Navy. One suspects that he was, at first, somewhat out of his depth. He could not, however, have been more fortunate in his choice of a wife. Margaret was not only charming but highly intelligent and would undoubtedly have obtained a good Economics degree from Cambridge had she not abandoned Newnham for marriage in her second year. Calm, patient, an excellent organiser (as was to be proved during World War II), a splendid hostess and a wonderful mother, she was devoted to John and was, and is, loved and admired by all who have ever come in contact with her.

Godfrey spent just under two years in the Home Fleet and although he did not dislike it and got on well with his messmates, he found the routine work in a highly centralised regime dull and unrewarding after the freedom and responsibility which he had enjoyed under Wemyss, Gough-Calthorpe and Burmester. "There was little scope for initiating anything, neither was one exactly encouraged to start new hares even if one had wanted to. Never before or since have I been so near the heart and core of all things Naval and yet I can remember very little of what went on." He was, moreover, somewhat anxious about his chances of being promoted to Commander. This step was the first one that did not come automatically; it was by selection. In 1920 only about one in three were being promoted. He had missed his time as an executive Lieutenant-Commander and three years of uninterrupted staff work still appeared to him to be more likely to be a handicap than a recommendation. As it turned out, all went well, and he got his step in rank on 30 June 1920, just before his thirty-second birthday, after only three and a half years as Lieutenant-Commander. He was in fact one of the youngest Commanders in the Service.

In 1921 Godfrey's former colleague from the Mediterranean, Gerald Dickens, now Deputy Director of Plans at the Admiralty, invited him to join Plans Division, an invitation he was delighted to accept. He served there from September 1921 to August 1923, firstly under Captain Barry Domvile and then for the first but by no means the last time under Captain Dudley Pound. Work in Plans Division was interesting but tended to be frustrating. The Division was concerned with policy-making, with the future, with strategy and its effects on bases, depots, stores and administration and with the naval aspects of international affairs, treaties and agreements, but this was a time when British policy was in a state of flux and indecision. The Navy, which for the last twenty years had been preparing for or actually fighting a war in the North Sea, had once again to think in terms of world strategy. There was a real danger of a naval race with the United States replacing the pre-war one with Germany. The old friendship with Japan was fading and relations with France were sour. Disarmament was competing with rearmament. "In the absence of an obvious enemy each Service chose the one that seemed to suit it best. The Army picked on Russia, the Air Force (surprisingly) on France, and the Navy—after considerable research, on Japan." In consequence one of Godfrey's main preoccupations was with the question of establishing a great naval base at Singapore. "For the first time in history a major question of Imperial Defence became (because of the opposition of the Labour Party) the subject of party wrangling. Every single paper about Singapore passed through my basket or was initiated by me or by the Deputy Director, and I attended as expert adviser all Parliamentary debates on the Navy, sitting in an uncomfortable box behind the Speaker's chair. Every Admiralty Department had to be alerted, and in doing so I learnt a great deal about the Admiralty and Government procedure, and about the indispensability of personal contact to supplement the written word."

In 1922 Britain was very nearly again involved in war with Turkey, when Kemal Attaturk came face to face with British troops at Chanak. Although inter-Service co-operation on the spot was excellent, the same could not be said of the state of affairs in Whitehall. To Godfrey it seemed incredible that there was so little contact between the Admiralty and the War Office and in the absence of "any stimulus from on high, I took the unusual step of finding out which particular lieutenant-colonel on the General Staff was dealing with Chanak, rang him up and went over and saw him. He was delighted and in that particular sphere, the dividing line in Whitehall having been successfully crossed, we established a strong, friendly and fairly permanent link."

Unfortunately, relations with the young Royal Air Force were not so good. "Opposed at every turn, Trenchard over-emphasised the independent role of the Air Force and in order to assert this, deliberately preached a doctrine of non-cooperation especially with the Navy; this doctrine permeated the higher ranks of the RAF, and was injected into the blood stream of future RAF staff officers at the Andover Staff College."

Towards the end of Godfrey's time in Plans he was notified that he was to join the staff of the Royal Naval College at Greenwich. He must have impressed Pound with his ability because, before he left Plans Division, Pound asked him to come with him as his Staff Officer (Operations) when he took up his next appointment as Chief of Staff, Mediterranean Fleet. Godfrey had to point out that by the time he had finished at Greenwich it would be essential for him to serve as Executive Officer, that is second in command, of a battleship or cruiser. Pound, of course, agreed and offered the post instead to Godfrey's friend and contemporary Tom Phillips who accepted and thereby 'hitched his waggon' to Pound's star. When, in 1939, Pound became First Sea Lord, he selected Phillips as his Deputy Chief of Naval Staff.

The Staff College had only recently been established. Its object was to impart higher naval education to officers of commander's and lieutenant-commander's rank and to assist in producing competent staff officers. One of the first Directors of the College explained that 'The idea is to give officers a broad outlook on all subjects connected with the influence of sea power, and a good general knowledge of the affairs of the day. In the old days naval officers had a much larger knowledge of affairs than naval officers of the present day. They spent a considerable part of their time ashore and while on shore mixed with men of affairs, sat in Parliament or travelled or lived abroad, and there is little doubt that part of their success was due to the fact that they were men of the world with wide general knowledge. They did not suffer from over-specialisation, because specialisation was not necessary. Specialisation is now necessary; it absorbs a lot of time and if we can allow officers an opportunity to study quietly or think about other subjects, it is to their advantage and, moreover, is of value in the training of staff officers. Therefore these two aims (staff training and higher education) fall naturally together.'

It was, therefore, something of a feather in Godfrey's cap that he should be appointed straight to the directing staff and permitted to put the letters PSC (Passed Staff College) after his name without ever doing a qualifying course. He again earned the golden opinion of his superiors and four years later he returned to Greenwich as Deputy Director. He and Margaret had been married on 15 December 1921 and their first child, Kathleen, had been born the following year. They had built a comfortable house, Braddocks, at Sevenoaks in Kent, and their second daughter, Eleanor, was born in November 1924. Greenwich was not far away, so these were years, all too few in a naval officer's life, when he was able to enjoy his young family. In one respect, therefore, it must have been something of a wrench when, in the middle of 1925, the time came to apply for a commander's job at sea.

Godfrey had, of course, long since resolved any doubts he might formerly have had about making his career in the Navy. He was ambitious and obviously well thought of. Nevertheless, in applying for the appointment of second in command of the 4765-ton cruiser *Diomede* on the New Zealand station he took, as he subsequently admitted, "a calculated risk in ignoring the maxim that the way to get promoted was to seek the fierce light that beats round the Commander-in-Chief of the principal fleets. The price I had to pay was to wait for my 'last shot' [for promotion to Captain] which came in 1928 when I had attained eight years seniority." One must conclude that he preferred the freedom to exercise his own initiative and the chance to see another and very beautiful part of the world, which service in New Zealand and Pacific waters would provide, to what he felt would be the rather stultifying atmosphere of the Home or

Mediterranean Fleets. At any rate, in spite of the fact that he lost ground compared with some of his near contemporaries such as Tom Phillips, it was a choice which he never regretted.

The commission, which lasted from October 1925 to October 1928, took *Diomede* and her sister ship *Dunedin*, whose commander was his old friend and *Britannia* choirmate Arthur Peters, through the Panama Canal to almost all the fabulous South Sea Islands as well as to New Zealand. The Royal New Zealand Navy at that time consisted of only a few very small ships, and the cruisers were 'on loan' from the Royal Navy, partly British and partly New Zealand manned. Margaret followed her husband out to New Zealand and they rented a house in Auckland where they soon made many friends, although *Diomede* was frequently away showing the flag in the Pacific. In February 1928 the two cruisers were sent in a hurry to Samoa where what amounted to a peaceful rebellion had broken out. Samoa, a pre-war German colony, which had then been excellently administered, had been handed to New Zealand as a Mandated Territory in 1919, but the New Zealanders proved unpopular and the local opposition party, Mau (no connection with Mau-mau), petitioned the League of Nations to transfer the mandate to Great Britain and adopted the tactics of passive resistance to the Government. Finally the situation became so serious that the Navy had to be sent to assist the tiny local police force, and four platoons of bluejackets and marines were landed under Godfrey's command. There was no fighting and the sailors in fact established excellent relations with the Mau Party. Godfrey spent two months ashore, for the second half of which he was without the support of the ships, which had returned to New Zealand. He made a number of friends with the German and New Zealand planters, many of whom had Samoan or half-caste wives, and he seems to have performed his rather invidious task with considerable tact and complete success.

The only other point which needs to be recalled about Godfrey's time in *Diomede* was his enthusiasm, which he shared with his Captain, J. M. Ritchie, for the 'divisional system'. This system whereby a ship's company was divided for man management purposes into Divisions, each with a lieutenant or lieutenant-commander in charge, was in contrast to the old tradition of the commander, or second in command, dealing direct with all problems. It was by no means universally adopted at this time, but it fitted in perfectly with the ideas of devolution of responsibility and the exercise by junior officers of initiative and judgement which Godfrey had learned from Burmester and Marriott in *Euryalus*. He was to remain one of its keenest advocates in his two subsequent commands.

As already noted, Godfrey had to wait for his promotion to Captain and he tells us that he "had begun to think I had been forgotten and was greatly relieved when on my way home in *Diomede* I received news at Jamaica of my promotion to Captain on 30 June 1928." He was informed that he was to return to Greenwich as Deputy Director of the Staff College, and discovered that one of his duties would be to deliver two series of lectures; the first on the French Revolutionary War of 1792 to 1801; the second on the Battle of Jutland. Conscious that he knew very little even of the maritime side of the former (ignorance of naval history was and remains the rule rather than the exception among serving naval officers), he suggested to his Director, Rear-Admiral Little, that he should first spend two months at Cambridge familiarising himself with the subject and "especially the inter-relation of politics and strategy, statesmen, soldiers and sailors". Thanks to his Director's broad-minded outlook and Godfrey's friendship with Jim Passant, a Fellow of Sidney Sussex College, this was quickly arranged. At Cambridge Godfrey met most of the historians, Holland Rose, Temperley, Butterfield and Brindley going out of their way to help him. He also got to know Rutherford, G. M. Trevelyan, and Admiral Richmond, later Master of Downing College. He enjoyed University life and dining at the High Table and writes that "this brief glimpse of the workings of a University was of great help to me when, ten years later, as Director of Naval Intelligence innumerable links were to be established with Cambridge, Oxford and London Universities, who contributed so much towards the founding of the Inter Service Topographical Department."

In the 1920s the Battle of Jutland was still very much a matter of controversy between the rival supporters of Beatty and Jellicoe. Having spent the whole war in the Mediterranean Godfrey was able to approach the question with an open mind, and was fortunate in having at his disposal not only the recently released German account of the battle but in being allowed access, for the first time, to the decrypted German signals "without which the progress of the battle and the decisions of Admirals Jellicoe and Beatty are incomprehensible". This, also, was knowledge which was to prove useful to him when he became Director of Naval Intelligence. Quite apart from this and the broadening of his mind and outlook which resulted from work at the Staff College, Godfrey was brought into contact with a large number of outstanding officers in all three Services. The total of four years which he spent at Greenwich was not wasted.

Early in 1931 he was informed that he was to be appointed to the command of a 10,000-ton cruiser in the Mediterranean, but this was soon changed to one on the China Station, firstly because the Mediterranean appointment was required for a more senior captain, and secondly because it was felt that as 'a young captain it is a good thing for you to go to a foreign station where you will get away on your own a good bit and have more responsibility'. This was of course entirely to Godfrey's taste and so, like all 'old China hands', he returned again to China.

It was arranged that he should recommission the cruiser *Kent* and take her out for a further period of service as flagship of Admiral Sir Howard Kelly, Commander-in-Chief of the China Station. On arrival he would exchange into *Suffolk*, also a 10,000-ton County class cruiser. *Kent* was completing a minor refit at Chatham, and thanks to the kindness of Admiral Sir Reginald Tyrwhitt, Commander-in-Chief the Nore, Godfrey was able to continue to live ashore at Braddocks, a privilege which enabled him to continue to enjoy the company of his family, which had been increased eighteen months earlier by the birth of his third daughter, Christina. He was also able to entertain some of his officers there, and one of his junior officers recalls with gratitude the hospitality which he and his messmates received from the Captain and his wife. The Admiral Superintendent of the Dockyard was 'Snatcher' Stirling, Godfrey's CO in *Welland* in 1908. Both he and Admiral Tyrwhitt ensured that *Kent* received preferential treatment and was not subjected to all the usual delays and annoyances associated with re-fitting. As a flagship, her officers had been carefully selected and Godfrey pays tribute to their quality. *Kent* was his first command and although the voyage east would be a short one he was anxious to hand her over to his Commander-in-Chief in as efficient and fully worked-up state as possible. *Kent* sailed for Hong Kong at the end of August 1931. Some four hundred of her ship's company had volunteered to rejoin her, which speaks well for the previous commission, but Godfrey was not content to rely on this and from the word go kept everyone very much on their toes. Efficiency almost always breeds happiness and this proved to be the case with *Kent*. It was just as well, because while she was passing through the Mediterranean news was received of the drastic and extremely unfair pay cuts imposed in consequence of the serious financial crisis of that year. The Home Fleet at Invergordon, where matters were not well handled either by the Admiralty or the senior officers on the spot, was in a state of semi-mutiny for the best part of four days. Thanks, however, to a good crew and first class officers there was no similar trouble in *Kent*, a happy outcome for which Godfrey, as commanding officer, must also be accorded a good deal of credit.

After a quick and uneventful passage, Hong Kong was reached on 9 October, and when Godfrey transferred to *Suffolk* he received a pleasant send-off from *Kent*'s officers, who pulled him across to his new command in a cutter. It was also rewarding to receive a letter from the Commander-in-Chief stating that by the end of the month *Kent* 'had worked up to a very satisfactory state of efficiency. The average loss of output during the three working up practices was 7 per cent. This constitutes a record for the 5th Cruiser Squadron.'

Godfrey's first duty, although interesting, was not a very pleasant one; it was to act as Prosecuting Officer at the Court Martials of the Commanding Officer and Navigating Lieutenant of the sloop *Petersfield* which had run ashore and become a total loss while on passage from Shanghai to Hong Kong. The matter was greatly complicated by the fact that the sloop was employed as the Commander-in-Chief's yacht and Admiral Kelly with his wife and daughter were on board at the time. The defence was that Admiral Kelly, a very dominant and awe-inspiring personality, had, in effect, issued orders to the commanding officer to steer a course which had led to the disaster and had, to all intents and purposes, himself assumed command. This the Admiral indignantly refuted. It cannot have been an easy task for the prosecutor to present a just and fair case without either offending his new Commander-in-Chief or arousing the resentment of the accused, but he seems to have managed to do so with a very fair degree of success.

For the Royal Navy, and indeed for most of the foreign community, life in China had not greatly changed in the twenty years since Godfrey had navigated *Bramble* up and down the Yangtse. The gunboats were still patrolling the great rivers and the cruisers, destroyers and submarines of the China Fleet dividing their time between visits to Canton, Shanghai and Hankow and exercises off Hong Kong or Wei Hai Wei, the former British base in North China, now only leased from the Chinese. Piracy was still not uncommon but the great city of Shanghai with its large International Concession flourished, displaying tremendous contrasts of luxury and squalor, enormous wealth and abject poverty. Sun Yat Sen had died in 1925 and, although various war-lords disputed the authority of the central government, Chiang Kai Chek was gradually asserting his supremacy which was seriously challenged only by the Communist leader Mao Tse Tung. There was, however, one major and very ominous difference from 1911, the growing and aggressive Imperialism of Japan. Economically and militarily Japan was determined to dominate China and to bring the whole of this vast and ancient country within its own and exclusive sphere of influence. Starting with the virtual occupation of Manchuria and the establishment there of the puppet state of Manchuquo, clashes with the Chinese became more and more frequent, leading in the north to a state of undeclared war which the League of Nations proved impotent to resolve. The Chinese very naturally became increasingly resentful and clashes began to occur in many other areas where the Japanese were established. At the end of January 1932 an incident in Shanghai led to serious fighting between the Chinese and the Japanese, who decided that the time had come to teach the Chinese a lesson and to establish, once and for all, their paramountcy in the city and its surroundings. Japanese marines and sailors were landed and aircraft from Japanese aircraft carriers bombarded the Chinese suburb of Chapei mercilessly. The Chinese reacted stubbornly and the possibility that the whole city would become involved in the fighting became very serious. The highly efficient Shanghai Volunteer Defence Force,

which included a regiment of Cossack mercenaries, was mobi-
lised to defend the perimeter of the International Concession
against incursions by either side and urgent appeals made for
help to the British, French and American Governments whose
nationals dominated the European business community. Small
forces of British and French troops and American Marines were
already stationed in the city, but reinforcements were urgently
needed and as so often in the past, it fell to the Royal Navy to
give swift and immediate aid.

Suffolk had been due to take over the duties of Senior Naval
Officer Shanghai on 12 February, but as the crisis exploded she
was ordered to proceed there immediately. Leaving Hong Kong
on the morning of 29 January she steamed at twenty-eight
knots and secured alongside Jardine & Mathieson's wharf in
Shanghai on the afternoon of 31 January.

This is what Godfrey found when he landed and made
contact with the British Consul General, Mr Brennan. "China
and Japan are at war and an extraordinary state of affairs has
arisen. Superimposed on the map of London, Shanghai,
through which flows the Whangpo River, about the size of the
Thames at Richmond, with a population of nearly four millions,
would stretch from Shepherd's Bush on the west to Greenwich
on the east and from Hampstead on the north to the banks of
the Thames. The foreign settlements occupy most of this area
with a French settlement in Kensington-Bayswater, and the
ancient Chinese city in Hyde Park. The Japanese, as the self-
appointed defenders of foreign interests and already deeply
committed in Manchuria, have staged a limited naval operation
from within the Settlement area with seaborne lines of communication. They have landed Marines and carried out operations from carriers cruising in the Yangtse estuary, concentrat-
ing on the Chapei suburb, a residential and industrial area of
no military significance. Our object is to keep the Chinese and
Japanese armies as much outside the western i.e. the big
business part of the settlement as possible. The Japanese appear
to be acting vigorously and to be determined to embroil us.
Our aim is not to get involved but to preserve as much as
possible of our considerable interests from depredation."

Godfrey immediately landed marines and seamen to reinforce the defences of the International Settlement and to man
observation posts so that *Suffolk* could provide artillery support

if required. Reinforcements of British, American, French and Italian troops were rushed to Shanghai and by the middle of February over eight thousand troops and two thousand of the Shanghai Volunteer Corps were involved. The British provided the largest contingent and its commander, Brigadier Fleming, was requested to exercise overall command of the mixed force. Godfrey took an immediate liking to him and they became firm friends. The Japanese had originally deployed about 800 marines and were opposed by some 2000 Chinese. Both sides brought in more and more men until something like 15,000 Japanese were confronting 60,000 Chinese. After the 'incident' was over Godfrey again met his old friend from the Mediterranean, Sakano, who had been appointed Rear-Admiral Yangtse. At the time he had been Director of Naval Intelligence in Tokyo and he was very outspoken to Godfrey about the mismanagement of the whole affair. Apparently the Japanese Admiral, Shiozawa, had been told to make a 'demonstration', had got too deeply involved and made a mess of things. Naval opinion in Tokyo favoured a withdrawal but the Army felt that such a loss of face could not be tolerated and this opinion prevailed so that the operation escalated out of all proportion. Sakano felt that more than a division of troops should have been sent in the first place, and this view was shared by Brigadier Fleming and the other military commanders of the International Force, all of whom formed a very low opinion of the performance of the Japanese, who were considered to have learned nothing since 1918. It seems at least possible that this impression, which was by no means ill-founded, contributed to the very serious underestimation of Japanese capabilities ten years later. The Japanese, like the Russians during the Finnish campaign, learned from their mistakes but the Western powers appear to have failed to notice the change.

However, if the Japanese showed themselves inept on this occasion, the Chinese were even more so and by early March they had been driven out of the Chapei suburb and the fighting receded some twenty to thirty miles away from Shanghai, where life, for the Europeans, rapidly reverted to normal. For various reasons *Suffolk* remained there for several months, acting for a time as Admiral Kelly's flagship.

What impression did Captain Godfrey make on those who knew him at that time? To his officers he was something of an

enigma. On the voyage out in *Kent* he had insisted on a very
high standard of efficiency, earning the praise of his Commander-in-Chief when he handed the ship over on arrival at
Hong Kong. *Suffolk* equally was a 'taut' ship, winning the
competitive firing trophy which was the big test of a warship's
fighting efficiency in all branches, and in addition a special
prize for night fighting and most of the other competitions open
to her, both sporting and technical. Godfrey proved himself
kind and thoughtful in many ways; and he was liked by many
and respected by all, but he seems to have been a shade remote
and conscious of the dignity of his rank. He could not stand
noise and became very irritated if fans or other items of ship's
machinery disturbed his sleep. He gave many talks to his
officers on Jutland and other matters of professional interest,
including one on the dangers of venereal disease which was rife
in Hong Kong and Shanghai. These lectures were not always
as gratefully received by his audience as he supposed. He was
not particularly interested in competitive sport and always put
ship's duties ahead of the requirements of the rugger or soccer
teams, and this was a time when, all too often, a ship's reputation depended on such matters. *Suffolk* was all the same a happy
ship. It is perhaps revealing that on arrival in Hong Kong,
Godfrey received an application from Chan Ah Say who had
been the Chinese number two steward in *Bramble* to serve him
again. In 1911 Ah Say had fallen ill and fearing that he was
going to die, had deserted in order—in the Chinese fashion—
to do so at home. He recovered and Godfrey had sent him a
message that if he would return to duty he would not be
punished. Ah Say had not only done so but had never forgotten
Godfrey's understanding attitude. Although by 1931 he had
retired from the Navy and was steward of the Kowloon Cricket
Club, as soon as he heard of Godfrey's arrival he asked to be
taken on as the Captain's steward and not only gave Godfrey
two years' perfect service in this capacity but kept in touch with
him for another fifteen years. In March 1946 he wrote, 'My
family and I were overjoyed to learn of your appointment as
Flag Officer in charge of the Royal Indian Navy and the
victorious news on both the European and Burmese fronts. . . .
We were much pleased to hear about your children getting
along alright in England. . . . It is very proud to your family to
have a daughter in the Women's Auxiliary Air Force.'

Someone else who was to give Godfrey years of faithful and friendly service was his coxwain, Petty Officer Finnecy. He had been Captain of the Top in *Diomede* and they had formed a liking for one another. As Captain's coxwain, first in *Kent* and then in *Suffolk*, he was in charge of the Captain's motor boat, whose crew also looked after the Captain's quarters. Finnecy and Ah Say between them ensured a very high standard of comfort. In 1939 Finnecy came out of retirement to serve Godfrey again in an unusual position of trust in the Intelligence Division, and the two of them remained friends until Finnecy's death.

Ashore in Shanghai Godfrey found some old friends and many new ones. There was Neilage Brown, now the head of all the Butterfield Holt enterprises in China. He had become "a very rich man with a chateau-like mansion at the back of the French concession, where he entertained lavishly and filled his house with beautiful things. He dined or lunched with me and I with him two or three times a week. His mind was ranging far ahead of the thinking of his colleagues in business. He forsaw the end of the 'gunboat' policy and was a pioneer in filling most of the important and all the subordinate posts in Butterfields with Chinese. Socially NSB was forgetful. He would ask people to dinner and then forget all about it and would be seen the same evening entertaining someone quite different at one of Shanghai's innumerable night clubs. Nevertheless we met some very nice and interesting people at NSB's house, including many of the leading Chinese in Shanghai." A couple who were to become lifelong friends were the young Chancellors. Christopher was the head of Reuter's Shanghai office and was later to become the Chairman of Bowaters. His charming wife, Sylvia, was the sister-in-law of a connection of Margaret Godfrey's and this had provided the initial introduction. The Chancellors had a wide circle of cultivated and unusual friends of all nationalities, very many of them Chinese, to whom they introduced Godfrey. They found him a very untypical naval officer. Sir Christopher writes that 'During my eight years in Shanghai I met a whole procession of naval officers—but I met no officer in the same class as John, whose outlook was so original, whose interests so embracing and whose mind was so stimulating. He wanted to know *everything* and to talk to people who were "in the know". Through me he met all the newspaper publishers in

Shanghai—German, French, Chinese and Japanese and a number of Americans as well as leading civilians such as Tony (now Sir William) Keswick. I introduced him to a close American friend, C. V. Starr, who owned the Shanghai *Evening Post* and was an exceptionally brilliant man. John met him again in World War II when he worked for Donovan. He also met the Cianos and some of our special Chinese contacts such as General Wu Teh Chen, Mayor of Shanghai.' Lady Chancellor's impressions are also illuminating. 'Being highly strung as well as highly intelligent he found it hard to release his social inhibitions in the company of other men. With women, however, he could quickly graduate to friendship. Of course, with the great *Suffolk* looming up on the horizon her Captain was—inevitably—an awe-inspiring figure (he was not unaware of nor displeased by this) but he was a singularly modest man and relieved to find someone who did not take him too seriously. I would not have called him exceptionally good-looking but his appearance was undeniably impressive. He could not utterly banish his inbred air of authority, but when he came to see me—unfeignedly on holiday—he was happy to listen to any nonsense that came into my head and I was certainly not unconscious of his charm.' In 1932 Margaret came out to join her husband and the friendship of the two couples was firmly cemented.

It is clear that Godfrey was something of an intellectual, although he himself detested that description. He had an intensely enquiring mind and was always anxious to explore as fully as he could new places and new ideas. He did not suffer from the average naval officer's lack of interest in such matters or from his contempt for foreigners, particularly those of another colour. Admirable qualities one might suppose, but not ones which were always greatly appreciated, or even understood, by many of his Service contemporaries.

After the Shanghai incident *Suffolk*'s programme reverted to the normal; visits to Hankow, Wei Hai Wei, the old German colony of Tsingtao and Hong Kong; exercises and regattas; entertaining and being entertained by the British communities, still the most numerous foreigners in China. It was a pleasant enough existence, but, like all commissions, it came to its end and in September 1933 *Suffolk* sailed for home and paid off at Portsmouth.

Godfrey then returned to Plans Division in the Admiralty, this time as Deputy Director. His Director was first Captain E. L. S. King and then Tom Phillips, both of them old friends. The principal difficulty with which the planners in all three Services had to contend was still the infamous 'Ten Year Rule'. First instituted, not unreasonably, in 1919, it was a directive to the Service Departments that, when preparing their annual estimates, they were to do so on the assumption that Great Britain would not be involved in a war with any major power for ten years. In 1928, at the instigation, most surprisingly, of none other than Winston Churchill, this rule was made self-perpetuating. Although this edict was in fact more or less allowed to lapse, by late 1933 the damage caused by fourteen years of starvation of the Defence Services had been done. "We had", wrote Godfrey in his Memoirs, "been eating into our reserves since the war and the ten year rule had prevented replacement and thrown some of the smaller firms out of business. The abrogation of the rule in 1933 did not mean that things would return to normal straight away. It would take nearly ten years to catch up and it did not seem as if we were going to be allowed the time. In the meantime there was only enough ammunition for the anti-aircraft guns of the Fleet to fire for twenty minutes; there was only one gun-pit in England; only one factory that handled some essential process in the manufacture of aluminium; only one very small firm that made the anti-torpedo net defence for harbours and only one motor landing craft. The know-how and expertise were confined to so very few people. In recent history no measure can have done more to undermine the foundations of Imperial Defence and, by its brutal, callous and indiscriminating impact spread more frustration among those who were doing their best to protect British territories and interests at a time when they were most vulnerable to attack. The assumption that there would be no major war for ten years deprived our preparations not only of all sense of urgency but ensured that the essentials of a rapid expansion were absent."

These were however the conditions under which the planners had to work in the mid thirties, and even after the ten year rule was dropped and the threats from Nazi Germany and Imperial Japan began to become more and more apparent, successive Chancellors of the Exchequer ordained that the restoration of the financial strength of the country along traditional lines must take precedence over rearmament.

As Deputy Director of Plans Godfrey was concerned once more with his old friend, the Singapore Naval Base. He found that "during the twelve years since its inception the Singapore scheme had been delayed, stopped, truncated and subjected to every sort of privation. What remained of the plan was a shadow of what was needed. Considerable progress had been made with the dockyard and naval establishments but no provision had been made for attack from the landward side across the Johore Straits." The Air Force were confident that they could prevent this.

Another typical problem was that of building up sufficient stocks of oil at strategic points in Britain and abroad. "The Admiralty had thought up a way of integrating the creation of a fuel reserve with the ten year rule and had suggested a ten year inclined plane programme starting with a substantial yearly provision which would be reduced year by year until at the end of ten years very little would remain to be done. When this had been proposed in the twenties the opponents of the plan had recruited a powerful and resourceful ally in Mr Churchill. The Chancellor said in effect; yes, I like your inclined plane, but will turn it round and go uphill instead of down. In other words, very little now and a vague undertaking, to be agreed with the Treasury every year, of more in the future." The result was, of course, that the reserve was never built up to the figure envisaged.

Another of Godfrey's concerns was the provision of seaward defences of ports in collaboration with the War Office and the Air Ministry, represented by Colonel Tom Hutton (later General Officer Commanding Burma) and Group Captain Bert Harris (the wartime Commander-in-Chief of Bomber Command). Hutton became a lifelong friend but Godfrey confesses that "threesomes are never very happy; they almost always tend to become two against one and I suppose Tom Hutton and I ganged up and it put Harris on the defensive. This may have made his attitude more challenging. In addition to expounding the air case and trying to extract money from the Treasury, Harris had the difficult task of predicting what the air bomber components of Britain and Germany would be able to do in five or ten years time, and I must confess to a feeling of slight irritation when he told us again and again that within a very few years German bombers would reach out well into the Atlantic beyond the Outer Hebrides. In 1933 they could hardly reach Birmingham. Of course he was perfectly right, but one got the impression that no defensive measures were any good and attempts were made to curdle one's blood by tall stories about the colossal damage that would be inflicted on London and other cities in the first twenty-four hours, and how it would go up and up during the ensuing week. It was the same on other committees with other Air Force representatives: Air Defence of Great Britain: Air Raid Precautions: defence of home ports: always these astronomical tons and tons of German bombs." The official history of The Strategic Air Offensive against Germany 1939–1945 remarks: 'This exaggeration of the number of casualties which strategic bombing was likely to produce was a major factor in all strategic thinking before the Second World War and exercised a profound influence on the minds of the Services, and the political chiefs and, being translated with even more sensational language by journalists and publicists, on public opinion at large.'

Other problems which Godfrey dealt with were the responsibility for the provision of landing craft and the defence of the Suez Canal. In the first case, by agreement with Hutton, Godfrey, with memories of the Dardanelles, got the responsibility transferred from the War Office, which had exercised this function since the days of the old 'Horse boat' of the Crimean War, and which was even more dominated by the Treasury than was the Admiralty, to the Navy. Even so it took two years to get formal government approval and only a dozen landing craft were available at the outbreak of war. So far as the Suez Canal was concerned, "single ships scuttled in the right place could block the canal for months. Some sort of partnership between the three Services and the Foreign Office on the one hand, and the French Canal Company and the Egyptian Authorities on the other was needed as a basis, and the possibility of the Navy alone having to take arbitrary action in an emergency could neither be ruled out nor openly admitted. With the consent of Admiral Little, the Deputy Chief of Naval Staff, I established an unofficial liaison with the British Director of the Suez canal company and, later, with the French Chairman and Managing Director in Paris. Lieutenant-Commander

Tony Simpson was appointed Naval Liaison Officer Port Said, and Jack Marriott, now a captain on the retired list, was given the dormant appointment of Senior Naval Officer, Suez Canal. He took up this appointment when our relations with Italy became strained. Thus, firm and reliable relations were established with the Canal officials in Egypt and with the Managing Director and Chairman in Paris without invoking the ponderous machinery of Government. Neither the Admiralty nor the Foreign Office were officially involved. My missions to Paris and contacts with the higher Suez Canal people gave me confidence in the reliability and integrity of the right sort of Frenchman."

Looking back long after the war on this period in its political context, of which he confesses that he and his colleagues were "only vaguely conscious", Godfrey remarks that "The country was deeply divided, and on the whole apathetic about defence. Our Prime Ministers were peace loving, pacifist or passivist and could not bear to think of war or the threat of war. Lacking firm and realistic leadership, the Government and Chiefs of Staff could give the planners no clear-cut objective or policy. Thus the planners found themselves working in a strange atmosphere in which past, present and future, facts, inferences and wishfulness became intermingled and all sense of purpose blurred. I was conscious of a certain lack of design which we did our best to mitigate by creating a future of our own devising, but one uncorrelated to the politics and temper of the country or to the personalities of succeeding Cabinets and Prime Ministers."

Early in 1935 came the promise of a new and most exciting appointment, command of the 32,000-ton battlecruiser *Repulse*, currently undergoing a major refit but destined when this was completed for the Mediterranean Fleet. This was not only one of the most desirable appointments which could be offered and an indication of official approval of his performance, but carried with it real hope of further promotion at its conclusion. Godfrey was, naturally, highly delighted. However, before taking up his new command and with what must have been a conscious effort to prepare himself for even greater responsibilities in the future, he determined to learn something more about Germany with whom he was now convinced war was inevitable. After cultivating the society of Germans living in London he secured a large number of letters of introduction and set out in June 1935 in the company of Colonel Tripp, Royal Marines, for an extended tour of Germany, Austria, Czechoslovakia, Yugo-Slavia and Poland. He confesses that "My attempts to penetrate the German way of thinking were not very successful. Those I met were pathetically anxious to talk about German politics but were not interested in the points of view of other nations and had no conception of the effects of Nazism abroad. They were badly informed about their own country and world affairs." He noted at the time that "Germany is not nearly so strong in a military sense as she makes out, but wants her surrounding countries to believe she is until she has had time to enlarge her Army and Air Force. In Berlin Densch, chief of staff to Admiral Raeder, said to me, 'I feel convinced that Germany really aspires to have the largest army in Europe and for England to have the largest navy and to rule the world together.'" Whatever the practical results of the trip, it demonstrated Godfrey's invariable passion for seeing for himself and forming his own judgements.

CHAPTER FIVE

Battlecruiser

Repulse was typical of much of the immediate pre-war Royal Navy. Despite her imposing size and the fact that she and the other two British battlecruisers, *Hood* and *Renown*, were at that time the fastest capital ships in the world, she had been designed in 1915 and was now verging on the obsolescent. Her long refit had been overdue but the money had not been forthcoming and not all the major work planned had been completed. Nevertheless she had been fitted with a hangar to take four aircraft and with a new and increased anti-aircraft armament. As her sister *Renown* was just about to undergo even more extensive modifications, considerable interest was being taken in the results achieved by those carried out in *Repulse*. Moreover the political scene was very threatening; Britain and Italy had been on the verge of war as the result of Mussolini's attack on Abyssinia. *Repulse* would be an important and much needed reinforcement for the Mediterranean Fleet and it was urgent that she should be worked up to maximum efficiency with the minimum of delay. This was a task after Godfrey's own heart, one calling for all his great drive and organising power. Most unfortunately he fell foul of the Commander-in-Chief Portsmouth, Admiral Sir John Kelly, brother of Howard Kelly under whom Godfrey had served in China. John Kelly was also a very dominant personality, a fine officer who had restored the discipline and morale of the Home Fleet after Invergordon. He was however mentally and psychologically completely different to Godfrey and reacted angrily to the latter's frequent requests for help in completing *Repulse*'s refit. So little did he think of Godfrey's ability that he wrote a special letter to the Admiralty suggesting, in effect, that although he was no doubt a brilliant staff officer, he was, in Kelly's opinion, quite unfitted for the command of a battlecruiser. This must have caused something of a sensation in the Admiralty and somewhat naturally the Board requested Godfrey's new Commander-in-Chief, Admiral Sir Dudley

Pound, to submit a special report on him at the end of six months. Pound's verdict was highly complimentary of Godfrey when it came, but until then it must have been a very discouraging start to a commission on which Godfrey's future prospects so greatly depended.

The ship had been two years in dockyard hands; she was filthy and everything had to be tested and proved; the ship's company were, of course, new to her and to themselves. Godfrey was again very fortunate in his officers, several of whom subsequently reached flag rank. The Commander was 'Hooky' Bell, who, if he did not always manage to move quite as fast as his Captain wished, was excellent with the men and quickly created a happy ship. The heads of departments, amongst them the present Admiral Sir Robin Durnford Slater and Vice-Admiral Sir Robert Elkins, were exceptionally able. Godfrey himself drafted in great detail the working-up programme and checked, at every stage, that the planned progress was being achieved. He was a master of detail, and unlike some commanding officers, carefully studied and made sure he understood the reports and suggestions of his subordinates. He was absolutely determined that *Repulse* should be the finest fighting machine in the Fleet. Once out of dockyard hands his programme was pressed forward relentlessly and there were constant exercises even when other ships remained in harbour, a feature which was to continue throughout the commission. Perhaps with memories of the British failure at Jutland in mind, Godfrey was particularly keen on night fighting exercises. He told his officers that unless one practised this art constantly the whole idea of a night exercise became 'repellent', a tendency all the more prevalent in the social atmosphere of Malta in those years. Nevertheless Godfrey retained his belief in devolution and although he drove his officers very hard in some ways, he basically trusted them to get on with their own jobs without constantly 'breathing down their necks'. He was himself a superb ship-handler and never put a foot wrong in manoeuvring the enormous bulk of *Repulse* either at sea or when entering or leaving tricky harbours like Grand Harbour, Malta, without the aid of tugs. He expected his principal subordinates to be able to do the same, and, conscious of his own apprenticeship with 'Snatcher' Stirling in *Welland*, would on occasions hand over to Elkins or one of the others leaving full control to them without comment or interference. Similarly, in practice night actions, he would remain silent on the bridge, allowing his gunnery officer to decide the exact moment to give the order to open fire. This not only created an air of quiet efficiency but built up a feeling of mutual confidence between the Captain and his specialists.

The result was that when *Repulse* joined the Mediterranean Fleet, she soon earned the confidence and approval of the Commander-in-Chief, Admiral Sir Dudley Pound, and of the two flag officers who commanded the Battle Cruiser Squadron, Sir Geoffrey Blake and, after he went sick, that even sterner critic Sir Andrew Cunningham. According to some, doubtless partial, accounts she performed better than her flagship, *Hood*, and in a simultaneous 'throw off' shoot she 'sank' Pound's flagship, *Queen Elizabeth*. All the evidence confirms that *Repulse* reached a quite exceptional standard of efficiency. It is perhaps worth adding that when *Repulse* met her end in the China Sea with the much more modern *Prince of Wales* in December 1941, her ship's company was basically unchanged. The older ship put up a magnificent performance and was fought and manoeuvred as gallantly and ably by Captain Tennant as Godfrey could possibly have desired.

Of course it would be idle to suggest that Godfrey alone was responsible for *Repulse*'s success in the Mediterranean. A great deal was due to his officers and to the long service regular ratings who formed the crew. Nevertheless a commanding officer is rightly held responsible if his ship performs badly and it is equally proper that he should be accorded a major share of the credit if she excels. *Repulse* excelled, and in consequence, as both Durnford-Slater and Elkins have testified, the commission was a happy one.

As in *Suffolk*, Godfrey remained something of an enigma to his officers. They found it difficult to sum up his personality. There is general agreement that he was immensely able and capable of frequent acts of personal kindness and thoughtfulness. He constantly attempted to improve not only the ship's fighting efficiency but also the well-being of her people. He gave many lectures on a wide variety of subjects such as 'The duties of Divisional Officers, Petty Officers and Leading Seamen', 'The training of Ordinary Seamen and Boys', 'Naval Discipline' and 'Mutinies'. They all contained a great deal of excellent advice and displayed a markedly liberal and forward looking outlook. Of course Jutland figured among them and once again one fears that this subject at least fell on somewhat stony ground. He also encouraged informal debates on less conventional topics, for example whether naval officers drank too much or the value of studying Naval history. Some resented these incursions into their free time.

He was an excellent host and frequently entertained his officers and male and female friends from on shore. On the latter occasions he would, if Margaret was not with him, ask one of the officer's wives to act as hostess, and as he kept a first class table and a fine cellar and took great pains to attend to all details, the results were very enjoyable. His Maltese cook was a master of French cuisine, though less at home apparently with the Roast Beef of Old England. His day cabin, which had been remodelled for him to the design of Brian O'Rorke, the leading architect responsible for the latest Orient liners, was elegantly furnished with good books, good pictures and good music. One guest wrote in his diary, 'No night exercises tonight . . . atmosphere strangely perfect . . . have wallowed in Kreisler, Heifetz, Rachmaninoff, Toscanini and Suggia. The after cabin so shaped as to produce music in a mysteriously effective way. Indeed his quarters produce a strange little world most unlike the whole.'

This is what Captain Stephen Roskill has to say of Godfrey at this time: 'I first met John Godfrey in Malta in about 1936 when late one evening a mutual friend took me on board *Repulse*. I was then a Lieutenant-Commander and I remember very well my nervousness at being ushered into the Captain's cabin: for at that time a Post Captain was regarded as a person whose authority stood only a little below that of the Deity, and by no means all of them would welcome an interruption by unknown and uninvited junior officers. But I was very quickly put at ease by my host, and as I looked around his book-lined cabin I quickly realised that I was in the presence of someone who did not conform to the usual pattern of senior naval officers. I think that I then sensed what I did not come fully to understand until much later—namely that John Godfrey was not only a man of unusually wide interests, but also gifted with an exceptionally powerful and original intellect.'

Perhaps this intellectual streak in his character and a certain

reserve and shyness, when combined with an almost fanatical
insistence on the very highest standard, resulted in his never
mastering the art of the 'common touch'. He could also, on
occasions, display a vein of selfishness. The phobia about noisy
fans, the forbidding silences when conversation took a turn of
which he disapproved, the fact that his motor boat was irrever-
ently labelled by the crew 'licensed to carry one passenger only',
a sense of humour that verged on the sardonic, a lack of interest
in organised sport prevented him attaining the universal popularity enjoyed by more extrovert characters such as Sir James
Somerville. One officer who knew him at this period has written
that he 'found it difficult to throw off the trappings of authority
and be hail fellow well met with his seniors and juniors and
even with his contemporaries, but he was very kind, very shy
and a firm friend once he could trust you. He was keen on the
new Navy of his dreams and thank God there were enough of
us to be ready for 1939.'

Repulse finally joined the Mediterranean Fleet in June 1936.
The threat of war with Italy over Abyssinia had receded with
the virtual abandonment of any serious attempt to impose
sanctions, but Hitler was now openly re-arming at an alarming
rate. The Rhineland was reoccupied and the Anschluss with
Austria imposed. France was torn by scandals and by clashes
between the extreme left and right. In the Far East Japan was
continuing her policy of aggressive expansion and was soon to
be once more engaged in open if undeclared war with China.
America, while free with advice from the sidelines, was firmly
isolationist. Britain herself was only just beginning to emerge
from the depths of the great Depression and was united only in
a desire to avoid war at any cost. Countries at both ends of the
Mediterranean were in a ferment—Spain on the verge of civil
war and Palestine already in the throes of an Arab revolt
against the Mandatory Power, Britain, caused by the increasing
flow of Jewish settlers and Britain's ambivalent attitude. Some
new crisis seemed to hit the headlines every week. It was to be
an unusually eventful commission.

After a few weeks in Gibraltar Repulse proceeded to Alexandria, but when, in the middle of July, the revolution broke
out in Spain, she had to return at high speed to Gibraltar with
a battalion of the Gordon Highlanders on board. She was soon
ordered to Palma, Majorca. This island had declared for Franco,

but Minorca, with its great naval base at Port Mahon, so well known to Nelson and Collingwood, was in Loyalist hands. 'Red' aircraft were bombing Palma daily. There were then, as now, many foreign residents in Majorca. The British, who were numerous, were mostly old and poorly off financially. The French had already evacuated some of their own nationals, but in addition to the English, the Germans, Dutch and Swiss were appealing for British help. Godfrey rapidly summed up the situation and requested permission to evacuate all the British who were willing to come and as many of the foreigners as could be accommodated. Permission was immediately granted and, on 30 July, 194 men, 281 women and 28 children were embarked in *Repulse*. They included 209 British subjects, 101 Germans, many of them refugees from the Nazis, 81 French and 49 Americans and small numbers from most of the other European and some South American countries. Many of them brought their pet dogs and cats with them and a kennel was arranged on the boat deck. The Gun Room was turned into a crêche for babies and Godfrey's own quarters were allotted to the over seventies. An English artist and his wife were "charmed and surprised to find anything beautiful on board a warship including Roy le Maistre's 'Blue Tower' picture". Another English woman wrote later, 'We were landed at Marseilles and then *Repulse* steamed off to Valencia to pick up more refugees. As she sailed off some American and German men stood to attention and took off their hats. I rather wished that I was a man so that I could take off mine too.'

In contrast to Palma, Valencia and its port Grao were held by the Government forces, largely Anarchists. Godfrey at once landed and made contact with the Civil Governor and the able and energetic leader of the British community, the manager of the Anglo-South American Bank. Not only had Godfrey to persuade the local British colony to leave and to cajole the ragged and ill-disciplined anarchist guards into permitting them to do so, he also had to establish communications with Madrid where there were still some 240 British subjects left. The British Ambassador had already abandoned Madrid and Britain was at first represented there only by the Acting Vice-Consul, a Maltese. On Godfrey's insistence, the Foreign Office finally sent Ogilvie Forbes, the Councellor of the Embassy, back to take charge. In the meantime Godfrey had to press hard for the evacuation of the British residents while this was still possible by train to Valencia.

The Royal Navy has always, for some reason, excelled at handling this sort of situation. Thanks to the tactful firmness displayed by Godfrey and his officers and to the traditional good humour and kindness of the British seaman, friendly relations were soon established with the authorities in Valencia (who in fact had practically no 'authority') and, more importantly, with the Militia and all the self-appointed guards and police, who were only too anxious to smell out any enemy of the Republic and carry out immediate and summary executions. "Refugees arriving at Valencia by train", wrote Godfrey at the time, "have to run several gauntlets. Lieutenant Commander Sawyer meets each train and shepherds them through the station to the buses which are to take them to Grao. They are generally held up by an interested but not unfriendly rabble, firstly on the platform, secondly on a bridge that has to be crossed before they are clear of the town, and after that at the many barricades on the three mile road to the port. Tom Sawyer, and Inglis his predecessor, have shown great ingenuity, tact and initiative in overcoming these difficulties and have got on excellent terms with everybody, porters, ticket collectors, police and even ragamuffins at the barricades. The Anglo-South American Bank have provided funds with which to help and a kind word, a cigarette or glass of beer works wonders in Spain. But in the end our most potent ally has been the white uniform of the British naval officer which everybody respects. One is met everywhere with smiles."

After three weeks, when the situation had been more or less stabilised, *Repulse* was relieved by the Fleet Repair Ship *Resource*, but no sooner was she back in Gibraltar and able to give her crew some much needed and well earned shore leave, than a fresh emergency arose. A small British registered merchant ship, the *Gibel Zerjon*, bound with an innocuous cargo for the Franco held port of Melilla, had been stopped by the Republican cruiser *Cervantes* outside the three mile limit. *Repulse* was at four hours' notice with three hundred of her men ashore enjoying the bright lights of Gibraltar. They were speedily rounded up with the help of their friends the Gordons, and although a number of them had to be laid out on the quarter deck to sober up, *Repulse* was at sea and steaming at over twenty-eight knots to the eastward in under three hours. Among those who had indulged not wisely but too well were the Commander and the PMO (Surgeon). When one of the officers who had not been lucky enough to get ashore went to the Commander to tell him that he could report to the Captain on the bridge that the ship was 'Ready for sea', he found that officer 'sitting in his cabin resting his head against the cold strut of the mainmast and being offered strong tea by his servant—in no condition to see the Captain. I therefore reported to the latter that the Commander would be up shortly as soon as he had got into uniform. The Captain then sent for the PMO, but, as the latter recounted, he just could not find his way up to the bridge despite an accusing voice calling him from up aloft "*What* have you done to the Commander*". I don't know what was said afterwards, except that John Godfrey decided to overlook the whole affair, which I thought was a pretty good show.' By the time *Repulse* reached the *Cervantes*, the flotilla leader *Codrington* was already on the scene and her Captain Geoffrey Miles had made a vigorous protest. The sight of the great *Repulse* was all that was needed to decide the Republican sailors to leave well alone and release the wretched little *Gibel Gerjohn*. This was one of the first of many such incidents in which the Royal Navy was involved, most of the other ones resulting from Nationalist efforts to enforce a blockade of Government ports.

The autumn was spent largely on exercises in Greek waters but by December *Repulse* was back in the Western Mediterranean, where news of the crisis preceeding Edward VIII's abdication was received. Godfrey's own feelings were that "We pray so often that he may be 'happy and glorious, long to reign over us'. It will be interesting to see what is the British public's idea of happiness. It seems to me unreasonable to ask any man to be a permanent civil servant all his life and at the same time to deny him the essentials of a happy life. If he renounces Mrs S and acts constitutionally he will be very unhappy and quite useless as a monarch . . . all this about breaking up the Empire is nonsense: I feel that it will remain what it has been, a strong voluntary alliance." The ship's company, however, "reached the conclusion that King Edward should abdicate (or retire as they call it) . . . and the less spectacular qualities of his brother, and his simple domestic life and charming wife will soon re-establish the Crown in the minds of the middle and working classes both here and in the Dominions." As so often, the British matelot got it right.

The first four months of 1937 were spent at Malta or Gibraltar apart from a few days in Greek waters. In May, together with a number of other ships of the Mediterranean Fleet, *Repulse* returned to England for King George VI's Coronation Review. It was a tremendous spectacle, almost rivalling that of the King's father in 1911 and certainly outclassing those of his daughter in 1952 and 1977. Great lines of battleships and aircraft carriers, heavy and light cruisers, destroyers, submarines and a host of small craft stretched from Cowes to beyond Spithead. It did much to restore the faith of the public in the Royal Navy, somewhat shaken by the Invergordon mutiny and the claims of the more extreme advocates of air power. What the public, unfortunately, did not perceive was the undue proportion of ships which, like *Repulse*, dated from the last war and which, from false economy, had neither been replaced nor adequately modernised. Nevertheless it was a fillip to the morale of the Navy as well as to that of the country.

On returning to the Mediterranean at the beginning of June, Godfrey had with him, as his personal guest, a friend, Edward Merrett, who was to become his Private Secretary in 1940. 'Ted' Merrett, a solicitor by profession, was a man of great charm, a talented artist, an amateur musician, a born raconteur, someone who was rapidly on the friendliest terms with all the officers and indeed many of the crew. Godfrey had brought with him his Hillman Minx car and on arrival at Malta took Merrett and sometimes some of the younger officers on many sightseeing and bathing expeditions. There were visits to friends on shore and delicious dinners, often with two or three of the officers, on board. This pleasant existence was suddenly interrupted at the beginning of July when *Repulse* was ordered to Palestine, where a new Constitution meeting some Jewish aspirations was to be announced. Disturbances by the Arabs were therefore anticipated.

A large, fast ship, capable of reaching the scene quickly and of landing marines and seamen in force was obviously required, but it is an indication of the confidence which the Commander-in-Chief, Sir Dudley Pound, already had in Godfrey's ability and powers of co-operation with the civil and military authorities that *Repulse* was selected for this as for so many other special missions. She reached Haifa on 7 July where her presence immediately had a calming effect on the local Arabs and a very reassuring one on the Jews. Godfrey, after making arrangements for the protection of the Mount Carmel Power station and the Oil Tank Farm, drove up in his own car with Merrett and some of his officers under a strong military escort to Jerusalem to meet the High Commissioner, General Wauchope, and the General Officer Commanding, General Dill (later to be Chief of the Imperial General Staff). Merrett's diary makes clear that Godfrey neglected no opportunity to see what he could of the Holy Land, but, of course, this was no sight-seeing jaunt, and when he reached Jerusalem, Godfrey learned that within the next few days the High Commissioner intended to arrest and deport to the Seychelles the 'Grand Mufti' of Jerusalem, an action which was likely to spark off violent Arab riots and even wholesale revolt. "A Mufti is strictly speaking a religious appointment, a Moslem jurist whose duty it is to give canonical rulings on points of Moslem Religious Law. It was a previous High Commissioner, Sir Herbert Samuel, who had appointed Haj Amin el Husseini to be Mufti of Jerusalem. He cannot have foreseen that el Husseini would have intensified the anti-Jewish and anti-British movement among the Palestinian Arabs and become such a thorn in the side of the Mandatory Power." The plan resulted in a flurry of signals between *Repulse* and the Commanders-in-Chief, Mediterranean and East Indies and the Colonial Office, but in the event the secret seems to have leaked out in advance, the Mufti evaded arrest, and escaped to Syria. During World War II he caused much trouble in Iraq and then took refuge in Berlin.

Repulse remained for a few weeks in Haifa until it became obvious that, for the moment, serious trouble was unlikely, and was then ordered to Corfu, to 'hold the hand' of the King of Greece, spending the summer there in the Royal Villa, formerly the property of the Kaiser. Godfrey of course knew Corfu well from the time when it had been the base of the French Fleet in World War I. Visits were exchanged and His Majesty was entertained to dinner on board and a showing of his favourite film, *Mr Deeds goes to town*, which Merrett and most of those on board had already seen more than once. 'A splendid little meal', wrote Merrett in his diary, 'commencing with the famous cold clear bortsch. HM delighted by the fish and surprised it was a local product—I'm not surprised, it's the cooking on board that is really so good.'

There were picnics ashore, calls to be made on the officials as well as cricket matches to be arranged with the local inhabitants who have played the game ever since the British occupation in the previous century.

Repulse's departure was somewhat complicated by the necessity of collecting the PMO who for several days had been attending one of the King's English guests, Mrs de Gay Fortman, who was ill, and whom the local doctors did not seem able to cure.

After a spell in Malta, where two new friends of the Captain, Sir Percy Mackinnon, a former Chairman of Lloyds, and Tim Foster, the son of a friend, were embarked, *Repulse* sailed for the Aegean to take over duties as Senior Officer of the Nyon Patrol in that area. In accordance with resolutions agreed at the Nyon Conference a system of naval patrols had been established throughout the Mediterranean to prevent acts of 'piracy', principally carried out by Italian submarines assisting Franco. One of the zones allocated to Great Britain was the Aegean, an area Godfrey knew well from his time in *Euryalus*. Pound again showed his confidence in Godfrey by instructing him to make contact with the Turkish authorities to obtain permission for British warships and their seaplanes to use Turkish coastal waters, and for their crews to land for rest and relaxation as they were accustomed to do in Greek waters. Turkey was also a party to the Nyon agreement, but no British warship had been allowed to visit a Turkish port, even on a courtesy visit, since Great Britain and Turkey had been on the verge of war during the Chanak affair in 1922 after the ill-fated Greek invasion of Anatolia. A good deal of diplomacy was therefore called for, all the more so as similar negotiations were being conducted in parallel, but with markedly less success as it turned out, by the Chargé d'Affaires in Ankara. The local Turkish officials proved to be extremely co-operative, and Godfrey went by car to Smyrna. In his hotel there he got into conversation with an old gentleman who proved to have been the Vali, or Governor, of the city when *Euryalus* had so unsuccessfully bombarded the forts just before the Dardanelles. A curious coincidence.

In between these emergency operations *Repulse* was of course constantly engaged with the rest of the Mediterranean Fleet in exercises to prepare for the war which seemed more and more inevitable. In March 1938 Godfrey remarked in his diary that "the last three days and nights have been spent at sea in the Atlantic doing combined exercises with the battlefleet. To command one of our capital ships, and especially a battle-cruiser, is thrilling enough, and to see this battlefleet and take part in its exercises is a grand experience which I shall never forget." He may have had many interests outside the Navy, but his true love was the Service and his burning ambition was to fly his flag as an Admiral at sea.

By the spring of 1938 the Spanish Republicans were losing ground and the prospects of a Nationalist attack on Catalonia and the south seemed imminent. "Non-intervention in the Spanish Civil War means that we intervene on either side in pursuit of our objects which are to exert a stabilising influence and to protect distressed British subjects, of which there seems to be an inexhaustible supply. Two years ago we thought we'd squeezed Majorca dry, but hundreds have remained tucked away in out of the way places. Others have returned." *Repulse* was therefore again sent to Palma, and there Godfrey made the acquaintance of the new British Consul, Alan Hillgarth, a retired Lieutenant-Commander. He had managed to win the confidence of the Spanish Captain General Majorca and of the commanding officer of the Italian bomber force which operated against Republican mainland Spain from an airfield just out-side Palma. When after a week *Repulse* left Majorca to make contact with John Leche, the newly appointed British Chargé d'Affaires and Minister Plenipotentiary to the Republican Government at Valencia and Barcelona, Hillgarth persuaded the Italians to refrain from bombing raids while this mission was being undertaken. Godfrey was highly impressed with Hillgarth's talents and arranged, when he became Director of Naval Intelligence, ten months later, for Hillgarth to be appointed Naval Attaché, Madrid, where the Franco Govern-ment was by then installed. It was an inspired choice.

After a very successful visit to Monaco, which no British warship had visited for many years, the next emergency proved to be Palestine again. Rioting had broken out in Haifa resulting in some eighty casualties and the High Commissioner had urgently appealed for a warship. The light cruiser *Emerald* was on her way home from the East Indies and was immediately diverted to Haifa, but she did not have sufficient marines or seamen for the purpose, so once again *Repulse* was rushed there. Pound gave Godfrey wide discretion to summon greater strength if he considered this necessary. *Repulse* arrived on 8 July for an indefinite stay. Godfrey wrote in his diary, "The state of the country is worse all round than it was a year ago: there is more bitterness between Jews and Arabs, trade is less good, uncertainty greater. Last year *Repulse* was a precaution in case of trouble. This year our job is more definite, and 150 seamen and marines have relieved the *Emerald*'s patrolling the streets at night, and occupying the points near the various storm centres where Jews and Arabs rub shoulders . . . The prospect of any sort of settlement seems more dim than ever, and so far no one has produced any constructive idea how to solve this problem . . . On Monday I shall fly to Jerusalem and meet General Haining who has relieved General Dill, and the new High Commissioner, MacMichael. Haining I know well having worked with him at the Staff College and at the Admiralty . . . The Brigadier thinks that sailors and marines are better at this sort of work than soldiers. It involves a lot of moving people on with the minimum of friction. Sailors and marines are more mature than soldiers whose average age is only about twenty-one, and by nature they seem to be more kind and tolerant . . . There's always plenty going on here to amuse the sailors who are soon on excellent terms with all and sundry and have no Arab-Jew inhibitions . . . The ship is quite transformed, everyone in khaki, and the sailors turning their hands to all sorts of queer jobs such as lorry drivers, customs searchers and railway guards. Although as lorry guards they are not supposed to go beyond the suburbs of Haifa, several have already found their way to Jerusalem and to the remotest parts of Palestine . . . Our howitzer is now installed on the Syrian frontier and two more are coming from Malta. The sailors get on very well with the Ulster Rifles and are teaching them how to use these handy weapons . . . The soldiers operating in the country don't get much sleep and I am having batches of them to live on board during their rest periods to give them a complete change of surroundings and get their minds off their work. I have also asked all the married NCOs and men and their wives to tea next Tuesday . . . I like Evetts, the Brigadier, more and more. He always asks me to go on expeditions with him, or when he

visits troops or is staging some small operation . . . The Brigadier and I have at last persuaded the District Commissioner to
agree to Commander Bell being appointed 'Town Commander'
and to preside over the Security Committee and I have asked
the C-in-C and he has agreed to him becoming an acting
Captain. So Bell is established ashore and Robin Durnford-
Slater takes over executive duties of a much depleted ship's
company . . . An early start today with the Brigadier through
Nazareth and down to Tiberias, and then into Transjordan for
a conference with Colonel Crystall commanding the Transjordan frontier zone. I met a remarkable young soldier, Orde
Wingate, in charge of a mixed force of British and Jews with
which he carries out night raids and reprisals on recalcitrant
Arabs. A sort of Lawrence, but on the other side, and rather
like L with a big nose, high cheek bones and sombre deep-set
eyes. The Arabs say 'He does not even fear God' . . . On the
whole the atmosphere in Haifa is less tense, and since the day
of the throwing of the big bomb things have been comparatively
quiet. This is to a great extent due to Bell who has made a
success of his job as Town Commandant . . . I enjoy meeting
friends from last year, and they seem pleased to see us back.
The Ruthenbergs, Jews from Vilna: he runs the electric power
station, and she a baby clinic: Von Marx his financial adviser
and a friend of the Rothschilds: the old etcher von Struck, a
great artist and friend of Einstein, with his most comfortable
and sweet Jewish wife. He has finished my portrait and is
urging me to take up wood or linoleum engraving. He tells
me that the particular sort of drawing that gives me pleasure
is susceptible to reproduction and is actually improved and
given a quality which is very satisfying and not difficult to
achieve . . ."

The commission was by now drawing to a close, but with the
international situation becoming ever more tense over Czecho-
Slovakia, *Repulse*'s return to England was hastened. She left
Haifa for Malta on 25 August. General Haining paid a special
visit to the ship before she sailed to address the ship's company
and present scrolls to eighteen officers and men commending
them for their work. He wrote later to Godfrey, 'I want to
thank you, and those under your command . . . for all they did
for us. I think the record of your various activities during your
seven weeks with us makes those who read it rub their eyes.'

During the seven weeks' stay *Repulse*'s ship's company had assisted at 26 bombings, 30 deliberate fires, 7 shootings, 12 stonings and murders and 8 lootings. As Godfrey remarked, "It's very lucky that no one was killed or even seriously injured, and we managed to remain on good terms with the Arabs who are genuinely sorry to see the sailors leave."

On leaving the Mediterranean he received the following letter from Admiral Pound: 'When you first came out here you will remember that I had to make a special report on you after six months. All I will say on this point is that the report should never have been called for—anyway all that nonsense has been dead a long time. You have commanded *Repulse* brilliantly and not only made her into a fine fighting machine but also into a ship which I knew would never let me down whatever duty she was employed on. The truth of this has been proved many times during the commission. I expect to see you go from success to success and from one important command to another and I am sure you will leave each one in a better state than you found it. You will always carry with you my very best wishes and grateful thanks for the loyal and whole-hearted service you have given me during the last two years . . .' Admiral Cunningham, commanding the Battle Cruiser squadron, was no less complimentary: 'I am sorry not to have seen *Repulse* again . . . I should much have liked to say a few words to your ship's company to tell them what a high opinion I hold of *Repulse*. It has been a great pleasure and privilege to have you in my squadron, and I can never be sufficiently grateful to you for your steady and loyal support and wise judgement. That we have not always agreed on every subject has been all to the good. It takes many opinions to make up a balanced judgement . . .'

A final proof of a highly successful commission was the fact that within a short space of time Commander Bell and all the heads of *Repulse*'s departments were promoted—almost a record for a private ship.

Repulse was due to pay-off when she reached England, but when she in fact did so the Munich crisis intervened and she was almost immediately ordered to join the Home Fleet at Scapa Flow. It was not until 19 December that Godfrey was able to hand over to his relief, his old friend Ernest Spooner. "No one", he wrote, "had any delusions that Munich meant a change in German policy. We were annoyed at the wishfulness of the politicians and especially of the Prime Minister, Mr Chamberlain." But for Godfrey himself there was an exciting prospect ahead. He had been appointed Director of Naval Intelligence.

CHAPTER SIX

Director of Naval Intelligence

ALTHOUGH AT the beginning of 1939 most of the British public still clung wishfully to the belief that Neville Chamberlain had indeed secured 'Peace in our time' at Munich, the Prime Minister himself and his principal advisers were no longer under any such illusion. The Diaries of Sir Alexander Cadogan, Permanent Under-Secretary at the Foreign Office, bear ample testimony to the atmosphere of crisis in which the year opened and of the despairing attempts of the Government to make up its mind whether to oppose the dictators with Britain's still quite inadequate resources in order to prevent a further accession to their strength or, alternatively, to delay the inevitable as long as possible to gain time for an improvement in her own military and diplomatic position. The Chiefs of Staff had already made it clear that even with France as an ally (and no formal alliance then existed) Britain could not simultaneously oppose Germany, Italy and Japan. Despite the many measures to rearm which had now been taken no real improvement in the position could be expected until the beginning of 1941. Nazi Germany was the most pressing and dangerous enemy, so every effort had to be made to restore Britain's traditionally good relations with Italy and to avoid, at almost any cost, presenting the Japanese with an excuse to attack her possessions in the Far East or Australia and New Zealand in the Pacific. In February the Spanish Republican Government had collapsed and it looked as though Franco would join the 'Pact of Steel' between Hitler and Mussolini and so imperil Britain's position in the Mediterranean. On 1 March Germany occupied the rump of Czechoslovakia. On 31 March, in an effort to remove any doubts in Hitler's mind that Britain would fight if necessary, Chamberlain gave Poland a unilateral guarantee. On 3 April Italy occupied Albania and on 27 April Germany denounced the Anglo-German Naval Treaty. From then on Hitler's verbal attacks on Poland and Great Britain became more and more strident and menacing. The War of Nerves, sustained by a rash of rumours, carefully planted by Admiral Canaris, the Head of the Nazi Secret Service, alarmed and confused the Western Democracies and kept the atmosphere at fever pitch. War seemed more and more inevitable. Confidential staff talks had been going on with the French for some time and in June even more secret naval conversations were resumed with the Americans. These were followed by negotiations with Soviet Russia, culminating on 12 August in the despatch of an Anglo-French Military Mission to Moscow. Due to deep-rooted suspicions on both sides and to the obduracy of the Poles the matter dragged on inconclusively until, on 24 August, the announcement of the Russo-German Pact made it clear to everyone that, unless Britain and France again gave way, war could not be delayed for more than a few days. Hitler invaded Poland on 1 September and Britain and France declared war on Germany on 3 September. Italy and Japan decided to bide their time before joining in, and the United States, while offering moral support and much advice, was not prepared, at this stage, to become more than the 'Arsenal of Democracy' on a 'cash and carry' basis.

Godfrey's first nine months as Director of Naval Intelligence were therefore passed under the louring and ever more threatening clouds of what Churchill has called the 'Gathering Storm'. He had been notified while *Repulse* was in Haifa in August that it was intended that he should relieve Vice-Admiral J. A. G. Troup as Director of Naval Intelligence early in the New Year. His immediate reaction was that it would be "quite the most interesting job for a director at the Admiralty". There was one drawback. Although customarily a Rear-Admiral's appointment, it was usually a prelude to retirement, carrying with it no prospects of flying one's flag at sea, an essential requirement for promotion to Vice-Admiral on the active list, let alone for attainment of the rank of full Admiral. Despite his long association with Pound, Godfrey had never been able to establish close personal relations with that austere and very reserved man. Pound had no interests outside the Service, except shooting and fishing, sports which held little appeal for Godfrey. Once, during a run ashore at Malta, the barriers had been lowered and a more intimate and friendly attitude adopted, but on the next occasion they met, Pound had reverted to his usual taciturn professionalism, as though the previous informal interlude had been a regrettable aberration. Nevertheless Godfrey decided to ask Pound's advice. He replied, 'I think your prospective appointment as DNI is an excellent one and when I go to the Admiralty I will make certain that it is their intention to send you to sea afterwards.' This was enough for Godfrey, but it so happened that, as a result of the death of Sir Roger Backhouse, Pound, who had been due to remain as C-in-C Mediterranean until 1940, in fact became First Sea Lord in June 1939, and so was in a position to make assurance doubly sure.

Two other events must have added to Godfrey's confidence and have removed the last traces of the inferiority complex from which he confesses he had suffered as a young officer, and which must have been revived by Kelly's damning report at the beginning of 1936. He was made Companion of the Bath in the New Year's Honour List. The whole system of Honours and Awards has been so debased in recent years that it is now difficult to realise the importance which was then paid to these matters. The CB was normally only awarded to officers of Rear-Admiral's rank. For a Captain it was most unusual. Pound wrote, 'I was really delighted at seeing you got a CB. It means so much more when you get it before you are due for it by seniority and in this case it was a fitting reward for the high state of efficiency you brought *Repulse* to and all the good work you did in her.' The second happy omen was Godfrey's promotion on 22 February to Rear-Admiral. Only once since World War I had a Captain been appointed DNI and he had promptly been made Commodore 1st Class. Backhouse, however, considered that Commodores 1st Class should only serve at sea, and arranged for Godfrey's immediate promotion to Flag Rank without waiting for the normal half-yearly promotions in July. Among the many letters Godfrey received was one from Tom Phillips who wrote, 'Another letter of congratulations after such a short period! but none the less sincere for that. I am delighted that they have broken away from the six months rule and promoted you when they wanted to do so.' In fact Godfrey asked for the promotion to be delayed for one week so that, as Naval ADC to the King, he could attend on Their Majesties when the Queen launched the battleship *King George V*; probably the only occasion on which the Senior Captain in the Navy has asked for his promotion to be deferred! The appointment of the new DNI had attracted an unusual amount of interest in the national and the Service press. Typical were the remarks of the *United Services Review* which, after commenting on the fact that the choice had fallen on a Captain rather than a Rear-Admiral, expressed the view that 'the answer must be that the post is given to the officer who is best fitted to hold it'. A report which Godfrey did not see until after the war was that made by the German Naval Attaché, who wrote to Berlin, 'Rear-Admiral Godfrey is an upright, charming and intelligent officer who . . . is at pains to test out circumstances personally and form his own opinion from experience . . . The Admiralty appears to have exerted itself to place one of their best officers in this important position.'

It was indeed a key post. The Intelligence Division was the senior one of the Naval Staff and its Director the only one to hold the rank of Rear-Admiral, but, it has been only too truly remarked, 'there was a grave disparity between the importance of the job in time of peace and in time of war. Intelligence deals with the enemy and the potential enemy . . . When there is no enemy it languishes and its importance is forgotten. Its strategic functions are only vaguely apprehended by those—and this includes the real talent of the Navy—who have no personal experience of Intelligence in war. In war time the position entirely changes . . . War in fact changes the Intelligence Officer from Cinderella to Princess. To vary the metaphor, Naval Intelligence changes in time of war from a sluggish brook to a raging torrent.' A very fair description, except that it fails to point out that the 'raging torrent' could not be released simply by opening a sluice gate: the level of the waters had first to be raised by sinking fresh wells, by digging out old channels and by re-building all the aqueducts which had formerly fed the brook. In 1939 the whole system had been neglected for a generation and it required someone with the ruthless energy and creative imagination of Jacky Fisher to effect the transformation not only of the NID but of the whole stagnant pool of British Intelligence.

Unfortunately this fact was only partly appreciated by the majority of the Navy's senior officers. Most of them, conveniently forgetting their previous contemptuous disregard of the needs of NID, confidently expected that if war should come they would immediately be fed with the 'raging torrent' of information which had poured forth in the days of the famous

Blinker Hall in World War I. The great reputation of British Intelligence stemmed almost entirely from his achievements. His brilliant team of cryptanalysts in Room 40 OB, the network of agents he built up in Greece, Spain and South America, the organisation created in the United States by the Naval Attaché and Sir William Wiseman had placed weapons in his hands which he had used with devastating effect not only in the purely naval sphere but in the political and diplomatic field as well. Acting on his own initiative and without much reference to higher authority, it was Hall who had nearly succeeded in bribing the Turks to abandon the war just before the Dardanelles (he would have succeeded if the Foreign Office had not already promised Constantinople to the Russians): it was Hall who was responsible for the downfall of Sir Roger Casement: it was Hall who handled the notorious Zimmerman Telegram which finally brought a reluctant America into the War. No wonder Dr Page, the American Ambassador in London, wrote to President Wilson, 'Hall is one genius the war has developed. Neither in fiction nor in fact can you find any such man to match him . . . All other secret service men are amateurs by comparison . . .' Unfortunately Hall's amazing triumphs aroused alarm and jealousy in many quarters in Whitehall. The Foreign Office, for one, was determined that no future Director of Naval Intelligence should ever again be permitted to wield such power and influence. Hall's incomparable organisation was transferred to the Secret Intelligence Service and placed under the control of the Foreign Office. There was much to be said for this attempt to unify the covert Intelligence organisations, but the Foreign Office was certainly not the right Department of State to act as overlord to clandestine, nefarious and sometimes distasteful activities. At least, the Foreign Secretary did not follow his American counterpart's example, who closed down his country's cryptanalysis department on the grounds that 'Gentlemen do not read each other's mail'! Ironically the only recognition which Hall received for his tremendous achievements was a Foreign Office decoration, the KCMG. He was not popular with the Naval Staff and was retired from the Navy at the end of 1918. The Hall tradition withered for lack of money, personality and opportunity. There was no threat to other parts of the Intelligence 'establishment', to the hegemony of the Foreign Office, or to the other divisions of the Naval Staff. But Hall was not forgotten. In 1939, in the growing atmosphere of crisis and impending doom, with the need for first class Intelligence again becoming apparent even to the most obtuse, and with the appointment of a Director of Naval Intelligence as able and dynamic as Godfrey, all the old fears and jealousies re-emerged. Any move to expand inside the Admiralty or to increase co-operation outside would be in danger of arousing suspicions of 'empire building', whispered charges of 'personal aggrandizement' and subject to misinterpretation of motive by those who feared that their own performance would not measure up to the standard of the new DNI.

Godfrey has stated that he did not know much about Intelligence when he became DNI. It is true he had little experience of the internal workings of the Division, of the nuts and bolts of the business, but his past service in the Mediterranean in World War I, his time in Plans Division and at Greenwich, his commissions in China and the Pacific had given him certain clear ideas of what Intelligence ought to do, the lines along which he would have to proceed, and the need for help and support not only from other departments in the Admiralty and Whitehall but from organisations and individuals unconnected with the government machine. He was well equipped to secure what he needed. He was just over fifty, full of energy and ambition and with the tough mental and physical constitution essential to a wartime leader. An innovator and a builder, with an open and enquiring mind, fully prepared, indeed anxious to use his own initiative, and act on his own responsibility, a talented and experienced staff officer, accustomed to co-operating with other Services both British and foreign, civil and military, his whole career seems, in retrospect, to have been a preparation for this appointment and the appointment itself to have been predestined.

One thing that Godfrey certainly realised was that time was running out. He took only a few days leave over Christmas and the New Year and then early in January, without waiting for the official date of his take-over from Troup, threw himself into the task of discovering what needed to be done and the order of priority in which the various tasks should be tackled. His appointments diary for January shows that before the end of that month he had met, among others, Sir Warren Fisher,

Permanent Secretary to the Treasury: Admiral Quex Sinclair, head of the Secret Intelligence Service, the mysterious 'C', and his deputy Colonel Stewart Menzies: Commanders Denniston and Travis, head and deputy head of the Government Code & Cipher School, the code breaking organisation, and one of their most talented cryptanalysts, Nigel de Grey: the French and American Naval Attachés. Early in February he reported to the First Sea Lord, Admiral Backhouse, and the Deputy Chief of Staff, Godfrey's former chief in the Battle Cruiser Squadron, Sir Andrew Cunningham. This was followed by a press conference presided over by the First Lord, Lord Stanhope, and then by meetings with Sir Robert Vansittart, Diplomatic Adviser to the Government, and Sir Alexander Cadogan, Permanent Under-Secretary at the Foreign Office. There were calls on Colonel Vernon Kell, head of MI5, the counter-intelligence service, and on Ronald Howe, Head of the Special Branch at Scotland Yard. It was clear that all official doors were open to the Director of Naval Intelligence, and, as he was soon to discover, not only official ones. Many important people in the city, in industry, in Fleet Street, and other centres of influence were anxious to help in any way they could.

One of the first to offer to do so was the great Blinker Hall himself. He was at this time nearly sixty-nine but as alert and full of vitality as he had been when he had sat in Godfrey's chair twenty years earlier. "He came to see me", wrote Godfrey, "on 22 March and from then onwards we met frequently. He very unobtrusively offered me full access to his enormous store of knowledge, wisdom, cunning and ingenuity. He told me that DNI should act on his own initiative, obtaining permission, if necessary, afterwards: that DNI is entitled to enlist the help of anyone inside or outside the country from the Archbishop of Canterbury and the General of the Jesuits downwards and that they would all be delighted to help me, and that boldness always pays. He emphasised the importance of my office and of having plenty of contacts in the City, Foreign Office and foreign capitals, and strongly advised me to establish a personal link with the American Ambassador. It was through him and his one time deputy Admiral Sir Aubrey Hugh-Smith [by then a power in the City] that I met Sir Montague Norman, Governor of the Bank of England, Sir Edward Peacock, Chairman of Barings, Olaf Hambro, Chairman of Hambros Bank, and Lionel and Tony Rothschild, all of whom helped me in a variety of fruitful and unexpected ways, particularly in the recruitment of wartime staff. He told me that my job had more kicks than half-pence and that I should not try to model my NID on *his* experience. He said, 'You have enough personality of your own to form your own department'. Above all he warned me of some of the political pitfalls that lay in my path in war time; and experience soon convinced me that I had an awkward commodity to sell, that the cupboard was bare and DNI extremely vulnerable. When in doubt I often asked myself what would Hall have done."

However, before Godfrey could get down to serious work in his Division he was involved in a secret and largely unofficial visit to Paris. "As we had no alliance or agreement with France, the knowledge that unofficial conversations were taking place with the French Admiralty would have been embarrassing to the First Lord, Lord Stanhope, who would have been the first to agree that he had better not be told. My mission was approved by the DCNS (Cunningham) with the knowledge of Backhouse. Its object was to devise the machinery of collaboration with the French DNI, Rear-Admiral de Villaine. Collaboration between Intelligence staffs, unlike Operations Staffs, commits the Service departments to nothing. In the course of a cordial and co-operative visit we agreed to exchange information about Intelligence centres abroad and to devise a simple method of communication. I met Admiral Darlan and at his invitation visited the Ministry of Marine and saw the elaborate underground arrangements that the French had devised, including the protected teleprinter communications to all naval bases which, as a result of my visit, were extended to London. They were much better equipped than we were at that time. Whatever Darlan may have done or thought subsequently I am sure that in 1939 he meant to be a good ally." At the same time arrangements were also made in the greatest secrecy for a French signal officer, Lieutenant de Vaisseau Toulouse Lautrec, to come to London to work under the auspices of NID10 on the preparation of an Anglo-French Naval Cipher. It was perhaps symptomatic that, despite the excellence of their arrangements, the French abandoned their subterranean command headquarters immediately war broke out and evacuated their Intelligence and Operations departments to the Chateau of

Marceau, some thirty miles outside Paris. The British did exactly the opposite. The Naval Staff remained in the Admiralty throughout the war. Although arrangements were made for alternative accommodation only the technical departments were evacuated to Bath.

What did Godfrey find when he officially took over the Naval Intelligence Division from Troup? It was always emphasised that in peace time the Division was 'not a Secret Service . . . and no one engaged on Intelligence work is to lay himself open to the suspicion of espionage.' Although this ruling was occasionally bent a little, it was broadly true and most of the information which trickled in was obtained from perfectly open and legitimate sources: announcements of foreign governments, press reports, appreciations by British naval attachés, observations by British warships visiting foreign ports. Covert intelligence sources were the responsibility of the Secret Intelligence Service.

The Director had two naval and one civil assistants. The Deputy Director, a Captain, concentrated largely on administration; the Assistant Director, usually a Colonel of Marines, was responsible for security and the control of the world-wide Reporting Organisation; the Civil Assistant dealt with civilian staff and all Civil Service matters. In this connection it should be emphasised that the Admiralty was a Civil not a Naval establishment and that Naval Officers serving in it were often regarded by their Civil Service colleagues as no more than 'professional advisers'.

The Division was, at this time, divided into about ten very small sections. Sections 1 to 5, the Geographical Sections, between them covered the whole world. They produced and kept up to date the Confidential Books which contained the details of foreign fleets, harbours, coast defences, building programmes and so on: they maintained contact with British naval attachés abroad and with the foreign attachés stationed in London: they studied Foreign Office telegrams and other information from abroad and circulated anything of interest to the appropriate members of the Naval Staff. The normal complement of a Section was one Commander, one Marine Major and one clerk. Section 6 looked after the so-called Geographical Handbooks which had first been produced in World War I and gave general information about foreign countries for the benefit of visiting British warships. Section 7 dealt with engineering and other technical information. Section 8 was the Operational Intelligence Centre,* recently formed to try to keep track of the day to day movements and intentions of German, Italian and Japanese warships and merchantmen. Section 9, a joint Signals and Intelligence Section, was responsible for the development and administration of the few Naval Direction Finding and 'Y' stations. Section 10 was responsible for signal security and liaison with the Government Code and Cipher School. None of these sections, with the exception of OIC, which had a staff of five, was manned by more than two officers and a clerk. There was a small secretariat to serve the DNI, DDNI and ADNI and to handle the more highly confidential typing, but all other typing requirements had to be met by the central Admiralty pool. A two- or three-man drawing office had to cope not only with the Division's own requirements but those of other Admiralty departments as well. Finally there was a small press department, for at this time DNI was responsible for the release of information of naval interest to the press and the BBC. The total strength of the Division within the Admiralty was under fifty men and women. Outside the Admiralty there were Staff Officers (Intelligence) on the staff of every Flag Officer and Commander-in-Chief, the Naval Attachés and Reporting Officers, many of the latter working on a part-time and unpaid basis in British Consulates in all the major ports. There were also Intelligence Centres at Alexandria and Singapore, the last of which was an inter-Service organisation which included a cryptanalysis department. Close touch was maintained with the Australian, New Zealand and Canadian Naval Intelligence Departments.

It was far too small an organisation to cover all the ordinary peacetime needs so that many of those considered less urgent had perforce to be dealt with in a very sketchy manner or not tackled at all. The Division was patently unable, for lack of men, money and materials, to meet the greatly increased demands which were now being made on it as a result of the emergency situation which was rapidly developing, let alone to face the test of actual war.

---

* For a full description of the work of OIC, see the author's *Very Special Intelligence* (Hamish Hamilton, 1977).

Nor were the other British Intelligence departments in any better state; most of them were in even worse condition. The Secret Intelligence Service, where naval influence had remained strong (its head since the war had always been a retired naval officer and many of the staff of GC & CS were old Room 40 hands), had been as crippled as NID by lack of money, and at Foreign Office behest had been compelled to concentrate its limited resources more on diplomatic than military Intelligence and to ignore altogether countries which it was thought would be either neutral or allied in the event of war. Both MI5 and MI6 tended to be amateurish and old-fashioned in their outlook and methods, a weakness that was to become painfully apparent before the war was three months old. The Foreign Office itself had no central body charged with assessing the validity of the reports which came to it from its ambassadors abroad, many of whom were starry eyed about the governments to which they were accredited. The Ambassador in Berlin, for example, struck out from the Naval Attaché's annual report remarks to the effect that the Germans would ignore the terms of the Anglo-German Naval Treaty just as soon as it suited them to do so, while even as late as June 1939 his colleague in Paris was continuing to sing the praises of the French Army and to report that its morale, like that of the French nation as a whole, was excellent. In the War Office Intelligence was subordinated to Operations and therefore lacking in independence and objectivity, while the Intelligence Corps, as such, was not even in existence. (It was not formed until 1940 when the inadequacy of the previous arrangements could no longer be ignored.) The Royal Air Force, which should have been one of the greatest providers of the raw material of Intelligence, from photographic reconnaissance, was neither prepared to devote any of its limited resources to this essential task nor to permit either of the other two Services to do so for themselves. Intelligence, the keystone of any efficient Defence policy, had been, like all other branches of the Armed Forces, hamstrung by the infamous 'Ten Year Rule'. Efficient Intelligence organisations could no more be provided overnight than could warships, tanks or aircraft.

It would be grossly unfair to Godfrey's predecessor, Troup, and to the previous Deputy Chief of Naval Staff, Sir William James, to suggest that none of NID's shortcomings had been perceived or that no attempts had been made to remedy them.

James, who had been in charge of Hall's Room 40 in 1917 and 1918, had, in 1936, directed Troup to form the Operational Intelligence Centre. This was certainly the most pressing need if the Division was to be transformed from a peace to a war footing. The young officer charged by Troup with this task, Paymaster Lt Commander N. E. Denning, had carried out his instructions brilliantly and the organisation which he had proposed and created, at least in embryo, had already functioned with considerable success at the time of Munich. The foundations laid by Denning were so sound that although the Centre's man-and-woman-power had to be increased from five to seventy-five during the next three years, its basic organisation required very little subsequent modification and the principles on which it worked no major change throughout the war. What Godfrey did was to recognise at once the key role which the OIC would be called upon to play and to ensure, so far as was humanly possible, that it did not lack, when the time came, the material resources and the right type of staff to enable it to perform its full role and influence events at sea in a way that Hall's Room 40 had never been able to do. Troup had also initiated plans for the conversion of the Admiralty basement into an underground complex to house not only OIC but the Operations and Trade War Rooms and the civilian-manned War Registry which logged and distributed the vast number of incoming and outgoing signals received or sent by the Admiralty. Nor had Troup been unaware of the needs for expansion of the staff of all Sections and he had begun somewhat tentatively to build up a register of civilians who would be prepared to offer their services if it did come to war. The skeleton of the organisation was there, but it still lacked a number of essential bones and a very great deal of flesh.

"One of the problems of an expanding department", wrote Godfrey after the war, "is the point of view held by many civilians and naval officers, especially after many years of peace and pruned estimates, that it is no good asking for this or that because the Admiralty or the Treasury is sure to turn it down. It is an insidious form of defeatism." Reluctance to press for something which he considered necessary was not a weakness of which Godfrey could be accused, but there is no doubt that he was greatly aided in achieving his objectives by the excellent relations he enjoyed with the DCNS, Admiral Sir Andrew

Cunningham. Backhouse's illness soon resulted in ABC having to take charge of the Admiralty pending the appointment of Pound as the new First Sea Lord. "There was a great deal to be done and a number of far-reaching and expensive decisions to be taken. Thanks to Admiral Cunningham's support, encouragement and disregard of red tape, I was able to make considerable progress. With his approval I used to preface my requests by the words 'By direction of the DCNS', which ensured them a quick passage. This was against all the rules. He was a most helpful person to serve, and very straightforward; when he praised he praised wholeheartedly, especially if things were going badly. He would browbeat people if they let him. This was the moment when you had to persist and refuse to be browbeaten. He did not favour a too ready acquiescence."

Godfrey was a firm believer in devolution. "It was clear from the first", he wrote, "that any system of organising an Intelligence service which did not embody a very large measure of decentralisation would fail. I was fortunate that both Backhouse and then Pound fell in with my idea that DNI should be regarded more as an administrator and organiser than as a moment to moment Intelligence officer. In this respect we differed from the War Office and Air Ministry where the DMI and DAI spent long periods expounding the current situation and had insufficient time left to look after their departments and outstations. Sea Lords were encouraged to send for Sectional heads and did so; this was good for both of them and gave the heads of Sections confidence. This freed me for my rightful duty, which was to organise, sustain and supervise a machine that was to grow from a few dozen to over a thousand individuals in three years of war." Much as Godfrey profited from Hall's advice, he realised from the start that circumstances had changed and that, unlike Hall, it would be a grave mistake to try to keep all the threads in his own fingers.

The first task to be tackled was that of recruitment. It was obvious that NID would have to rely mainly on civilian volunteers. The specialist skills even of retired naval officers would be at a premium in the Fleet and the technical departments. Moreover Godfrey was already conscious that the right type of civilian might have knowledge and experience essential in the new sections that he planned to create which no naval officer could supply. In this respect there is no doubt that Godfrey was a pioneer. By good fortune the author Charles Morgan, who had started life in the Navy and was determined to serve it again if war came, was introduced to Godfrey. He was immediately given the responsibility with Commander Caspar Swinley, head of NID1, of discovering, interviewing and allocating suitable volunteers. There was no lack of applicants and the Division was brought up to its permitted establishment by the outbreak of war.

In World War I, when a number of civilians had also been brought into NID, the practice of giving some of them commissions in the Royal Naval Volunteer Reserve or in the Royal Marines had led to certain difficulties. Godfrey avoided this problem by supporting the creation of a new branch of the RNVR, the Special Branch, whose members were recruited specifically for Intelligence or Meteorological duties and wore green cloth between their wavy gold lace to distinguish them from their brethren of the Executive branch. Ian Fleming and the author were two of the earliest recruits on the Intelligence side. The Special Branch was later enormously expanded and its members carried out a very wide range of technical duties, including mine disposal, but the original intention was a small example of Godfrey's ability to foresee and provide for unusual circumstances.

Although some additional staff, mostly retired naval officers, had been earmarked for OIC, and an active service Commander, Geoffrey Colpoys, was in charge of the small section, Godfrey, with his knowledge of Room 40's work at Jutland and after, saw at once that OIC must be made into the nerve centre of the Admiralty, which, unlike the War Office and the Air Ministry, was an operational authority. The Centre would have to expand into a Division within the Division, and unless he was going to abandon his policy of devolution and become himself a 'moment to moment' Intelligence officer, he must put in charge of it an officer of sufficient seniority and ability to hold his own with the Assistant Chiefs of Staff, and even the Deputy Chief of Staff. He recalled that when he had visited Room 40 in 1917 he had found there one of his contemporaries, Jock Clayton, who only two years previously had also been a navigator at the Cape Helles landings. Now Clayton had been placed on the retired list and so was available. In March he was given the dormant appointment of head of OIC with the grade of Deputy Director. It was to prove a splendid choice.

Godfrey showed equal flair in selecting Paymaster Captain Thring, who had been the U-boat Tracking expert in 1918, to head the re-formed Submarine Tracking section of OIC. Godfrey also put all his weight behind the drive for the expansion of the Direction Finding stations and the creation of a Civilian Wireless Service to man them, for which Denning and Commander Sandwith, head of Section 9, had been vainly pressing for some time. It took months to overcome the obstruction of the Treasury, so that the organisation was far from complete at the outbreak of war, but at least the wheels had been set in motion.

Satisfied that he could rely on the combination of Clayton, Colpoys, Sandwith and Denning, Godfrey then turned his attention to other areas. He had been much impressed by Hall's account of the value he had derived in World War I from the services of his Personal Assistant, Claud Serocold, a stockbroker. It was through him that Hall had gained contact with the City, and Serocold had carried out all sorts of unofficial and unorthodox tasks for his master with tremendous success. Hall strongly advised Godfrey that in this case at least, he should follow his example. So Godfrey appealed to Sir Montagu Norman and Sir Edward Peacock. "I was very touched by the way these two eminent men, overburdened with work, turned their minds to the problem of finding me a personal assistant. Norman rang me up and said, 'We've found your man'. I thanked him and asked when I could come and see him, to which he replied 'On no account. You are much too busy to waste a morning in the City. *I* will come and see you.'" This was how it came about that NID's best-known recruit, the subsequent creator of James Bond, Ian Fleming, joined the Division. Fleming, like his master, was a complex character. To some he seemed a 'bit of a mountebank' or a 'chocolate soldier'. Even his own wife is quoted as saying that Ian could suffer anything except discomfort. Others found him supercilious and aloof. Those of us, on the other hand, who saw Ian at close quarters during the war, are agreed that he was another of Godfrey's inspired choices and that he made a very great contribution indeed to NID's success. This was certainly Godfrey's own view and he appears to have looked on his talented PA almost as the son he had never had. He even remarked after the war that "Ian should have been the DNI and I his naval adviser", a truly remarkable over-statement from one so hard-headed and dispassionate. Fleming achieved far more than Godfrey could reasonably have expected of him when he took him on in the summer of 1939, but he would have been the last to claim that he would have made a successful DNI.

In World War I those at sea and serving abroad had suffered from a frustrating lack of reliable or even of any news of the progress of the war and of events at home. Godfrey was determined that this should not happen again. After some difficulty he secured Board approval for the formation of an Information Section to provide for the dissemination of this type of information to the Fleet, to naval attachés, the Cabinet, and the BBC, by means of daily and weekly summaries of naval events. Charles Morgan had no difficulty in assembling a most talented band of men and women, who included Hilary St George Saunders, Librarian of the House of Commons, Pirie-Gordon from *The Times*, Professor and Mrs Webb, Robin Barrett from Reuters, William Plomer, the author, Mrs Urwick, later to become Mrs Hilary Saunders, and yet another of Hall's old team, Marjorie Napier.

A Section which by its very nature could have no raison d'être in time of peace but which would be vital in war, was that concerned with the interrogation of prisoners of war. Plans for an inter-Service organisation to be administered by the War Office were drawn up and the officer Godfrey selected to head the naval side was a Colonel Trench RM. In 1913, as a young captain, Trench and Lieutenant Brandon, RN, while making a clandestine reconnaissance of the coast defences of the North Sea and the Frisian Islands, a real life *Riddle of the Sands*, had been arrested and imprisoned. Trench knew the Germans and the team he built up between 1939 and 1941 was to extract an astonishing amount of information of the greatest value.

Something to which Godfrey gave very early attention was the establishment of good relations with the press. He consulted Lords Rothermere, Camrose and Kemsley, Garvin of the *Observer* and Sir Roderick Jones, the head of Reuters and his General Manager, Godfrey's old friend from China, Christopher Chancellor. He was already in touch with *The Times* through its Naval Correspondent, Admiral Thursfield, who introduced him to the Deputy Editor, Barrington Ward. He does not seem to have been able to contact Lord Beaverbrook, which may well have been a tactical error, but the others all welcomed the idea of co-operation on a rather higher plane than had previously been customary. Sir Roderick Jones placed his foreign organisation entirely at his disposal. Godfrey also called on all the editors and started a series of informal press conferences so that a valuable two-way exchange of information was successfully created. The editors "would often give me a tip if some particularly juicy morsel of naval news was about to break. In return I was often able to confirm information of doubtful currency and I had no hesitation in ringing up an editor direct and in a friendly way discussing some item of mutual concern. What is more, they would sometimes tell me in confidence the source of their information." He also discussed plans with Thursfield for creating a corps of naval war correspondents afloat. The disaster to the submarine *Thetis* early in the year gave a foretaste of the demands which would be made on the Press Department in time of war and exposed the inadequacy of the existing arrangements. It at least gave Godfrey the opportunity of providing the excellent head of the Department, Captain Brooking, with a slightly more adequate staff.

All these various steps to make good twenty years of neglect in the space of a few months and to equip the Division for its future task, had to be taken in an atmosphere which was a curious mixture of crisis, confusion and a continuing reluctance to abandon the comfortable habits of peace. Despite the increasing number of short cuts which he was taking, Godfrey had to compete with the claims of every other department of the Navy and to fight through any proposal for expansion against the dead hand of the Treasury. But many of the Whitehall Establishment were still operating on a peacetime basis. Ministers left for week-ends in the country on Friday afternoons and, incredibly, the Admiralty telephone exchange closed down completely at noon on Saturdays. A relic of Hall's days, a small private exchange, with direct lines to the Foreign Office, 'C', MI5 Scotland Yard, etc., did give DNI some independent means of communication, and as Hitler and Mussolini often chose the week-ends for their coups, Godfrey got quite used to spending Saturdays and Sundays at the Admiralty in the company of Cunningham or the Assistant Chief of Naval Staff on the end of this line. Apart from actual moves by the dictators, such as the occupation of Prague or the invasion of Albania, there was also the War of Nerves mentioned at the beginning of this chapter. David Dilks, the editor of the Cadogan Diaries, writes, 'The British Government heard every kind of rumour, some accurate, more not. What was lacking was a machinery for the collation and assessment of Intelligence.' A typical example of this was the report planted on the British Embassy in Berlin that the German Air Force was going to make a surprise attack on the British Fleet during the Easter leave period. Had the Foreign Office had some section capable of evaluating the truth of this and other such reports before giving them circulation, much trouble would have been saved, but they had not, and the Ambassador's telegram was placed before the Cabinet, which, without even consulting the DNI, gave orders for some of the Fleet's anti-aircraft guns to be manned and for the First Lord to make reference to the fact in a speech he made on board the new aircraft carrier *Ark Royal* at Portsmouth. This of course caused a sensation, followed by considerable official embarrassment when the falseness of the rumour was recognised. A similar sort of report that German U-boats were patrolling in the Channel and off the mouth of the Thames, planted in this case on Vansittart, caused equal excitement. Two good results did ensue. Godfrey managed to get a direct line installed from his private exchange to Sir Horace Wilson, so that Chamberlain's adviser could verify such rumours. He also arranged for a duty commander to be available night and day in NID, and got the Civil Service to agree to keep an operator on duty in the main exchange during week-ends. Perhaps of greater importance was his suggestion for the establishment of a Situation Report Centre, consisting of a representative of the Foreign Office and the three Service Intelligence Directors 'to collate intelligence received from abroad and to issue daily secret situation reports in order that any emergency measures which may have to be taken should be based only on the most reliable and carefully co-ordinated information'. There was already another inter-Service Intelligence body in existence, the Joint Intelligence Committee. This had been formed in 1936 and consisted of the Deputy Directors of Intelligence of the three Services. It met on an *ad hoc* basis to prepare reports for the Joint Planning Committee, and had therefore been concerned only with long-term intelligence. It was Godfrey who had suggested the inclusion of a Foreign Office representative in the Situation Report Centre, and when, after a couple of months, this body suggested that it should be amalgamated with the JIC, it was again Godfrey who pressed strongly that the Foreign Office should provide a Chairman for the revised JIC as "the only way to secure Foreign Office collaboration, previously lacking in Intelligence work". His suggestion was adopted and a Counsellor of the Foreign Office, Mr Stephenson was duly appointed. He was succeeded soon after the outbreak of war by Cavendish Bentinck, who held the position throughout the rest of the war. The work of this Committee will be referred to later. Suffice it to record at this stage the debt it owed to Godfrey.

There were other rumours about the German Navy current in the summer of 1939. The Secret Service was insistent that German U-boats were cruising in the South Atlantic and that secret re-fuelling bases had been established at various remote points overseas. Coupled with this was a strong belief that the Germans had built more U-boats than the number permitted under the Anglo-German Naval Treaty. There was absolutely no truth in either of these stories, but NID lacked any independent means of verifying them and could not therefore ignore them.

Another question was the exact size of Germany's two projected battleships of the *Bismarck* class. These should not have exceeded the tonnage laid down by the Washington Treaty, 35,000 tons. The Germans truthfully disclosed their proposed length, beam, armament and certain other particulars but gave a totally false dimension for their draught, 26 feet instead of the actual figure, 34 feet. Admiral Raeder personally assured the British Naval Attaché, Captain Troubridge, that the former figure was correct and that the new ships would conform to Treaty limitations. As the two ships were longer, beamier and carried a heavier armament than the new British *King George V* class, the only possible explanation for the lighter draught had to be that their armour, speed and endurance would be correspondingly reduced. The British technical departments were

naïvely reluctant to believe that the Germans were deliberately
lying. It would have been inconvenient politically and would
have meant, as in fact was the case, that the German ships
would be well over 40,000 tons and would therefore outclass
their British equivalents. The German Section of NID were
highly sceptical, but unfortunately could not prevail on NID7,
the technical section, to support them against the considered
views of the rest of the Naval Staff, an example of the dangers
of relying on one's 'experts' and of the folly of trusting to
the good faith of foreigners.

There is an intriguing footnote to this. Although the Naval
Staff may have been convinced of the Germans' good faith,
NID was not and asked the SIS to try and get more information.
Some time in the middle of 1939 Godfrey was informed that
they had found a contact who, for a large sum, would hand over
plans of the ship. Godfrey waited for several hours, with a
member of the SIS, in his father-in-law's flat over the Turkish
Baths in Jermyn Street. Had this been a James Bond story the
gallant agent would have won through against fearful odds in
time for Britain's battleships to be redesigned and war prevented.
Unfortunately it was the real life Secret Service of 1939: the
spy failed to turn up and Godfrey never knew whether the
whole thing was a plant, whether the plans were only for the
ship's bakery or whether Himmler had got there first.

By the middle of June international tension was reaching
breaking point. Anglo-French conversations had started with
Russia but were making little headway, a situation in no way
aided by the fact that someone in the Foreign Office Communication Section was disclosing to the Soviets the instructions sent to the British delegation. German claims for Danzig
and the Polish Corridor were shrill and insistent and were being
backed by Mussolini. A serious situation had arisen over the
arrest of British subjects in China by the Japanese. War drew
ever nearer. There were, however, some Germans with cooler
heads, or less nerve, than Hitler. Admiral Canaris and the
German General Staff were by no means as confident as the
Führer and the egregious Ribbentrop that Britain would not
honour her obligations to Poland and declare war on Germany
if she should attack Poland. So, early in July, Canaris and his
associates despatched a trusted representative, Lt Colonel

Count von Schwerin, head of the British Section of German
Military Intelligence, to try to find out what the true situation
was. Von Schwerin came quite openly but without any publicity, but there were two curious aspects to his visit. He was not
sponsored by the German Military Attaché, von Scheppenburg,
and his first British contact was not the Director of Military
Intelligence but the DNI, Godfrey. Godfrey later recalled that
"he was a very acceptable type of German, had charming
manners, spoke English perfectly, was unobtrusive and receptive
and a good mixer. He explained quite frankly what he was
trying to find out and that his enquiries were entirely open and
above board. I arranged three or four small parties for him to
meet representative people. Foreign Office, business men, MPs,
members of the Services, so that he could form his own opinion
by listening to and joining in the conversation which I undertook to lead in the right direction. It seemed to me that this
method would carry conviction better than my bald assertion
that we *were* in earnest and always honoured our obligations,
however quixotic they happened to be. Admirals Hall and
Aubrey Hugh-Smith very kindly lent me their flats and staffs,
and I asked (among others) Gladwyn Jebb from the Foreign
Office, James Stewart the chief Conservative Whip, the Director
of Plans from the Admiralty, the Director of Military Intelligence and R. A. Butler. The talk was frank and objective and
von Schwerin was obviously impressed. We asked what Britain
could do to convince the Führer that Britain and France would
act if Poland were invaded. He suggested a British air demonstration over Paris, a visit of the French Air Force to London
or of the French Fleet to a North Sea port. All these things
were done. DMI arranged for him to inspect training units
and the Air Ministry showed him air stations. Before he left
von Schwerin said that it was most difficult to get unwelcome
intelligence past his immediate chiefs to the head of the Army
and the State, that he personally was quite convinced that we
were in earnest, and that he would do his very best to inform
those above him and would let me know if he succeeded. Later
in the year, after war had been declared, an anonymous
message of unmistakable origin reached me via Switzerland to
the effect that the message had been delivered but not believed."
Von Schwerin apparently also told Jebb that Hitler was convinced 'that it was the British intention to surrender at any rate

Central and Eastern Europe to Germany' and pressed the British to 'take Winston Churchill into the Cabinet'. This, of course, was not done until the day war was finally declared.

As noted previously, some of the very first people on whom the new DNI had called were 'C', the head of the SIS, and Denniston, head of the Government Code & Cipher School. Although, at that time, the GC & CS had not had any success in cracking German ciphers it was obvious to all concerned that if a breakthrough could be achieved the immense advantage which Room 40 had given the Allies in World War I might be repeated. All three Service Intelligence Directors were concerned, but the DNI probably most of all, partly because of the continuing strong naval presence within GC & CS itself and partly because the code breakers were still largely dependent on the Navy's 'Y' stations, particularly that at Flowerdown, for the supply of their raw material—the enciphered texts of foreign wireless messages. GC & CS was just as much in need of expansion and extra funds as NID. Some of the old hands had been recalled to the colours at the time of Munich, but many more were needed and the headquarters in Broadway, Victoria Street, left little scope for expansion. There was also the exaggerated fear of the effects of an all-out bombing attack on London. Plans were therefore made to transfer the establishment to what was to become its famous wartime home, Bletchley Park. Godfrey writes, "Procurement and processing of Special Intelligence [the term used during the war by 'insiders' for what has now come to be known as 'Ultra'] is, perhaps, the most esoteric of all sciences. It was only by bringing its exponents together under one roof that we could, in 1939, create a team sufficiently numerous and expert to deal with the great diversity and volume of Special sources. This was the practical issue which was put to me when I became DNI and as soon as I had mastered this fundamental principle I agreed to the concentration of all our resources at an outstation in the country, with means of rapid and secure dissemination through OIC (proper ciphers, special transmitting stations and so on) to the appropriate authorities all over the world." Godfrey in fact saw from the outset that concentration of effort in the cryptanalysis field was essential but that the best means of disseminating and making use of the results might well vary. So far as the Navy was concerned there could be no doubt that the Operational Intelligence Centre was the right place for this important function to be performed. The best of Intelligence could have no value unless it reached the operational authorities who had to make use of it swiftly, by secure means, and in a form which carried conviction to the recipients. At some stage in the process information from many sources would have to be co-ordinated, analysed and evaluated, the wheat separated from the chaff and the probabilities carefully assessed. The Admiralty, unlike the War Office and the Air Ministry, was itself an operational authority, in fact so far as war at sea was concerned, the supreme one. Only in the Admiralty's OIC could the full overall position be seen, only there could informa tion from *all* sources be assembled and considered. Only in the light of *all* the information available in OIC could decisions be taken as to which ships and which authorities would require specific items of information, and only the Naval wireless system could pass on the necessary information to the Fleet. For these reasons Godfrey insisted that NID must have full and sole responsibility for analysing and disseminating items of Special Intelligence bearing on the future war at sea. He thereby incurred the enmity of some who saw this as a barrier to the growth of their own 'empires'. Paradoxically it gave rise to charges that he was the empire builder and that it was he who was acting from a sense of pique and a desire for personal aggrandisement. Godfrey stuck to his guns and events were to show that he was completely right to do so.

Godfrey may also have had a hand in the first decisive step made by GC & CS towards their eventual penetration of the German cipher system, Enigma. This step was the pre-war meetings with Polish Intelligence, who were far ahead of the British and French cryptographic organisations in their attack on Enigma. On 24 July British and French delegations met the Poles at their secret headquarters outside Warsaw. The French delegation consisted of Colonel Bertrand and Captain Braquenie. The British one certainly included Commander Denniston, head of GC & CS and his chief cryptanalyst, Dilwyn Knox, but there was a third member of the party whose identity has never been satisfactorily established. Some, including one of the Poles who was present, claim that this mysterious individual, who was introduced as 'Professor Sandwich' a Cambridge mathematician, which he most certainly was not, was in fact Colonel

Menzies, 'C''s deputy. It is possible, but Godfrey once mentioned, casually, to the author that he had sent Humphrey Sandwith, who was the head of DSD/NID9, the section responsible for the 'Y' and D/F stations, to a meeting in Poland just before the war, which had resulted in the Poles presenting to the French and British two of their reconstructed Enigma machines. The coincidence of the names is remarkable and it would not have been unreasonable that the British party should have included someone who could speak with authority about the British capability to achieve the very first step needed to decrypt foreign ciphers, namely the interception and recording of the enciphered wireless messages. This was, after all, a meeting of specialists, of technicians, not of amateurs.

By August the grains of sand in the hourglass had almost run out. Godfrey, typically, saw that he must seize the last opportunity to make a personal reconnaissance and assess for himself the possibilities and cement relations in countries which might continue to give Britain a window into Germany, particularly from the naval point of view. On 1 August he left London for Copenhagen. From there he went on to Stockholm and then to Helsinki. On the 9th he was in the Hague and on the 11th in Paris. In all these cities he made contact with British ministers or ambassadors and our naval attachés and the local heads of the SIS. He also talked to some of his opposite numbers in the countries concerned. On his way home he spent a whole twenty-four hours at Le Zoute conferring with the head of the SIS section attached to the French Deuxième Bureau. He had first met the officer in question, Commander 'Biffy' Dunderdale, RNVR, at Nicolaief in December 1918 when he and his father had acted as interpreters for Godfrey and Captain Chetwode.

Godfrey was back at the Admiralty by 13 August. General mobilisation had not yet been ordered, but retired officers and civilians earmarked for service in NID were now called in: the Information Section started to function: Fleming and one or two others on DNI's personal staff began to work full time: above all the OIC was brought up to strength on the excuse of a large-scale coast defence exercise and its new recruits were given intensive instruction in their duties. The Naval Intelligence Division was on a war footing before the end of the month.

As Charles Morgan later wrote, Godfrey's task had been 'to make preparations for war which were practical and imaginative, practical in the sense of putting to the fullest possible use material already available, imaginative in the sense that the machinery set up must be of the kind that could be adapted to the needs and opportunities of war.' That much he had certainly achieved. If the cupboard was still a long way from being fully stocked, at least it was not as bare as it had been eight months earlier. On 22 August 47 naval or marine officers and 56 civilians, male and female, were borne on the Division's books. A very great deal had been accomplished in a very short space of time. Godfrey, however, was only too conscious that a very great deal remained to be done.

CHAPTER SEVEN

Winston is Back

'WINSTON IS BACK'. The Admiralty's signal to the Fleet on 3 September is almost as well known as Nelson's famous 'England expects . . .' before Trafalgar. Nelson said he wished to 'amuse the Fleet'. Their Lordships in 1939 are usually credited with a desire to encourage the Royal Navy, but were they in fact perhaps only intending to warn senior officers to keep a weather eye open for unusual squalls? Certainly it was not long before a number of them, confident that they were acting in an entirely proper and seamanlike manner, found themselves caught aback, dismasted and on a lee shore as a result of an icy and totally unexpected blast from Whitehall. Some managed to club haul themselves away from disaster by their own exertions; others were towed out of danger by brother officers; the least fortunate were lost without trace.

Godfrey, in a hurried note to his wife dated 3 p.m., Sunday, 3 September, wrote, "'Going to War' has been quite eclipsed by the announcement that Winston is coming here as First Lord. Stanhope told me this at the Club just after he had heard. He seemed rather sad. It was decided on the spur of the moment —so like our methods. Geoffrey Dawson [Editor of *The Times*] whom I met shortly afterwards told me that Neville [Chamberlain], whom he had seen the previous evening, had assured him that Winston would be a Minister without Portfolio in the War Cabinet. Later—Just met the great man in the passage. The first person he asked for on arrival was the DNI." Another and more junior officer of NID also encountered the new First Lord in one of the Admiralty's innumerable and depressing passages. Bricklayers were at work building blast walls. As a paid-up member of their Union, Winston Churchill could not resist picking up a trowel and adding a few bricks to his new Department's very inadequate defences.

Despite Godfrey's efforts in the preceding seven months, not all the problems had been foreseen and not all preparations completed. The problems, some of which were not finally resolved for more than two years, fell into five categories. Firstly, it soon became apparent that the sources on which NID had to rely were in the main incapable of supplying the information required. The SIS's agents, GC & CS's crypt-analysts, the RAF's Photographic Reconnaissance Units (PRU) and the Navy's own Direction Finding organisation at first produced little, in some cases nothing, of any value. This greatly handicapped the work of the Operational Intelligence Centre, the section of NID to which, quite rightly, the largest effort had hitherto been devoted. Secondly, and arising out of the first, was the difficulty of verifying the flow of rumours and doubtful reports which poured in, some planted by the Germans, some originating in the fertile imaginations of well-wishers at home and abroad. Thirdly, there was still a lack of proper machinery for inter-Service co-operation and co-ordination in Intelligence matters. Fourthly, there were administrative problems such as co-operation with the French, and, very soon, of exchanging information with the Americans, and the need to rearrange and expand the network of British naval attachés abroad to meet the new situation. Last but not least was the question of satisfying the urgent and peremptory demands of the new First Lord, both in the realms of publicity and in connection with his burning but often impractical desire for offensive action.

All these tasks had to be tackled not against the comfortable background of the 'drôle de guerre' on land, but under the constant pressure of immediate attack and counter-attack at sea. Dönitz had placed almost the whole of his small U-boat fleet on patrol by the end of August: the liner *Athenia* was sunk by one of them on the very first day of the war. Two pocket battleships, *Graf von Spee* and *Deutschland* were ranging the Atlantic and Indian Oceans. Magnetic mines were immediately laid in British coastal waters. Merchant shipping losses in the first three months of the war totalled 222 ships of three quarter of a million tons. The Royal Navy's losses included the battleship *Royal Oak* and the aircraft carrier *Courageous*, and those of the Germans *Graf von Spee* and nine U-boats. There was no 'phoney war' for the Royal and Merchant Navies! As Godfrey put it, "the Admiralty had to go to action stations without any 'working up' period. Among other tasks it had to learn how to deal with its chief asset, the First Lord, Winston Churchill."

Winston's departure from the Admiralty in 1915 had not been regretted by the majority of the Navy, and in the immediate post-war years, as Minister for War and Air and as Chancellor of the Exchequer, he had done little to endear himself to naval opinion. On the other hand, any task he undertook was performed with such immense gusto and enthusiasm that it became for him the only thing that mattered. Now he was, again, a 'Naval Person'. He was determined that he would not leave the Admiralty a second time under a cloud of failure. Godfrey sometimes wondered "if Mr Churchill's long years in opposition to all governments had left him with a feeling that during his early days at the Admiralty we all shared the delinquencies of those politicians he had so consistently bastinadoed in public. Certainly his written words gave the impression that he thought that we all needed a good shake up and comb out, and the procession out of the Admiralty at very short notice of Directors, Sea Lords and others lends colour to this belief." Godfrey was probably lucky that he was not one of these early casualties.

The First Lord's attitude to NID was considerably affected by the fact that its Director was responsible for naval publicity and press censorship. Realising the importance that this would assume, particularly with a First Lord who rightly regarded himself as the British Empire's foremost propagandist, Godfrey had arranged for the appointment of an old friend, a retired Rear-Admiral, Patrick Macnamara, to deputise for him in dealing with the newly formed Ministry of Information and to handle the weekly naval press conferences. The Ministry of Information, an entirely new Ministry, was going through a lot of teething troubles but Macnamara's cautious and phlegmatic nature, his ability to get on with Americans and his unruffled demeanour were just what was required in such a 'vulnerable' post. Unfortunately, just when things seemed to be settling down satisfactorily, Macnamara was posted elsewhere and his successor, Vice-Admiral Theodore Hallett, personally selected by Pound, proved an unfortunate choice. The trouble was that the First Lord "always remembered that he had been a journalist and thought he knew best, as indeed he did, how to present news to the Press and the public. It became his habit to cheer

everyone up in his Wednesday broadcasts—good news was
made to seem better; bad news was toned down, delayed or
sometimes suppressed. Any particularly spicey bits might be
held up for three or four days until it could be included in the
First Lord's broadcasts and no one was more conscious than
Mr Churchill of the popularity of the bringer of good tidings.
Hallett had a lively and impatient temperament and in his
Monday afternoon talks at the Ministry of Information to the
Press he failed to realise not once but twice or three times that
it was unwise to steal the First Lord's thunder. There was a
lively scene in which a deluge of wrath descended on my head,
and next morning I had to tell Hallett that the First Lord was
appointing him to sea. I was extremely sorry to lose Hallett,
but he was happier at sea and did splendid work in charge of
Combined Operations training." At the same time responsibility for press and publicity was taken away from DNI and
placed under the Vice-Chief of Naval Staff. Godfrey regretted
the change because he felt that publicity and security should
come under one person, but there can be little doubt that with
Winston as First Lord, or even as Prime Minister, the responsibility was an invidious one and would have taken up far too
much of the DNI's time and energy. Before this had happened,
Godfrey had already incurred the First Lord's wrath over his
plan for a corps of naval war correspondents afloat. He had
asked Thursfield, of *The Times*, to discuss this with the Commander-in-Chief of the Home Fleet whom he happened to be
visiting. When Churchill heard of this he "was furious. It had
never occurred to me that I was 'favouring' *The Times* at the
expense of papers like the *Daily Express*. How easily one can put
a foot wrong!" For all his earlier experience of Whitehall,
Godfrey still had a lot to learn.

It was also about this time that Godfrey found another of his
sections taken away from him, and this was to have more
serious consequences. He had been well aware that one of the
reasons for the failure of the Admiralty to introduce the convoy
system earlier in World War I was due to the lack of any
department capable of assembling, analysing and disseminating
statistics about merchant shipping losses. That had been
remedied in 1917 when Geddes had brought in George Beharrel. Beharrel was by now Chairman of Dunlop and Godfrey
had been to see him to learn exactly what was needed to start

such a section again and how it should be run. It formed part of the new Information Section and was intended to serve not only NID but the Admiralty as a whole. It soon attracted the attention of Professor Lindemann who removed it from NID and installed it in the Private Office under his own direct control. It became a private piece of machinery and only information that the 'Prof' considered would be to Mr Churchill's liking emerged from it. For example, on Lindemann's express instructions, for a long time stragglers and ships dispersed *from* convoy were, if sunk, included in the figures of ships sunk *in* convoy. It was not until Professor Blackett's Operational Research Department began to delve into matters that the truth began to emerge and the correct conclusions could be drawn. Certainly, the Statistical Section under its new master did nothing to illuminate the truth in the controversy which soon arose over the size of the U-boat fleet and the number of losses inflicted on it.

Godfrey was determined from the outset that in this, as in all other matters, NID must speak the truth without fear or favour. Only by sticking to the known facts and by avoiding any tinge of wishful thinking and 'Very Senior Officer Veneration' (the tendency to accept that not only is the Senior Officer always right but that only the Senior Officer is right, a great 'hate' of Godfrey's) could the Division establish a reputation for integrity and earn the trust and confidence of the Naval Staff and the Fleet. Naturally enough, reports by officers who had carried out attacks on U-boats at sea tended, for many months, to be over-optimistic. All these attacks were considered by an Assessment Committee, presided over by the Director of the Anti-Submarine Warfare Division and comprising representatives from NID and other interested Divisions of the Naval Staff, Coastal Command of the RAF and the French Naval Commission.

Three things were needed accurately to assess the current or future threat posed by the U-boats; their number at the beginning of the war; the monthly rate of loss they suffered; the rate at which those losses were replaced by new building. Germany actually started the war with 57 U-boats, but NID had unfortunately been confused by the spate of pre-war reports from the Secret Intelligence Service that U-boats were operating in the South Atlantic. A careful check of the numbers definitely located in Home Waters showed that such operations could only be possible if the Germans had secretly built U-boats in excess of the numbers permitted by the Anglo-German Naval Treaty. This theory was supported by a further crop of SIS reports that the Germans were using duplicate numbers, and NID, much more sceptical of German good faith than the Constructor's department had been over the size of *Bismarck*, tended to accept these stories and came to the conclusion that, on 3 September, the Germans possessed not 57 but 66 U-boats. NID also overestimated the German rate of building. Understandably they believed that the enemy would accord a much higher priority to U-boat building than was at first the case. Godfrey had warned the Deputy-Chief of Naval Staff that, with no means of checking the building programme, because neither the SIS nor the RAF Photographic Reconnaissance Units were capable of obtaining the necessary information, NID's estimates would have to be a 'best guess' which would be modified, either up or down, just as soon as reliable information could be obtained. In their estimate of U-boat sinkings, however, the Assessment Committee, much influenced by the sceptical approach to 'claims' of Paymaster Captain Thring in OIC, were very accurate indeed. They quickly came into conflict with the First Lord, who was anxious to establish his own reputation and encourage the nation with announcements of substantial successes.

DNI issued a weekly tabular statement of the U-boat position, based on the Assessment Committee's findings, and his own estimates of new commissioning. This return listed not only 'Known' sinkings but 'Probables' and 'Possibles' as well, giving the name of the ship or aircraft involved. The object was both to encourage our Anti-Submarine forces and to keep the magnitude of the problem before the eyes of all concerned. The return received a pretty wide circulation. On 4 November it stated, correctly, that only 6 U-boats had definitely been sunk. On the same day the First Lord broadcast that 'The attack of the U-boats has been controlled and they have paid a heavy toll'. 6 out of 58 completed, let alone out of 77 completed (which was NID's estimate at that time), hardly seems to justify Winston's claim. Perhaps he realised this because, on 24 November, he gave instructions that the Weekly Return was in future to be circulated only to himself, the First Sea Lord and the Deputy-Chief of Naval Staff.

On 18 January DNI circulated a paper giving his opinion on U-boat numbers. It ran as follows:

In existence on 1.9.39	66
Increase 1.9.39 to 1.1.40	9
Known losses	9
Plus probables	17
Probable increase 1.1.40 to 1.7.40	48
Anticipated total on 1.7.40 without making any	
allowance for losses between 1.1.40 and 1.7.40	109

These figures did not meet with the approval of the First Lord. On 22 January he criticised them in a personal minute. His remarks and Godfrey's comments on them, made to the DCNS on 26 January, with the true figures established after the war in brackets, are set out below.

First Lord
DNI's paper is really intended to announce the good news that his previous forecast of building was excessive.

Godfrey
Our September estimate was a best guess that would need monthly modification. The object was not to convey good or bad news but to state as truthfully as possible views based on NID and Ministry of Economic Warfare investigations.

To obtain the figure of 109 in July it is necessary to assume that not more than 26 U-boats were sunk before the end of 1939, whereas 35 is the lowest acceptable figure.

35 is an overestimate, and it would be unwise to base our policy on wishful thinking.
[The correct figure is now known to have been 9]

It is absurd to present figures on the assumption of no further losses. At least 5 probables have occurred since 1.1.40.

It is obviously possible to scale down the number of 109 depending on how optimistically or pessimistically one regards our effort. I think 5 probables is an overestimate.
[In fact none had been sunk]

First Lord
If we assume the same rate of loss for the next six months as for the first four, namely two per week, 52 would have to be deducted from 109, making 57 on 1.7.40.

A new statement should be prepared which gives due consideration to all factors at work. This should be discussed between 1st Sea Lord, DCNS and myself before being widely circulated. *The statement of U-boat losses is a matter of high policy.*
[Author's italics]

Godfrey
2 per week is probably an overestimate. Most unwise to assume loss of 52 in the next six months.
[In fact only 14 U-boats were sunk in that period]

I feel somewhat doubtful of its efficacy, as it is based on assuming unknown factors, but unless we assume the Germans are going to make a considerable effort to increase their numbers of U-boats, there will be no incentive to make the corresponding effort ourselves to overcome the menace, and this will sooner or later have an effect on our preparations. I feel strongly that it is important that the probabilities as seen by the Naval Staff should be presented without bias or wishfulness.

In the meantime, on 20 January, Churchill had told the nation on the radio that 'It seems pretty certain tonight that half the U-boats with which Germany began the war have been sunk, and that their new building has fallen far behind what we expected'. Even by adding the 16 'probables' to the 9 'known' sinkings the total only reached 25, not 33 as implied by the First Lord. The true figure was of course 9.

On 7 February NID estimated that Germany had 56 U-boats in commission. The actual figure was 49. The report which had caused NID's comments had mentioned U88 and this gave rise to the possibility that 32 U-boats might be unaccounted for. NID was unwilling to accept this theory, but Sir Dudley Pound seized on the 'missing' 32, added on three known sinkings since the date of the report, and assumed that 35 had now been sunk.

Churchill commented on this figure, 'A working hypothesis: but I think 45 will be nearer the truth'.

On 15 April, documents were captured from U49 (sunk during the Norwegian campaign) which revealed that Germany at that time had only 43 U-boats in commission; her losses up to that point had been 22, a figure which did not compare very favourably with Pound's 35, let alone Churchill's 45, of February. The whole episode reminds one of *Alice Through the Looking Glass*. 'When I use a word,' Humpty Dumpty said, in a rather scornful tone, 'it means just what I choose it to mean—neither more nor less.' 'The question is,' said Alice, 'whether you can make words mean so many different things.' 'The question is,' said Humpty Dumpty, 'which is to be master—that's all.' Who was to be master was soon demonstrated. The revised figures (which for some reason gave only 19 sinkings) were issued on 24 April over the signature of Captain A. G. Talbot, the Director of the Anti-Submarine Warfare Division. On the following day the First Lord minuted: 'As we know from wrecks, corpses or survivors that we have 15 U-boats sunk for certain, Captain Talbot's estimate of 19 in all indicates that only four others have been sunk by the British and French activities. The ordinary accidents of the sea and the Service would, according to the figures of the last war, have accounted for all this number. Therefore the conclusion to which this officer comes is that all the attacks, except the actual 15 of which we have remnants, have failed. This conclusion leads me to think that it might be a good thing if Captain Talbot went to sea as soon as possible.' Talbot was relieved by Captain Creasy at ten minutes notice.

One would have thought that the firm evidence of the comparative lack of success of British anti-U-boat measures would have now been accepted, but in his last minute on the subject as First Lord, Churchill characteristically refused to accept defeat. 'It does not follow', he wrote, 'that sunken U-boats have not been replaced by others of the same number', a myth which NID had long since abandoned. It is only fair to record that in one respect Churchill was nearer the truth than NID, who on 15 July estimated that replacements had increased the total number of boats in commission to 60 or 65. Winston, by this time Prime Minister, considered the figure excessive. He was right. The Germans did not regain the number with which they had started the war until September 1940. From then onwards they began to give the sort of priority to U-boat building that NID had always anticipated, so that the U-boat fleet grew increasingly rapidly month by month. However, it was not until January 1941 that Godfrey was officially permitted to revert to the procedure in force at the beginning of the war and circulate to all those officers and departments responsible for providing the ships, aircraft and trained men, so desperately needed to defeat the U-boats, the true facts and figures on which they could formulate their plans. He had never taken the First Lord's ban too literally and had kept the more senior officers verbally au fait with the real situation. Today it seems quite incredible that such subterfuge should have been necessary to meet a threat which Churchill himself described as 'The only thing that ever really frightened me during the war . . .'

Churchill may possibly have had good reasons for the attitude he adopted, but what about the professional head of the Navy, Admiral Pound? Throughout all this controversy he does not seem to have cross-questioned Godfrey or his experts at all. His February figure of 35 U-boats sunk was plucked out of the air. If he attempted to protect the unfortunate Talbot, he certainly did not succeed. Perhaps he did Godfrey a good turn by not passing on to the irate First Lord DNI's shrewd comments on the minute of 22 January. At any rate, rather surprisingly one must now conclude, Godfrey, who had throughout stuck to his guns, survived to fight another day.

We must now turn to another controversy in which Godfrey played a prominent part but one in which, on this occasion, Churchill actively supported instead of opposing the NID view. With the creation of the Royal Air Force in 1918, the Navy had lost control of the 2500 aircraft and 55,000 men of the Royal Naval Air Service. For the next twenty years relations between the two Services had been bedevilled by arguments about the maritime air contribution which the RAF should or could make to meet the Navy's needs. There was a good deal of strength in the Air Force's argument that the 'air was indivisible' and in the fact that it was so starved of funds that it could not possibly honour all its commitments. The Senior Service, less concerned at threats to its very existence, continued to proclaim that it was not getting, and under the existing arrangements never would get, the skilled men and suitable aircraft which it knew it needed. In 1937 a belated and not very satisfactory com-compromise was reached; the Royal Navy regained control of all ship-borne aircraft and their crews—the Fleet Air Arm—but the RAF retained all shore-based aircraft, including those of Coastal Command which were employed on purely maritime duties.

One of the many drawbacks to this typically British solution was that the Navy remained completely dependent on the RAF for all forms of air reconnaissance, other than the purely close range tactical reconnaissance which could be provided by its own obsolescent ship-borne aircraft. Long range recon-naissance, particularly photographic reconnaissance, could only be achieved by land-based aircraft. It was the failure of the RAF to supply this that had so inhibited NID's efforts to give an accurate estimate of the U-boat building programme. Even more serious, in the short term, was the fact that, in the absence of any effective SIS organisation in Germany, photographic reconnaissance gave the only hopes of ascertaining the where-abouts of the major German surface ships. Complete and regular coverage of *all* German ports would have shown which ships were safely in port and which were missing and therefore likely to be at sea on operations. This was a service to the Navy which the RAF could not provide.

At the outbreak of war the need for photographic recon-naissance not only for the Navy but also for the Army and the RAF itself at once became obvious. The only aircraft available were Blenheims, which had neither the ceiling, range nor speed required. Casualties were heavy. Nor had the RAF developed the techniques of high altitude photography. There was only one single officer in the Air Ministry with any training in the art of interpreting such photographs as could be secured. The situation was saved by the Secret Intelligence Service, or to be more precise by a twentieth-century buccaneer, Sydney Cotton. Cotton was an Australian and an extremely experi-enced civilian pilot. In World War I he had served with distinction in the Royal Naval Air Service and had invented the universally used Sidcot flying suit. Since then he had been involved in many enterprises, latterly in connection with aerial survey work. In 1938 he was recruited by Squadron Leader

Winterbotham, the RAF liaison officer with the SIS, to fly a private Lockheed plane in co-operation with the French Deuxième Bureau to obtain clandestine aerial photographs. Cotton was a complete individualist, impatient of red tape and any form of bureaucracy. He found the French old-fashioned and impossible to work with. The joint project was abandoned, but Winterbotham, with Admiralty support, managed to secure a second Lockheed and early in 1939 was again in business. Cotton was himself a commercial photography expert, and developed a system to prevent cameras icing up at high altitudes. He made many flights over and into Germany (his aircraft was the last civil plane to leave Berlin before war broke out), and carried out a survey of parts of the Mediterranean and of the Red Sea and Italian Somaliland. He was also connected with the Aircraft Operating Company, a Wembley based company engaged on processing aerial survey photographs which possessed the only Swiss Wilt photogrametric machine in the country. This instrument could measure the height of objects on the ground revealed by photographs taken at 30,000 feet, an accomplishment unknown to the Air Ministry.

Godfrey had first met Cotton in April 1939 and had been very impressed with the results of his work. He continued to give him all the support possible. On his way back from Berlin at the end of August, Cotton, from a range of fifty miles, had secured excellent photographs of German main units anchored off Wilhelmshaven but out of sight of land, and thus inaccessible to any agent. NID were delighted with these photographs which established the whereabouts of at least some of the German heavy ships, but it was important to establish if and when they left their anchorage. A further set of photographs was secured on 2 September which confirmed that no ships had left. This was exactly the type of information which the Operational Intelligence Centre needed. Godfrey, briefed by Denning and one of the retired officers recalled for duty in NID, Commander Charles Drake, who acted from then on as the link with Cotton, began to press strongly for Cotton to be provided with suitable aircraft and all the necessary resources to act as 'the eyes of the Fleet'. The trouble was that Cotton's Lockheed and his little Beechcraft, while excellent for clandestine operations in peace time, were obviously unsuitable under war conditions. The Air Ministry, confronted by Godfrey with

Cotton's photographs and demands from the Naval Staff for reconnaissance of all German ports, were forced to admit that Cotton was achieving results which the Air Force could not equal, and on 22 September granted Cotton an Honorary commission in the RAF and put him in charge of a special Photographic Reconnaissance Unit (PRU). Unfortunately, due in part to scepticism and also, one must say, jealousy in certain quarters, they would not for some time supply him with the only type of aircraft suitable for his purpose, Spitfires. Contrary to RAF practice, Cotton could see that unarmed, stripped down, 'Cottonised' Spitfires would have the increased performance required. Eventually he appealed to the head of Fighter Command, the Command which was rightly crying out for every Spitfire and Hurricane it could get. Air Marshal Dowding recognised more clearly than the Air Staff the vital importance, to all the Services, of the information which only Cotton seemed able to obtain. He gave Cotton his first Spitfire, but although it was stripped down and ready for operations by the late autumn, it did not, for some reason, carry out its first PR flight until 10 February 1940.

In the previous December Drake had made contact with the Aircraft Operating Company and learned that they had offered their services to the Air Ministry back in August but that the offer had been rejected. Because the company's techniques of interpretation were so much in advance of those of the RAF, Cotton had been making use of them, but the company simply could not continue in business on this basis: it must have official funds and status. Godfrey again drew the attention of the Director of Air Intelligence to the value of its methods and by the end of January had persuaded him to press the Air Ministry to take the company over. Unfortunately, Air Commodore Buss put the proposal to the Vice Chiefs of Staff Committee without telling Godfrey that he was going to do so. In consequence Admiral Phillips, the DCNS, was not briefed and when the proposal was considered the Vice-Chief of the Air Staff, Air Marshal Sir Richard Peirse, failed to explain clearly what was at stake and, for the second time, the proposition was turned down.

On Saturday, 10 February the Admiralty's pressing request for photographs of Emden was at last met. Cotton telephoned Drake to say that the photographs were being rushed to the

Aircraft Operating Company for development and interpretation, processes which would be completed by the early hours of Sunday morning. Drake confidently expected their arrival at the Admiralty by nine o'clock. Nothing happened because in the meantime the Air Ministry had expressly forbidden the Aircraft Operating Company to deal direct with NID. The whole of Sunday morning was wasted in a search for charts and a North Sea Pilot, immediately available in the Admiralty, but not, apparently in the Air Ministry. In the meantime the interpreters had discovered a concentration of craft which they at first took to be U-boats. They again appealed to be allowed to contact NID for help, but were again curtly refused permission to do so. Finally, on Sunday afternoon, Cotton lost patience, ignored his instructions and got in touch with Drake. Denning, OIC's expert, hurried down to Wembley and at once confirmed what the interpreters had already begun to suspect—the alleged U-boats were merely river barges.

The delays which had been caused by the Air Ministry's attitude seemed intolerable not only to Godfrey but to Admiral Pound, who informed the First Lord and pointed out the danger of the Aircraft Operating Company folding up. Churchill instructed him to call an urgent high-level conference that very evening. The matter must be resolved once and for all and if the Air Ministry would not act, the Admiralty must take over the company itself. Pound specifically instructed Cotton to attend and to take the seat next to him usually occupied by the Vice-Chief of Air Staff. Godfrey brought along Drake. When Air Marshall Peirse arrived he was surprised and furious to find Cotton there and to learn that he had disobeyed his instructions and had gone direct to the Admiralty. He had perforce to accept Churchill's ultimatum and the Aircraft Operating Company was incorporated into the RAF, but Drake always considered that Cotton's chances of continuing to run PRU vanished from that moment. He was sacked on 16 June, after successfully evacuating his men and aircraft from France.

Although the future of the Aircraft Operating Company and its valuable techniques had been assured by the decisions reached at the meeting on 11 February, the problem of obtaining sufficient reconnaissance flights had by no means been overcome. Godfrey continued to urge in and out of season for pressure to be put on the Air Ministry. On 26 March, for example, he pointed out that specially equipped, long-range 'Cottonised' Spitfires could cover Kiel (which had never so far been photographed) and that if photographs were obtained they could be accurately interpreted by the Wilt process. But, he went on, the machines were lacking so that the Navy had "only very scanty ideas of the whereabouts of important enemy ships." He asked for bi-weekly reconnaissance of all German ports to be carried out on the same day and urged that this be given "absolute priority". The Air Ministry reply was not encouraging. It was that only 'one long range Spitfire would be in commission by the end of the month'. The first photographs of Kiel were not in fact obtained until 7 April. They showed the harbour full of shipping and the nearby Holtenau airfield crammed with aircraft. With no previous photographs with which to make a comparison the interpreters were unable to state whether the situation was normal or abnormal. Two days later the Germans invaded Denmark and Norway. Godfrey's pleas for regular cover of the German ports had come too late.

We must now leave the struggle to obtain adequate photographic reconnaissance for the Navy (which was not in fact brought to a successful conclusion for another three years) and return to other problems which confronted Godfrey in the early months of the war. One of them was Ireland. "In 1939", he admits, "we knew very little about Ireland or the Irish; had we known more we might have tackled the problem more effectively from the start." The Irish Free State, as it was then known, was quite determined to stay neutral and not become involved in 'England's war'. The situation was, however, full of the anomalies and paradoxes always present in Anglo-Irish relations. The Free State was a member, in theory at any rate, of the British Empire. The border with Ulster was open and nearly a quarter of a million southern Irishmen were to enlist in the British armed forces. The country was economically bound to and completely dependent on the United Kingdom. As recently as 1938 the Royal Navy still had bases at Queenstown, Berehaven and Lough Swilly but these had somewhat needlessly been given back to the Irish. On the other hand, de Valera and his government could not forget their history and the continuing 'Partition' of the country. They looked anxiously over their shoulders at the 'new' IRA and at that section of the electorate which was not only sentimentally but actively anti-English. The German Legation remained open in Dublin and was a centre of Axis propaganda and, it was feared, espionage. The trouble was that the Free State could not be treated either as any other small neutral nor as an allied country. Neither the SIS on the one hand nor MI5 on the other felt that they could operate in southern Ireland, but Godfrey soon found that he "had a very definite anti-submarine and coast watching problem to solve, plus a complicated security situation if at any time we took over the ports. Neither did we feel then that the Irish government could be trusted to counter German penetration. No other department in Whitehall could give us much help or was in fact particularly interested, although the War Office became interested when we planted a large army in Ulster."

That Ireland could not entirely isolate herself from the war was immediately demonstrated by the sinking of the liner *Athenia*. Survivors, many of whom were Americans, were landed in Galway and, at Godfrey's request, Alan Kirk, the US Naval Attaché, went there to interview them and counter the accusations that it was the British who had sunk the ship. This incident at once revived fears, which were eventually proved to be quite unfounded, that U-boats were using Ireland's west coast to refuel and shelter. An efficient coast watching organisation was needed as much by the Irish as the British. A British Naval Attaché, Captain Greig, RN, was appointed to Dublin (a patent anomaly in the circumstances) and he soon established close unofficial relations with the Defence Department there. Colonel Archer, of the Irish Army, visited London and arrangements were made to help him with advice and equipment for the coast-watching force which he was establishing. Exchanges of information were undertaken and the Royal Ulster Constabulary encouraged to co-operate with their colleagues south of the border. At DNI's request, Sydney Cotton carried out an aerial survey of the west coast, which revealed no signs of any German activity. A yacht was chartered to make a clandestine investigation, but when the skipper landed to pursue his enquiries ashore he was arrested, although quickly and politely released, by the Irish police! For some time, however, 'Potato' reports, as they were code named, continued to arrive and much energy was wasted in trying to investigate them. By the spring of 1940 alarm over German activities had somewhat subsided, unofficial co-operation with the Irish authorities was increasing, the Army and the Air Force followed the Navy's example and appointed attachés to Dublin, and the situation seemed to be more or less under control. With the fall of France, of course, all the old fears were revived. Godfrey himself visited Dublin and established personal relations with the less violently anti-British members of de Valera's government to whom he had been introduced by Frank Pakenham, now Lord Longford, whose wife, Elizabeth, was one of Margaret Godfrey's many cousins. Godfrey also worked very closely with the American Minister, Mr Gray, and with the Vichy French Naval Attaché. He appointed a Staff Officer (Intelligence) in Belfast to get information on all questions affecting Ireland which concerned the Admiralty and to maintain overt, as opposed to covert, contacts, throughout the country. By August 1941 DNI was able to report that "Ireland still clings to neutrality but this attitude rests largely on fear, and practical evidence of our ability to give them immediate protection against air attack would reduce their fear, and greatly increase the chances of a favourable reaction if we were compelled to demand bases in Ireland."

Looking back now it would seem that British fears about the Irish attitude and German activities were exaggerated, but the possibilities could not be ignored at the time. The problem was only partially a naval one, but owing to the unwillingness of other departments to take any action, NID, as so often happened, was compelled to involve itself in matters not all of which lay strictly within its normal sphere of responsibility.

Even further removed from the purely naval sphere was the question of 'irregular' activities on the Continent. There seemed to be a general assumption, doubtless a carry over from Blinker Hall's day, that the Director of Naval Intelligence handled sabotage and clandestine operations, or should at least take the lead in co-operation with the Director of Military Intelligence and the SIS in formulating plans and initiating action. As no one else seemed anxious to set the ball rolling Godfrey records that "I took it upon myself to initiate the poising of a number of clandestine operations aimed at cutting off the supply of Swedish iron ore, blocking the Danube, crippling the Rumanian oil refineries (on which the Germans were very dependent), sabotaging barges on the Danube and double agent chicken food. It was difficult to obtain official approval on a high plane for such operations. Senior officers desired the end but hesitated at the means. The Director of Military Intelligence set up a small department called MIR under Colonel Holland, but by and large the 'top brass' were apathetic, the Foreign Office were hostile and, of course, resources were then meagre. Clandestine warfare and double agent exploitation needed a lot of money and this did not become plentiful as long as Simon was Chancellor of the Exchequer. As First Lord of the Admiralty Churchill only made marginal incursions into these realms. My guess is that he liked to think that such things were going on but was cautious about getting personally involved." Although Churchill may not have taken much interest in some of the plans for irregular warfare—this was before his instructions after the Fall of France to 'set Europe on fire'—he was very much involved in the plans to cut off the Swedish iron ore by mining Norwegian coastal waters, Operation Wilfred, and in a scheme to sow mines in the Rhine, Operation Royal Marine. Both were delayed by the opposition of the Foreign Office and the timidity of the French. An attempt to block the Danube at the Iron Gates did go ahead but miscarried. Godfrey confesses that he was "not sorry when" in 1940 "the whole paraphernalia of subversion, sabotage and clandestine warfare was turned over to the 'Special Operations Executive' (SOE). I continued to keep in touch with their activities through liaison officers." If this was 'empire building', it was obviously undertaken with some reluctance!

One other small incident in connection with clandestine Intelligence should perhaps be recorded at this point. Towards the end of 1939 Admiral Quex Sinclair, 'C', died and the question of his successor had to be considered. Contrary to previous custom a soldier, his deputy Colonel Stewart Menzies, not a sailor, was appointed. The canard has been put about that Godfrey had coveted the appointment and was much upset that he did not get it. Nothing could be further from the truth. His wife recalls clearly that he was indeed approached to learn whether he would like his name to go forward for consideration but he firmly rejected the suggestion. It would have meant the end of his naval career and of all his hopes of the sea appointment which Pound had promised him. It would also have involved abandoning the work of re-creating the Naval Intelligence Division, which he had only just begun. Godfrey was not the man to leave a task, particularly one so important to his own Service, half-finished.

Godfrey did not see much of his wife or family at this time. In the summer of 1939, when war seemed inevitable, Margaret had decided that she ought to do a war job. She had met Quex Sinclair and he had arranged for her to have some training in the work of the Commercial Section of GC & CS on a half day a week basis. On 1 September she reported to Bletchley Park. Godfrey himself was still living in a flat in Cadogan Street which they had taken before the war, and the three girls, when not away at school, were looked after by friends or aunts of Margaret in the country. After a time the Commercial Section of GC & CS returned to London and for some months Margaret lived with John in a furnished flat in Buckingham Gate from which they could both walk to their offices. When the Blitz started the Commercial Section returned to Bletchley again and the flat in Buckingham Gate, which had a glass roof, began to seem less attractive. When Godfrey and his wife saw an airman parachute down through the roof of a similar flat next door, Blinker Hall's generous offer of his own rather more solid flat, 36 Curzon Street, was gladly accepted. It was small but very comfortable and Godfrey was admirably cared for by an excellent housekeeper, Dulcie, whom Margaret had engaged. Margaret snatched what time she could to get up to London, but such visits were necessarily brief and infrequent.

One of Godfrey's many imaginative ideas was the creation of the Information Section. The Section was designed to satisfy a number of different needs for information. Firstly, to keep those at sea and overseas informed about the progress of events not only at sea but on land and in the air, and to give an intelligent commentary on diplomatic, political and economic affairs both at home and abroad. It was intended for officers of all ranks and was Confidential but could be used by officers to inform their men. Its first editors were Charles Morgan and Hilary Saunders. Their staff were of equal calibre and its literary standards were therefore understandably high. Their medium was the weekly *Summary of Naval and Political News* (*SNPN*). Secondly there was a *Daily Summary of Naval Events* (*DSNE*), a Secret sheet for circulation to senior officers at home. Thirdly there were periodic 'Natel' telegrams for naval attachés containing entirely secret information about recent events for their own information only, and other less but still confidential news for their use in discreet conversation with selected foreigners. Fourthly came a weekly Top Secret summary of all operations which affected the Navy, for the benefit of the Joint Planning Committee, who in turn used it in producing the *Weekly Cabinet Resumé*. The Information Section also advised the War Cabinet Secretariat about naval news sent to Dominion Prime Ministers. There was also a weekly illustrated news sheet, the *Naval Bulletin*, for the information of ships' companies at sea. Finally the Section was responsible for scanning and circulating to other sections of the Division and to the rest of the Naval Staff information culled from BBC Monitored Intercepts, BBC Digests and news received from Reuters and the Press.

Inevitably, the Information Section, and particularly *SNPN*, experienced teething troubles. Morgan and Saunders were determined to make it readable and enjoyable as well as informative, with cartoons, pictures and articles ranging from the state of the Stock Market to an occasional book review. This was well received in the wardrooms of the Fleet, but incurred the displeasure of some of the more crusty Commanders-in-Chief. More serious was the rumpus in the spring of 1940 caused by an accurate and all too revealing account of the political difficulties being experienced by Monsieur Daladier's government in France. Once again Godfrey's head came near the chopping block. "Our Ambassador, paying a courtesy call on Mr Daladier was, to his dismay, confronted with the offending copy of *SNPN* which the Prime Minister, registering hurt feelings, produced from the drawer of his knee-hole table. History does not relate how the Ambassador dealt with the situation. France fell within a few weeks; the incident was forgotten; but the interim was filled, from DNI's point of view, with the poisonous dust of acrimony. The powers that be were not amused, and said so one after another. First on Counsellor level—a 'phone call from the Foreign Office; then the Permanent Secretary, Cadogan; then the Secretary of State; and finally the Prime Minister, relayed through Pound. They were all determined to have DNI's guts for a necktie. There did not seem any point in passing all this on to Charles and Hilary who already had their work cut out in disentangling truth from falsehood and propaganda, without being bothered about expediency. What was important was that the British Navy should know what was going on. The French were told that *SNPN* no longer existed and it was left to them to infer that it was no longer any good asking for copies. It died and in its place, with a revised circulation that did not include foreigners, appeared a smaller periodical called *Weekly Intelligence Report*." *WIR* continued to appear for the rest of the war, reporting with great freedom and skill the truth as the editors and their staff saw it. The work of the Information Section, in all its aspects, probably never received the recognition it deserved, but the Navy, and many others besides, would have undoubtedly complained loudly if it had not so admirably fulfilled the purposes for which it was created. Once again, NID showed the way.

The Naval Intelligence Division had, of course, many contacts, at all levels, with the Foreign Office and the Diplomatic and Consular Services. British naval attachés served two masters: the Ambassador or Minister to whose staff they were appointed and the Director of Naval Intelligence. Their duties were many and important and they did not, on the whole, suffer in peacetime from the disadvantages of Admiralty based members of the Intelligence Division, lack of promotion prospects. They were hand-picked officers of captain's or commander's rank, except in Washington and Tokyo which called for a rear-admiral. Some were accredited to more than one country. In a few cases their duties could hardly be described as naval: for example, the naval attaché in land-locked Hungary was there because the Regent, Horthy, was a former Admiral of the Imperial Austro-Hungarian Navy, and still enjoyed talking naval 'shop'; a useful way of establishing friendly and intimate relations. In almost all cases a good naval attaché could exert considerable influence outside his purely professional ambit.

With the declaration of war, new problems arose. Naval attachés in enemy countries were repatriated with the rest of the staff of the Embassy concerned. The valuable flow of information which they had previously supplied ceased. Posts in allied and some neutral countries then became more important. Some attachés were soon required for sea service: all of them, as good naval officers, longed for it. A general reappraisal of the position was needed, a reappraisal to which the DNI had to give his close personal attention. Blinker Hall had built up an exceptionally talented team. Godfrey was to do likewise.

A country which had been sadly neglected from this point of view during the inter-war years was Spain. No naval attaché was resident in Madrid: the Naval Attaché, Paris, was also accredited to Spain. He was not able to pay more than an occasional visit there and had in consequence few contacts and no influence. This was a weakness which Godfrey determined to remedy as soon as he became DNI. By June 1939 he had persuaded the Treasury and the Foreign Office to appoint an Assistant to the NA Paris, to reside in Madrid. This was merely a first step. The proud Spaniards did not relish receiving a mere Assistant who was subordinate to Paris, and were even less impressed when the 'overlordship' was transferred to Lisbon, geographically and linguistically closer. Finally, Godfrey was able to obtain agreement to the upgrading of the post, and the Assistant NA, Lisbon and Madrid, became Naval Attaché, Madrid. Important though this was, the choice of the officer concerned was even more so. Godfrey had not forgotten Commander Alan Hillgarth, whom he had met as Consul at Palma during the Spanish Civil War. He understood the Spaniards, spoke excellent Spanish and was well known to and respected by senior Spanish naval officers and other members of the new regime. Hillgarth's knowledge of Spain and his influence with the authorities did a very great deal to counteract German influence and to persuade the British Government that, despite outward appearances, Franco's policy was to avoid any involvement in the war. Godfrey wrote later that "Hillgarth was rather a super-Attaché for several reasons; (a) I encouraged him during his periodical visits to London to report direct to the Prime Minister after seeing me; (b) I had an A1 source in Spain whom I kept in contact with through him and Gomez Beare [Lt Commander RNVR, the Assistant Naval Attaché]; (c) Hillgarth was uniquely the co-ordinating authority in Spain for the Secret Intelligence Service and SOE as well as NID; (d) Hillgarth was the only member of the Embassy staff who knew Spain and had many contacts in high places, political and social. Don Gomez Beare linked up with commerce and could go anywhere as he looked like a Spaniard. Actually he was a Gibraltarian."

The A1 Spanish source mentioned by Godfrey was Don Juan Marsh, a "multimillionaire owner of banks, oil and shipping companies, a tobacco monopolist and friend of Franco. Don Juan was also an admirer of British institutions and believed that it would be to Spain's advantage to be on good terms with Britain. On 23 September (1939) he had come to see me accompanied by an interpreter. He explained that he 'had control' of all Spanish ports except on the north and north west coasts (meaning I suppose from Vigo to San Sebastian) and, believing that the future of Spain was bound up with that of Great Britain, he would do all in his power to help us. If we received reports of U-boats taking in fuel from a Spanish oiler or in a Spanish port, he asked us not to sabotage the ship or create fires and explosions in the port as we used to do in World War I. Instead would we let him know and he would see that it did not happen again. The same applied to 'incidents' in Spanish ports which should be minimised rather than exaggerated. He explained that the port authorities were under his control. He said that Franco would never let the German Army into Spain. He wished the relations of Spain and England to be friendly and tranquil and would do all he could to achieve this end. We kept in touch and he passed me valuable information which was never incorrect."

In Paris, Captain 'Hooky' Holland, with his execrable but fluent French, had long since won the confidence and esteem of Admiral Darlan and the French Naval Staff. He now became in effect the head of a naval mission and therefore required a considerable increase in staff in the shape of retired regular and Volunteer Reserve Officers. In addition liaison officers had to be appointed to French ships and commands, and each one of them had to be carefully selected.

In other countries active service officers, needed at sea, were replaced by retired Flag Officers. One of these was Godfrey's old friend Vice-Admiral Sir Gerald Dickens, who went to the Hague. In Turkey, the Naval Attaché was naturally enough stationed in the inland capital, Ankara. The importance of Constantinople and the Dardanelles called for an officer there and the very able Commander Wolfson, RNVR was appointed as Assistant Naval Attaché for this purpose. Not all these

changes were made at once and many others were needed as
the war progressed and the situation changed. Naval attachés
played a vital part not only as observers of the enemy through
the windows into Germany and Italy of Madrid, Stockholm,
Athens and Constantinople, but as ambassadors of naval goodwill in Paris and Washington, or in almost operational roles as
in Buenos Aires and Montevideo during the events leading up
to the scuttling of the pocket battleship *Graf Spee*.

The reader will by now, it is hoped, have realised the large
number and wide variety of the problems with which the DNI
had to concern himself in the early months of the war. His
Deputy took as much of the routine administration off his
shoulders as possible, but much of his time was taken up with
the abortive Operation Catherine, Churchill's plan to send old
battleships into the Baltic. The famous co-ordinating staff in
Room 39, next door to Godfrey's own room, was still in the
process of being formed. The head of the Secretariat, Paymaster Captain Woodhouse and his assistant, Paymaster Lt
Commander Pearce, were first class, as were the two secretaries
Miss Cameron and Miss Gavin. Lieutenant Fleming rapidly
found his feet, but at this time Godfrey was just not able to
delegate and rid himself of detail as he would have wished and
later succeeded in doing. Clayton was well established in OIC
but the idea that Pound and Phillips should visit the OIC on
arrival each morning to find out the latest position never
materialised and the special door which had been provided for
this purpose was never used by them. It was a pity in more
ways than one, because neither of them ever really came to
understand the strengths and the limitations of the information
available to OIC. Nor did they learn to appreciate and rely on
the great ability of that department's principal officers, as they
would have done had they made daily visits to the Centre.
Fortunately, the Assistant Chiefs of Staff and the Directors of
Divisions did not follow their example so that at a lower level
at least an atmosphere of trust and understanding between
Intelligence and Plans, Operations, Trade and Anti-Submarine
Warfare was gradually created exactly as Godfrey had hoped
it would be.

In one area, that of the Geographical Sections, it had not
been possible to make very much progress. NID1, the German
and Scandinavian Section had a new and extremely able head,

Commander Ian Campbell who had been Godfrey's number
one in Kent in 1931. It was a key appointment and Campbell
went on to become DDNI, but despite some modest increases
in personnel all the sections remained insufficiently staffed to
do much more than keep their heads above water; they could
do little to cope with the accumulated backlog of work or
prepare for the 'hot war' which was soon to engulf them.

Godfrey later summed up this period as follows: "During the
first six months of the war the development of Naval Intelligence in its true sense, i.e. the extraction and distillation of
information about the enemy and about the lands and seas on
which we might have to fight him, was hampered by lack of
experience, co-ordinating staff and money, and by my preoccupation with administrative side-lines such as security, press,
postal and telegraph censorship, propaganda and so on. All
these activities were feeling their way rather uncertainly; the
machine creaked a good deal and every day brought its crop of
problems which called for my personal attention, not only to
decide what to do at the moment, but to devise or revise
procedures or methods which would ease the handling of
similar problems in future. Amid so many creaks, groans and
headaches it was difficult to decide which ailment to tackle
first or how to cure it." The Intelligence problem is always
most difficult when the enemy holds the initiative. The weaker
side, on the defensive, tries to be prepared everywhere, and
inevitably fails. The aggressor, knowing precisely where he
intends to strike, can concentrate all his resources on a single
objective. Nevertheless, as Godfrey had told Captain Siemens,
the German Naval Attaché, when he came to say farewell on the
outbreak of war, "Germany couldn't win a short war and was
bound to lose a long one". Only once, at the height of the
Norwegian campaign, did Godfrey seriously wonder whether
he had been right.

CHAPTER EIGHT

Wilfred to Sealion

ON 9 APRIL 1940 the Germans invaded Denmark and Norway. On 10 May they opened their attack in the west with the assault on the Low Countries and France. On 11 May Churchill succeeded Chamberlain as Prime Minister. By 4 June the evacuation from Dunkirk was over and on 10 June Mussolini thought it was safe to declare war. On 17 June Pétain sued for peace and on 22 June the French surrendered. 'Nous vaincerons parce que nous sommes plus forts' they had proclaimed. Now General Weygand thought that Hitler would ring England's neck like a chicken's. 'Some chicken—some neck,' replied the new Prime Minister. Not only his but his country's greatest hour had arrived. The British people were curiously confident. They comforted themselves with the thought that they always lost every battle but the last and that at least they no longer had any 'damned allies to let them down'. Most of the rest of the world, however, including Ambassador Joseph Kennedy, shared Weygand's opinion.

It had been a staggering ten weeks; surprise after surprise, defeat after defeat; blunders, muddles, misconceptions; crisis succeeding crisis with bewildering speed. No one, from Chamberlain and Churchill downwards, could disclaim responsibility. How much did faulty Intelligence contribute to the débâcle?

A good Intelligence organisation depends on good sources; it must have the ability to draw the right conclusions from the information which it receives; it must persuade those who have to take the operational decisions to accept and rely on the appreciations which it produces. Intelligence, on its own, cannot win battles; it cannot even prevent defeats if the enemy has overpowering strength or if the High Command ignores the advice it tenders. It is unlikely that the best of Intelligence could have saved France, but a month earlier it might have prevented the German success in Norway.

Churchill had been pressing the Cabinet since September

1939 to agree to some offensive action that would halt the important flow of Swedish iron ore from Narvik in the north of Norway to Germany. The iron ore ships, and German warships and auxiliaries, crept down the Inner Leads, the coastal water-way inside the islands along the Norwegian coast. The Norwegians were not prepared to object to such infringements of their neutrality, but the British Foreign Office was strongly opposed to any possible violation on Britain's part. Then had come the Russo-Finnish war and a plan, provided the Norwegians and Swedes would agree, to help the Finns by sending British and French troops through Narvik and Sweden to their aid. With the Finnish collapse this had come to nothing, but Churchill at last won his battle and the Cabinet approved his plan, Operation Wilfred, to mine the Inner Leads. The possibility of a violent German reaction was not ignored, and troops were held ready to land at various Norwegian ports if, but only if, the Germans violated Norwegian territory. Despite this contingency planning, it is clear that the attention of the First Lord, and of Pound and Phillips, was concentrated far more on Operation Wilfred than on any possible German counter-move, let alone on the chance that Hitler might entirely forestall them. There was also a very real fear that the Germans might succeed in sending one or more of their heavy ships out on a commerce raiding cruise into the Atlantic.

By a curious coincidence, Admiral Raeder had been conducting a similar campaign to persuade Hitler to occupy Norway. It was Raeder who had introduced Quisling to him and who had gradually won the Führer over to a daring scheme for invasion despite all its obvious dangers. The Germans had learned of the Anglo-French plans to send troops through Narvik to help the Finns and their fear of British action was reinforced by the rescue of British Merchant Navy prisoners from *Spee*'s supply ship *Altmark* in Jössing Fjord on 14 February by HMS *Cossack*. Plans for the operation, Weserübung, were therefore rapidly completed. Five groups of ships, comprising almost every available warship in the German Navy, were to land troops at Narvik, Trondheim, Bergen, Christiansand and Oslo. Supplies and other troops were to be transported concealed in merchantmen. The landings would have to be made simultaneously at all points with the result that the more northerly groups would have to sail at least two days before

D-Day. The Narvik group was to be covered by the battle-cruisers *Scharnhorst* and *Gneisenau*, which were then to decoy the British fleet away to the north-west and so permit the safe return to Germany of the other forces. All groups would have to reach their destinations undetected by the British and unsuspected by the Norwegians. Surprise was essential to success.

The winter had been exceptionally severe and the Baltic and the Belts had been frozen over. This and other factors had caused postponements by both sides. Operation Wilfred was finally fixed for Monday, 8 April, Operation Weserübung for the 9th. Both sides deployed submarines to report any counter-moves made by their opponents and attack any targets sighted. The Germans had some suspicions of British plans. The British had last minute clues which should have, but did not, alert them to the intentions of their enemy. What were these clues, and why were they ignored until it was too late?

The last five months had been full of rumours of sudden German attacks. Indeed Hitler had wished to attack the Low Countries and France in November, but bad weather and the pleas of his High Command had caused a postponement until May, one month after the Norwegian venture. This war of nerves had made the Western Allies highly sceptical of such reports; they had become complacent. It was not easy to disentangle fact from fantasy and reports emanating from Copenhagen had been particularly difficult to evaluate. Both the British Consul and the Naval Attaché were sure that they had excellent sources of information but many of their tele-grams had been proved quite unreliable. The Naval Attaché, a retired captain, was convinced that he was regarded by the Gestapo as such a danger to them that he used to lock up his shaving brush each night in case some German agent should impregnate it with anthrax! Godfrey had replaced him early in 1940 with an officer of his own choice, Captain Henry Denham, who was later to demonstrate his great talents for such duties in Stockholm. At the beginning of April, however, it is possible that he had not had time to eradicate all traces of NID's scepticism about reports emanating from Copenhagen. The Foreign Office, for its part, showed no signs of alarm. Very soon the British were to develop two sources of information, photographic reconnaissance and cryptanalysis which, if they rarely revealed the whole picture of enemy intentions, almost always provided a check on the seemingly and often inaccurate reports of diplomats and agents. At this juncture, unfortunately, neither photographic reconnaissance nor cryptanalysis was capable of giving such an invaluable service. For NID it was largely a question of 'By guess and by God', and God seemed to be more 'Mit Uns', as the Germans might have put it, than with us.

Nevertheless, in the first days of April reports began to come in of German concentrations, naval, military and air, in the western Baltic and in the north of Germany. The ice had melted and German minesweepers were active in the Belts. On 4 April a report was received that the Germans intended to attack Norway. On the 6th there were further signs that something unusual was afoot. These reports were not entirely ignored. Air patrols were sent out during the forenoon of Sunday, 7 April to reconnoitre the Heligoland Bight and reported a cruiser and six destroyers steaming north. A subsequent bomber attack on these vessels was unsuccessful and unfortunately their report that the formation had included a battlecruiser was not received until they had returned to base. In the meantime the Admiralty had sent a signal to Admiral Forbes, Commander-in-Chief Home Fleet, which accurately described the German intentions but which contained the very unfortunate qualification 'all these reports are of doubtful value and may well be only a further move in the war of nerves'. Neither the Admiralty nor the C-in-C appear to have taken this information seriously because the Home Fleet remained in Scapa and did not even start to raise steam until several hours later.

In Copenhagen that Sunday morning Denham had set off for Gedser to try to verify rumours of German minesweeping activity in the Belts. He soon found ample evidence not only of this but of heavy German ships steaming north. He hurried back to Copenhagen and signalled the facts, and his suspicions that this portended a German attack on Norway, to London. His signal was received late that night and was seen by Captain Ralph Edwards, who had just taken over as Director Operations Division (Home). Edwards later told Denham that he had taken the signal to the First Lord, but that Churchill's comment on it had been 'I don't think so'. The following entries in Edwards' diary* strongly suggest that whatever NID's view on the accuracy of these reports may have been, the reports themselves were not acceptable to the First Lord, the First Sea Lord or the Deputy Chief of Naval Staff.

'4 April. A story has been produced that Hitler is to attack Narvik and the coast of Norway on 8 April. In the opinion of Intelligence and the High Command the German Military Chiefs would never allow such a 'mad expedition to sail'. I pointed out that if there were any truth in the story Operation Wilfred would clash with the German move. It was suggested that the operation should be postponed for twenty-four hours. First Sea Lord and First Lord would not agree.'

'6 April. Further indications from Denmark and from DNI that very considerable movements are taking place in north German Baltic ports.'

'7 April. I recommended that Operation Wilfred be postponed, but the 1st Lord and DCNS would not agree. The 1st Sea Lord was away down at Broadlands fishing for salmon and arrived back rather late in the evening . . . dead beat. DCNS was tired and the 1st Lord well dined. The result was they all failed to come to any useful decision . . . In the earlier part of the evening DCNS and the 1st Lord agreed with me that this might be a part of the heralded attack on Norway . . . I tried to interest them in Norway but they were only interested in the battlecruiser problem.'

The battlecruiser problem was of course the sighting by Bomber Command earlier that day, which was already fulfilling the German intentions of causing a diversion: Phillips and Churchill preferred to regard the sighting as the prelude to an Atlantic break-out, not as a move against Norway. Although their conviction may have begun to weaken they were still not prepared to cancel Wilfred or to order the Home Fleet to the centre of the North Sea to counter any invasion threat.

Next day, perhaps as a result of Denham's signal and of the receipt of the interpretation of the first photographs of Kiel referred to in the last chapter, the truth began to dawn on all concerned and Forbes was advised that the information contained in the previous day's signal might, after all, be correct. The break-out theory was not however entirely abandoned. The

* Rosk 4/75.

Home Fleet had sailed from Scapa at 8.15 p.m. on the 7th, but on a north-easterly course to prevent a break-out. Churchill, usually so anxious to take charge and issue instructions, did not for once attempt to interfere. The opportunity to deal a decisive blow against the invaders while they were still at sea, laden with troops and equipment and without effective air cover, had been lost. Had it been seized it is just possible that Weserübung would have been dealt a smashing blow from which it could not have recovered. Who can say what effect such a defeat would have had on Hitler and the German plans for the offensive in the west?

There was undoubtedly an Intelligence failure, but was this failure due to a faulty appreciation by NID, or was it the result of a refusal by the First Lord and his two principal advisers to act on the information placed before them? To judge by Edwards' comments NID may have been sceptical of the truth of the report received on the 4th but by the 6th had swung round to acceptance that something unusual was in the wind. The crucial signal was that sent to Forbes on the 7th. Without the fatal qualification all might yet have been saved. With it the Admiralty was as good as telling Forbes to ignore it. Who was responsible? It can only be a matter of speculation because the original of the signal has apparently been destroyed. Neither Campbell, head of NID1, nor Denning, the expert in OIC, have any recollection of it. Godfrey makes no reference to it at all in his Memoirs. The impression Captain Roskill formed when he was working on his official history, *The War at Sea*, was that Godfrey had at least approved the caveat—though he found no evidence that he had originated it. To that view he has recently added the rider that it is unlikely that Godfrey was solely responsible for this serious error of judgement. In the author's opinion it is highly improbable that Godfrey had anything to do with this signal at all. He refused to adopt the role of 'moment to moment Intelligence officer' and specifically left such duties to Clayton, Colpoys or Denning in OIC or to Campbell or one of the other Section heads as appropriate.* The wretched sentence was almost certainly

* By a coincidence Godfrey was absent from the Admiralty during two crucial operations. He was in America throughout the *Bismarck* operation and on tour in the UK during the disastrous PQ 17 Convoy. In the author's opinion it is very doubtful whether his presence in the Admiralty on the

added by Pound or Phillips on the instructions of Winston, who just did not want to believe the contents of the report.

Whoever was responsible for this Intelligence failure—for failure it was—the result was that it was the British not the Germans, who 'missed the bus'. The Germans seized the airfields and the British troops and ships were totally deprived, not for the last time, of any effective air cover. Whether, in view of this, better direction of the campaign could subsequently have retrieved the situation is doubtful, but as it was order and counter-order made confusion worse confounded and for this no one was more to blame than the First Lord. As Sir John Dill, soon to succeed Field Marshal Ironside as Chief of the Imperial General Staff, sadly remarked to Godfrey, "all the careful teachings of the Staff College were ignored, the chain of command disrupted and, he might well have added, every military sin perpetrated at the Dardanelles repeated on a rather more extended scale". As the losses of and damage to ships mounted so did unease among the Naval Staff below Board level until, finally, at the end of April or the beginning of May, Godfrey, as the senior Director, felt that he must express the alarm felt by all the others present at a morning Staff Meeting. His remarks were not well received by the DCNS, Phillips, who was in the chair. It was, Godfrey later confessed, the only occasion throughout the war that he felt serious doubts about Britain's ultimate victory.

The sudden extension of the war of course put heavy pressure on every Section of NID, pressure which became greater every week and reached a peak with the Blitzkrieg against the Low Countries and France. No pre-war plans had remotely envisaged a campaign in Norway (or for that matter a war in which France was occupied by an enemy). "A lot of nonsense has been written about Norway", wrote Godfrey. "Charts are meant to keep ships outside the 5-fathom line but the sort of information we needed for the Norwegian Campaign would have involved the laborious survey of the whole coast and all its fjords and inlets, which could not have been carried out secretly and would have been out of the question in peace time without the full collaboration of Norway. WSC, in a rage,

---

latter occasion would have caused Pound to alter his decision to scatter the convoy.

sacked people most unjustly and I suppose I was lucky in not getting chucked out as well", all the more so because he had specifically advised against the campaign because of the paucity of information! Donald McLachlan in his *Room 39* states that the War Office folder on Norway contained only a sheet of paper with the letters 'SFA' in it. The German and Scandinavian Section of NID was slightly better equipped than this. Commander 'Scottie' Campbell, its head at that time, recalls that one of his new recruits, Todd, peacetime head of Thomas Cook & Sons' Egyptian Department, was able to provide much information and maps from his old employers! Campbell gives another example of NID's initiative in overcoming the lack of information from official sources such as the SIS and the RAF at this time: 'Very early one morning in the first days, Admiral Godfrey came to the night desk with the First Sea Lord and other senior officers. Had the Germans got to Trondheim? It seemed so petty to say I don't know, so I picked up the telephone, asked for Continental Trunks and got through in a few minutes to the Vice-Consul there in Trondheim, a naval officer. "Any sign of the Germans?" I said breezily. "Yes," was the reply, "I can see the Huns coming up the hill and I've just burned my books."' NID2, the French and Low Countries Section, in which the author was at that time serving, was in no better state. We were reasonably well informed about Belgium and the Netherlands, but there had been a gentleman's agreement with the French of long standing that the two countries would not spy on each other and once France became an ally we merely had to ask for any information that was required. That obviously did not include information about the coast defences of French ports. One report, it may have been on Oran, dated back to pre-Entente Cordiale days! Curiously enough, the British section of the German General Staff was equally small and equally ill provided with information about England. So far as British Intelligence was concerned, the blame did not rest with pre-war Intelligence chiefs, but with the lack of funds and very low priority accorded to them.

It should not be supposed that NID entirely failed to provide the Naval Staff and the Fleet with any useful information during the Norwegian campaign. On 15 April Bletchley Park succeeded in cracking the new 'Yellow' Enigma key which the Germans had just introduced for their land and air operations in Norway. This was read with few delays for the next month and sometimes contained some information of naval interest. Whereas the British War and Air Ministries were quite unprepared to handle the quite considerable volume of priceless intelligence now made available to them, Godfrey had long since foreseen the problems which would arise and had made the necessary provisions. Back in January he had insisted, as already noted, that if decrypts of naval interest should ever be produced they must be telexed, translated but otherwise in full and as received, to OIC, the Section of his Division specifically created to handle this and all other forms of operational Intelligence. He had gone further. Realising not only that a security problem would arise—the need to protect the source—but also on the other hand that, if decrypts were to be put to really effective use, all operational authorities involved must be swiftly informed and must realise the complete authenticity of the information sent them, he had warned the Commander-in-Chief Home Fleet and certain other flag officers that Intelligence of this type would be signalled to them with the prefix 'Hydro'. The system was immediately put into effect. For example, on 30 April the C-in-C was warned that Vaernes aerodrome was ready for operations by enemy bombers and fighters; on 3/4 May destroyers were sent to intercept a German convoy, although without success; and on 9/10 May the cruiser *Birmingham* with destroyers that included Lord Louis Mountbatten's *Kelly*, attempted to intercept a force of German minelayers. On 13 May the prefix was changed from 'Hydro' to 'Ultra', which has now come to be the term used to describe all forms of cryptanalysis, although in fact Special Intelligence was the description used throughout the war in the British Navy. There was also a foretaste of things to come when, as a result of the capture of a German patrol boat, German naval Enigma traffic for a few days of April was read in early May. Unfortunately the German Navy's system was much superior to that of the Army and Air Force and it was not until a year later that BP was really able to make much of a contribution to OIC and the war at sea.

Although, therefore, the practical results achieved were meagre, it should be emphasised that Godfrey had devised the right system in advance, a striking contrast to the SIS and the other two Services who took another twelve months to introduce and perfect the Special Liaison Unit organisation which eventually functioned so well. By a remarkable coincidence the British prefix 'Hydro' was almost duplicated by the Germans, who subsequently gave the code name 'Hydra' to their main naval cypher.

Other valuable intelligence was recovered from U49, including a copy of the German naval gridded chart, a list of all U-boats in commission and the dispositions of all those on patrol in the North Sea. It is true, as the official History of British Intelligence claims, that OIC failed to pay sufficient attention to BP's theory, based on a study of changes in the volume and type of German wireless traffic, that a movement of heavy German units was underway in the North Sea early in June, and that had they done so the aircraft carrier *Glorious* might have escaped from the *Scharnhorst* and *Gneisenau*; but the art of making deductions from the study of wireless traffic, which BP incidentally had learnt from NID10's attempts to frustrate the Germans doing the same with British traffic, was still in its infancy and highly unreliable unless confirmed from other sources. Nevertheless, and this too was in marked contrast to the attitude of the other Services, Godfrey immediately arranged for someone from the Naval Section at Bletchley to visit the C-in-C Home Fleet and explain the work of the Section to him.

No, despite mistakes and weaknesses, NID did a good deal better than some of its critics will allow. The trouble was that not only were the providers and analysers of Intelligence struggling to find their feet, to improvise and deal with unforeseen situations, the users of Intelligence, both political and Service, the very people who had neglected to supply the directives and the means in peacetime, now expected immediate and perfect service. "Many of my colleagues", Godfrey wrote, "seemed to think that I ought somehow to produce information out of a hat and there was an exaggerated belief in the efficacy of spies. Straightforward reconnaissance by surface craft, submarine or aircraft, the traditional observation of the approaches and 'looking into' the enemy's ports, was allotted a secondary role. Thus we never got more than half-hearted support in the long drawn out campaign to persuade the Air Staff that the

Admiralty, having lost control of all shore-based aircraft, needed the help of the Air Ministry to provide the Navy with photographic reconnaissance . . ."

However, if British reactions to the German invasion of Norway were slower than they should have been, they were swift enough over the Danish Faroe Islands and Iceland. The Faroes were occupied on 13 April. Iceland took a little longer. On 4 May, Humphrey Quill, then a Major Royal Marines, serving in the Far Eastern Section of NID, was told that he was to lead an 'irregular' operation to Reykjavik to arrest the German consul and any other German nationals and secure the country for Britain. The Foreign Office still had scruples about the infringement of 'neutral' territory and this was why NID with a small force of marines was to carry out the mission. Before leaving Quill was sent for by Godfrey. 'He greeted me by saying that I would want some money for "special purposes" and then turned round to a filing cabinet behind his left shoulder and extracted a huge bundle of notes which he presented to me.' Quill, who accomplished his mission with complete success, never knew where the five hundred pounds came from. They may have been provided by 'C', but it is more probable that they were part of a private fund established early in the war for Godfrey, and subsequently replenished from time to time, by a wealthy individual whose name remains a secret. His object was to enable the DNI to carry out just these sort of enterprises without having to justify the expenditure to the Treasury or his own superiors. An extraordinarily patriotic act which also displayed great faith in Godfrey's ability and integrity.

The very heavy losses suffered by the German Navy during the Norwegian campaign meant that it could do little to support the Army in the Low Countries and France. This did not, however, greatly relieve the strain on NID. Communications tended to break down quickly and the author can well remember receiving an urgent telephone call from Admiral Dickens in the Hague demanding air support for the Dutch. What was unusual was that the connection was by radio telephone via New York: neither of the speakers could properly hear the other but a delightful lady in New York kindly acted as a relay point, despite the Admiral's somewhat sulphurous language.

On another occasion, during the battle for France, it was the teleprinter which miraculously kept us in some sort of touch. By the middle of June, the French Admiralty had evacuated Marceau and was very temporarily installed at Tours. The Naval Attaché, Hooky Holland, had been relieved two months earlier by Captain Pleydell Bouverie, who had not yet had time to establish the same close relations with Darlan and his Staff as had his predecessor. He was by no means sure of the will of the French to carry on what every day seemed more and more a losing fight. The eventual disposition of the French Fleet had become a matter of pressing concern to the Admiralty and Prime Minister Churchill. Very little reliable information was reaching London about the true military and political situation. Godfrey felt strongly that he must be able to give the best possible advice to the First Sea Lord, but as it was impossible for him to do as he would have liked and personally investigate the matter on the spot, he did the next best thing and sent his Personal Assistant, Ian Fleming, to France. When Fleming arrived in Tours, he pretty quickly summed up the situation, but was in something of a quandary as to how to make an immediate report to his chief. He then found that the Naval Attaché's private teleprinter line to the Admiralty had been re-established and was working. This, in effect, would enable him to talk to Godfrey with complete security if suitable 'operators' could be found. It so happened that the author had, quite illicitly, formed the habit of chatting over the teleprinter to his opposite numbers on the NA's staff, and it was with some anxiety that he received a message one evening to go down to the Admiralty teleprinter room. He was relieved to find that he was to act as operator for the Director of Naval Intelligence for half an hour's very confidential conversation with the great man's PA in Tours. Fleming confirmed that France was on the point of collapse, but suggested that he should attach himself to Darlan to act as a link and exert whatever influence he could on the head of the French Navy. This was of course a job for the Naval Attaché, not for an RNVR Lieutenant from NID, but in any case Darlan seems to have done his best to withdraw from contact with the British and all touch with him was lost. However, Godfrey, who had been much intrigued by this rather unorthodox means of communication, was by now a good deal better informed about the state of French morale and was far from confident that, if it came to it, the French Fleet would sail for British ports. When the new First Lord, A. V. Alexander, and Pound were about to fly out to Bordeaux in a last desperate effort to stiffen French resolve, Godfrey caught the First Sea Lord just as he was leaving the Admiralty to give him an urgent message. It was from Lord Tyrrell, a former Ambassador to France and a good friend of Godfrey's, who was sure that "Darlan was a twister. Pound was incredulous— to him it seemed unbelievable that Darlan was anything but an honest, straightforward sailor . . ."

The terms of the Armistice imposed on the French by the Germans provided for the demilitarisation of the efficient and largely intact French Navy under German and Italian supervision. The danger of the Axis powers obtaining some if not all of the French ships and so tilting the maritime balance against Britain seemed very real at the time. The British had assurances from Darlan that he would never allow this to happen but would he, or could he, honour them? Good intelligence might provide the answer but it would have to be firm and unimpeachable. The surest source would obviously be knowledge of instructions sent by the French Admiralty to its ships in North African and other overseas ports. There was no time for the cryptanalysts to set about breaking French naval cyphers, to which they had naturally devoted no effort hitherto. A 'coup de main' was needed, but one which the French would never suspect. Churchill suggested the sudden arrest of the French Naval Mission in the Admiralty, breaking open their safes and seizing their cypher books or assaults on those French ships which had taken refuge in Portsmouth and Plymouth. Both plans foundered on the fact that the French would be bound to discover at once what had happened and would immediately introduce fresh cyphers. In Malta, however, lay a single French vessel, the submarine *Narval*, which declared for de Gaulle. Godfrey saw that here was the one chance. He persuaded Churchill to hold his hand and obtained Pound's agreement. Confidential Books from *Narval* ensured that during and after Somerville's attack on Admiral Gensoul's squadron at Mers El Kebir, the British were able to read some of the messages transmitted by wireless by and to the French Admiralty. For the first, but by no means for the last time, Churchill was able to lean over the shoulder of his Commander and demand action which the man on the spot was reluctant to take. The officer who actually conducted the negotiations with Gensoul, was the late Attaché in Paris, Captain Holland. It broke his heart. Godfrey always felt that it had been a mistake to entrust Holland, who knew and liked the men to whom he was delivering a humiliating ultimatum, with this mission. Attachés, in Godfrey's opinion, almost always tended to identify themselves too closely with the nation to which they were accredited.

It is impossible to say what influence, if any, Godfrey had on Churchill's and Pound's decision to strike at the French at Mers El Kebir, or Oran as it is wrongly called by the British. Pound had apparently disbelieved the warning that Darlan was a 'twister', but the First Sea Lord seems to have changed his mind later because he told Godfrey that, in his opinion, the 'best place for the French Fleet was at the bottom of the sea'. It is impossible to say whether the action was necessary; Admiral Cunningham, turning a deaf ear to instructions from London, achieved better results at Alexandria without bloodshed, but he was not dealing with Admiral Gensoul and was a long way from Toulon.

By the end of June, for the first time for one hundred and twenty-five years, the whole western coast line of Europe, from the North Cape in the Arctic Circle to Hendaye on the Franco-Spanish frontier was in enemy hands. An attempt at invasion of the British Isles seemed both inevitable and imminent, but Britain was without any adequate means of obtaining advance warning of it. At the end of May the Joint Intelligence Committee, prompted by Godfrey, had reviewed such means as she had. The Secret Intelligence Service's organisation on the Continent, which had never been very effective, was now completely disrupted. Information from decrypts of German Air Force signals was growing in volume but the brief penetration of Naval cyphers had ceased. The only certain way to discover the concentrations of troops, aircraft and ships which would be needed to launch the assault was photographic reconnaissance. The JIC had recommended that the Air Ministry and the Admiralty should at once establish a regular and systematic photographic watch on the 'invasion' coasts and that an inter-Service Intelligence organisation should be created to analyse the results obtained and prepare regular appreciations for the High Command. On 28 May Godfrey drew attention to these recommendations and stated that some of them had already been put into force in anticipation of approval. A Joint-Services Intelligence Committee had begun to meet daily in the Operational Intelligence Centre under the chairmanship of Clayton's deputy, Commander Colpoys, assisted by Denning. But Godfrey had also suggested that the Naval Air Division should provide naval observers for reconnaissance of maritime subjects. Not only did the Director of the Naval Air Division fear that this would arouse opposition from the Air Ministry but he considered that Coastal Command, responsible for PRU, was already overburdened. His solution was to rely on the SIS and so 'reduce the necessity for so much air reconnaissance'! Fortunately other members of the Naval Staff took a less negative attitude and the First Sea Lord formally requested the Air Ministry 'to provide frequent photographic reconnaissance of German, Dutch, Belgian and appropriate French ports'. DNI was instructed to report the results. He did so on 17 June. The Combined Intelligence Committee was meeting daily and working well. The situation had improved considerably but had not yet properly settled down. During the next few months coverage of Dutch, Belgian and French Channel ports was indeed fairly good, but reconnaissance of Norwegian, German and French Atlantic ports was to remain highly unsatisfactory for another year or more. We shall have to return to this unfortunate story again. Three things should be noted at this stage: the renewed attempt by Godfrey to get the RAF to provide the information which the Navy and indeed both the other Services desperately needed if invasion was to be thwarted; the somewhat muted support he received from the rest of the Naval Staff; the fact that, once again, it was Godfrey who initiated a further move to secure inter-Service Intelligence co-operation.

Godfrey was also striving in other ways to secure information about occupied Europe. The French Naval Attaché, Capitaine de Vaisseau de Rivoyre, "through tradition and upbringing instinctively gave his allegiance to the constitutional rulers of France, but nevertheless during that agonising period when it was obvious that the French Army was collapsing, he made a point of maintaining daily personal contact with me. Thereafter he gave his allegiance to Pétain and we had a very sad and final meeting after Mers El Kebir, when he called me an 'assassin' . . .

I am glad to say that eventually he bore no umbrage. The French section had also been keeping very closely in touch with Lieutenant de Vaisseau Bedin, his assistant attaché for air and a man of very different temperament. NID2 had formed the opinion that he was a potential recruit for whatever emerged in the way of a French resistance movement. I saw him several times. Naturally he did not air his views with his French colleagues. When it had been decided to intern the French diplomatic staff I phoned Bedin and asked him and his wife and family to stay away in the country until I told him to return—he had a cottage near Godalming—so that when the internment took place Bedin was missing. The French, as we learnt later, were not suspicious. They considered him as pro-Vichy as the rest and without any prompting appointed him Naval Attaché in Dublin." Bedin provided NID with much useful information from Vichy until it was feared that his masters were becoming suspicious and he left Ireland for a job with Ferry Command of the RAF.

Hillgarth, in Madrid, provided other sources. There was, of course, no direct official contact with Vichy, but on those occasions when the French Admiralty felt the need to inform the British concerning the movements of French warships or other similar matters, they did so via their own Attaché in Madrid and Hillgarth. Hillgarth gradually managed to win the confidence of his opposite number and was then the recipient of quite a lot of useful information. His American colleague was even more helpful by allowing him, quite unofficially, to see the reports made by the US Naval Attaché in Berlin. For some reason, the Vichy authorities allowed the Canadian Minister, Monsieur Dupuy, to remain in Vichy, and to go backwards and forwards between Vichy and London via Lisbon. "He brought us", says Godfrey, "first hand information of what was going on and about the attitude of Pétain and Laval towards the Germans. I am not sure if the Foreign Office believed him implicitly . . . but what he told me during his visits to 36 Curzon Street fitted fairly accurately with Fleet Admiral W. D. Leahy's account of his experience as American Ambassador to the Vichy Government."

In the summer of 1940, however, few of these contacts had been properly established. The attention of British Intelligence was concentrated on the preparation for Operation Seelöwe, the invasion of England. The Combined Intelligence Committee at its daily meetings in OIC now had the benefit of an increasing flow of decrypts of Luftwaffe signals. Although many of these were of a routine or administrative nature, some were more important, and when considered in conjunction with the evidence obtained from photographic reconnaissance enabled far better appreciations of German intentions to be produced than ever before. On 17 September Hitler issued instructions that Seelöwe was to be postponed indefinitely and shipping gradually dispersed, although the threat of invasion was to be maintained as a diversion. Evidence reaching British Intelligence about German intentions was, however, very contradictory and Army and Air Intelligence in particular remained convinced until well into October that the invasion was still 'on'. Indeed on 18 October the Chiefs of Staff ordered a return to the highest state of readiness. Three days later, according to the official Intelligence history, the 'Chiefs of Staff, and especially the CIGS, were perturbed about the widespread feeling that the danger had passed.' It was not until the end of the month, on the insistence of Churchill, that they somewhat reluctantly accepted that the danger had passed at least for the time being and authorised the relaxation of some of the defensive measures and a much overdue redisposition of naval forces.

Before this, however, some of those involved in Intelligence had already become highly sceptical about the degree of the threat. The Chairman of the Joint Intelligence Committee, Cavendish Bentinck, writes, 'I can remember a JIC meeting in September when Paddy Beaumont Nesbitt, then Director of Military Intelligence, explained, "Anyone who says the Germans will not invade is mad", to which I replied, "Then I ought to be removed to a lunatic asylum."' Of course the Joint Intelligence Committee had to produce an agreed and unanimous report but Godfrey, in his Memoirs also shows that opinion must have been very divided. "On 20 October I received completely reliable information that the German invasion of England was 'off' except as a diversionary threat. I naturally lost no time in telling Admiral Pound and Tom Phillips, at the same time explaining how we knew. Such stupendous news is not easily forgotten. We later heard that it had been postponed until June 1941 and that there was no immediate danger was amply confirmed by the dispersion of invasion craft in Dutch, Belgian and French ports. In March 1941 certain German activities were alerted and I informed Admiral Pound that we could no longer count on the state of immunity from danger which had existed since October 1940. It was then that he surprised me by saying that I had never told him that the threat of invasion had receded last October. Moreover, he warned me to be more careful in future. I pointed out to him how impossible it would have been for me to withold information of such magnitude, but he was not appeased." In another account of this episode he refers to the information having reached him on 13 October, which in fact seems more probable, since on that date a report was indeed received from the SIS's most reliable Czech source stating that the invasion had been put off until 1941.

The official history is somewhat critical of the Joint Intelligence Committee's inability to come forward with firm appreciations for the Chiefs of Staff. The answer would seem to be that, as was to be demonstrated again and again from this time onwards, the Director of Military Intelligence was not given the same freedom to form his own judgements by his superiors as were his Naval and Air Force colleagues. Pound always tended to accept the Army view in such matters but it is incredible that he should have entirely forgotten Godfrey's advice on such a supremely important question even though he personally did not agree with it. Can he already have been suffering from the symptoms of the tumour on the brain which was to prove fatal two years later?

Before leaving the first nine months of 1940 the question of the security of British naval cyphers must briefly be considered. After World War I the German Navy had become aware of the great successes of Room 40 and determined that they would never again be put at such a disadvantage. On the one hand they adopted, in common with the other German Services, the highly efficient and sophisticated Enigma machine cypher system; on the other, retaining full control of their own cryptanalysis department, the xB Dienst, they made a determined attack on British cyphers. Aided by British signal security failures during the Abyssinian crisis they had, by 1939, penetrated some of the Royal Navy's operational and administrative cyphers. This, combined with other forms of radio intelligence, such as direction finding, traffic analysis and study of call signs (which they themselves had abandoned), enabled the xB Dienst to supply Admiral Raeder with much useful information about British naval dispositions during the first ten months of the war. British submarine losses in the Heligoland Bight were largely made possible by German knowledge of their patrol areas and during the Norwegian campaign the location and movements of the Home Fleet were accurately deduced. In August 1940, however, changes in the British cyphers were introduced which were, according to a post-war German comment quoted by Captain Roskill in his *War at Sea*, 'a great set-back for German naval strategy . . . The insight into British movements, which had lasted so long, thus came to an end. Knowledge of British movements had spared German vessels from many a surprise encounter with superior forces and this had become an element in operational planning.' Unfortunately, although these and subsequent changes thereafter prevented the xB Dienst from achieving much of operational value from these particular cyphers, the Germans began to bite into another British cypher, Naval cypher No. 3, the cypher provided by the Admiralty, with US agreement, for use between the two Navies. A large proportion of the traffic concerning North Atlantic convoys was sent in this system and from the latter part of 1941, throughout 1942 and until mid 1943 German decrypting gradually became sufficiently timely to be of great importance to Admiral Dönitz in his conduct of the U-boat war. It has been estimated that the work of the xB Dienst cost the Allies at least sixty more merchant ships sunk on the North Atlantic convoy routes alone than would otherwise have been the case. Then, early in June 1943, the cypher was changed and, to all intents and purposes, the xB Dienst was a spent force.

These failures in British naval cyphers have quite naturally attracted much unfavourable comment. What organisations and which individuals should be held to blame? The whole question of cyphers and their security is highly technical and complex and continued reticence by the British authorities does not make it easy to disentangle exactly what happened. It is clear that the department which devised and produced not only naval but all British Government cyphers was the Government Code and Cypher School, and to this extent that body must accept the primary responsibility for any shortcomings.

Although the Navy's communications security has been particularly singled out for censure it should not be supposed that that of the other Services, both military and civil, was necessarily inviolate. Far from it. Nor were British weaknesses any greater than those of any other nation. The harsh fact is that no country, whether belligerent or neutral in World War II, had completely secure systems and some British cyphers, notably the machine cypher used by the Army and RAF from the beginning of the war, were in practice better than most. Wireless telegraphy, which had vastly increased the amount of raw material for cryptanalysts, was barely a quarter of a century old, and in 1939 both cypher makers and cypher breakers were confronted with all sorts of unforeseen problems.

One of these problems which does not seem to have been properly appreciated was the vast increase in the volume of wireless traffic which war conditions would create, and volume is essential to successful cryptanalysis. This does not seem to have been envisaged by the Royal Navy in the thirties. Fleets at sea were expected to maintain strict wireless silence and indeed when Godfrey was pressing for the expansion of the direction finding organisation he was told that it was unnecessary for this very reason. Because the threat from U-boats had been grossly underestimated little thought had been given to the need for ocean-wide protection of convoys against attack by U-boats and in consequence no estimate had been made of the volume of signalling which this would generate. Nor with British ships, both naval and mercantile, moving constantly all over the world could the Admiralty do what the Germans did and reduce the load by introducing different cyphers for different geographical areas and different forces. In the Royal Navy the need to bring ships together at short notice from widely separate areas as the operational situation demanded necessitated cyphers held in common on a much wider scale, even world wide in some cases. This lack of understanding of what was going to be needed, was perhaps partly due to the fact that it was only shortly before the war that all the Royal Navy's vessels were fitted with high frequency wireless transmitters which permitted the Admiralty to keep in direct touch with ships no matter how distant. Previously long-distant communications had been by cable and then by purely local onward transmission by wireless.

Britannia and *Hindustan*, Dartmouth 1897

Britannia cadets, 1902. John is standing on extreme left

Lieutenant, 1909

HMS *Bramble*, Yangtze 1911, recently fitted with W/T

HMS *Swiftsure* (nearest camera) and HMS *Euryalus* proceeding to bombard Smyrna, March 1915

ommander, 1921

John and Marga[...]
15 December 1[...]

The Captain of *Suffolk* in a light-
hearted mood ashore, 1932

Repulse leaving Portsmouth, 8 June 1936

Refugees from Majorca on the quarterdeck of *Repulse*, 1936

DNI, 1942

Recruiting in the Punjab, 1943

Inspection. Navy Day, 1945

With Princess Alexandra at the Cheyne Spastics Clinic, July 1956

John and Margaret in the garden at
Wilmington, 1969

If any of these problems had been foreseen there certainly had not been sufficient money to carry out the research and development required to improve British cypher systems, but the Signal Division's pre-war rejection of Lord Louis Mountbatten's recommendation that the Navy should follow the example of the Royal Air Force and the United States Navy and go over to a machine cypher system, was simply due to typical and misguided naval conservatism. Such newfangled inventions would never stand up to the arduous conditions at sea, it was maintained.

One can hardly blame the Director of Naval Intelligence for any of this, but he was responsible for security in all its aspects, so should he not have immediately detected the weaknesses and have taken action to have them put right? Various other departments had a say in the handling of naval cyphers. GC & CS devised and produced them. M Branch of the Admiralty distributed them to those who had to use them. The War Registry logged, received, despatched and distributed signals within the Admiralty. The Signal Division was responsible for the mechanics of transmission. But the responsibility for security seems to have been blurred. Section 10 of NID was certainly responsible for ensuring that these instructions were followed and for considering any case where compromise might have occurred as a result of physical capture. There is no evidence of any failure here. But what about the silent and secret work of enemy cryptanalysts? So far as can be ascertained at present, it was generally assumed in 1939 that this was a responsibility of GC & CS. This had definitely been one of Room 40's duties and it seems reasonable to suppose that when GC & CS took over all cryptological work after World War I, it took on this responsibility along with the rest.

Certainly when Paymaster Lieutenant-Commander D. A. Wilson joined NID10 in 1935 he was not briefed that this aspect of signal security was one of his duties. His main, and at that time not very onerous, task was to ensure that GC & CS was kept up to date with the Navy's requirements in respect of its cyphers, ships' call signs and so on. The Section then consisted of two officers and was located in GC & CS's headquarters at Broadway, Victoria. On the outbreak of war, by which time Wilson was in charge, Godfrey authorised an increase in the strength of the Section in the shape of a number of junior RNVR officers. Some members of the Section accompanied GC & CS to its wartime stations at Bletchley Park and Mansfield College, Oxford, but Wilson and most of his new recruits moved back to the Admiralty. This splitting of the Section did not, of course, imply the acceptance of any additional responsibilities; it was merely the result of GC & CS's move to the country. Godfrey also displayed his awareness of the importance of the Section's work by agreeing to it becoming a joint Intelligence and Signals Department and it was in fact housed in the Signal Division. Much of its work was taken up with traffic analysis and the prevention of accurate deductions being drawn by the enemy from these means.

However, by early 1941 the DNI does seem to have felt that he was responsible, at least in part, for more than just the physical security of cyphers. In a general review of the work of his Division issued at this time, Godfrey stated that NID10's work "also includes the scrutiny of all our W/T traffic with a view to spotting mistakes in cyphering, coding, etc. and *estimating possibilities of compromise by the enemy.*" (Author's italics.) It seems probable that this did in fact represent a change from the 1939 position and that this change was brought about because Wilson came to the conclusion that some of Britain's cyphers were vulnerable. Wilson's own recollection is that no one at BP was doing anything about it so that he, obviously with Godfrey's approval, assumed responsibility for improving the co-operation between NID10 and BP.

Just how the successes of the xB Dienst at this time were spotted is another matter which is far from clear. The fact that British cyphers were weak was demonstrated in a very practical way by Paymaster Lieutenant Dudley-Smith while serving in the battleship *Resolution*. He amused himself when off duty with some amateur cryptanalysis and, without too much difficulty, succeeded in cracking the Flag Officers' cypher. Such talent could not be wasted at sea and he was immediately posted to Bletchley Park where he became Travis's Personal Assistant and, amongst other duties, he gave particular attention to signs of weaknesses in the security of British communications. It is not, however, easy to discover if an enemy is reading your cyphers. Cryptanalysis is always a closely guarded secret and operational instructions sent out as a result of cypher breaking are carefully worded to conceal this fact not only from the other side but from one's own. In any case, Britain was not at that time reading the enemy's signals. All that can at present be said is that Godfrey, no doubt primed by Wilson, was aware that all was not well not only with naval but with many other cyphers. In addition to the changes made in August 1940, Godfrey proposed that an inter-Service cypher security committee be set up and in January 1941 arranged for the appointment of a signalman, Captain Jasper Haines, RN, to be its Chairman with appointment as Assistant Director in the Operational Intelligence Centre. Doubts had gradually arisen about the security of the so-called 'Long Subtractor' system and early in 1941 consideration was given to the question of replacing it by something better. The fact that it took something like two years before the new 'Stencil Subtractor' was introduced into use does seem excessive, but the difficulties of devising, testing, producing and distributing all over the world an entirely new cypher should not be underestimated. BP's resources were concentrated far more on the offensive side of the work, on breaking the enemy's cyphers rather than on the defensive task of improving Britain's. There were also difficulties with the Americans to be overcome, for in 1941, before the United States had come into the war, it had been decided to establish a joint Anglo-US cypher, and No. 3 had finally been chosen for this purpose. In so far as the Americans, on instructions from the very top, accepted cypher No. 3 and continued to use it rather than disclose to their Ally the secrets of their own superior machine cypher, ECM, they too must accept a share of responsibility for its deficiencies.

It will be clear from what has been said that Godfrey cannot in any way be held responsible for the original weaknesses in the Royal Navy's cyphers. These were due to pre-war failures to visualise the needs of war, to naval conservatism and to Treasury parsimony. Can he be held responsible for the length of time taken to remedy the situation? With hindsight it is easy to say Yes, but in fact it was not easy at the time either to discover that changes ought to be made or to get those changes introduced in a flash once the weaknesses had been recognised. The delays that did occur were largely outside DNI's control and Godfrey and Wilson in fact did well to achieve as much as they did and as quickly as they did. It is quite clear that the xB Dienst, even at its most successful, never managed to penetrate British Naval cyphers in the same comprehensive and consistent way that Bletchley Park decrypted the German Enigma traffic; isolated messages did provide the German Naval Staff with information of great importance, but a large amount escaped them entirely and much that they did decrypt arrived too late to be of any operational importance, although it did help to build up a background picture of the convoy cycle and procedures. This failure on the part of the Germans to achieve complete success was partly the result of the construction of the despised British system and partly due to the frequent changes and modifications introduced by Wilson. At the very least it can be said that Godfrey and Wilson became concerned early on that the Royal Navy's cyphers might become vulnerable and took effective steps to strengthen and eventually replace them. The German experts simply never admitted that their vaunted Enigma system could be compromised.

It should not be supposed that the account given so far covers all the activities of the Naval Intelligence Division during the first nine months of the war. A number of other important changes and developments were taking place, but it will be more convenient to examine them in the next chapter. It may, nevertheless, be useful to try to summarise the progress which had been made up to this time. NID had been 'blooded', and its staff, most of them quite new to Intelligence work, had settled down and had learnt rapidly. OIC, despite very inadequate sources of information, was beginning to function with a fair degree of efficiency. Godfrey's insistence on integrity, on an analytical and sceptical approach to information was permeating the Division, which, if still understaffed in some sections, was now receiving much needed reinforcements. Some of the major deficiencies, for example lack of topographical information, were largely the result of the rapid extension of the war into areas never envisaged either by the politicians or the Chiefs of Staff in peace time. A great deal of flesh had been put on the skeleton, but more flesh and more muscle were still needed. Mistakes, some of them avoidable, some of them not, had been made and a good deal of criticism, some of it just, more of it unjust, had been incurred. What can now be seen is that the Division had been developed on the right lines. Growth in scope and expertise in the next six months would turn it into a real 'war winner'.

For Godfrey himself the period had been one of great strain. Success was expected of him but when achieved was taken for granted; failures attracted instant notice. His dealings with the First Lord had not been always smooth but he had courageously stuck to his principles and, unlike some of his less fortunate colleagues, he had survived. The new First Lord, Alexander, was much more disposed to accept the advice of the Naval Staff and allow them to carry out their duties without constant interference. From Phillips, the DCNS, Godfrey, after one or two brushes, had received much help and support, but the attitude of Sir Dudley Pound must have appeared rather more ambiguous. It had been a very testing time but Godfrey, like his Division, was finding his feet, and if he had on occasions been compelled to drive as well as lead, he had inspired his staff with his own energy and enthusiasm and was at last beginning to get the results he desired.

CHAPTER NINE

It Does Work. That's the Main Thing

THE FRENCH surrender changed the position not only for the British but also for the Americans. If the British were concerned about the fate of the French Fleet, the Americans were equally worried about what would happen to the Royal Navy after the British collapse which most of them considered inevitable.

Anglo-American naval relations, which had not been particularly harmonious in the twenties, had improved in the thirties, not out of any 'blood is thicker than water' sentiment but because both navies desired some reinsurance against the Japanese and the Germans. The secret and unofficial Phillips-Ingersoll conversations in 1938 had broken the ice but had led to no conclusive result. In June 1939, Commander Hampton was sent to Washington and with the Naval Attaché, Captain Curzon-Howe, held even more highly secret discussions with Admiral Leahy and Rear-Admiral Ghormley which took matters a stage further but which again produced no binding commitments on either side. President Franklin Roosevelt, who had been Assistant Secretary of the Navy in 1918, had taken a close interest in this preliminary sparring, which he regarded quite as much as a means of advancing the interests of his own country as a way of stiffening British resolve to resist the Dictators. On the outbreak of war, however, he immediately instituted the 'Neutrality Patrol' in the western Atlantic, which in practice if not in theory was extremely helpful to the British. He also wrote a personal and very friendly letter to Churchill, the new First Lord, suggesting that they keep in close personal touch with each other; this was the origin of the famous 'Former Naval Person' correspondence. And so, from the outset, contact between the Admiralty in London and the Navy Department in Washington was a good deal closer than the laws of strict neutrality would normally suggest. Contact was at two levels, Churchill—Roosevelt, and Naval Staff—Naval Staff. Important links in the lower level were the British DNI and the American Naval Attaché.

Before the war Godfrey had quickly followed Blinker Hall's advice and had made a point of getting into personal touch with the American Ambassador, Joseph Kennedy. Kennedy gave him the name and telephone number of one of his confidential secretaries to whom Godfrey could communicate anything of special significance and seek a personal interview. Godfrey did not neglect this direct access to Grosvenor Square, but of more practical benefit were the close and friendly relations which he established with the Naval Attaché, Alan Kirk. Godfrey describes Kirk as a "modest, shrewd and kind-hearted man. He was one hundred per cent co-operative and invariably met me more than half way." He was well thought of by his superiors in the Navy Department and appears to have had a direct line into the White House. Both men were ardent advocates of closer liaison between the two navies, which they felt would be to the mutual advantage of their respective countries. Kirk had interviewed the survivors of the *Athenia* and had also publicised a visit he had made to the aircraft carrier *Ark Royal*, when the German propaganda machine was claiming that she had been sunk. Kirk realised early on that in some respects the Royal Navy was ahead of his own Service and could see that the US Navy could learn much from British war experience, particularly in respect of magnetic mines and anti-submarine defences. Godfrey, for his part, was convinced that the British goal must be to draw the Americans closer and closer and that this could best be achieved by providing them with as much information as possible. There were two objections to this. Firstly, American security was considered to be lax. Secondly an important body of opinion, shared at times by Churchill, was averse to giving away any British secrets except on a strictly quid pro quo basis. Others even felt that the Americans had nothing to offer the British. But, as early as 11 December 1939, Godfrey had minuted that "the more the Americans have the feeling of being 'In' with us—without necessarily getting the impression that we are under an obligation to them—the more easily and fluently will the countries merge, if need be, as allies". There were, however, possibilities of leaks in American security through the US press. Kirk encountered similar difficulties with the Navy Department's technical bureaux when he suggested that, if the Americans would only be more forthcoming he would be able to secure more from the British. For the first six months of the war both sides were anxious to receive but loath to give. Godfrey continued to urge on the Board of Admiralty that a balance must be struck between the political gains and the technical losses involved in a more liberal attitude on revealing secrets to the Americans. It was obvious, he wrote, that America would not enter the war against Britain and it was to Britain's advantage to assist the Americans to increase the efficiency of their Fleet. Any information imparted to the Americans would draw them closer to Britain and personal friendships, which would be valuable if the United States did enter the war, would be formed between American and British officers. Kirk's views were precisely the same, but whereas there were already some American observers in British ships, the United States Navy would not reciprocate. However, on a personal and non-technical plane things gradually improved. Godfrey states that "During 1939 and 1940 he (Kirk) used to see me for half an hour once or twice a week and I told him pretty well everything".

Godfrey's sensible and long-sighted views were shared by many of the scientists such as Sir Henry Tizard and Professor A. V. Hill and were gradually gaining acceptance with the Naval Staff and Board of Admiralty when the whole situation was dramatically changed by the onrush of the German Panzers through France. For the British it was no longer a question whether they should or should not give their secrets to the Americans. The possibilities of horsetrading had all but vanished. With France out of the war it was a question of survival and it was worth paying any price to obtain American help and to persuade them to join in the shooting war. The Americans, somewhat naturally, did not see things in quite the same light. It was all very well for the British to ask for old destroyers, aircraft, even rifles; if Britain was going to suffer the same fate as France any weapons, munitions or secrets which might be supplied to her, assuming that any of them reached her before she was overrun, would fall into the hands of the Germans. America was woefully unprepared to stand alone against the Axis, and would have need of everything she possessed for her own defences.

It all depended on what assessment one made of Britain's chances of preventing or defeating a German invasion, and Godfrey had a share in persuading the President's advisers that these chances were good if the United States would give all support short of war to Britain. Godfrey's influence could not, unfortunately, be exerted through Ambassador Kennedy or Alan Kirk. Both Kennedy and Kirk were profoundly pessimistic about the chances of British survival. Kennedy, a second generation Irish-American, while no doubt relishing the social and diplomatic power inherent in his post, was not by nature or upbringing, an Anglophile. He was a shrewd and successful American politician and business man, who had fought his way to the top by backing winners not losers. In the early summer of 1940 he judged Britain was a loser. Ambassadors, after all, are appointed to give their governments objective advice. It was unfortunate for Joe Kennedy that his advice, however objective, was wrong. To what extent he influenced his Naval Attaché, or how far his views were influenced by Alan Kirk, is impossible to say, but Kirk, too, thought the battle on Britain's side of the Atlantic was lost unless the United States immediately entered the war. Kirk had a strain of pessimism in his nature and had never been really convinced, although he obviously wished to be, that the British and the French were setting about things in the right way. For that one can hardly blame him. When the attack in the west opened he saw all his worst fears realised. Godfrey's judgement was that he "seemed well balanced and imperturbable until things went wrong—then he went completely to bits. When the Germans were sweeping across France both the Ambassador and he got into a panic and he told me that he was convinced that unless America came in the British would be defeated by August. This was at a time when the morale of the country was (perhaps rather irresponsibly) going up by leaps and bounds after the frustrations of the first eight months of the phoney war. To make light of his fears I got him to bet me half-a-crown (and write it down and put it in an envelope to be opened on 4 August) 'that, unless the United States joined the Allies, Great Britain would be defeated by 4 August'. He thought it a great joke when I produced this and tore it up on 4 August." Alan Kirk was a good friend of Britain but his job was to form dispassionate judgements, and viewed dispassionately Britain's prospects seemed bleak.

In Washington alarm mounted. If Britain were defeated and the remnants of the British Fleet came under German control, the combined naval strength of the Axis would be formidable. But if Britain could be kept in the ring there might yet be time for America to plug the gaps in her own defences before she was attacked. Churchill, in an endeavour to obtain immediate material aid, more than once nearly overplayed his hand by pointing out that he could not guarantee what would happen if his Government fell and was replaced by one that would use the British Fleet as a bargaining weapon to secure the best possible terms from Hitler. Roosevelt was in a difficult position. He was about to stand for an unprecedented third term. Anything which could be construed by his political opponents as likely to involve the United States in war was hardly a vote-catcher. Fortunately neither he nor his Secretary of War, Stimson, nor the Secretary of the Navy, Knox, was entirely convinced that all was lost. At the suggestion of William Stephenson, head of the British Secret Intelligence Service in the Western Hemisphere, it was decided to send a certain Colonel William Donovan to make a personal assessment for the President of the chances of British survival and the desirability, from the American point of view, of supplying Britain with the means to carry on the fight. This is what Godfrey, who met Donovan within a day of his arrival, has to say about a mission which was to have decisive results for Anglo-American relations:

"The object of Bill Donovan's mission was to discover if we were in earnest about the war, and if we were worth supporting, to enquire into our methods in adopting conscription, the difficulties we experienced and how they were overcome, our anti-fifth columnist methods and to establish intimate collaboration with the British Navy both in the spheres of technical development and intelligence.

"A soldier, he did very well as 'Fighting Bill' in 1917–1918, became head of the large firm of lawyers, Donovan Leisure Inc, was a Republican, a Catholic, a Southerner, a great divorce lawyer and a personal friend, in spite of politics, of the President. Before he left the USA he was told that he would find us 'difficult', secretive and patronising. His actual experience, so he said, was exactly the opposite.

"I was one of the first people to meet him, and, without the help of the American Ambassador, he quickly established contacts with important people in this country. Donovan sensed the general air of defeatism at the Embassy and felt it to be more marked among the Naval than among the Army representatives. Undeceived by appearances he quickly became aware of the spiritual qualities of the British race—the imponderables that make for victory but had evaded Mr Ambassador Kennedy, for whom he seemed to have very little use. Kennedy reckoned the big attack was coming soon and wanted to clear out before it materialised—he thought his mission was complete and was anxious for a relief.

"I saw a lot of Donovan during his month's visit and he dined with me at Sevenoaks and sat up to 2 a.m. on 3 August talking before catching the aircraft back to the States next morning. He then told me what he intended to report to the President. One of his first tasks would be to urge the appointment of a 'sensible Ambassador', and of someone who could travel backwards and forwards ('a sensible Colonel House') and keep the feelings of each country fresh in the minds of the other country's rulers. The need was for someone who could readily detect all the various ways by which the two countries could concede to each other and co-operate, whilst insisting and explaining to each other the prickly matters where national sovereignty and prestige were involved, and where perhaps the ignorant and too peremptory demand for concessions should be avoided. His answers to the questions 'were we in earnest about the war and were we worth supporting' were 'definitely Yes', and in this respect one must regard his influence as decisive, as Kennedy and others had been feeding the President very different information. Donovan also took back with him definite proposals regarding the following matters, concerning all of which he considered that the USA should help us in every way:

(a) Bomb sights
(b) Flying boats
(c) 50 destroyers
(d) Squadrons of Flying Fortresses with if possible pilots and certainly mechanics and technical maintenance staff
(e) 25 pdr and 105 mm guns
(f) Motor boats—release from US Naval service
(g) All surplus material including Lee Enfield rifles
(h) Use of American airfields for training of Canadian, Australian and British pilots

"In addition, he urged full intelligence collaboration and the placing at our disposal of reports by US Consular officers, especially in French ports, direct liaison between myself and the United States DNI, and the establishment of safe and direct methods of communication. In the sphere of technique and material, Donovan said he would be able to smooth out difficulties, as he had among his clients and his clients' relatives such a large number of industrialists of all sorts, many of whom were carrying out contracts for the British Government.

"It was obvious that we had a good friend in Donovan and one who had the ear of the President and knew how to work with the British.

"Not only did Mr Roosevelt accept Donovan's appreciation of our war effort, but he approved in principle the supply of material on a large scale, which developed into 'Lease Lend' and later full alliance."

It would obviously be wrong to over-emphasise Godfrey's part in all this. Donovan was assisted in his mission by the well-known American journalist Edgar Mowrer who conducted his own independent enquiries and came to exactly the same conclusions. Nevertheless it is indicative of Godfrey's standing and reputation that, as was the case with von Schwerin's mission twelve months earlier, he was one of Donovan's first and closest contacts. In his letter of thanks to Godfrey Donovan wrote, 'I shall always remember most gratefully your many courtesies and kindnesses to me. Certainly you aided me in getting a perspective that I could not have done otherwise.' There is no doubt that Donovan greatly influenced his friend the President, but negotiations at the highest level, with the Prime Minister, the Foreign Secretary, Lord Halifax and the British Ambassador in Washington, Lord Lothian, all playing vital roles, continued until, on 2 September, the destroyers for bases deal was finally signed. Shortly before that Rear-Admiral Robert Lee Ghormley, Assistant Chief of Staff in the Navy Department, had been sent to London for discussions with the British Naval Staff. The British expected that these discussions would develop into full-scale Staff talks and to definite commitments by both sides, and Admiral Sir Sidney Bailey was appointed head of a committee to conduct the negotiations. In fact Ghormley's terms of reference were much more limited than the British had hoped and no firm decisions were reached until the highly secret American-British-Canadian meeting in Washington in March 1941, at which the British delegation was led by Rear-Admiral Bellairs. However, one result of Ghormley's arrival in London was that the First Sea Lord gave clearance for the communication to the Americans of almost any information they might require, a vindication of the policy which Godfrey had been advocating for the past ten months. Ghormley's staff, originally half a dozen in number, expanded quite quickly to forty and most of them came to the American Section of NID to receive introductions to the appropriate Admiralty Department or to have tours to shore bases and establishments arranged for them. One of the other results of the ABC conference was the establishment of a British Admiralty Delegation in Washington. This was at first small and disguised as part of the purchasing Mission, but it grew until it included representatives of twenty-three Admiralty Divisions, including an NID section, Section 18, under Captain Eddie Hastings.

Before this happened, however, various other changes had taken place. Alan Kirk had returned to Washington in December 1940 to take up the post of Director of Naval Intelligence, where he was confronted with problems as daunting as those which Godfrey had encountered in 1939. He was armed with all the knowledge and advice which Godfrey had imparted to him, aid for which he was always most grateful. He was followed in March 1941 by Ambassador Kennedy, whose departure was less regretted. His successor, John G. Winant, was a man of very different character and temperament. Godfrey secured an immediate introduction to Winant through one of Margaret's many relations, Mrs Carnegie, formerly Joseph Chamberlain's third wife. Born Mary Endicote, the daughter of an American Secretary of State, she had been a pillar of Boston society and still knew everyone of importance in both American and British political circles. "It was not difficult", Godfrey wrote, "to establish close relations with Mr Winant. He was a very welcoming person and valued the informal liaison which frequently took the form of his dining or dropping in to see me at 36 Curzon Street. I saw that he got all the news, good and bad, and took him into my confidence before my 1941 and 1942 missions to America." Winant was to prove a good ally of Godfrey.

Although Donovan had been greatly intrigued by and full of admiration for all he had seen of British Intelligence and had advocated a free two-way exchange of information, it soon became clear to Godfrey that, despite Kirk's efforts, all was not well on the other side of the Atlantic. Something more than was at present being done was necessary. On 28 April he proposed the "complete fusion of the British and American Intelligence Services . . . What I have in mind is not liaison but complete co-operation, with US officers attached to NID sections and vice versa. In certain special categories this co-operation exists already and we have derived benefit from it in the Far East. It is up to us to return their services in the Atlantic." He may well have been referring to Special Intelligence, cryptanalysis. The Americans had already broken into Purple, the Japanese equivalent of the German Enigma cypher system, and the American officers had delivered two Purple machines to Bletchley Park by the end of January 1941. The British had not as yet had much success with German naval cyphers, but were well into the Luftwaffe and Army ones. Where the Americans were far behind the British was in their general Intelligence expertise, in inter-Service co-operation and co-ordination and effective use of results obtained from many different sources. In a report dated 4 May 1941, the new British Naval Attaché in Washington, Rear-Admiral Pott, had stressed these shortcomings, which naturally were not only to America's own disadvantage but which also greatly hindered the British in obtaining information from a country which was by now an ally in all but name. There was great jealousy between the State Department and the Armed Services, between the Armed Services and the FBI, between the Army and the Navy, and between the Operations and Intelligence Departments of the Navy itself. Pott did point out that, thanks to Kirk, co-operation with the Office of Naval Information was excellent and that his Assistant NA, Lieutenant Peter Smithers, RNVR, was receiving some extremely valuable information, but this was on a completely unofficial basis and only as a result of the first class personal relations Smithers had established with his opposite numbers in ONI. The situation overall was far from satisfactory.

Godfrey's proposals, for which he had secured the backing of his colleagues on the Joint Intelligence Committee, went to the

Chiefs of Staff who not only approved them but agreed that Godfrey should go to Washington as their emissary and with their full authority. His mandate was 'to set up a combined intelligence organisation on a 100 per cent co-operative basis'. Godfrey, accompanied by his Personal Assistant, Ian Fleming, left London on 15 May and reached New York a week later. Godfrey had decided that one of the things he must press for would be a unified American Secret Intelligence Service which exercised the functions carried out by no fewer than four different bodies in Britain, each under a different political master— sabotage and resistance in occupied territories (SOE), political warfare (PWE), economic warfare (MEW), and covert intelligence gathering (SIS). The obvious candidate to head the new organisation was Donovan, who "had the ear of the President and knew how to work with the British". Godfrey had discussed these ideas fully with Winant before he had left, and in New York Stephenson and Sir William Wiseman, the British business man who had occupied Stephenson's post in World War I, had come to very similar conclusions and had even talked to Donovan about them.

On arrival in the States Godfrey recalls that "I found everybody—War, Navy, and State Departments—most helpful and ready to take anything we were prepared to offer. As far as I was concerned we had no secrets; we gave them the JIC-JIS set-up, which they adopted, appreciating for the enemy [attempts by a small inter-Service section to put themselves in the position of the German General Staff and forecast their plans], all prisoner of war interrogation techniques, the OIC which surprised them as they regarded it as part of 'operations', and of course copies of a brochure on NID organisation specially prepared for the occasion. We already knew that the relations between the Army and Navy were bad, but we did not realise how bad until we tried to get them to see eye to eye and collaborate with each other and with the State Department about this supremely important matter of Intelligence and its allied activities. After a fortnight it became clear that I was up against a brick wall. I discussed my dilemma with Mr William Stephenson and Sir William Wiseman. They told me that the only person who could and would handle this question with any hope of success was the President and that somehow I must meet Mr Roosevelt. Wiseman spoke to Sultzberger, the Editor of the *New York Times*, whom I had met, saying that it was important that I should meet the President, but not saying why. Sultzberger rang up Mrs Roosevelt and asked her to ask me to dinner and make sure that I had an hour with the President afterwards. All went according to plan. I received the invitation—the White House: 7.30: dinner jackets. I was received by Mrs Roosevelt and taken care of by two ADCs. Then the President was wheeled in. I had been warned that he would almost certainly pull my leg and make some provocative remarks about the British or Imperialism and that I must on no account allow myself to get 'mad' as the Americans say. So there was the inevitable 'Hallo, Admiral, how did you come out?' and when I mentioned the Clipper via Bermuda he said 'Oh yes, those West Indian Islands; we're going to show you how to look after them . . . every nigger will have his two acres and a sugar patch.' Rough stuff and rather brash, but having been warned by Willie Wiseman, I kept my eye firmly on the object of my visit and mustered up the semblance of a laugh . . . By some unobtrusive process FDR was got into his wheeled chair and a lift took us up to a drawing room . . . For an hour we looked at a rather creepy crawly film of snake worship . . . and then, with a warning from Mrs Roosevelt not to keep her husband up too late, I was directed into the adjoining Oval Room—the President at his desk and me sitting in the famous Lincoln chair. Now, I thought, the moment has arrived for me to say my piece. But no: the President felt reminiscent and described to me in some detail his visit to London in 1917, when he was Under Secretary for the Navy, and his admiration for Blinker Hall. I ignored the remark 'Of course, Hall had a wonderful Intelligence Service but I don't suppose it's much good now', and then had to listen to a long description of how spies crossed the German-Danish frontier every night and then by boat to Sylt and flying boat to Harwich. Blinker Hall must have deployed some fantastic cover story and the young Under Secretary of the Navy not only swallowed and believed it, but remembered to recount it to Hall's fifth generation successor twenty-four years later. At last I got a word in edgeways and said my piece. More reminiscences—I said it a second time and a third time—one intelligence security boss, not three or four. I'd been in the Oval Room for an hour and a quarter. Mrs Roosevelt came in—time for bed.

"Driving home to the Potts I felt doubtful if I'd really made the point, but within three weeks Big Bill Donovan had been nominated, with three million dollars to play with, as head of a new department, later to be called the Office of Strategic Services. I fear that for the time being, by meeting the President, I made myself unpopular with Secretary of the Navy and with my old friend Kirk, who was very cool and stoney-eyed when I went to say goodbye ten days later. However that wore off and our close collaboration was resumed in London when he returned as Number Two in the US Naval Mission."

Godfrey makes it clear that he did not himself suggest Donovan, he was content to have achieved his major objective —a single chief for the Intelligence organisations. Donovan's name was probably put forward by Winant, who was in Washington at the time, and by Stephenson who had his own ways of getting news and views into the right quarters. All the same, it was no mean achievement to have secured a private interview of more than an hour with the President. One wonders whether the British Chief of Defence Staff (Intelligence) could do the same today. OSS became, after the war, the CIA.

There were of course other results from Godfrey's mission. Intelligence of all sorts from American officers and officials in Europe and Vichy Africa began to trickle into NID. The Anglo-American cypher, mentioned in the last chapter, was introduced. Officers from the Office of Naval Information, including the head of the Far East desk, visited London and were shown all the British secrets. Their reactions seem to have been mixed, perhaps well summed up by the officer who remarked 'Like everything British, you get the impression that it's not very well organised, that it's rather diffused, but it does work—that's the main thing.' The Americans were now much more ready to exchange Intelligence, and in respect of the Japanese they had a great deal to offer, but it was too much to hope that a completely integrated Anglo-US Intelligence Service could be created before the Americans were involved in the shooting war. When they were, full integration was achieved in some areas. In others, notably in the field of Atlantic operational Intelligence, although an American had been designated to take up an appointment in the British OIC, it never proved necessary; the very intimate, day to day collaboration built up between Rodger Winn in the Admiralty's Submarine Tracking Room, and his opposite number, Kenneth Knowles, in OP 20G in the Navy Department, rendered such an exchange unnecessary. But in other areas, and not only purely naval ones Godfrey's ideas of inter-Service and inter-allied integration did bear fruit to the great benefit of both countries.

It goes without saying that the policy of trying to bind the Americans closer to the British was being pursued at the highest level by the Prime Minister and in all sorts of other ways, notably in the scientific field, but the Royal Navy had so far tended to make the running. There were obvious reasons for this. The English Channel may have been a tank trap but the Atlantic was a bridge. The whole move to Anglo-American co-operation had started with the 1938 secret naval conversations, and Roosevelt's Neutrality Patrol was bound to involve liaison with the Royal Navy even though it was publicly justified as a means to keep the war away from America's doorstep. In many respects, therefore, the steps leading to closer and closer co-operation were taken in operational and technical fields. Godfrey did not give a repeat performance of Hall's role in 1917, confronting an American President 'too proud to fight' with a Zimmerman Telegram. Roosevelt was certainly no great admirer of the British Empire. England's misfortune was America's opportunity. But he was a dedicated opponent of the Nazis, and to this extent the British were knocking on an open door. Godfrey saw that what was needed was to create conditions which would make it easy for the President, militarily, diplomatically and above all politically, to utter the words 'Come in'. Many others had the same idea, but Godfrey did have a share in producing a situation in which the Americans involved themselves in undeclared war in the Atlantic nine months before Pearl Harbour and which in turn led to Hitler declaring war on the United States.

This brief account of Godfrey's share in the early development of Anglo-US naval co-operation has led us away from the growth and organisation of NID inside the Admiralty at the end of 1940. One of the difficulties of producing a chronological record of Godfrey's activities as Director of Naval Intelligence is that they were so widespread and varied. However, before attempting to describe their ramifications, it may be helpful to remind the reader of some of the principal events during 1941.

With Operation Sealion postponed (in fact abandoned), the German Naval Staff were glad to concentrate on attacking Britain's sea communications upon which the country was, as she still is today, completely dependent. Pocket battleships, battlecruisers and disguised armed merchant raiders, eluding the inadequate British air and sea patrols, ranged the broad oceans where U-boats could not yet reach. The U-boats themselves, although still comparatively few in number, now had the French Biscay ports at their disposal and the Battle of the Atlantic began in earnest. At the end of May the battleship *Bismarck*, after sinking *Hood*, met her end at the hands of the Home Fleet, a final British triumph to which the Operational Intelligence Centre made a notable contribution. In the same month, after Wavell's spectacular victories in the Western Desert over the Italians and the conquest of the whole of Italian East Africa, the ill-conceived expedition to Greece had enabled Rommel's newly arrived Afrika Corps to recapture all the lost territory in Libya. The British defeat in Crete had equally nullified the effects of Cunningham's triumphs at Taranto and Matapan, successes in which Intelligence had also had a share. Malta was besieged, the Middle East in a ferment, Egypt threatened. The whole situation was gloomy in the extreme. On 22 June, Hitler repeated Napoleon's mistake and invaded Russia. By the beginning of December the Germans had reached the gates of Moscow. The German Air Force, which had pounded Britain in the Blitz of the winter of 1940/1941 was now occupied elsewhere, but Russia seemed doomed and the United States still gave no indications of being prepared to come to Britain's or to Russia's aid. All this changed when, on 8 December, the Japanese, without waiting to declare war, struck at the American Fleet in Pearl Harbour and crippled it. Hitler immediately declared war on the United States. Whether they liked it or not, the Americans were at last involved in the fighting. However bleak the immediate prospects, eventual victory over the Dictators was assured.

Godfrey was a many-sided man prepared to examine any theory or proposition. In the summer of 1940, one of the most critical periods of the war, his mind turned to the question of astrology. If, he thought, astrology and the casting of horoscopes was an exact science, as its practitioners claimed, then British astrologers, given the necessary data, should be able to say what advice Hitler, reputed to be much influenced by such matters, was receiving. After all, as Godfrey said, "under certain circumstances it is what people believe that matters, not what is". Some time and effort was therefore devoted to exploring this question, and Godfrey was somewhat intrigued by the results. The British astrologers foretold that 'All that Hitler wants to achieve must be done by the end of February 1941. All that has not been done yet will have to be done now quickly . . . We must not give up now—very soon he will be under most discouraging influences. After March 1941, Hitler's luck will be out.' What the First Lord's and First Sea Lord's reactions were, when this very encouraging piece of information was reported to them, has not been made public, but an unknown commentator referred to this flirtation with astrology as 'NID at its most unexpected'.

If resource to astrology did not produce any very positive results, another of Godfrey's bright ideas certainly did. Reports received in NID from 'C', the Foreign Office or indeed any other source rarely contained any very precise or clear indication of their authenticity or probability. 'From a usually reliable source', 'From an unknown source' and similar expressions were helpful in their way but such qualifications were not always included and were in any case too long-winded and imprecise for incorporation in signals to ships and Flag Officers at sea. Godfrey wanted something short and concise which would immediately convey to the recipient the exact degree of trust which should be placed in any particular piece of information. Like all great ideas it was so simple that one cannot understand why it had not been thought of before. Each item of Intelligence received in NID was assessed and graded for reliability from A to E for source and 1 to 5 for contents. Thus A1 would indicate that a report had come from a completely reliable source and that the information it contained was regarded by NID as factual. B4 would show that though the source was good the information itself was thought to be unlikely, while a D2 assessment meant that despite the poor or virtually unknown nature of the source the report itself seemed highly probable. Furthermore, any deductions drawn from the information contained in the text had to be separated from the facts by the word 'Comment'. An additional virtue of the system was that it compelled Intelligence Officers to consider all information they received with great care and to accept a degree of personal responsibility when giving it further circulation. Godfrey was very insistent on the use of the system in NID and succeeded in getting the other Services to follow suit, although not without great difficulty so far as the Army was concerned. "The War Office", Godfrey considered, "issued their communiqués with the reliable items mixed up with the less reliable, ungraded, and with inference and comment interjected in a way which made it impossible for the recipient to distinguish between advice, disguised as inference or comment, and facts, that is straightforward Intelligence. Thus the identity of a piece of information and maybe its integrity was lost sight of or blurred by the personal views of the commander." The lack of independence of Military Intelligence from Operations and its subservience to the views of the CIGS exacerbated this tendency. The old newspaper motto, 'Comment is free, facts are sacred' never seems to have been held in much regard on the other side of the Horse Guards.

Nor, unfortunately, does it seem to have been one of Sir Dudley Pound's favourite precepts. Three weeks before the German airborne invasion of Crete, Special Intelligence revealed the enemy's intentions to the British. Naturally a signal was drafted in NID to inform the Naval Commander-in-Chief Mediterranean, Admiral Sir Andrew Cunningham. As it was so important the draft signal was passed to the First Sea Lord to see and note before despatch. It read 'German airborne troops will attack Crete on 20 May . . .' Next morning, when he saw the typed copy of the out signal, Godfrey was amazed to see that the word 'Crete' had been altered to 'Malta, Crete or Cyprus'. "An element of untruth had been injected into a high grade intelligence report which, if discovered, would cast doubts on future reports from the same source. I pointed this out to Admiral Pound and he admitted that he had inserted the words 'Malta and Cyprus' to 'put people on their toes'. He realised that he had done wrong but would not admit it." In the event it is unlikely that any harm was done because the correct version reached Wavell, and Freyberg in Crete, direct from BP, but Pound's amendments may have shaken Cunningham's faith in the efficiency of NID in the same way that Captain

Jackson's wretched signal to Jellicoe on the morning of the Battle of Jutland caused him to ignore subsequent accurate information sent him by Room 40. The Crete telegram is a sorry commentary on Pound's understanding of the aims and purpose of Intelligence.

Godfrey certainly did not suffer from a one-track mind. During the Blitz of 1940/41 he had been introduced to Tom Harrison, the creator of the organisation Mass Observation, by Captain Charles Lambe, the Deputy Director of Plans. Mass Observation was widely used during the war by the Home Intelligence Section of the Ministry of Information, but was nevertheless an independent body. It produced more than 400 reports on a wide range of subjects dealing with morale, rumour, war dislocation and frustration, industrial difficulties and general propaganda effects. Godfrey decided that "the conditions of the war threw an obligation on the Services to reassure personnel afloat and abroad as to the effects of enemy action on their people at home. In other wars it was the people at home who felt concern for their men afloat: in the present war it was more general for the men afloat to be concerned at the reports, garbled and otherwise, of the effects upon their people at home of the heavy bombings. I was able to obtain the services of Mass Observation to carry out investigations into post-blitz conditions at Coventry, Southampton, Portsmouth, Plymouth, Swansea, Cardiff, Clydebank, Manchester, Bristol, Liverpool, Hull and the reactions of the inhabitants to ARP and relief measures. They also did investigations into public opinion about the escape of *Scharnhorst* and *Gneisenau* from Brest to Germany, a seaman's first two months in the Navy and security investigations at Hull and Liverpool. The latter were particularly useful and revealed many gaps in our shipping security arrangements.

I decided personally how each report should be handled; the more sulphurous portions might be passed to Sea Lords and selected Directors and parts suitable for inclusion in WIR to the Information Section for final editing and issue. As they were, quite rightly, often criticial of Local Authorities they needed careful handling. For example, C-in-C Portsmouth was indignant about criticisms (fully deserved) of the Town Council's relief measures and had to be placated. Herbert Morrison, Home Secretary, regarded any criticism of ARP anywhere as a personal insult. Nevertheless the reports went on, people appreciated them and I had the support of the First Lord, A. V. Alexander. In sending more or less unexpurgated reports to C-in-Cs of home ports I felt that an account of the reaction of local inhabitants to heavy bombing could not but be of value especially as they provided the background for letters which would be sent to personnel afloat. In the early stages of the war there was no sure indication of the effects which bombing would have on civilians. I also felt it was the duty of the Service to keep track of the cumulative effect which depressing or fearful correspondence might have on men who were already worried about their families at home." WIR of 14 March 1941 contains reports on Southampton, Liverpool, Manchester, Portsmouth and Plymouth which make interesting reading today. Southampton, Plymouth and Liverpool seem to have had the highest morale. The centre of the last named city after dark was described as being 'a mixture between a bump supper night at Cambridge and a Bank Holiday at Blackpool. Nowhere have I seen more drunkenness, more singing and shouting and catcalling, more picking up, or more people being sick . . . The impression on a critical person might be unfavourable, but there was no sign that the people disliked this sort of behaviour. The sailors brought an atmosphere of revelry and holiday, which they continued throughout the air raid warnings.'

NID served the Royal Navy in many ways but in none more direct or important than in the supply of 'operational intelligence', the day to day and week to week information which enabled convoys to be protected and diverted away from danger or enemy surface ships and U-boats brought to action and destroyed. At the beginning of 1941, BP had not, except for one very brief period in 1940, succeeded in penetrating German Naval cyphers. The Operational Intelligence Centre was therefore still dependent on four main sources—direction finding of enemy units' wireless transmissions, wireless traffic analysis, action reports from ships and aircraft at sea, and photographic reconnaissance. At this period of the war the German U-boat fleet, although growing fast, was still limited in numbers and Admiral Raeder was intent on making the fullest possible use of his large surface ships and of disguised merchant raiders. The battleship *Bismarck* was operational, her sister ship *Tirpitz* working up. The battlecruisers *Scharnhorst* and *Gneisenau* had at last repaired the damage they had suffered in the Norwegian campaign and were again ready for operations, as were two pocket battleships, and two heavy cruisers. Half a dozen merchant raiders were at sea. Regular, frequent and efficient air reconnaissance of every enemy port to establish which ships were present and accounted for and which were missing and must therefore be presumed to have sailed for operations was essential if these powerful and dangerous corsairs were to be prevented from cutting off the flow of seaborne imports on which Britain's ability to carry on the war, in the air, on land and at sea, utterly depended.

On 19 March 1941 the First Lord, Alexander, enquired of DNI 'whether you are satisfied with regard to the size of the PRU organisation and the reconnaissance achieved. If you are not satisfied, perhaps you could suggest ways in which an improvement could be made.' The First Lord went on to ask for DNI's opinion 'about the arrangements, such as they are, for aerial reconnaissance over the seas through which raiders operating from German ports would pass into the Atlantic. Is there any possibility of increasing the reconnaissance force available for this work?' Drake, in Room 39, drafting a reply for his master, started succinctly with the single word 'No'. Despite all the pressure applied during the past ten months, both by the Joint Intelligence Committee and the Chiefs of Staff, Coastal Command's PRU had only nineteen Spitfires, none of which was capable of operating further east than Kiel, further north than Trondheim or as far south as Bordeaux. It was not Coastal Command's fault. Air Marshal Sir Frederick Bowhill and all his staff were most anxious to co-operate: they simply could not obtain the necessary priority from the Air Ministry. Not only PRU but the whole of Coastal Command was starved of suitable long range aircraft. Bomber Command's requirements to meet Churchill's desire for area bombing of Germany took precedence over everything else.

On 27 March the VCNS, Tom Phillips, minuted that the inadequacy of PRU was 'not due to any lack of pressure by the Admiralty on the Air Ministry . . . We have repeatedly stressed the vital importance of this reconnaissance but have not yet succeeded in getting our requirements met . . .' Coastal Command was at last about to come under Admiralty operational control and Phillips suggested that the first item to be discussed with Bowhill should be how to improve PRU, but he was

neatly checkmated by the Air Ministry who, without consulting
either Coastal or Bomber Commands, let alone the Admiralty,
took PRU away from Coastal Command and assumed direct
control of it.

On 15 April VCNS, at the First Lord's request invited
Bowhill to a meeting in the Admiralty. Godfrey, accompanied
by Drake, attended. The aircraft available for PRU at that time
were 25 Spitfires with no reserves; 5 Blenheims with 3 reserves;
this the Air Ministry considered adequate to meet the needs of
the Army and Navy and those of both Bomber and Coastal
Commands. Bowhill estimated that to meet the naval requirements alone he would need 27 aircraft with 10 in reserve.

And so it went on. In August 1941 the new AO C-in-C
Coastal Command, Sir Philip Joubert, who had regained control of PRU, again discussed the whole question with Phillips
as the result of further complaints to the Chiefs of Staff by the
JIC. Joubert stated that he would shortly have 87 aircraft,
including 5 Mosquitoes, available for photographic work. He
was taken aback when DNI proved that the current figure was
44 and that the plans for the future would only increase this
figure to 58, and that furthermore, the 5 Mosquitoes, so valuable because of their long range, had been diverted, once
again, to Bomber Command.

Suggestions had already been made that, if the Air Staff
would not allow the Navy to develop its own Photographic
Reconnaissance Unit, perhaps it would be less of an affront to
RAF pride if the SIS took on the job. The Navy had long been
accustomed to providing the Secret Service with craft for
special purposes. This suggestion got short shrift.

The Naval Staff were so dissatisfied that at the end of
September 1941 they reverted to Godfrey's previous suggestion
of creating their own PRU within the Fleet Air Arm. Sydney
Cotton was engaged in an honorary capacity as an adviser,
having refused the doubtful honour of being made a Proba-
tionary Temporary Acting Sub-Lieutenant, RNVR(A). A
suitable machine, a Douglas Boston, was obtained 'under the
counter' from the Ministry of Aircraft Production, but the
scheme was surrounded by too much secrecy, the machine was
damaged, eventually irretrievably, by inexpert handling, and
finally the project was abandoned. The only result was to
increase the hostility of the Air Staff and the First Sea Lord was

compelled to give the Chief of the Air Staff a promise that the Admiralty would have no further dealings with Sydney Cotton.

Thanks to constant pressure, exerted by Godfrey in the JIC, matters gradually improved at home and by early 1942 the situation there was more or less satisfactory. This was not so much due to any increase in the number of reconnaissance aircraft but was the fortunate result of increased bombing raids, for which damage assessment reconnaissance was required. This could often be combined with cover of naval requirements. In the Mediterranean and elsewhere abroad, on the other hand, the situation remained highly unsatisfactory for at least another twelve months.

It must, of course, be recognised that particularly in the early years, Britain just did not have sufficient aircraft to meet all the demands placed on the Royal Air Force. Co-operation between the RAF and the Navy at lower levels was always excellent, but in the highest echelons, over the question of reconnaissance, to quote Godfrey, it reached "its nadir". The whole question was bedevilled by the mistaken priority given to Bomber Command by Churchill, and the almost paranoiac fear of the Air Ministry that the Navy would regain control of land based maritime aircraft. Godfrey, accurately briefed by Clayton and Denning in OIC and by Drake in Room 39, was only concerned that the Navy should have these modern versions of Nelson's frigates. No one would have been better pleased than he if the Royal Air Force had supplied them, but his constant reminders that the photographic reconnaissance needs of the Navy were not being met did nothing to increase his popularity with the Air Staff.

The need for proper air reconnaissance was in no way lessened when the German Navy's Enigma cypher system was penetrated; the two sources complemented each other, cryptanalysis taking over where PRU left off. Nevertheless the information with which OIC was able to provide the Naval Staff and the Fleet was certainly greatly increased both in quality and quantity when German cypher material was captured which enabled BP to make a permanent break into the naval system which had in effect defeated them for so long. This invaluable booty was secured by the boarding of three German trawlers, *Krebs* on 4 March 1941, *München* on 7 May and *Lauenberg* on 25 June. The first capture was made during the course of the Commando raid on the Lofoten Islands; the second two were the result of operations carefully planned by Captain Haines, whom Godfrey had appointed Assistant Director Intelligence Centre (Y) in January of that year. As Godfrey took a very close interest in the work of GC & CS and was well aware of the difficulties being experienced, it is reasonable to suppose that Haines's terms of reference specifically included the planning and execution of just such 'pinches', and Haines himself went to sea with the cruisers which caught *München*. It is now clear that they were even more successful than has previously been supposed and that the very gallant boarding of U110 on 8 May, which also yielded a valuable haul of cypher material, was only an added bonus. These were coups in the true Hall tradition and their importance to the eventual defeat of the German Navy can hardly be over-estimated.

Godfrey was rightly confident that Clayton, Denning and Winn would make effective use of this new source of knowledge, but there were serious problems about how and to whom it should be communicated. Room 40's greatest weakness had been that it was too secret, but too wide a distribution of the golden eggs of cryptanalysis would sooner or later result in the demise of the goose which laid them. A carefully chosen list of officers to be indoctrinated was submitted to the Prime Minister. Churchill had of course, and very properly, been kept fully informed of GC & CS's successes and was already accustomed to receiving all the significant information provided by the 1940 breaks into the German Air Force and Army cyphers. Indeed, he had commanded that he be shown all the most important decrypts raw and in full as soon as received and translated. Like many others in positions of supreme authority, he distrusted the views of his Intelligence staffs and preferred to make his own evaluation of the material. Individual German naval decrypts did not lend themselves to such a procedure. They were almost always meaningless unless studied as a whole and in conjunction with every scrap of information from all other sources. Godfrey eventually managed to obtain the great man's agreement to his suggestion that a daily summary of digested naval information be prepared for him by NID. Two other minor problems arose. The list of individuals to whom it was proposed that the knowledge of this Special Intelligence should be imparted had to be submitted for the Prime Minister's approval. It was returned with the name of Clayton, Deputy Director Intelligence Centre, the one officer above all others concerned with its use, struck through in red ink. This was quickly put right but the incident did not show any great understanding on the part of Churchill of the workings of NID. Secondly, A. V. Alexander, the First Lord, was not included on the list. This must have been done on the instructions of the Prime Minister, but it caused Godfrey some difficulty. Alexander was at least aware of the existence of Special Intelligence and made repeated demands to see it. Godfrey eventually approached Sir John Anderson, the overlord for Home Affairs. "I needed advice, and if necessary backing, and thought that I could not do better than consult Sir John, who had the reputation for great wisdom combined with a deep knowledge of the workings of government both on the ministerial and on civil service level. He received me promptly and very cordially. I explained my dilemma and, as was his custom, he turned the problem over carefully in his mind and asked me to come and see him again in three days' time. When I returned and before he delivered his judgement (he looked rather like a judge without a wig), I felt perfect confidence that he had got the right answer and a watertight reason. And he had. The job of the minister in question is, he said, to defend the vote of his department in the House. He has no authority outside that orbit. The acquisition of the information in question is not paid for out of his vote and therefore he has no valid claim to have access to it." Alexander does, in fact, seem to have received some Special Intelligence summaries, but he never had the run of the OIC where all operational decrypts were handled, and many of OIC's most secret appreciations and summaries were specifically stamped 'Not to be shown to 1st Lord'. It all seems a little strange and cannot have helped Godfrey's relations with Alexander, with whom, in all other respects, he seems to have got on very well.

Godfrey did not regard himself as a 'moment to moment' intelligence officer but he was a believer in seeing for himself and forming his own judgements about where his Division needed strengthening or expanding, and in discovering in what respects it could more satisfactorily meet the demands of its 'customers'. He disliked intensely the idea of being desk-bound and made a point of visiting Commanders-in-Chief, Flag and Naval Officers in charge round the British Isles at least twice a year. "I made sure", he wrote, "that their organisa-tion fitted in with NID's and with each others. On these visits I tended to become a sort of unofficial emissary of the Board. Senior naval officers used to pour out their troubles on all sorts of matters unconnected with Intelligence which I was able to convey to the right quarter when I returned to Whitehall. Perhaps they talked more freely to me as I had no personal responsibility for their administration. Naval ports are potential training grounds for Intelligence Officers. A good officer may languish after he has broken the back of his job and Intelligence officers generally told me if they had not got enough to do or were hankering after new experiences or wanted to go to sea, and although this method of gaining information may not be orthodox it seemed to work all right so long as I was completely frank with the senior officer regarding my talk with his subor-dinate. It was after all a compliment that one should value the services of someone he had trained. On the whole senior officers were helpful and as a result of my visits Tower (from Scapa), Birley (from Gib), Montagu (from Hull), Pyke-Nott and others joined NID or were transferred to more important jobs. These visits earned good dividends and when the invasion period started they had given me an invaluable knowledge of our coasts. I also established a personal link with the Fairlight Coastguard station near Hastings and at 8 a.m. daily the Coastguard officer gave me by telephone a weather report, thereby perpetuating a custom that must have been in force in 1066." Godfrey greatly regretted that he never managed to visit either the Mediterranean or the Far East, but although air travel forty years ago in the middle of the war was not quite what it is today, he was in fact planning to make trips to these areas in 1943.

In addition to all these calls on his time, Godfrey had other preoccupations—visits to Bletchley Park and to the Inter Service Topographical Department at Oxford, meetings of the Joint Intelligence Committee, and of the inter-Service Security Board, the setting up of new Sections to deal with propaganda and the work of double agents—and it may well be asked how he was able to keep his finger on the pulse of his Division and not only keep it running sweetly but plan for its future. In the first place he was served by some very talented Deputy and Assistant Directors, Cooke, Clayton, Lamplough, Craig, and Campbell, and by an excellent Civil Assistant, Johns. An extra DDNI (Foreign) had been appointed in the early days and as the Division and the size and number of its component Sections increased, additional assistant directors were also recruited or promoted to take responsibility for specialist functions. They relieved Godfrey of a great deal of administrative work, represented him on some high-level committees, and in the realms of operational intelligence and security handled all day to day matters. This deliberate policy of devolution and delegation did not stop at this level, but was carried down to heads of Sections and even further.

On 1 August 1939, five weeks before war was declared, Godfrey had issued the following instructions: "Each Section is responsible for the collecting and sifting of information. . . . Inside the Admiralty, I wish each Section to be responsible for the promulgation of its own intelligence, and for this purpose the Heads of all Sections have access to members of the Board and Heads of Departments, subject only to the proviso that I am kept informed afterwards. Outside the Admiralty promulgation is initiated direct as in the case of OIC, or through the Information or Geographical Sections, e.g. to Naval Attachés, for work of less immediate nature." In a report to the First Sea Lord at the end of 1942, he wrote, "It was always my aim to select and build up into these posts [Section Heads] men with the right sort of personality and knowledge and, as we do at sea, to thrust responsibility on them even before they were quite ready for it, on the principle that it is only by experiencing responsibility that one can learn to be responsible."

The author can give a small personal example of the lengths to which Godfrey carried this policy. When, in the latter half of 1940, as a very newly promoted RNVR Lieutenant, he was made OIC's 'expert' on merchant raiders, Godfrey arranged that he should submit reports direct to the Assistant Chief of Staff (Foreign), Godfrey's old friend Bobbie Harwood, the victor of the River Plate, and that he should even give a brief talk on the problem to the assembled Naval Staff at the end of one of the VCNS's regular morning meetings.

The process of fitting round pegs into round holes was not easy and in some cases it took a little time; but after twelve months special talents and qualities had mostly been recognised and transfers and promotions had resulted in key positions being filled by an exceptionally able band of officers whether active service or retired regular naval officers, RNVRs or civilians. The appointment of Rodger Winn to take over from the ageing Thring in the Submarine Tracking Room is an example of this. Godfrey was a pioneer in delegation and in 'dilution' by giving opportunities to civilians. Having satisfied himself that a particular individual was capable of running his section or department Godfrey left him to it, not without support, that was immediately forthcoming whenever requested, but without day to day interference in matters on which the responsible officer was expected to be more of an expert than his Director. This was a bold decision: Godfrey was consciously and to a very unusual extent placing his reputation in the hands of his subordinates. He was very rarely disappointed. Those, and there were a few, who felt that Godfrey did not interest himself sufficiently in their affairs, failed to realise the compliment that was being paid them. Godfrey correctly saw his task as that of a creator, a builder; once he was satisfied that a particular function was being capably performed, he turned to the next problem that seemed to call for him to put his drive, his influence and his authority behind it.

If the Deputy and Assistant Directors and Section Heads represented the engine room and the armament of this increasingly powerful ship, the bridge, with its radar and signalling apparatus, consisted of Godfrey's personal staff and his 'Coordinating Section', the famous Room 39. Ian Fleming has already been introduced, but this is a short description of his duties which he himself wrote at Godfrey's request after the war: 'In wartime much use is made by the DNI of civilian contacts outside Whitehall and a large proportion of his contacts in his own Division are with civilians in Naval uniform. The DNI found it convenient to canalise the majority of these through an RNVR officer who acted as his Personal Assistant. This officer had command of three languages and widespread outside interests and contacts. As a result "bright" suggestions by the many brilliant civilians working with junior rank in the NID often received more encouragement than if they had gone through the normal Head of Section channel to the DNI. In fact the DNI found his PA of use in most matters not directly connected with the naval Service. This officer was also a convenient channel for confidential matters connected with subversive and clandestine organisations and for undertaking confidential missions abroad, either alone or with the DNI. The DNI also found it convenient to have an officer not connected with ordinary Sectional duties to represent him on Inter-Service and Inter-departmental Committees at a level not requiring his presence or that of the Deputy Director.' Fleming also took over the function of Intelligence planning for which, in Godfrey's words, "he had a very marked flair".

Fleming was complemented by a Personal Secretary, Ted Merrett, the Captain's guest in *Repulse*. Godfrey was a believer in Jacky Fisher's theory of the benefits of intelligent nepotism and he had recruited Ted at the beginning of the war to investigate rumours that the skippers of Dutch coasters were acting as German spies. Merrett had a Dutch wife and business connections in the Netherlands and was soon able to prove that these reports, like so many others at the time, were completely without foundation. After the Fall of France he became Godfrey's Private Secretary. If Fleming was often the spark in the magneto of the DNI's machine, Merrett was the oil can. He was the kindest and most understanding of men with the ability to make friends everywhere and had at least one amiable contact in almost every Admiralty Division, Government Ministry, Foreign Embassy or local police force, who would willingly accede to unusual requests for help at short notice and without going through the official channels. He smoothed feathers ruffled by his master's impatience or irascibility, he helped solve the personal problems of NID's expanding and very mixed staff, he arranged details of Godfrey's official and personal entertaining and travelling, drafted letters of condolence, congratulation and assisted him in his intimate relations with his staff by bringing to his attention cases of loss, illness, bereavement or hardship. Godfrey referred to Merrett as "the benevolent spirit. Not being in uniform was a source of strength. By some process, of which he alone knew the secret, he succeeded in gaining the confidence and affection of the heads or subordinates of all the civilian branches which serve the Navy so loyally. All opposition to his demands melted when subjected to his benevolent approach—an approach which paid such attention and solicitude to the feelings, rights and prestige of others. Those whom he visited knew perfectly well that his object was to get something out of them without using the cumbersome official channels, but they enjoyed his visits, he made them laugh and they did what he asked. Ted was also very good at conveying unpleasant messages and pieces of information in a way that left no sting, a quality which, I am afraid, I exploited mercilessly." An Admirable Crichton if ever there was one, without whose devoted services both Godfrey himself and the Division as a whole would have been greatly the poorer.

The Co-ordinating Section, NID17, grew up gradually. This is how Donald McLachlan, who was one of its members, describes it in his book whose title, *Room 39*, was taken from the number of the room it occupied: 'NID17 . . . has been called a power station, a clearing house, a brains trust . . . It is true this personal staff generated much power, representing as they did the Admiralty's interest on some of the most important committees of the British and Allied war machine . . . Keeping the machine working; receiving ideas and facts; and seeing that they reached the right departments and were not then ignored; forming a body of day to day opinion which could be quoted as the NID view—this was also part of the function. . .'. Godfrey himself has this to say about the section which "occupied the big room next door to my office. As far as I know it never had a head, nor would a 'head' in the way that the word is usually accepted in the Service, have been tolerated. Room 39 consisted at one time of two stockbrokers, a schoolmaster, a KC relieved by a most eminent barrister, a journalist, a collector of books on original thought, an Oxford classical don, a barrister's clerk, an insurance agent, two regular naval officers, an artist, two women civilian officers and several women assistants and typists. The atmosphere was more like a commune than one would expect in the nerve centre of an important Division. The noise was terrific. It got so bad that I had a green baize door installed between Room 39 and my room. Everyone had a telephone of his own; some had two or three; they used them incessantly and relentlessly—almost savagely. They enjoyed the click, the clank of the typewriters, and the ebb and flow of humanity and it was with the greatest difficulty that I persuaded them to banish the typists and institute some control over the nomadic marauders from other sections who camped out in the narrow defiles between the desks or crowded around the fireplace . . . They worked like ants and their combined output staggered the imagination. They put up patiently and kindly with my admonitions and upbraidings. Individually and collectively they always made me feel at home and showed no signs of annoyance when the one, two, three or four strokes on my bell summoned one of their company to my room . . . How was it that this Section, which grew up in almost ragamuffin conditions, with so little parental guidance, except rebukes and recriminations—how was it that Room 39 achieved such phenomenal success, and was so much admired inside and outside the Admiralty? The answer may be found in the mutual respect and the close personal friendships which grew rapidly between the naval officer and civilian, whether in the uniform of the RNVR or not. The keeness to understand the ways of the Navy and to submit to its discipline were evidence of their eagerness to pull their weight and to accept as big a share of responsibility as could be entrusted to them. The atmosphere of cheerfulness and mutual aid, which emanated from Room 39, was not without its effect on me and on the rest of the Division."

By the spring of 1941 Godfrey had completed more than two years as DNI. The Division had fully found its feet and although much work still remained to be done it was now functioning with great efficiency. Godfrey therefore had every reason to expect that he would soon receive the sea appointment in command of a cruiser squadron promised him by Pound and which he so greatly desired. However, sometime in the middle of the year the First Sea Lord sent for him to explain that it was now his policy to appoint to important sea commands those who had already done well at sea under war conditions and to retain in key jobs ashore officers who had given evidence of their aptitude for such work. It was a sensible enough policy but it was a great disappointment for Godfrey. Splendid staff officer though he was, he longed to be back at sea, while the lack of such an appointment appeared to rule out any hopes of eventual promotion to the rank of Vice-Admiral on the active list. However, he had had to refuse requests from many of his own staff to go to sea and he accepted Pound's decision loyally and without question. It was, after all, a sign of approval of his performance during the past two testing years.

CHAPTER TEN

Three Views or One

THE END of 1941 and the opening months of 1942 were marked by a series of crushing disasters for Britain and America. Four hours after the attack on the US Pacific Fleet at Pearl Harbor on the 8 December the Japanese had invaded the British Crown Colony of Hongkong. Two days later they sank Tom Phillips' flagship *Prince of Wales*, and Godfrey's old command, *Repulse*, while they were attempting to interfere with reported Japanese landings in Siam and north Malaya. Within two months Singapore, the supposedly impregnable fortress, had capitulated and it was not many more weeks before the Phillipines, the Dutch East Indies and Burma had been subjugated. Could these catastrophes, which had more far reaching effects on the British Empire than any defeat it had suffered since Cornwallis surrendered at Yorktown in 1781, have been foreseen and prevented? Was faulty Intelligence to blame? Did the Naval Intelligence Division, with its world wide responsibilities, fail?

The short answer to the last question is No. The potential threat from Japan had been fully recognised as long ago as the twenties and much thought had been given by the Chiefs of Staff as to how it could be met. The oft delayed creation of the Naval Base at Singapore, the first tentative conversations with the American Navy, wartime plans to reinforce the garrison and to increase the RAF strength in Malaya so that the territory could be held until a strong British fleet had been assembled and brought to the scene, all these show the concern of the authorities in Whitehall. The course of the war in Europe in 1940 and 1941 unfortunately proved to the hilt the contention of the Chiefs of Staff that Britain, on her own, could not successfully resist a simultaneous attack by the Germans, Italians and the Japanese. Without the whole-hearted and active co-operation of the United States British possessions in the Far East could only be defended if the Mediterranean were to be abandoned. The crippling of the US Pacific Fleet at Pearl Harbor removed this last hope of avoiding wholesale disaster.

In 1936, in the face of the growing menace from Japan, an inter-Service Intelligence centre, the Far East Combined Bureau, had been set up in Hongkong, a compromise between the Army's desire to locate it in Shanghai and the Navy's preference for Singapore. It was, however, realised from the outset that Hongkong would be indefensible in any war with Japan and on 29 August 1939 the FECB moved to Singapore. The FECB, which contained a cryptanalysis section in direct touch with GC & GS in London, and a replica of the Admiralty's Operational Intelligence Centre, was headed by a naval captain who was responsible to the DNI but who was also Chief of Intelligence Staff to the naval Commander-in-Chief, China Station. The FECB nevertheless served all three Services, and kept in close touch with all the local Intelligence organisations throughout its vast area, which extended from Suez eastwards to Panama, and with our Embassies and Legations and with the Secret Intelligence Service. It drew information from as well as supplying information to London. It was a well thought out and comprehensive organisation, the first example of integrated inter-Service effort in the Intelligence field, and so far as NID was concerned its most important out-station.

Regrettably it was more difficult to extract information from Japan than from any other country in the world, not excluding Soviet Russia, and this difficulty increased every month from 1939 onwards. It is unlikely that the cryptanalysts either in the FECB itself or in GC & CS in England had much success until, in January 1941, the Americans, who had broken into the so-called Japanese 'Purple' diplomatic cypher, supplied the British with two of their Purple machines, probably in exchange for the secrets of the German Enigma system. Just under a year later the Americans cracked the 'Red' cypher used by the Japanese naval attachés and once again passed on their success to the British. The Americans may also originally have been ahead of the British in certain other aspects of Japanese Intelligence, but with a free exchange of information from 1940 onwards both countries should have been equally well informed. Unfortunately the Japanese Navy was considerably more circumspect in its use of wireless than its German counterpart, and the OIC in Singapore did not enjoy the same priceless flow of Japanese naval decrypts as its parent in London did of German ones.

Despite the comparative paucity of information, there was no doubt, either in London or Singapore, about Japanese intentions. An Anglo-Dutch-American conference in Singapore in April 1941 appreciated that Japan's objective was the complete domination of the South East Asia area. Although it was felt that, if the Japanese could be convinced that any aggression would be met by a united response from the three Associated Powers and in view of their commitment in China and the uncertain attitude of Russia, an immediate attack was unlikely, it was recognised that 'such is the national psychology of the Japanese, acts of hysteria which might lead to war must be faced'. It was also clearly stated that in such an event the Japanese could be expected to make a dead set against the US Pacific Fleet upon which the safety of the area principally depended. A surprise attack of the type the Japanese had employed against the Russians at Port Arthur in 1904 and more recently against the Chinese in Mukden and Shanghai was clearly envisaged. By the end of November the FECB had noticed a homeward movement of all Japanese merchant ships which would be completed by the first week of December. They concluded that war would follow almost immediately. Certain precautionary measures were therefore taken. One of them was increased air reconnaissance, which in fact detected the large Japanese Malayan invasion convoy and caused Phillips to sail on his ill-fated attempt to intercept it.

It will be seen that there are no grounds for accusations of Intelligence failures here. The three-way exchange of information between the FECB and NID and GC & CS was in fact excellent, but there have been suggestions that Godfrey was not interested in the Far East and that, as a result, the Naval Staff were not kept as fully informed as they should have been. To anyone who had known Godfrey during his two commissions in China such an accusation would be surprising and it is categorically denied by Commander Patrick Barrow-Green, who dealt with all the most secret Japanese operational intelligence in the OIC. He was responsible for briefing the First Sea Lord and the Naval Staff and his chief, Godfrey. The suspicion probably arose from a misunderstanding of the DNI's policy of devolution and of his insistence that his 'experts' should deal direct with the authorities rather than that he should do so himself. Quite apart from this, information was also reaching the War Office, Air Ministry, Foreign Office and the Joint Intelligence Committee and any shortcomings on the part of NID would have been quickly noted and castigated.

There were, of course, some mistakes. The efficiency of the Japanese Navy's Air Arm, the great superiority of their 'Long Lance' torpedo and the skill and boldness of the high command were underestimated, but such underestimates were shared by the US Navy and similar misapprehensions existed about the Japanese Army. Probably no one had realised how much the Japanese had improved since their poor performance in Shanghai in 1932. It is nevertheless interesting to note that in September 1940 Churchill considered that 'The NID are very much inclined to exaggerate the strength and efficiency of the Japanese' and his decision to despatch *Prince of Wales* and *Repulse* to the Far East in the mistaken belief that two unsupported capital ships would deter the Japanese was taken against the advice of the Naval Staff. No, the inevitable gaps in British knowledge of the Japanese Navy and its movements cannot have influenced the final outcome. Political miscalculations in London and the unrealistic attitude of the civil authorities on the spot made it all the more disastrous, but its basic cause was the stark fact that the British just did not have the sea and air forces available to defend the area. The totally unforeseen crippling of the US Fleet in Pearl Harbor made a desperate situation hopeless.

It is impossible to describe Godfrey's career as Director of Naval Intelligence without constantly reverting to the early months of the war because so many of the developments which he initiated, both in purely Naval and in inter-Service Intelligence, had their beginnings before the middle of 1940. Although this does not make the task of his biographer or that of the reader easy, it does show his unusual ability not only to see what was required at any given moment but, even more, to forecast what was going to be needed in the future. It is also a tribute to his exceptional drive and energy that so many different projects were pushed forward successfully at one and the same time.

One of the most brilliant and successful of his creations was the Inter Service Topographical Department. Topography, according to the *Concise Oxford Dictionary*, is the 'detailed description, representation on map etc. of natural and artificial features of a town, district etc.'. Accurate information of this sort, essential for the success of any landing on enemy territory, whether large or small, had been entirely lacking at the Dardanelles in 1915 and, again, in Norway in 1940 where some officers are said to have had little more information than that contained in the 1912 Baedeker and the majority even less than this. Total war demands total Intelligence, but this need had not been foreseen in the inter-war years or if it had no funds had been provided to assemble and keep up to date information of this type about almost every country in the world. The ISTD was conceived, nurtured and brought to maturity, in the face of initial apathy in other departments, almost entirely as a result of Godfrey's vision, drive and enthusiasm. Starting in March 1940 with a staff of one, its numbers had grown to 17 by the end of that year, to 72 by the end of 1941, and were then doubled and redoubled to reach a figure of 541 on 31 December 1944. This was empire building on a grand scale, but then, from June 1940 onwards, no single Commando, hardly an agent of SOE and certainly no major Allied force set foot on German or Italian held territory without the benefit of detailed information about the terrain and its natural and man-made features and characteristics supplied by ISTD. Admiral Sir Andrew Cunningham said that the work of ISTD got 'Torch', the invasion of North Africa, off to 'a flying start' and that it had been executed with 'speed and great accuracy'. Godfrey drew the attention of the Board to this in a minute dated 17 November, in which he wrote, "As a comprehensive piece of good craftsmanship and editing the work is probably unique and I doubt if a commander of an expedition has ever before been given his intelligence in such a complete and legible form. General Eisenhower has written a very nice letter of thanks." Pound remarked 'This is a great achievement' to which, Alexander, the First Lord, added 'I agree'. The value which came to be attached to the work of ISTD is also shown by the fact that it was copied by the Americans in the Pacific, that Eisenhower readily agreed to the attachment of American officers to its staff, and that Mountbatten insisted that one of its leading members, Commander Hughes, establish a similar organisation for him in his South East Asia Command.

The story of ISTD is told in some detail in one of the most fascinating chapters of Donald McLachlan's splendid book, *Room 39*, but here we must confine ourselves mainly with Godfrey's achievement in establishing and developing an inter-Service organisation which enormously aided the ability of the Allies to go over to the offensive, which facilitated the task of the Commanders concerned and thereby must have saved thousands of British and American lives.

When fully developed ISTD consisted of a number of geographical sections, each under an editor, producing final reports for specific areas from information assembled from a variety of sources—its own experts on beaches, port facilities, climate, railways, economics, geology, fire susceptibility etc., and from its Contact Register, which contained the names of thousands of individuals and organisations with specialist knowledge of particular areas and installations. In addition the Admiralty Photographic Library, another wing of the department, contained an absolutely unique collection of photographs, which were used to illustrate the Inter Service Information Series or *ISIS* reports as they were appropriately named, since the Department was located at Oxford. The Oxford University Press was responsible for printing and binding the final versions giving them that touch of authority and authenticity which no 'amateur' production could ever have achieved. The head of the Department was a Colonel of Marines, S. J. Bassett, the chief editor, an Oxford classical don, A. F. Wells, and the staff included not only Naval hydrographers, Royal Engineers and RAF specialists, but some of the brightest minds from the Universities, and experts from the publishing and advertising world. Although, from the very beginning the Department set out to serve the three Services equally, and to provide topographical information to SOE, the SIS or indeed to any 'customer', it grew from a tiny section of the Naval Intelligence Division and was paid and administered until the end by the Admiralty.

Godfrey was well aware at the outbreak of war that NID was sadly lacking in topographical knowledge and within a few weeks he had approached the geographical departments of Oxford and Cambridge Universities for help. Several reports were prepared but the difficulty with such limited resources was to predict in advance the areas on which to concentrate. In January 1940 Godfrey asked the Operations and Plans Divisions of the Naval Staff for as much notice as possible of their likely requirements but very soon afterwards received a rebuke from Tom Phillips for NID's inability to produce information about the Finnish arctic port of Petsamo. Godfrey countered by pointing out that all the staff of his Division were occupied on current intelligence and that they simply had no time for research, even on areas actually affected or threatened by war. He therefore requested and obtained permission to recruit one or two specialists to collect and collate topographical intelligence to satisfy current and future needs.

In World War I Hall had set up a section, NID32, composed mostly of part-time civilians recruited from the Universities, to produce a series of geographical handbooks, but, like so much other valuable intelligence work, this had perforce been discontinued after 1919 and was in any case more of educational than operational value. However, an ex-member of the Section, H. J. Paton, White's Professor of Moral Philosophy at Oxford, was available to give Godfrey advice and on his recommendation, A. F. Wells, Fellow and Praelector in Classics at University College was selected to tackle the job. He joined NID on 28 March, less than a fortnight before the German invasion of Norway. Once again, by knowing where to go for advice, Godfrey had made a superb choice. Margaret Godfrey, who was herself to become an invaluable member of ISTD, writes, "Freddie was a perfectionist. The clarity of his mind was mirrored in the clarity of his writing where he insisted on the right word and the highest standards. He analysed the reports of the other experts and no discrepancies slipped through. Rather frail with fair hair and blue eyes with a boyish twinkle, he looked too young to hold the post of principal editor (which he eventually occupied), but this he did with distinction. He recruited other distinguished classical scholars with double firsts who were the ideal editors of the different geographical Sections. The complete reliability of all the ISTD reports stemmed from his example."

Wells, however, had to start from scratch and he was entirely a one man band. Godfrey was convinced that "somewhere in Great Britain there was an authority on any subject or place if one could only find him or her". The terms of reference he gave Wells were to discover and make contact with any sources of topographical intelligence in the country which might be exploited to fill the empty files in NID; sources such as shipping companies and business firms engaged in foreign trade, magazines, newspapers and technical publications, tourist and photographic agencies, travellers and explorers, and geographical and other learned departments of the Universities.

In the middle of May 1940 the Chiefs of Staff instructed the Joint Intelligence Committee to examine the state of topographical intelligence in the three Service ministries. The answer was not, of course, at all satisfactory. Godfrey suggested to his colleagues on the JIC that each Intelligence Director should be assisted by an Assistant Director for Topography and that a small inter-Service committee be formed to work under the JIC. This was far-sighted because events were to prove that of all fields of Intelligence Topography most demanded an integrated, inter-Service approach. Unfortunately his recommendations did not find favour with the others, who thought that *ad hoc* co-operation would meet the mark. The JIC did however recommend that all three Services should increase their staffs to deal with the subject. Godfrey did not wait for higher authority but at once created a new Section, NID6, consisting of Wells, Captain E. F. B. Law RN, borrowed from the Hydographer, a secretary, Mrs Pipon, and, to head the new unit, Sam Basset, who he knew had carried out a useful coastal survey of Madagascar and who had been one of his students at the Staff College. Sam Bassett, like Freddie Wells, was the right man for the job. The only office that could be secured for the new section was a converted lavatory outside Room 39!

NID6 was immediately inundated with requests for information—about the Rhine-Main-Danube Canal, the Canary Islands, the Azores, the Zeiss works at Jena, bridges in Iceland, corn-growing areas in Italy, Irish lochs and the height of the breakwater at Mers-el-Kebir behind which Admiral Gensoul's squadron lay. But when it tried to co-ordinate its work with that of the parallel sections which it was assumed would have been set up in the War Office and the Air Ministry, it was found that neither of these Ministries had created or intended to create such specialist organisations. They would be content to rely on the services of NID6. This was an unexpected compliment but it did not help to lessen the pressure on the Section. The first beach reconnaissances of the French coast were carried out between 11 and 18 June just ahead of the advancing Germans, and with this and information obtained in London, NID6 produced its first consecutive beach report in the form of photographs pasted into brown paper of folio size linked by text. It covered, by a curious coincidence, the same stretch of coastline as that for which a report was demanded four years later by the planners of Operation Neptune, the invasion of France. And so it went on—Dakar, the inland waterways of Germany, the Corinth Canal, Tangier-Ceuta, and Malaga were some of the areas upon which information was requested in the hectic summer and autumn of 1940. Somehow it was all assembled and supplied, often at only forty-eight hours notice.

For some time Godfrey had been considering moving the Section to Oxford and with the onset of the Blitz this became urgent. After consultation with Professor Kenneth Mason, who had already done work for Godfrey, the Section was successfully moved in the middle of October to the School of Geography at Oxford. The advantages, apart from the freedom from bombing, were obvious. Not only was all the expertise of the University readily at hand but so also were the services of a first class printer, the Oxford University Press. Godfrey had not forgotten the help he had received from the Egyptian Government Press twenty-five years earlier and was fully conscious of the greater confidence which professional presentation would give to the users of NID6's reports. Not only did the Oxford University Press have an unrivalled reputation for the quality of its work but it was already printing the Navy's codes and cyphers and was thus accustomed to the stringent security procedures which the Section's work demanded. It was this, as much as anything else, which prompted a move to Oxford rather than to Cambridge, where the Scott Polar Research Institute and Geographical Department had also been carrying out work for NID and where Godfrey had maintained the contacts he had made during his few months at Sidney Sussex before his time at Greenwich. The work of his new Section fascinated Godfrey and he gave it a great deal of attention, negotiating personally with Douglas Veale, the Registrar of the University, and with Dr J. Johnson, the head of the OUP, who appointed his deputy Mr Batey, the Assistant Printer, to carry out liaison with the Section. Godfrey visited Oxford regularly every Wednesday on his day off, "a weekly interlude in the academic atmosphere of the great University much to my liking and a real and very acceptable change and refreshment". On his return to the Admiralty he was completely up to date with the needs of the new Department and able to tackle the Admiralty Secretariat, the Treasury, the Chiefs of Staff Committee or the JIC to secure the man and women power and the space and equipment which NID6's rapid expansion demanded. Stereoscopic and photographic equipment, a Wild machine similar to that used by the Aircraft Operating Company at Wembley, the requisitioning of Manchester College, supplies from America—these were but a few of the problems with which he dealt.

The Section was receiving imperative requests for information from the War Cabinet Offices, the Joint Planning Committee, Combined Operations Headquarters, the Admiralty, the War Office, the Air Ministry, the SIS, and SOE, and it was obvious that it was hopelessly understaffed. One of the first reinforcements it received was the DNI's wife, Margaret, who became Bassett's Personal Assistant. Bassett was at first a little worried that she had been sent there as a 'spy', but when he found that she would tackle any job, no matter how humble or at what hour and that she was the soul of discretion, he realised that he had got a treasure. She soon graduated from sticking in photographs to acting as liaison officer with Godfrey's own co-ordinating Section, Room 39, through whom requests for information were channelled. She also took over the task of liaison with the OUP. In an official report written towards the end of the war, Wells said that 'She used to receive Mr Batey or Mr Thompson, his deputy, and hand over to them the text, photographs and maps ready for printing and go the rounds of the sections with them to discuss with the editors any points of printing on which the editors wished to give special instructions or required technical advice. The editorial system was the natural outcome of the production of comprehensive reports compiled by many contributors (and therefore bound to be inconsistent in material and formal respects), and also of the decision to print. It was therefore valuable to the editors, who to begin with knew little or nothing about printing, to have direct consultation with the printers, which liaison through Mrs Godfrey allowed. She herself controlled the printing-timetable as a whole and took special responsibility for preparing all the maps and photographs or other illustrations for the Press. In this she relieved the editors of a great deal of complicated work which would otherwise have fallen on them.' After she left to join her husband in India it was found necessary to form a Central Administrative Unit under a Lieutenant Colonel to carry out the duties she had performed almost single-handed, though it is true the volume of work had continued to grow by leaps and bounds.

This is, however, to anticipate. By September 1940 the short-comings of the compromise put forward by the JIC in May were becoming apparent, and, once more prompted by Godfrey, the Committee recommended the formation of a combined topographical organisation to act as a Central Clearing House for all requests. It further proposed that these requests be channelled through the JIC and that a liaison officer be appointed to act as a link between the Central Clearing House and the Joint Planning Committee and to produce lists of priorities. By December the Directors of Intelligence at the War Office and the Air Ministry had at last accepted the need to expand the Section on proper inter-Service lines, something which Godfrey had advocated from the outset, and some Army and RAF officers were appointed. It was not however until October 1941 that the Section was given the name which correctly reflected its constitution and responsibilities, the Inter Service Topographical Department. As already remarked it continued throughout to be administered and paid (miserably) by the Admiralty.

Three essential adjuncts to ISTD, equally creations of Godfrey's, must be mentioned. Wells' efforts to obtain information from all and sundry in the early days had been most rewarding but he had only been able to scratch the surface, and with the move to Oxford a new Section, NID21, had to be set up in London to exploit all these sources to the full. First under Lieutenant Robert Harling RNVR and then under Lieutenants Hippesley-Cox and Reilly RNVR, the Contact Register grew in an astonishing manner until by 1943 there was hardly an area in the world or a likely subject without the name of some specialist recorded on the 10,000 cards in its index. Experts of all sorts, whether employees of engineering or commercial firms, refugees from Europe, or retired Merchant Navy Officers were relentlessly tracked down and interviewed. Godfrey's belief that somewhere in Britain an expert on almost anything could be found was proved over and over again. It was safer and far more efficient than sending a spy to try to obtain the information on the spot.

Illustrations were an essential part of all the *ISIS* reports and the Admiralty Photographic Library which remained an NID Section, housed in the basement of the Bodleian Library at Oxford under F. M. Wonnacott of the British Museum, contained and reproduced the thousands of photographs obtained not only from commercial firms and agencies but sent in by private individuals who had responded in an unprecedented way to an appeal by the DNI over the radio. The collection was far and away the largest and most valuable of its kind ever assembled in Britain or for that matter in any other country.

The third Section which supplemented, in a rather more permanent form, the work of ISTD was NID5, the successor to NID32. NID5 under Professor Mason at Oxford and J. Wordie at Cambridge produced a fresh and up-to-date series of Geographical handbooks. They were designed for the use of an occupying power and contained all the information needed by a temporary or permanent civil or military government. Godfrey had wanted the series to be world wide, but after he left NID and despite the protests of his successor, a short-sighted Deputy Secretary of the Admiralty considered that 'the Geographers have dug themselves in to a congenial task, and have no incentive to complete it and be thrown out of Government work'. This extremely short-sighted and unjust judgement resulted in the work being closed down before the series was finished, but copies of the Handbooks still surviving are collectors' pieces, eagerly sought after by officials of other governments and by private individuals.

The real proof of the need for ISTD and its associated Sections, and of its complete success in satisfying that need, is shown by the countless demands for its services made from its inception in 1940 right up to VE Day in 1945 by all the Services and by almost every Commander-in-Chief. The Department's creation, administration and growth owed so much to Godfrey's personal interest that if this had been his only achievement as DNI, it would have been sufficient to establish him as a truly great Intelligence chief and one of the earliest and most ardent advocates of an integrated inter-Service Intelligence organisation.

Before turning to other examples of Godfrey's preoccupation with inter-Service Intelligence, it may be of interest to give his own impressions of a typical day in his life at this time. "I lived in a first-floor flat lent me by Reggie Hall at 36 Curzon Street, next door to the Curzon Cinema and over Martin's Bank. By installing a direct hand-operated telephone line in my bedroom I maintained touch with the Duty Intelligence Officer in Room 39 and with the Duty Officer in the Operational Intelligence Centre. Sleep was precarious due to air-raids but during periods of wakefulness the mind was very much on the alert and usually concentrated on some intractable problem which jostled for priority with the variety of things that must not be forgotten. To fortify my memory I made a pencil note of all these matters and can strongly recommend this method of putting one's mind at rest. I was apprehensive, not that a satisfactory solution could not be devised but that I might forget. Sometimes when I finally woke up I found that I had covered two or three sheets of foolscap.

"6.30. Woke up or was awakened by a telephone call from the Duty Officer who gave me a summary of events on land during the night and then switched me over to OIC who told me what had gone on at sea. I then browsed over my nocturnal notes for an hour or worked on some paper. I found 6.30 to 7.30 was the most prolific hour of the day.

"7.45. Breakfast.

"8.15. Walk to the Admiralty across the Green Park and sometimes round the pumped-out pond in St James' Park, but more often by the North West door or the private entrance (on the Horse Guards) and usually arrived just as the charladies were leaving.

"On arrival I finished off the notes on the brain waves accumulated during my wakeful hours and with the help of Joyce Cameron [his most efficient secretary] reduced them to memoranda, instructions or queries so that action could be initiated in the right direction. A quick visit to OIC and glance through the Foreign Office and other telegrams followed and at about 9 a.m. Mrs Fenley brought me the night's Special

Intelligence summaries from NID12 [Naval Section BP]. She
was followed by Paymaster Captain Woodhouse or Commander
Pearce [his Naval Secretariat] with current papers. Then a
word with Ted Merrett and Ian Fleming and the day had
really started.

"Churchill's 'prayers', so called because they usually started
'Pray inform me . . .' or 'Pray why has . . . not been done?' also
arrived at about 9.30. They were dictated last thing at night.
The wording was insistent, frequently harsh, and an answer
was usually demanded by a certain time, say 5 p.m. They were
ultimata with an imminent time limit but were usually irrelevant to the main issues with which we were struggling and had
no war winning potential. They put one on the defensive,
added greatly to the strain and provided an ugly ingredient in
our forenoon work. It was now that I appreciated the qualities
of Ian Fleming. He took the prayers in his stride and, being less
well disciplined then I, did not attach the same importance to
their menacing wording. Usually by lunch time he had got to
the heart of the matter.

"The period 10 a.m. to 12.45 p.m. was normally devoted to
conferences and interviews. The Joint Intelligence Committee
followed by the weekly meeting of the three Intelligence heads
with the Chiefs of Staff took place on Tuesdays.

"Afternoons were mostly taken up in pre-arranged interviews
and in meetings with members of my staff and it was not until
after 4 p.m. that I was generally able to cope with the contents
of my In-basket. Papers that needed prolonged study I took
home with me and worked at after dinner, returning to the
Admiralty about 9 p.m. for a couple of hours.

"About once a fortnight I visited Bletchley Park, Medmen-
ham [The Central Interpretation Unit of the RAF's Photographic Reconnaissance Unit] and [usually once a week] ISTD
at Oxford, and other country departments. The ISTD never
grew quickly enough and called for a good deal of personal
effort at all levels."

This long and tiring routine was perhaps no more demanding
than that of many other senior members of the Naval Staff.
What was unusual was the great variety of problems, many of
them quite outside the experience of the average naval officer,
to which solutions had to be found or on which decisions had
to be given or obtained. Godfrey wrote after the war that "The

real interest of a DNI's job consists not so much in the commodity with which he is dealing but with the constant calls it
makes on his judgement, energy, patience and courage at
uncertain and unexpected but very frequent intervals. Constantly at such times the human element is the main factor,
whether it is in your staff, your clients, your critics, your
colleagues, the enemy or yourself."

The problems of what would now be called 'man management' in NID were daunting. For three years the Division was
in a state of continuous, rapid and violent expansion. Old
sections doubled and redoubled in size. New sections were being
added, new responsibilities assumed, new methods employed.
It was all part of a disciplined, fighting Service but to an ever-
increasing extent its staff consisted not of regular naval officers
but of civilians, whether in or out of uniform, with different
backgrounds, ambitions and outlooks. Many were watch-
keepers, twenty-four hours on and forty-eight off; for all, the
working day was long and the physical conditions, by modern
office standards, shocking. There was no Mess, no organised off
duty recreation, none of the means by which a ship or regiment
or even a well-run civilian business normally builds up and
maintains esprit de corps or corporate spirit. The captain of a
battleship or aircraft carrier, with complements of up to two
thousand men, was necessarily a somewhat remote figure to
most of his crew, but at least they all saw him at Sunday
Divisions, ship's concerts or football matches from time to
time. DNI, however much he might try to pay regular visits to
OIC, ISTD or any other of the major departments of his
Division, had an even more difficult task in impressing his
personality on the staff of the twenty or so NID Sections within
the Admiralty, let alone those in the out-stations in this country
and overseas.

Despite all this, the spirit and morale throughout NID was,
with a few exceptions, excellent. Godfrey's own conviction that
the work of the Division was of supreme importance, that it
was, in its way, a 'war winner' spread downwards through his
Deputies and through Room 39 and the Section Heads to every
member of the staff, however humble his or her role. The fact
that the Director was irascible, impatient, at times unreasonably demanding and unsympathetic to excuses, that he insisted
on the highest standards, and did not suffer fools or the indolent

gladly, did not always inspire a great deal of love. But even those who most resented what they considered to be his 'ruthless, relentless and remorseless' drive for efficiency, recognised that it was achieving results and, however reluctantly, were unstinting in their admiration for their chief's ability. Godfrey certainly had a quick temper, no doubt as a result of the immense pressure of his work and perhaps also because of the piles from which he suffered throughout the war but which he would not have operated on until it was over. On one occasion he hurled an ink-pot, fortunately empty and badly aimed, at Captain Baker-Creswell, an officer whom he both liked and admired. Baker-Creswell prudently withdrew, but within thirty minutes was recalled to finish the interview as though nothing had happened. Campbell and Paymaster Commander Pearce also confess to adopting the technique of ignoring these sudden outbursts, refusing to allow themselves to be provoked and bearing no ill-will afterwards, but another officer recounts that on one occasion he was literally reduced to tears as the only alternative to striking a superior officer! But, as Godfrey himself remarked about Tom Phillips, "as a colleague he cannot have been easy, but then one does not want easy people in war time." McLachlan quotes this description (which Margaret, incidentally, considers inaccurate, not to say unintelligble) of Godfrey by one of his junior officers: 'A tall tapering man, with a head of imposing size and authority balanced upon a heroic torso and the legs of a dancing master. He looked like one of those Western Chinese that the French and Americans reckon Englishmen to be. This impression doubtless derived from the Admiral's unwavering pale blue-grey eyes, set beneath a domed cranium, which could be by turn merry and amused or cold and steely. He talked very clearly and fast in a misleadingly soft voice.' Another officer, however, felt that 'if he smiled he did so with his mouth and face; but not with his eyes; these remained cold, searching, mirthless and hard'. Ewen Montagu, in his book, *Beyond Top Secret U*, while admitting that, in most ways he disliked him as a person, considered that NID was 'a wonderfully efficient organisation, the brilliant creation of one man . . . Godfrey. I have never used the word genius of anyone else. I have been privileged to know many extremely able and wise men, at the Bar, among Judges and among statesmen who came to my father's house when I was a young man, but only to John Godfrey would I give that accolade, certainly as regards intelligence work.' Many of his officers, however, had a genuine affection for him. Campbell, Head of the German Section, and later Deputy Director, Fleming, who probably coined the nickname Uncle John, Robert Harling, who was fascinated by him and has described him as 'this most maverick of all Admirals, outdone in oddity only by Fisher and Hall', Merrett, a life-long friend, McLachlan, Johnson of the Oxford University Press, are some of those who realised that basically Godfrey was a kind and thoughtful man, seeking in many quiet and unexpected ways to promote the well-being and interests of his staff.

His secretary, Joyce Cameron, who was in an excellent position to judge, wrote when he left NID, 'There must be few heads of departments who have taken such an interest in the welfare of their staff as you have done . . .' and many of the other letters which he received at that time express the writers' gratitude for acts of personal kindness.

Godfrey concluded a letter to all members of the Division, written on the fourth anniversary of the outbreak of war, "In an organisation of the present size and distribution of the NID it is impossible for me to meet members of the staff as often as I would wish; but I know that in all its work, whether of administration or research, the human factor is the most important and that the successes which we can justly claim are due to the individual efforts of enthusiastic people who serve on my staff and will, I trust, continue to serve until the war is won."

As the war progressed and the period of desperate defence by Britain gradually changed to one in which plans to go over to the offensive began to assume some imminent reality, the tendency for NID to become involved in problems outside the strictly naval sphere became more pronounced. This was inevitable and desirable for many reasons. Not only did total war demand total Intelligence, but nothing that the Royal Navy did or contemplated doing was without its effects on the prosecution of the war by the other Services and Departments of State, nor was any action of theirs without some influence on the Admiralty. The incredible successes of Bletchley Park in penetrating the German cypher systems produced a mass of information about every aspect of the enemy war effort, army, navy, air force, secret service, diplomatic and economic. The naval content of this Golden Treasury was of course handled by the Operational Intelligence Centre, where immediate minute to minute action was taken to keep the operational authorities in the Admiralty and at sea informed, and where regular and ad hoc summaries and appreciations were also prepared and circulated to those concerned. Godfrey, however, saw that if the First Sea Lord and the other senior members of the Naval Staff were to be able to play their parts on the increasing number of committees, from that of the Chiefs of Staff downwards, by which the conduct of the war was controlled, they must be promptly and fully informed of all the other major facts gleaned from cryptanalysis, Foreign Office telegrams, reports from the SIS and so on. He therefore caused one of his staff in Room 39, the KC Ewen Montagu, whom he had brought into NID in 1940, to prepare daily a digest of all non-operational Top Secret information for circulation to Pound and the Sea Lords. These were the famous 'Orange Summaries' in which facts were clearly differentiated from inferences and deductions to provide an unimpeachable background for the naval decision-makers. Montagu also had to scan all this information with the greatest care to spot the slightest indication of changes in Axis policy and immediately brief his master on its significance. He was also the NID representative on the XX Committee, the inter-Service body concerned with feeding misleading information to the enemy by double agents, and it was typical of Godfrey that he not only selected the right man for the job but gave him great freedom of action and access to all the most precious and secret information so that he could carry out his devious duties with the maximum efficiency. The fact that neither man found the other entirely 'sympathique' in no way impaired an extremely successful working relationship in which each of them fully recognised the other's great abilities.

Another member of Room 39 personally recruited by Godfrey was Donald McLachlan. His wife was one of Margaret's many cousins. Learning that McLachlan was employed on some not very demanding duty in the Intelligence Corps, Godfrey 'cut him out' and got him into naval uniform before the Army realised the magnitude of their loss. After three or four months in the German Section Campbell reported that he was 'ripe' and Godfrey revealed to him his new job. "It was, by means of insidious propaganda, to undermine and destroy the morale of officers and men in the German (and for a time, the Italian) Navy. This was achieved by the use of overt and covert wireless broadcasts, by the distribution of leaflets from the air, by the spreading of rumours and other subversive means. Sefton Delmer, the arch operator of this technique, worked in the Political Warfare Executive (PWE). I had many talks with Tom Delmer and Donald McLachlan and after pondering over the matter for two or three months and familiarising myself with the workings of PWE I came to the conclusion that a small component of PWE, working as an undercover section in NID was an activity that had war-winning attributes, provided it was realistic, ruthless and was provided with an adequate sting. The chief difficulty in starting a new section to operate an entirely new process is to find the right sort of staff. The qualifications for the job were a deep knowledge of German mentality, a capacity to see things from the German point of view and to know what would hurt them most, combined with an instinctive flair for high grade journalism and 'putting things across' in a way that would influence public opinion. In this case public opinion was that of the German navy personnel, their wives and families, and particularly the U-boat fleet. McLachlan possessed these qualities to a marked degree. He had been on the editorial staff of *The Times*, *Times* correspondent in Berlin, a schoolmaster at Winchester and Editor of *The Times Educational Supplement* before he came to NID. He was a terrifically hard worker with very strong nerves. He was ready for the job and also ready to take great responsibilities. I think Donald was genuinely pleased when I asked him after dinner at 36 Curzon Street if he would like the post. He accepted and I then asked him and Ian Fleming to put the machinery in motion for creating a Naval Section (17z) in collaboration with PWE. I was greatly relieved and confident that there would be no lack of sting with him, Ian Fleming and Sefton Delmer in charge. As Section 17z developed I formed the personal view that an element of perfidy, verging on the unscrupulous, was one of the ingredients essential to its success, and that this was being adequately looked after. My principal function was to protect it from internal political interference, from depredations of people who said this 'isn't quite playing the game', and to preserve the anonymity of the men and women who actually did the work. We set up a high-powered cover committee (which never met) to whom was responsible a working group consisting of Captain Charles Lambe (a later and very distinguished First Sea Lord but at that time Deputy Director of Plans Division), Ian Fleming (who represented me as DNI), Donald and when necessary a representative of Operations and Press Divisions." As with Montagu, McLachlan had access to all Britain's most secret sources of information and was given a very free rein by his chief. Difficulties soon arose with the BBC who monitored the script of the German naval programme containing much unpublishable material, but these were overcome and McLachlan began to get involved in the release of special items of naval interest to the BBC in which all the necessary propaganda points were made but from which all material not available to the Press was excluded. This proved so successful that not only he but representatives from the other two Services became more and more involved in PWE's and the BBC's propaganda work.

Evidence regarding the effectiveness of the campaign are conflicting. It often provoked the German propaganda machine into ill-considered and unfortunate counter-action but German naval morale never broke as it had done in 1918. On the other hand there is no doubt that German sailors' relatives did listen to the clandestine broadcasts and it may have been a factor in persuading prisoners of war that their British captors knew all about them, even details of their personal lives, and therefore disposed them to talk more freely than they otherwise would have done. It is in any case an illuminating example of how Godfrey's mind worked, his views on his own role and the methods he employed in setting up a new section.

Several references have already been made to that important and eventually influential body the Joint Intelligence Committee. A brief account of its purpose, work and composition is now overdue. Once again it is necessary to retrace our steps, this time to 1936 when the JIC was formed as a Sub-Committee of the Committee of Imperial Defence. It then consisted of the Deputy Directors of Intelligence of the three Services and it was charged with the co-ordination of Service Intelligence, a task in which little progress was made in the next three years.

It also prepared ad hoc reports for the Joint Planning Committee. We have already seen how, at Godfrey's suggestion, the Situation Report Centre was set up in April 1939 and how this small body merged itself with the JIC. On the outbreak of war the Committee of Imperial Defence ceased to function and the JIC became a Sub-Committee of the Joint Chiefs of Staff, who were, so to speak, in permanent session. Just before this Godfrey had obtained agreement to the appointment of a Counsellor of the Foreign Office to act as Chairman, a position which was filled with great success throughout the war by V. F. W. Cavendish Bentinck. The JIC now comprised the three Directors of Intelligence or their Deputies, assisted by a few officers of Commanders rank from the former Situation Report Centre; it had power to co-opt representatives of any body whom it was desired to consult. The Committee's duties were:

1. To assess and co-ordinate Intelligence received from abroad with the object of ensuring that any Government action which might have to be taken should be based on the most reliable information available.
2. To co-ordinate any Intelligence data which might be required by the Chiefs of Staff or the Joint Planning Committee.
3. To consider any further measures which might be thought necessary to improve the efficient working of the Intelligence organisation of the country as a whole.

In May 1940 the JIC decided that representatives of MI5 (Security), MI6 (Secret Service) and Ministry of Economic Warfare should join the Committee but should attend meetings only when matters of interest to them were to be discussed.

It will be seen that these terms of reference were very wide, involving not only the presentation of an inter-Service Intelligence view to the planners and supreme policy-makers but also the duty of advising on means to improve the efficiency of all intelligence organisations including such bodies as GC & CS and, when it was finally formed, ISTD. There was obviously scope for disagreement within the Committee itself and for friction with departments who did not agree with the JIC's recommendations.

We must now digress briefly to trace the evolution of a subsidiary body which produced draft appreciations which the

JIC considered and, if they thought fit, amended before passing them on to the Joint Planners or Chiefs of Staff. This was the Joint Intelligence Staff. The Italian invasion of Greece at the end of October 1940 had taken Britain (and Germany, for that matter) completely by surprise. As a result it had been suggested that a joint-Service section should be formed to attempt to forecast future energy strategy and policy, and report thereon direct to the Chiefs of Staff, sending copies of their appreciations to the JIC. It was to be provided only with such information as would be available to the enemy. The naval representative was Captain Troubridge, late Naval Attaché in Berlin, and the first secretary was Donald McLachlan, both personally selected by Godfrey. The fact that Mountbatten's name was also considered and the seniority of the Army, Air Force and Foreign Office representatives shows the importance attached to the work of the Future Operations (Enemy) Section (FOES) as it was called. The Section did some useful work, but was unpopular with the War Office because its views, including those of the Army representative, General Mackesy, often differed from those of the CIGS. As a result FOES was summarily abolished and replaced by the slightly less high-powered Advanced Enemy Planning Section (APES) although Troubridge continued as its Chairman. APES was instructed to send its appreciations to the Service Intelligence Departments so that they could, if necessary, be amended before being presented to the JIC and, after still further consideration, to the Chiefs of Staff. This, naturally, resulted in delay and often in an unfortunate watering down of the conclusions in order to arrive at what was the lowest common denominator of agreement among the various Ministries. Eventually, in the spring of 1942, a proposal by Troubridge, strongly backed by Godfrey, was adopted as a result of which APES became the Joint Intelligence Staff of the JIC.

The JIS was given access to all information, not only that available to the enemy, and was able to cross-examine experts from all the Ministries before hammering out an agreed appreciation to send up to its parent, the JIC. Because the naval representatives on the JIS were generally members of NID Godfrey was kept well informed of their activities and the reasoning behind their appreciations, but he in no way influenced their views let alone imposed his own on them. On the contrary, he had the greatest confidence in Troubridge and in his successor Captain J. M. Baker-Creswell, and, having formed his own opinions on the basis of their briefing, refused to compromise or deviate from them. This, unfortunately, was not always the case with the Director of Military Intelligence, who was often subject to considerable pressure from his superiors to fall in with their own pre-conceived ideas. The Joint Intelligence Staff also served the Joint Planners and it was not always possible for them to obtain the approval of their Directors before advising the Planners, so that cases arose of their views being disowned at a higher level. This occurred mostly with the Director of Military Intelligence who did not have the same freedom of action or the same authority in the War Office as Godfrey did in the Admiralty. The Joint Planning Committee came more and more to rely on the Joint Intelligence Staff. Both organisations were located in the War Cabinet Offices, but on different floors and a considerable distance away from each other. The very able Secretary of the JIC, Lt Colonel Denis Capel-Dunn, felt strongly that their offices should be next door to each other. There was a good deal of opposition to this by the Joint Planners, but this was in the end worn down, chiefly by Godfrey and Capel-Dunn, and thereafter co-operation between the two bodies was extremely close.

There were according to Godfrey, two striking examples of outside pressure affecting the work of the JIS. First was the obsession of the soldiers that, during 1941, the Germans had an unlocated army, a masse de manoeuvre in the words of the CIGS, Sir Alan Brooke, of twenty-odd divisions destined for the invasion of this country and not involved as a reserve for the Russian offensive. The second was the War Office view that the German plan was to push through the Caucasus and Persia to Abadan and then to combine with the Japanese in a pincer movement on India. The JIS firmly rejected both these theories but despite this they were more than once advanced by the Director of Military Intelligence at the meetings of the Joint Intelligence Committee. The JIC stuck to the view that the furthest German objective was Baku on the Caspian and that in fact they would never reach it. There is no evidence that this myth of the 'Secret Army' was planted by the Germans. Nevertheless it has a curious parallel in the well-engineered deception foisted on the Germans by Operation Bodyguard that the non-existent First US Army was waiting in England at the time of the invasion of Normandy to descend on the Pas de Calais or elsewhere.

Godfrey's recollections of pressure on the JIS and JIC by the War Office are fully confirmed by Captain Baker-Creswell and his successor Commander Drake, and by their assistant Lieutenant-Commander Fletcher-Cooke, and, which is not open to the charge of Naval bias, by the extremely able Air Force representative, Wing Commander Millis. He writes that he was never subjected to pressure from his superiors 'calculated to impair my ability to exercise a free judgement on the subject under review. The attitude of the DMI, Major General Davidson, showed a marked contrast. I gathered that he invariably reflected the views of Alanbrooke who seemed obsessed with the idea that the Germans had almost to the end of the war a powerful undisclosed reserve of military strength. The result was that the obviously very embarrassed War Office representative was under constant pressure whenever matters of major military importance were under review, to seek to impose on the JIS the pre-conceived view put forward by the Director of Military Intelligence instead of allowing him freely to evaluate with his colleagues the information they had at their disposal from widely different sources. Indeed the DMI went further than that. I can recall three outstanding instances of the written conclusions of the JIS being referred back by him for complete reversal because apparently they did not accord with Alanbrooke's obsession in regard to Germany's undisclosed reserve of military resources.' The three cases cited by Millis were the continuing 'threat' of invasion, the ultimate objective of the German thrust into the Caucasus, referred to above, and the likelihood of a German invasion of Spain as a reaction to the Allied landings in North Africa. In each case the War Office view, or perhaps one should say that of Alanbrooke and Davidson, was eventually overborne by the representatives of the Admiralty, Air Ministry, and Ministry of Economic Warfare, whose appreciations were generally adopted by the parent body, the JIC. Nevertheless Baker-Creswell writes that 'there is no doubt that the JIC sometimes altered the wording of our papers before sending them to the Chiefs of Staff which made Millis absolutely furious. John

Godfrey had complete faith in the JIS and I have no doubt that he fought against these alterations and amendments.'

The task of the Chairman of the Joint Intelligence Committee, Cavendish Bentinck, was not an easy one. He not only had to represent the Foreign Office point of view but to endeavour to guide the Committee to a mutually agreed appreciation for submission to the Chiefs of Staff. He rather overmodestly wrote to Godfrey, 'I often feel the most awful fraud when discussing matters in which I have neither competence nor knowledge'. He certainly must have needed all his diplomatic skill to smooth over views so contradictory as those outlined above. He personally liked and admired Godfrey and states that he would have been prepared to serve under him, rating him in all respects a better Intelligence chief than his colleagues on the Committee, but felt that he did not make sufficient effort to disguise his impatience and sometimes contempt when the others failed to follow his arguments or agree with his views. Godfrey, for his part, had a high opinion of Cavendish-Bentinck. On 18 July 1942 he wrote to Sir Alexander Cadogan, Cavendish-Bentinck's Foreign Office chief, "I do not know if the Chiefs of Staff have ever mentioned it to you, but in case they haven't, I should like you to know how very much we all value the services of Cavendish-Bentinck and the excellent work he is putting in as Chairman of the JIC . . . I felt you should know how I feel about this, and I think I am speaking for my colleagues . . .", to which Cavendish-Bentinck replied, 'Cadogan has shown me the charming letter you wrote him about my work on the JIC. It was very nice of you to write that and I am most grateful . . . you have always been very kind to me, and I have known that if ever there were any problems or troubles, I had only to come to you in order to learn how to deal with them expeditiously and quietly.' Major General Sir Kenneth Strong in *Men of Intelligence* suggests however that Godfrey 'had inherited the traditional mantle of British Naval Intelligence with its air of superiority over the Army and the Air Force: he tended to regard those who differed from the views of the Navy as recalcitrant sailors who must be severely dealt with. He was undoubtedly the dominant personality among the three Service Directors of Intelligence and was a master of the 'broad brush' or sweeping generalisation: seldom did a problem present itself as wholly maritime, but any disposition to ignore the effects of sea power upon it was smartly dealt with. His colleagues were clever men of great detail—a common tendency at least in Army Staff Officers. The two attitudes, the general and the particular—or perhaps the Admiral and the particular, did not blend easily.' They certainly did not when the 'particular' happened to be in the wrong! After all the Joint Intelligence Committee existed to produce the best possible Intelligence appreciations upon which the Chiefs of Staff and the Prime Minister could take sensible decisions, and a compromise solution that 2 and 2 made 3, not 4, was hardly conducive to that.

Strong later remarks that meetings of the JIC with the Chiefs of Staff 'were often difficult as the Chairman, Field Marshal Sir Alan Brooke, was frequently very sceptical of the Intelligence estimates, particularly those produced by the Navy and the Air Force, and had a habit of gobbling like an infuriated turkey when he disagreed with anyone's remarks. He firmly believed that the Army produced the best Intelligence officers, but he was not allowed to have his own way for the Navy argued that because of the danger and unpredictability of the sea, even in peacetime, the naval officer was the more realistic in his estimates . . .' Pound never seems to have made much of a contribution to the meetings of the Chiefs of Staff other than on purely naval matters, indeed there are constant references to his dozing until something nautical was mentioned. It must therefore have been all the more irritating to a man of Alan-brooke's temperament to have his cherished views contested by the Director of Naval Intelligence whether in person or by the Naval and Air Force representatives on the JIS.

Churchill was not at first a great admirer of the Joint Intelligence Committee. He did not like what he called 'this form of collective wisdom'. In August 1940, shortly after the break into the German Enigma system, he had minuted, 'I do not wish such reports as are received to be sifted and digested by the various Intelligence authorities. For the present Major Morton will inspect them for me and submit what he considers of major importance. He is to be shown everything, and submit authentic documents to me in their original form.' Whether this was really the best way for the Prime Minister to receive information about the enemy and form appreciations upon which the proper conduct of the war in part depended is open to doubt. It may have caused him, on occasions, to form views on incomplete evidence, because although the German decrypts always told the truth, they did not always tell the whole truth. Those who differed from the Prime Minister were not popular with him, and the JIC of course considered Intelligence from all sources and arrived at joint, considered opinions as to their significance. It would appear that gradually Churchill came to accept the value of this method, which many now consider to have been one of the reasons for the great superiority of British over German Intelligence.

Godfrey's influence on the Joint Intelligence Committee may have been abrasive, but it was both necessary and, in the end, beneficial. It was essential to counteract the innate suspicion and dislike of Intelligence amongst many senior officers of all three Services, and of the Prime Minister in cases where Intelligence did not support his own views. There was far too great a tendency to rely on hunches rather than on a considered appreciation based on a factual examination of the wealth of reliable information that was increasingly available. Wishful thinking about the true size of the German Army, the effects of area bombing or the need for a greater maritime air effort could not be eradicated by a supine attitude of Very Senior Officer Veneration. On the contrary, it required a stubborn determination to face facts no matter how unpalatable or unwelcome, a high degree of loyalty to and faith in those who, at lower levels, produced those facts, and strong nerves and considerable moral courage to meet the opposition of more pliant colleagues and the hostility or indifference of superiors. Godfrey's refusal to compromise on matters of principle was to cost him his job, but it vastly improved the efficiency and eventual influence of the JIC.

CHAPTER ELEVEN

Dismissal

BY AUGUST 1942 the Naval Intelligence Division had virtually assumed the shape and size which it was to maintain until the end of the war. The many gaps in the organisation which Godfrey had taken over in February 1939 had been filled, weaknesses had been eliminated, new procedures devised and an extremely talented staff appointed to all the key positions. The machine was running smoothly and efficiently in top gear. The Operational Intelligence Centre, although temporarily deprived of decrypts of the Atlantic U-boat traffic, had won the full confidence of the Naval Staff and of the Commanders-in-Chief Home Fleet and Western Approaches and of the Air Officer Commanding-in-Chief of Coastal Command. Co-operation with Bletchley Park was excellent. The Geographical Sections were at last properly manned and able to respond to all the calls made on them. NID6 had been transformed into the Inter-Service Topographical Department, its reputation high with all its many clients. Security, Prisoner of War Interrogation, Deception, Propaganda, Information had all got into their stride. The Co-ordinating Section in Room 39 ensured that nothing was overlooked and that the views of NID were known and respected both inside and outside the Admiralty. Liaison with the other Services and with the Americans was good. The barometer in the Intelligence world seemed to be set fair.

The general war situation had also improved greatly since the beginning of the year. A period of balance had almost been reached. The Battle of the Atlantic had still to reach its climax, but at least the U-boats were being driven from the American coast, and, despite their losses, the convoys were battling through. Rommel had been held at the first Battle of El Alamein and plans for the invasion of North Africa were well advanced. Malta was still holding out. The Americans had won the Battle of Midway and were going over to the offensive at Guadalcanal. All Burma was in Japanese hands but they could advance no further. Russia, although badly mauled, had not collapsed; the Battle of Stalingrad was about to begin. Germany herself was now under nightly assault by Bomber Command. No one expected a swift Allied victory but no one doubted that it would finally be achieved.

Godfrey himself must have felt very satisfied. He had held the post of DNI for three and a half years, longer than any Director since Blinker Hall. Despite the fact that so many of his plans for his Division had now come to fruition, he was not the man to rest on his oars. No organisation was so good that it could not be improved and his restless and enquiring mind would soon discern new Intelligence fields to conquer. Amongst other things he was planning a second trip to the States and then ones to the Mediterranean and the Far East, two areas which he had not so far been able to visit. In May that year Ian Fleming, in a letter to his friend Peter Smithers, Assistant Naval Attaché in Washington and Mexico City, had written 'U.J. [Uncle John] continues in good heart. He is now only 2 from the top of the Rear-Admirals' list, so I don't know what will happen to him. I fancy they will rate up his job to ACNS (I) [Assistant Chief of Naval Staff (Intelligence)] and leave him there, but no one knows. He is a real war-winner, though many people don't realise it and are put off by his whimsey. He has the mind and character of a Bohemian Mathematician. At least, so I have decided after discarding many other descriptions.' There was indeed a problem because Godfrey was already senior to all the Assistant Chiefs of Staff and to his colleagues on the JIC and would soon be senior to any new VCNS. On 15 September he was promoted Vice-Admiral on the active list, which, in view of the fact that he had been denied the opportunity of a sea appointment as a Rear-Admiral, could only be taken as a mark of exceptional satisfaction with his performance.

But Godfrey was not destined to become the longest-serving Director of Naval Intelligence. On the very day that he was promoted Vice-Admiral, Pound sent for him and informed him that his appointment was to be terminated. On the following day he confirmed his decision in an extraordinarily curt and cold memorandum.

DNI
    I find that the papers you sent me today had been con-

sidered by VCNS before he made his recommendation to me that he considered that co-operation amongst the Members of the JIC which is important for its proper functioning was not possible as long as you were a member.

Taking into account the very thorough investigation which has been carried out by VCNS, I endorse his opinion and it is therefore with the greatest regret that I am informing the First Lord that I consider your relief is necessary.

I should like to take this opportunity of placing on record an acknowledgement of the most able and thorough way in which you have carried out the duties of DNI.

(Initialled) D.P.

16/9.

The true facts behind this harsh and, in many people's view, quite unjustified decision are hard to come by. Most of those principally concerned, including Pound, Moore (the VCNS) and Godfrey himself, are dead. It is understood that Godfrey's Personal file, retained in the Ministry of Defence, throws no light on the matter at all. Cavendish-Bentinck has told the author that the Assistant Chief of Staff (Intelligence) at the Air Ministry, Air Vice Marshal Medhurst, his deputy, Group Captain Inglis, and the Director of Military Intelligence, Major General Davidson, had found such difficulty in getting on with Godfrey that they had requested their respective Chiefs of Staff to ask Pound not to renew his appointment as DNI. Cavendish-Bentinck, although he personally got on well with Godfrey and greatly admired his ability, felt that, as Chairman, he should maintain a strictly neutral attitude in the matter, but when he was sent for and cross-questioned by Moore he reluctantly admitted that JIC meetings went more smoothly when Godfrey was not present. It is not certain what role Colonel Stewart Menzies played in all this. He was, according to Cavendish-Bentinck, not an outstanding man, and had it not been for the results achieved by Bletchley Park, for which he was nominally responsible, Cavendish-Bentinck thought it unlikely that he would have held the post of head of the Secret Intelligence Service for long. If this estimate of Menzies' ability is correct, it may well be that he regarded Godfrey as a threat to his own position and sided with the others.

It must therefore be admitted that Godfrey had, for one

reason or another, succeeded in stirring up a pretty angry hornet's nest. He was certainly in the dock and, apparently, without a defending Counsel. Moore does not seem to have regarded himself as occupying the position of Judge but rather that of Counsel for the Prosecution, because he never, so far as can be ascertained, cross-questioned the defendant. Nor did Pound. The 'accused' was charged with failing to get on with his colleagues on the JIC. He could hardly deny it; they said so. If the JIC existed solely to produce comfortable, acceptable, anodyne, lowest common denominator appreciations, he was guilty as charged. But did it occur to Moore that Godfrey might be right in the opinions to which he held so tenaciously, even aggressively? If there was dissension on the JIC, and curiously enough Cavendish-Bentinck denies that it was frequent, did either Moore or Pound pause to consider whether the right solution should not have been to replace one or more of the others rather than Godfrey?

A full and impartial examination of the facts would have revealed many things in Godfrey's favour; his consistent and ardent advocacy of inter-Service co-operation in Intelligence matters; his insistence on maintaining the integrity and independence of Intelligence; the fact that in the great majority of cases where there had been a difference of opinion among members of the JIC it was Godfrey who was right and his critics who were wrong; that Godfrey, for all his impatience and tactlessness, was a bigger man and a better Intelligence chief than any of his colleagues. Was the smooth functioning of the JIC more important, as Cavendish-Bentinck feels, than the contribution, however great, of any single member? The author believes that there can be no compromise in the presentation of the truth in matters of Intelligence.

In Godfrey's Memoirs there is more than one reference to Pound's understanding and support of NID. Godfrey regarded Pound as "an old friend". The author can see no evidence now to support either of these statements. Indeed elsewhere Godfrey himself remarks that "During 1942 I began to feel that I didn't know where I was with Pound. I was never quite sure if he had heard everything I said or . . . if he'd remember, or even if he was interested. I tried to find out if he was interested by the simple dodge of saying that the process by which we found out about what went on in a certain place [BP] was

rather complicated and interesting, and waiting to see if he
asked me to explain how it was done, but he never did. The
reaction was negative. He did not seem interested, much less
inquisitive." Pound's behaviour over the estimate of U-boat
sinkings and the likelihood of invasion in 1940, his additions to
the Crete telegram in 1941, and his handling of the PQ 17
operation in 1942 all display a complete lack of appreciation of
what Intelligence could and should provide or how it should be
used. His reactions to the accusations now brought against
Godfrey can hardly be described as those of a friend.

But, even if it was considered that the smooth functioning of
the JIC was important, was Godfrey's impatient and at times
overbearing behaviour the real reason for his removal? Viewed
dispassionately it hardly seems to justify the 'sacking', for this
is what it amounted to, of an officer whose appointment the
First Sea Lord had so recently renewed and whose most
exceptional promotion he had just approved. Captain Roskill,
who, in *Churchill and the Admirals*, considers that 'In retrospect
this was very unfair to Godfrey . . . and one does feel that
Pound and Moore should have given him support rather than
allowing the Generals to get him sacked', now feels that there
must have been 'more to it than meets the eye'. This was
certainly Godfrey's own view.

He has written that "I see now what I did not realise at the
time, that I was being subjected to a form of pressure by the
CIGS to agree that Germany had an uncommitted army in
existence and that this army was being held back from both
Eastern and Western fronts. This pressure was being exerted
through the Director of Military Intelligence and could not
be reconciled with the opinion of the JIC so long as the DNI
(a member of the JIC) held out. Admiral Pound was thus
receiving conflicting advice . . . and in a dilemma of this
sort the temptation is to support the more powerful of two
protagonists, CIGS-DMI rather than his own organisation
DNI-JIC." In addition there was the CIGS's belief in the
'pincer movement', a co-ordinated German-Japanese attack
on India, for which we now know there was absolutely no
foundation in fact. "The JIC was unable to find substance
for either of these reports, but they continued to be pressed
strongly . . ." In spite of the JIC appreciation Godfrey learnt,
when he reached India in the spring of 1943, "that Field

Marshal Wavell, the Commander-in-Chief, was told by the War Office to prepare for war on two fronts and the following steps, among others, were taken:

(a) The entire wooden shipbuilding resources of the west coast of India were turned on to the construction of lighters for use on the Tigris and Euphrates.

(b) A great naval base was planned, and partly prepared in the Gulf of Kutch (north of Bombay).

(c) Fifteen master mariners (RNR officers) were taken away from the Royal Indian Navy to command inland water transport craft on the Mesopotamian rivers.

(d) Millions of pounds were spent on the defence of the Khyber.

(e) Lay-back aerodromes with concrete overhead protection were constructed a hundred or so miles inland from the west coast of India.

. . . The Finance Department, manned by the able members of the Indian Civil Service, who were quite able to understand the elements of grand strategy, were sceptical and . . . were chary of finding money to finance further service projects."

A classic example of the unfortunate results of distorting or inventing Intelligence!

Nor was Alanbrooke the only member of the Chiefs of Staff Committee to whom Godfrey's addiction to the 'truth, the whole truth and nothing but the truth' was unwelcome. He had not endeared himself to the Air Staff by his campaign for better aerial photographic reconnaissance. As this controversy simmered down a new one sprang up—the efficacy of the Royal Air Force's bombing policy. According to Godfrey "Our knowledge of the strength and position of German air forces was pretty accurate, but when it came to assessing the accuracy of British air attacks on German ships and targets things were different. The Air Staff would naturally like to think that their attacks were successful and it was my staff's painful duty to assess results in terms of damage known to have been inflicted on ships, U-boat pens, shipbuilding facilities and so on. The sincerity with which claims were pressed and the heavy casualties among bomber crews created a tense and unhappy atmosphere in which the truth could only too easily

become obscured." Naturally enough proof that targets of
naval importance were not being hit cast doubts on the success
of the whole bombing campaign against Germany to which so
much gallantry and material effort was being devoted.

The last straw seems to have been the discovery that the
Director of Naval Intelligence was sending daily Special
Intelligence (Ultra) summaries, which as well as items of
purely naval interest contained others of army, air force and
political significance, to Admiral Sir Andrew Cunningham, by
now head of the British Admiralty Delegation in Washington.
The practice had started, with Pound's approval, when
Cunningham was Commander-in-Chief Mediterranean. "When
Cunningham went to Washington . . . it was even more
important that he should be kept thoroughly in the picture and
to ensure this I established a section of NID in his headquarters
in charge of Commander Eddie Hastings and quite clear of the
Embassy" (whose attitude to security was, in Godfrey's view,
suspect). "As was our custom a sharp line was drawn between
raw intelligence and inference . . . Military Intelligence were
also sending the War Office representative, Field Marshal Dill,
daily telegrams, but these were in the forms of appreciations in
which pure intelligence and inference were mixed up with
comments and advice, without being graded. Both Cunningham
and Dill liked my daily telegrams which were more factual than
those of the War Office." It is possible that Dill commented on
the superiority of the NID appreciations; if he did so it would
have been like a red rag to a bull in its effect on Alanbrooke.
One way or another the secret was out—not that Godfrey had
endeavoured to conceal anything; the telegrams were sent at
Cunningham's request and it obviously never occured to
Godfrey that they would arouse the wrath of the other Services.
He was, after all, circulating similar summaries to Pound and
the Naval Staff, so why not to the head of BAD? There can be
little doubt but that these were the papers referred to in
Pound's memo of 16 September.

One might have supposed that Pound, on receiving complaints against the senior Director of the Naval Staff, an
officer who had served him in one capacity or another for more
than eight years and on whose abilities he had reported in the
very highest terms, would, at some point, have discussed the
whole affair with Godfrey. Godfrey states, "I know he was

angry and unhappy, and his extreme reticence would not allow him to have a heart to heart talk with me". One must conclude that pressure was being put on the old man by the other two Chiefs of Staff and that Alanbrooke in particular was insistent that Godfrey must go. Pound does not have an enviable record for standing up for subordinates who incurred the displeasure of those in positions of great authority. If Tom Phillips could be sacrificed for daring to oppose Churchill over the policy of bombing Germany and the decision to send troops to Greece rather than to consolidate Wavell's victories in Cyrenaica, it is scarcely surprising that Pound should take the easy way out with a Director of Naval Intelligence who had got at cross-purposes with the professional heads of the other two Services.

It is impossible to say whether Pound's attitude was affected by the fact that he was already a sick man. Godfrey, like a number of others, had become seriously concerned about the First Sea Lord's health. "I used to see him three or four times a week and regularly every Tuesday morning when the three Directors of Intelligence met the Chiefs of Staff . . . even as early as the spring of 1940 it was obvious that the Chief of Naval Staff was very sleepy. That he used to doze was common knowledge, but what I find hard to believe is that he was mentally awake the whole time and was automatically alerted with full knowledge of what had been said and was taking place, by the mention of anything to do with the Fleet. In any case, this seems to me irrelevant as the three Chiefs of Staff met in order to bring their collective wisdom, experience and views to bear on all questions and not only those concerning their own Service. There were many besides myself who had come to the conclusion that his sleeping had some deeper significance; of course we were not sure, and it is not the sort of thing that should be discussed in a disciplined Service. Such discussions can easily drift into disloyalty and induce widespread lack of confidence. By the end of 1941 I felt that something should be done and confided my anxieties separately to two retired Admirals. Both these officers, whom I had known for years and who were very much nearer to Pound's age than I was, were in the habit of seeing him once a week. They were discreet and tactful and were just as conscious as I of Pound's infirmity. Although it had not occurred to them that he was already a

sick man, they were alive to the fact that his memory, judgement and mental alertness, but not his power of decision, were
waning. But neither was prepared to undertake the thankless
task I had in mind for them." Godfrey, of course, hoped that
they would persuade Pound to consult a physician. Had he
done so the advice he would certainly have received would have
been that, for his own sake, he should resign. If this had
happened early in 1941 a number of terrible mistakes would
almost certainly have been avoided. Cunningham, Horton or
Fraser could have taken over and would have made far better
Chiefs of Naval Staff.

Whether Pound's decision to terminate Godfrey's appointment as DNI was affected by ill health or not, and irrespective
of whether it was right or wrong in the circumstances, the
actual way in which he handled it can only be described as
callous. He refused to discuss the matter with Godfrey but
preferred to rely on the advice of Moore, who had equally given
the DNI no chance to state his side of the case. He announced
his decision, not in a personal and private letter but in a terse,
unfriendly and unforgiving memorandum. This was not the
way that Cunningham or Mountbatten would have handled
such a problem. The change of DNI was not announced
immediately—a successor had to be found—and naturally
enough no reasons for it were given when the news was made
public. What did strike informed observers was that it was not
accompanied by the award of the knighthood, a KCB or KBE,
which Godfrey's three and three quarter years' brilliant achievements had surely earned. That was a very public expression of
official disapproval, a gratuitous and deliberate slap in the
face, something that, ever since, has been greatly resented by
all wartime members of the Intelligence Division.

Godfrey, being the man he was, accepted Pound's decision
loyally and with dignity. Neither then nor at any time thereafter, either publicly or privately, did he express resentment at
the way he had been treated or display any animosity to
Pound. On the contrary, in 1954, when an attack on Pound
appeared in the *Sunday Express*, Godfrey immediately wrote to
the then First Lord and First Sea Lord urging them to take
steps to "right the wrong that is being done to his [Pound's]
memory", although it was in the end sensibly decided that the
'least said, the soonest mended' and no action was taken. He

also thought that Admiral Sir Dudley North and his supporters were mistaken in continuing for so many years to demand an official admission that he had been unjustly treated. In Godfrey's view the Board of Admiralty had every right to terminate the appointment of an officer in whom they had, whether rightly or wrongly, lost confidence and that in such circumstances, protests were in the interests neither of the Service nor of the individual concerned.

After such a body blow it cannot have been easy to carry on as though nothing had happened, but on 24 September, accompanied by Ian Fleming, Godfrey left by air for his planned visit to Washington and Ottawa. He has left no details of the purposes of the visit but his appointments diary records that he stayed with the Cunninghams in Washington and that he met, amongst others, Lord Halifax, the British Ambassador, Admiral King, Pound's opposite number, Field Marshal Dill, Paymaster Commander Travis, the Head of BP, and the NID representative on Cunningham's staff, Eddie Hastings. On 18 October Godfrey flew to Ottawa, where he lunched with the Governor General, Lord Athlone and conferred with the Canadian Chief of Naval Staff and his DNI. This was the first visit ever made by a British DNI to Canada. Godfrey subsequently recommended that Canada should be the first port of call for senior British naval officers visiting North America, which had for so long been our best 'window', from the Intelligence point of view, into the United States. The Royal Canadian Navy, as the author can testify from personal experience, was quite rightly very sensitive to any implied suggestion that, despite having been in the war from the very beginning, it was a poor relation compared to the mighty United States Navy. After three days in Canada, Godfrey flew back to Washington and on 27 October to England. A month later he turned over to his relief, Captain (later Rear-Admiral) Edmund Rushbrooke. Rushbrooke took over a Division which he himself would have been the first to admit was running on oiled wheels and required very little further propulsive effort.

Writing in 1964 Godfrey commented that "I had long realised that my strong suit was planning and nurturing new developments, and that I wasn't much good at expounding the day to day situation . . . My regrets at leaving NID were not therefore connected with the work itself but because it meant losing touch with such a gifted and loyal band of officers and civilians, most of whom I had myself had a finger in selecting. After four years we were a closely integrated group, the machine was working admirably and really delivering the goods. My regrets were, in fact, similar to those I had experienced so many times when a ship pays off at the end of a successful commission . . . After twenty years I think that it was a good thing for me and the Naval Intelligence Division that my Directorship was not prolonged until the latter stages of the war."

On leaving NID Godfrey said goodbye personally to as many of his staff and associates as he could, but he also wrote to a large number to express his gratitude for their services to him and to the Division. The replies which he received in return are a truly remarkable testimonial to the enormous respect and admiration which he had earned and to the universal sense of loss engendered by the announcement of his departure. The following excerpts are typical:

Captain Lewes, his ADNI (Security)—'It has been a joy for me to work for someone who knew his staff; trusted them; encouraged them and let them do the work.'

Colonel Bassett, Superintendant of ISTD—'I still feel like a clock which has lost its main spring and with it my regulator.'

Commander Loehnis, Head of DSD/NID9—'We could only have succeeded as well as we have through your interest and unfailing backing and support and it has been a great privilege to serve under someone who has understood our difficulties and problems so well and has invariably known how to achieve the object in view.'

Freddie Wells, ISTD—'I must think of your going as a tragedy, because I at least have not met or learnt of anyone else with your intellectual grasp of the problem of Intelligence and with your force in moving from the idea to action . . . I hope that Oxford will not lose you. There will always be a room for you at this College as long as I am here.'

John Johnson, Oxford University Press—'The Press feels forlorn at the prospect of losing you both . . . The truth is of course that you, if I may say so without impertinence, have learned the great secret of giving spiritual and human value to every side of life, including business life.'

Commander Rodger Winn, Head of the Submarine Tracking

Room—'It was you yourself who gave me the opportunity to earn distinction and who had the distinctly novel idea of entrusting an important Section of the Division . . . to a civilian. I shall always be grateful to you for having placed this confidence in me.'

Frank Birch, Head of Naval Section at BP—'Anyhow you know what we owe to you and how you nursed us through all that sickly infancy . . . I shall never forget—who could—all you did for us then and since and I only wish you were going to be with us to the end.'

Captain Charles Lambe, Deputy Director, Plans—'I feel I have lost a good friend in the Admiralty. It always did me the greatest good to come and talk things over with you and I, in my turn, am most grateful for all you did to help us. I must say the Intelligence forecasts prior to the North African operations have proved astoundingly correct and I take my hat off to Baker-Creswell and his party . . . I hope that you also know how much I should like to work with you again in the future.'

Perhaps Colonel Cordeaux, formerly head of a geographical section and then NID representative with MI5, summed it all up when he wrote—'There are very few officers who were serving in NID when you joined and who are still there or, like myself, so closely connected with it as to know all the details of its work and organisation. As one of that small group I should not like you to leave without paying personal tribute to the truly remarkable achievement for which you are responsible. Only a person like myself, who knew what the conditions were when you started, can understand the full meaning of that achievement. I will confess that personally I have often thought that some major decision of yours was mistaken but, looking back, I cannot recall one such case in which the results did not prove me to be wrong. It has been a great privilege to have witnessed the building up of the Division during the last three years and nine months.'

These and many other similar messages from men who really knew the immense contribution which Godfrey had made to the whole Intelligence organisation of the country must have more than made up for Pound's unfeeling, if not untypical, note of dismissal.

CHAPTER TWELVE

India's Coral Strand

It might have been supposed, after the events described in the last chapter, that Godfrey would have been placed on the retired list and offered no further employment. On the contrary, only three weeks later, while staying with the Cunninghams in Washington, he received the following personal telegram from A. V. Alexander, the First Lord: 'Subject to concurrence of Government of India I have pleasure in offering you the appointment of FOCRIN.' (Flag Officer Commanding, Royal Indian Navy). This had hitherto been only a Rear-Admiral's post, although regarded in peacetime as something of a plum from the social point of view. Now it was being up-graded, but what made the offer surprising was that although it demanded all the great drive and energy which Godfrey had so clearly displayed as DNI, it also called for the very qualities of tact and the ability to co-operate with other Services which Pound and Moore apparently considered he lacked. The current incumbent, Vice-Admiral Sir Herbert Fitzherbert, had, it is true, held the appointment for six years (he had been promoted in the normal course of events after three years), but he had done well in India, was generally popular and in no way anxious to be relieved. Was Pound secretly conscious that he had treated Godfrey unjustly and was seeking to make amends, or did the initiative come from Alexander? It is yet another mystery in an already puzzling affair.

After consulting Cunningham and pondering the matter for twenty-four hours Godfrey "came to the obvious conclusions, first that in war time you must do what you are told, and secondly that I was unlikely to get anything better. Moreover, I quickly realised that the prospects of three years or so in India appealed to me strongly. It was, in fact, the fulfillment of my childish wishes to 'see' China, the South Seas and India. China and the South Pacific I had had in full measure. Now it was India's turn." So he promptly replied that he "would be

pleased to fall in with Their Lordships' wishes and am much
honoured in accepting the appointment." The agreement of
the Government of India was delayed, apparently because of
some reservations on the part of the Commander-in-Chief of
the Eastern Fleet, Sir James Somerville, and did not arrive
until after Christmas. So it was not until the end of February,
1943, that Godfrey and his Secretary, Paymaster Captain
Tinniswood, set off from Bristol by flying boat, via Lisbon,
West Africa, Khartoum, Cairo, Basra and Bahrein for India.
They reached New Delhi on 16 March.

The Royal Indian Navy was both a very old and a very new
Service. It traced its history back to 1612, when the Honourable
East India Company's Marine had been founded. Since that
time its fortunes and functions had waxed and waned and its
name been changed many times—the Bombay Marine, the
Indian Navy, the Indian Marine and then the Royal Indian
Marine. After the Great Indian Mutiny it had become a
non-combatant service, providing troopships for the Indian
Army, station ships in the Persian Gulf and acting as a combina-
tion of Trinity House, the Board of Trade and the Royal Navy's
Hydrographic Department. Its officers came from the British
Mercantile Marine and its ratings from the Ratnigiri coastal
district south of Bombay, and its stewards from Portuguese
Goa. The men were excellent seamen, although their standard
of education and martial qualities were low. It was a tiny,
self-contained and inbred force.

In World War I its ships had been armed and had given good
service in the Red Sea (where Godfrey had first encountered
them) and in Mesopotamia. In 1919 Lord Jellicoe had proposed
that the RIM be expanded and transformed into a permanent
fighting force. This was summarily rejected by the Government of India on the grounds that the country could not afford
both an army and a navy and that it must, in consequence,
continue to look for its maritime defence to the Royal Navy,
for which India paid the Admiralty an annual subvention of
£100,000. The Indian Government went even further. The
troopships were sold and all officer recruitment suspended from
1921 to 1928. The Service almost ceased to exist. However, in
1926, agreement was reached in principle to start to build up
again into a permanent combatant Service and the Royal Navy
supplied a few small ships and a Rear-Admiral to fill the post of

Director of the RIM. Officer recruitment was resumed by participation in the Royal Navy's Special Entry cadet system, and it was agreed that the officers and men should have the same uniform as the Royal Navy, except for distinctive buttons, and that the ships should fly the White Ensign. Although the acquisition of two modern sloops was approved, costs were not permitted to exceed the £100,000 previously paid to the Admiralty. The purchase of one was therefore deferred and the cost of the other defrayed by the sale of the RIM dockyard at Calcutta, so destroying the organisation on the east coast. Bombay was left as the only base, with no training establishments except some converted godowns and sheds. In 1934 the Indian Naval Discipline Act was finally passed and the Service at last became in name as well as fact the Royal Indian Navy under a Flag Officer Commanding instead of a Director.

The British Admiralty was now pressing the infant Service to take on greater responsibilities but Munich showed that it was still far from ready to do so. The Chatfield Commission in November 1938, which reviewed the efficiency and future role of the three Indian Services, wrung from a reluctant Indian Government agreement to a considerable expansion of the RIN. Six more sloops and a number of minesweepers were ordered from Britain and a modest increase in personnel authorised, but this latter only after the Finance Department had demanded a detailed examination of and justification for the duties of every single rating already on the books. Fitzherbert, a vigorous not to say aggressive little man, was not one to hold back and readily accepted the new commitments thrust upon the RIN by the Admiralty. Recruitment had already been extended to the Punjab, since the Ratnigiris were no longer capable of meeting all the RIN's needs; training establishments were now planned and the enlargement and development of the Service pushed forward with great energy and enthusiasm. What was lacking was time; time for the new ships to be built; time for more ratings, particularly technical specialists for a modern navy, to be recruited and trained; time for a proper infra-structure to be created and tested; time to make good the appalling gap in the middle and senior ranks of the officer corps caused by the fatal suspension of recruitment in the twenties; time for loyalty and tradition to be nurtured. But time was one of the many things that was not available.

The RIN started the war with but eight small ships and only 200 officers and 1400 men, and with virtually no reserves such as the Royal Navy's Fleet Reserve, RNR or RNVR. It was, by any standards, far too small a base on which to build the organisation which the Admiralty wanted and which Fitz-herbert felt compelled to accept. It is a great tribute to his energy and determination and to the dedication and professional competence of his small staff that so much was in fact achieved in the first three years of the war.

Nor was the tiny size of the pre-war RIN its only problem. The subcontinent of India is vast. If superimposed on Europe it would stretch from Belfast to Malta and from Lisbon to Danzig. Delhi, the capital, is eight hundred miles from the sea. Until the arrival of the Europeans in the sixteenth century, its many invaders had come overland not across the Indian Ocean or the Bay of Bengal. From the end of the eighteenth century onwards India's enormous coastline had, thanks to the Royal Navy, again been secure. There was no consciousness of the importance of sea power, no maritime tradition and only a tiny proportion of the population, even of the educated classes, had ever seen the sea. Hindus were forbidden by their religion to cross it. Although many ships in the British Merchant Navy were manned by Lascars, the indigenous Merchant Marine was not much larger than the RIN; and many of its deck officers were Portuguese subjects from Goa. The great Indian ports of Calcutta, Madras and Bombay were filled with European, mostly British owned ships.

With the Army, however, it was very different. India had a splendid martial tradition dating back to her earliest recorded history. The British Indian Army was the premier, if not the senior, Service. In 1914 it had consisted of some 150,000 men and had expanded, without too much difficulty, to ten times that number by 1918. Reverting to its old strength after the war it was still one hundred times as large as the RIN in 1939. It was to expand again to a strength of two and a half million men in the next five years. Every man was a volunteer and, when properly equipped, more than capable of holding his own with his British and American comrades or his German, Italian or Japanese enemies. Despite India's great size, she was a poor country. It was an astonishing achievement.

Nor was the young RIN the only new Service competing

with 'Big Brother'; there was also the Royal Indian Air Force demanding the same type of technically skilled, intelligent recruit as the Navy.

The head of all three Services was the Commander-in-Chief of the Indian Army, constitutionally the War Member of the Government and head of the War Department. There was no separate Admiralty with its staff of civil servants: no First Lord to fight the Navy's battles in Parliament: everything went through the War Department and despite much good will the outlook of the officials concerned was a military not a naval one.

It was, therefore, no easy task to create a sizeable fighting Navy out of the tiny Royal Indian Marine in a country with no maritime tradition, under the domination, no matter how benevolent, of a large and expanding Army, and against a background of pressing demands for Indian independence from Britain. The surprising thing is not that difficulties arose and that mistakes were made but that such a very great degree of success was achieved in such a very short space of time.

By early 1943 when Godfrey arrived in Delhi, the RIN's personnel had grown to over 20,000. A Royal Indian Naval Reserve and a Royal Indian Naval Volunteer Reserve had been formed, the latter now providing the bulk of the officers up to Lieutenant-Commander's rank, of whom nearly 40 per cent were Indian. Recruitment of ratings was no longer confined to the Muslim Ratnagiris and the Punjabis, but was on an all India basis so that soon nearly half the lower deck came from southern India, and Hindoos and other religions almost equalled the Mohammedans, with all the problems of messing, religion and language which such a mixture involved. The six newly built sloops were in commission (although not all of them had yet reached India) and modern minesweepers, trawlers, motor torpedo boats and small craft of all sort were beginning to come forward to replace the little ships hastily requisitioned for local defence at the beginning of the war. Depots and training establishments were being brought into service and Naval Officers-in-Charge, with appropriate staffs, had been appointed to all the principal ports, at some of which full scale RIN bases had been established. The headquarters of the RIN had been transferred from Bombay to Delhi, although this had been carried out on a rather piecemeal basis and was by no means complete. Shortly before Godfrey's arrival, under pressure from the Admiralty, Fitzherbert had agreed to the establishment of a Landing Craft Wing to permit effective RIN participation in the projected reconquest of Burma and Malaya. This was something not previously envisaged and quite outside the RIN's capability without considerable help from elsewhere. The Admiralty, as always, wanted bricks, but was not prepared to supply even a modicum of straw. Fitzherbert was reluctant to reject any request for a contribution to the Imperial war effort. Understandably but, with hindsight probably wrongly, he accepted the new commitment and turned to the Indian Army for help. The men of two regiments were permitted, indeed encouraged, to transfer en masse to the RIN to become shallow water sailors. The change to naval procedures and discipline was not easy for them and difficulties with the Landing Craft Wing persisted throughout its existence, adding yet another set of problems to those with which the Navy was already faced. Nevertheless, the Landing Craft Wing gave yeoman service in the Arakan campaign and won high praise from Lord Mountbatten.

The RIN was responsible for the local defence and control of Indian ports, but its seagoing ships were attached to and under the operational control of the Royal Navy. At the outbreak of war, once it had become clear that there was no immediate danger from Japan, the great majority of British warships had been recalled for duty in home waters and the Mediterranean. Then in 1941, as the threat from Japan grew more alarming, attempts were made to reverse the process. Unfortunately the Royal Navy's resources were now stretched to the limit. The loss of *Prince of Wales* and *Repulse* and the crippling of the US Pacific Fleet at Pearl Harbor were followed by the Battle of the Java Sea and the virtual destruction of the remaining British, Dutch and American squadrons in the Far East. Sir James Somerville's hastily constituted Eastern Fleet of Jutland veterans was in no position to dispute control of the Bay of Bengal and the eastern Indian Ocean with the Japanese when they despatched a strong carrier force there in April 1942. Somerville only narrowly escaped complete disaster and was compelled to withdraw for a time to East Africa to await reinforcements of modern carriers and battleships. Luckily the Japanese were too preoccupied in the Pacific to renew operations by their major surface forces in the Indian Ocean. The

Eastern Fleet returned to its main bases at Colombo and Trincomalee in Ceylon to build up its strength for the coming offensive against Burma, the Dutch East Indies and Malaya. The Royal Navy also used all the main Indian ports and made use of the RIN's shore facilities and signals organisation. The relationship between the two Services was not always an easy one; the RN expected much but gave little.

Godfrey, therefore, was taking over a newly created Navy which, from a tiny base, had already expanded twelvefold in three and a half years and which was suffering from a grave lack of experienced officers and fully trained men; a Navy which was subordinate to and greatly dependent on the Indian Army for backing and many administrative functions, but which was competing with that Army both for recruits and supplies of all sorts; a Navy of a country with no maritime tradition whose better educated citizens, the very men needed for the new officer corps and technicians, were increasingly demanding that the British should quit India; a Navy based on the traditions and practices of the Royal Navy which was however generally unable and sometimes unwilling to give its young sister Service the support and sympathetic understanding which the situation demanded. It was a daunting prospect but, to Godfrey, a much more appealing one than the pre-war 'plum', with its not very onerous professional duties and its social attractions of cocktail and bridge parties, pig-sticking, polo and shooting.

The Flag Officer Commanding the Royal Indian Navy had a variety of functions. He was responsible for the organisation, training and administration of the RIN. He was also Principal Sea Transport Officer (India) and Naval Adviser to His Excellency the War Member (Commander-in-Chief, India). He had to maintain liaison and close co-operation with the senior Royal Navy officer, previously C-in-C, East Indies Station, but now C-in-C, Eastern Fleet, and to act as a link between the Admiralty and the Government of India. On some questions a final decision rested with the Secretary of State for India and the India Office in Whitehall. Godfrey soon decided that there were several similarities between his new and his previous appointment. "Both were constructive jobs. One sat down with a clean sheet of paper and had to produce something out of nothing. For example at the beginning of the war the RIN had no medical service, no accountant service, no welfare or amenities, no womens' service, no anti-submarine school, no tactical unit, no mechanical training establishments. My predecessor laid the foundations of many of these branches and I had to do my best to build them up. Apart from being constructive offices the two jobs of DNI and FOCRIN were minor autocracies. One had an entirely free hand in engaging and appointing staff. Both entailed the acceptance of responsibilities which you could not share with your immediate superior, VCNS and C-in-C India. In other words they could do little to supplement your wisdom if things went well or mitigate your lack of wisdom if you ran into trouble. Both were full of snags which could only be dissolved by un-orthodox methods." Despite this emphasis on independence and the acceptance of responsibility, Godfrey does seem to have been more conscious as FOCRIN than he had been as DNI of the need to protect his rear (or perhaps one should say his head) by better personal 'public relations' with his immediate superiors. His early dealings with Churchill had not encouraged him to exercise his right to frequent private interviews with that great man and one senses a certain feeling of relief when Winston left the Admiralty for No. 10 Downing Street. Mis-takenly, as it turned out, Godfrey had believed that Pound understood his problems and could be counted on for sympathy and support when the inevitable difficulties arose. Although he never mentions the question specifically in his Memoirs, Godfrey must have been aware of this mistake and there is no doubt that he took great trouble to keep both the Viceroy and the Commander-in-Chief very fully informed of the RIN's problems and progress by means of regular personal interviews and frequent written reports.

As soon as Godfrey arrived in Delhi Fitzherbert took him to pay his respects to the Viceroy, Lord Linlithgow, and to report to the Commander-in-Chief, Field Marshal Lord Wavell. The next ten days were taken up with other official calls and introductions and to getting to know his own small staff at Naval Headquarters. He writes in his Memoirs that "knowing next to nothing about India, or the Royal Indian Navy, I was fortunate in finding already in existence the nucleous of a first class staff. The senior British officers in the very young RIN had had administrative responsibilities thrust on them very much earlier in life than their contemporaries in the Royal Navy. They matured earlier and their judgement was mellower. Lieutenant-commanders were doing the work of captains in charge of shore establishments. My Chief of Staff, Commodore J. T. S. Hall, RIN, was not only a very experienced staff officer, but he knew a great deal about India and how to get things done, and about the working of that strange machine, the Government of India at Delhi or Simla, ruled, as regards Army and Navy, in the last resort by a general on the staff of the Secretary of State for India in Whitehall. When it became necessary to strengthen our liaison with Whitehall, Hall was the obvious choice for the post of RIN Liaison Officer in London, where he not only handled the Whitehall end of our affairs with conspicuous success, but became my personal link with the Admiralty."

FOCRIN's second in command was the Commodore, RIN, at Bombay, A. R. Rattray. "Jack Rattray was the last of the bucanneers and would have fitted well into the Elizabethan navy. Starting in the Merchant Navy in sailing ships he had joined the Royal Indian Marine in 1912 but during the Kaiser War became a fighter pilot in the Royal Flying Corps in Mesopotamia . . . He had a difficult job at Bombay with many conflicting interests to co-ordinate, not least of which was the Royal Navy, who behaved as if they owned the place and were slow to realise that Bombay was under the Government of India. But Rattray knew Bombay from A to Z, got on well with everyone, never bellyached, was extremely executive and prompt however exacting the demands of Delhi or the exigencies of the war might be . . . A more wholehearted and loyal friend and second in command I could not wish to have." It is quite clear from Godfrey's letters that his friendship with Jack Rattray developed quickly. He usually stayed with him on his fairly frequent visits to Bombay in his house close to the exclusive Bombay Yacht Club, whose members Rattray liked to bombard after dark with a powerful pea shooter, although not perhaps when his Admiral was present. Rattray was a rumbustious extrovert, an unusual friend for someone so reserved as Godfrey.

Godfrey found his official bungalow in Delhi, No. 12 King George's Avenue, "charming and the garden full of flowers and birds, the latter rather quarrelsome and squeaky. They fly in and out of the house seeking some shade and perch on picture rails and other projections. I have a partridge, two hares, a hoopoe, a mongoose and a handsome green parrot in the garden . . . At least 15 servants are needed to run my simple bungalow, and it takes four people to deal with flowers in the house. The mali (gardener) plucks and arranges them, the masalchi (house boy) throws dead flowers and wet moss out onto the verandah. The 'sweeper' sweeps them off into the garden and the assistant mali throws them onto the rubbish heap . . . The horse wanders about the garden and crops the grass. If you want the grass cut you must indent on the Public Works Department and after a lapse of some days a cow arrives towing a victorian lawnmower in charge of a very old man. During the hot part of the day—9 a.m. to 6 p.m.—the cow can be seen reclining under the best shade tree, chewing the cud contentedly, while the old man prepares innumerable meals for himself and smokes a very long pipe."

Any newcomer to India was inevitably confronted with many strange problems; the great variety of peoples, languages, customs and religions, climate and, perhaps above all, size. Godfrey certainly did not waste time getting to know his new command. A fortnight after reaching Delhi he left to spend ten days in Bombay, followed by three in Karachi. After a week back in Delhi he set off again for the east coast, Calcutta, Chittagong and Vizagapatam. These were the first of innumerable visits, or 'tours', during which, in the space of three years, he was to cover more than 114,000 miles. He summed up his first impressions in a letter at the end of April to Margaret who was still waiting in England for a passage to India. "The heat has come and surges about in great puffs. Politically things are slack and the wealthy Hindoo business men who back Gandhi are finding that riots and strikes don't pay and are withholding the recognised payment of one rupee a day to the trouble-makers—called ghoondas. This poorly-paid occupation is now manned by professional thugs, not by an outwardly respectable crowd. My Naval destiny has certainly brought me to a strange land where, as Europeans, we live a life completely remote from the country itself. The procession of Government Houses, Bombay, Karachi, Calcutta, the princely hospitality of the Jam Sahib, the vigour and enthusiasm of all that appertains to the RIN against an impossible political background and non-existent public opinion provide a stern assortment of contrasts. One is encouraged by the rather naïve way that people accept one's opinion without questioning or opposition. Dudley Pound said that my position as a Vice-Admiral would be unassailable and he was quite right; he also told the Jam that he (DP) was sending out the best Flag Officer he had to help India create its Navy. I am no longer sorry I left the NID—it isn't sour grapes—I find in this job *almost* everything that I like and look forward to . . . I only wish you could be here to share the oddities and the humour in this strange land."

Almost immediately afterwards Godfrey went down with jaundice, traced to a smear of jaundice in the anti-cholera vaccine. It was practically the first time he had been off duty since the beginning of the war. He spent six weeks in hospital in Simla, which at least gave him the opportunity to consider what he had so far seen of the RIN.

He had quickly realised that the RIN was faced with a number of serious problems stemming from the very rapid expansion initiated by his predecessor and greatly aggravated by the cessation of officer recruiting in the twenties. Before the war the planning and administration of the tiny Service had been carried out by FOCRIN with a small staff at Bombay, organised on the lines of a staff for a Naval Squadron except that it was ashore not afloat. But FOCRIN was now required to collaborate closely with the Government of India and the other two Services in Delhi, and although a more or less piecemeal transfer from Bombay had been taking place in the last two years it was by no means complete and the organisation and administration of the Delhi Headquarters was still ill-designed to deal with the new situation. Godfrey therefore prepared from his sick bed a plan to transform Naval Headquarters into a miniature Admiralty but adapted to the procedures of the Government of India and existing organisations of the Army and the Air Force. The main proposal was to divide NHQ into two main parts, 'Operations' and 'Administration', each under a senior officer directly responsible to FOCRIN. The head of Operations was to be responsible for Intelligence, Training, Security, Operations Plans, and a number of specialist functions. The head of Administration was to have four main branches under him, Equipment, Engineering, Personnel and Administrative Planning, and also staffs dealing with Accounts, Medical and Regulations matters.

Despite the grave shortage of experienced officers, a problem which continued to bedevil the RIN up to the time of Indian Independence, Godfrey refused to abandon the principles of devolution which he had imbibed from Wemyss and Burmester a quarter of a century earlier and which he had applied with such success in NID. He was fortunate that the small corps of regular RIN officers were such a dedicated and talented body of men. As regards the completion of the move to Delhi Godfrey was able to call on Captain S. J. Thomson, RIN, newly designated as Chief of Personnel, who "used to come up to Simla about every ten days and discuss progress which was astonishingly rapid. Thomson was a very hard and accurate worker with a good grasp of principles and detail. He really worked too hard and made himself ill", but he achieved results. Thomson did not particularly like Godfrey. He describes him as having 'the dome of a prelate, the eyes of a devil and the mouth of a petulant child'; he thought his new chief was too impetuous, impatient, and ignorant of the slow workings of Indian bureaucracy. Despite this he had to admire Godfrey's obvious intelligence and the new impetus he immediately gave to the effort to provide the administrative and logistic support which the RIN still lacked.

In a letter to his second in command, Rattray, on 23 May, Godfrey summed up four other matters on which he felt they should concentrate; firstly to eliminate from the RIN all ships of *no* fighting value; secondly to obtain on loan from the Admiralty some officers of lieutenant-commander's rank; thirdly to devote much attention to discipline and morale; and fourthly to review all senior appointments, which were tending to solidify and be regarded as permanent irrespective of whether they were necessarily filled by the most suitable officers. Until the first point had been tackled no favourable response could be expected from the Admiralty, since the RIN would be accused of not making the best use of the officer material already at its disposal. Whereas there had in the past been a case "for boosting up the *number* of ships in the RIN to get people to play up, this no longer applies and we must go all out for quality as distinct from quantity." After only two months in India this was an astonishingly accurate appreciation of the basic problem confronting the RIN. As to discipline and morale, Godfrey also put his finger immediately on the sore points: food, pay, leave, discipline, complaints. It was, however, one thing to diagnose the weaknesses; it was quite another, in existing circumstances, to cure them. Godfrey took an early opportunity of discussing his first impressions with Lord Linlithgow. His recollection of this and other meetings, when the outside temperature was 102 degrees Fahrenheit, were "of a very cold air-conditioned room and a Viceroy wearing tweeds, a sweater and muffled in a scarf and always most interested in anything I had to tell him. He not only seemed to, but showed that he did, attach importance to what I had to say on non-naval subjects. He remembered that I had been DNI for nearly four years and that he had once been Civil Lord of the Admiralty and was sympathetic in an understanding way towards our Naval needs and aspirations. He and the Private Secretary to the Viceroy (PSV), Sir Gilbert Laithwaite, were prepared to write a demi-official letter to Mr Amery, the Secretary of State for India, backing up some plan that was taking shape. The PSV was a very powerful person with tentacles deeply entwined in the roots of Whitehall. Some people went so far as to say that the PSV really ruled India. Both Lord Linlithgow and Gilbert Laithwaite returned to England in October 1943 and the growing RIN lost two very good friends and a direct and executive link with the India Office and the Secretary of State, Mr Amery, who had been Parliamentary Secretary to the Admiralty in the twenties and maintained an abiding interest in Navies and sea-power."

In June Wavell, the C-in-C, returned briefly to England and Field Marshal Sir Claude Auchinleck became, for the second time, Commander-in-Chief in his place. In October 1943 Wavell returned, but this time as Viceroy. Godfrey seems to have got on well with both men, but while admitting that his experience with Wavell as C-in-C was too brief for an informed judgement nevertheless felt that "Auchinleck was the only Commander-in-Chief who took the slightest interest in the Navy", which was curious in that he was an Indian Army officer who might have been expected to take a slightly more parochial view than the British Army Wavell. Godfrey met Wavell daily while he was C-in-C but "very few naval questions arose. His regular meetings were", according to Godfrey, "tranquil but rather inconclusive. They dealt mainly with questions of military administration, security, transport and so on, but rarely with operations or politics. It was exceptional for a naval question to arise, as we tried to settle matters of Naval supply and maintenance direct with the Adjutant General, Quartermaster General, Engineer-in-Chief or other Head of Department.

"Two incidents stick in my memory. After a depressing recital by the CGS [Chief of General Staff] of the progress of the war in Burma, someone said 'well, things can't get worse'. Trivedi, [Secretary of the War Department], a realist, disagreed, observing that 'there is no upper limit to chaos', an aphorism which I have used with telling effect on several occasions. The other incident also concerned the Burma campaign, where the braying of our mules was apt to give away the position of troops. The Quartermaster General, Phil Vickers, announced triumphantly that the vets had succeeded in 'de-vocalising' the mules in Burma, whereupon Roone, Engineer-in-Chief, said that he hoped that one of the first acts in our post-war reconstruction programme would be to restore their brays. Everyone laughed except the Chief. I was sitting on his left and saw his hand creep forward and grind together some pencils, a sure sign that he was not amused. Chilled by his silence and the pencil grinding, laughter died out into a self-conscious simper.

"When he [Wavell] became Viceroy in October 1943 I made a point of seeking an interview every two or three months and giving him a short report on maritime affairs. I do not recall that he had much to say to me on these occasions and, after I had said my bit, silence prevailed until I departed. Sometimes he would call me back when I had almost got through the door and a lively and unexpectedly interesting conversation ensued. The silences were in no way unfriendly or embarrassing.

"The Commander-in-Chief exercised his functions through the CGS [Chief of General Staff], Quartermaster General, Principal Supply Officer, Master General of the Ordnance, Director of Medical Services and Engineer-in-Chief. All these officials gave the RIN a very high priority during the difficult years of expansion and consolidation—they gave us as much and more than we asked for and I can remember no occasion when I had to appeal to the 'Chief' [Commander-in-Chief] regarding any matter that concerned the Military Departments. The same could not be said of the Finance Department. The C-in-C exercised his function of War Member constitutionally through Trivedi (later Sir Chandulal Madharial Trivedi, KCSI, CIE, OBE, LLD), the Secretary of the War Department and his additional and joint secretaries, Hutchings, Irwin and, especially, Philip Mason, with whom our relations were uniformly good. I found Trivedi receptive and helpful and, if a question showed signs of going wrong in the lower echelons, a word with him would generally give it a slant in the right direction, that is, we hoped, in the direction that Naval Headquarters thought was right. The Commander-in-Chief's Committee met daily in the Chief's room at 9.30 a.m. with the CGS, the deputy C-in-C, the military heads of departments, Trivedi and FOCRIN and the Air Officer Commanding attending, with Mason as secretary until he was seconded to Mountbatten's staff. Under Auchinleck our meetings were frequently rather jagged. The Chief was not always prepared to listen to opinions that differed from those he had already formed. Listening to such opinions, especially those of Eric Coates, who represented the Finance Department, made him fidget. Very soon it was clear that he could not bear it a second longer and an explosion took place which more or less blasted that item off the agenda . . . imperceptibly we got into the habit of reserving controversial matters for occasions when it was known he would be on tour. The questions were then fully debated, all pros and cons being stated in the Minutes which the Chief could read at his leisure on his return. I must confess that the tendency to suppress the mention of unpopular points of view rather worried me, as it savoured of wishfulness, a vice I had been at some pains to discourage during my four years as Director of Naval Intelligence.

"After spending three years administering a small navy and a port and sea transport service from such a very Military Headquarters as New Delhi, it is legitimate to wonder if the Service was helped or hindered by subordination to a Supreme military command. Certainly we got every encouragement and all the help that it was in their power to give from the Principal Military Heads of Departments, but the sort of help we needed was just the kind that a military C-in-C finds it hard to give— to stand up and fight that cold-blooded machine, the Military Finance Department and, in doing so, to give the small Navy more than its fair share of support compared with the Indian Army in which he had spent forty years of his life. In a material sense we had as much support as a First Lord of the Admiralty can give his First Sea Lord. The Chief would always do all he could to help even in that tricky campaign, hag-ridden with misunderstandings, to persuade the authorities to agree to the formation of the WRINS (Womens Royal Indian Naval Service). But when all these comparitively straightforward issues had been met and making every allowance for the malaise and poverty of India, there remained a spill over of problems, fortunately infrequent, where morale, politics, castes, creeds, leadership and climate intermingled—the imponderables, in fact, that can make or mar a service. These imponderables provide the most searching test of any organisation—a regiment, a fleet, a hospital, an industry. A regimental officer who assumes that a navy is just another sort of regiment, is handicapped from the start in appreciating the difficulties and risks of a Maritime Service, or indeed of the morale of a ship's company. There are more differences than similarities, as Napoleon failed to realise. Unless there are over-riding considerations of State, I would say that it is unsound to make a soldier or a sailor the political head of his own Service, or to interpose a soldier between the professional head of a navy, or a sailor between the CIGS, and the Cabinet. It might work operationally, but it is less likely to produce successful administration. Neither am I a believer in attempts to standardise Army and Navy administration; such attempts produce neither efficiency nor economy . . . Although I felt able to advise the Government of India and initiate and carry to fruition action regarding purely naval objectives, there were still a number of political and purely Indian matters which remained mysterious and for which no solution seemed possible; discipline, religion, caste, aspirations . . . my relations with Wavell and Auchinleck were anomalous—almost a contemporary and yet subordinate to officers who could give me no guidance on politico-military matters."

Godfrey lost two of his personal staff, his Secretary and his Flag Lieutenant, after a few months when they had to return to Britain due to ill health. Tinniswood was replaced by Captain (S) R. S. Braine RN. Godfrey found that "in addition to being an exceptionally sound and able supply and secretarial officer, he was a man of most mature experience and good judgement, who knew how to get difficult things done with a smile and without rubbing people up the wrong way. He got on very well with Trivedi, Philip Mason and the staff of the War and Finance Departments. He was never at a loss to devise ways of getting Naval Headquarters' proposals accepted by discovering the line where resistance was least. If one's cause is just, any means to achieve one's ends are justified and the line of least resistance may be found, for example, during a carefully arranged cocktail party, or by waiting until the opponent of whatever one wants is on tour. Braine was very good at this sort of thing." Braine had been warned in the Admiralty that he would find Godfrey an extremely difficult master to serve. In fact he came to like him once he had realised that the sudden 'tantrums', usually occasioned by some 'pet project' being held up, were short lived and quickly forgotten. What he did find unusual was that he was not expected to carry out the conventional duties of an Admiral's Secretary, but was told to regard himself as the head of a Department, dealing with the legal and administrative problems of the RIN. He was given full authority to use his own initiative, and told his chief did not expect to see him more than once a week unless he ran into trouble. On Godfrey's instructions Braine signed papers 'By command of FOCRIN.' This was in marked contrast to the practice in the War Department where a Lieutenant-Colonel confessed to Braine that he 'was only there to open envelopes.' As head of the Legal Department Braine had a particularly heavy commitment since there were, according to Godfrey, "never less than twelve Court Martials pending for 'offences to the prejudice of good order and naval discipline'. Braine and I were particularly lucky in finding the post of Judge Advocate held by an ex-barrister from Madras, Commander George Walker, RINVR(S) . . . His legal advice was always tempered by sound common sense and, unlike Sir John Simon, he did not present both sides of the case and leave it to me to decide. He proposed action and I can recall no instance when his judgement was at fault. I got into the habit of leaning on him heavily and consulting him not only on legal matters but on all sorts of subjects on which his understanding of Indian politics and points of view was invaluable to me and the Naval Service. A man of great ability and charm who expressed himself very lucidly verbally and on paper, he would have done well in any walk of life."

The new Flag Lieutenant was Lieutenant-Commander John Dixon, RINVR. "Having been in the princely firm of Mackinnon Mackenzie, the agents for P & O and BI Steamship lines, what he did not know about getting about India and the personalities at Indian ports was not worth knowing. He got on with everybody extremely well, was tactful and considerate, ran my domestic staff at Delhi without a hitch and coped most adequately with the unpredictable moods of all those who inhabited No. 12 King George's Avenue and of our transient guests, and never bothered me. What he enjoyed most was organising a 'party' and he did it extremely well."

Indianisation had, of course, started in the RIN. Godfrey, who was singularly free of the racial prejudices not uncommon in the Royal Navy or among certain of the British in India at that time, soon made up his mind "that, from every point of view, I should acquire an Indian Additional Secretary and an Indian Additional Flag Lieutenant. I sought the advice of His Highness the Jam Sahib, who strongly recommended for the secretarial post Lieutenant (S) Chakrapani Srinivasan, RINVR(S). Teddy Srinivasan was a high caste Brahmin, a product of Madras and Balliol who, after leaving Oxford, had been working in the firm of Parry's in Madras for ten years. Coming from good legal country stock, his cousin was the Editor of the *Hindu*, the best English paper in South India. I shall always be grateful to the Jam Sahib for putting me in touch with this knowledgeable, shrewd and endearing person, who served me so loyally for nearly three years and relieved Braine of all the Indian side of my work, consisting of correspondence and liaison with Indian officials and businessmen, Chambers of Commerce, members of the Legislative Council and Indian princes."

The appointment of the additional Flag Lieutenant did not come about until the end of 1943. On a visit to Jodhpur Godfrey had been impressed with the son of the Prime Minister, one of the relatives of the Maharaja. The young man in question, Naha Singh (always known as Tiger) and his sister, Baiji, had both been educated in England and had acquired a great liking for the British way of life. Godfrey arranged for Naha Singh to be appointed a Midshipman in the RINVR and after suitable training promoted and appointed as an additional Flag Lieutenant. Both he and his sister became firm friends of the Godfreys, staying with them in Delhi and visiting them in England after the war.

These then were Godfrey's principal personal staff officers; an able and talented band of men. He was also fortunate in having a number of other first class officers to fill senior appointments; Captain J. W. Jefford, RIN, "an outstanding officer of robust temperament", who succeeded Thomson as Chief of Personnel and Post-war Planning and later became the first Commander-in-Chief of the Pakistan Navy, Commodore L. Sanderson, one of the older RIN officers who was Naval Officer-in-Charge, Calcutta, Commodore P. A. Mare, RIN, Chief of Administration at Naval Headquarters, Commodore H. A. B. Digby Beste, RIN, "a retired officer of distinction, who returned to India with great public spirit in spite of ill health" as deputy to look after the Sea Transport side with Sir John Nicholson, a partner of the firm of Alfred Holt & Co, shipowners of Liverpool. Digby Beste was later succeeded by a RNR officer, Commodore D. A. Casey, RNR. Captain John Ryland, RIN specialised in motor gunboats, under the C-in-C Eastern Fleet; he did so well that Godfrey had "great difficulty in getting him back into the RIN proper and out of the grip of Sir James Somerville." Two other RIN officers should be mentioned at this stage although they did not come onto Godfrey's staff until later. The first is Captain John Lawrence, RIN. Godfrey had met him before he left for India, when Lawrence was commissioning the new sloop HIMS *Narbada*. "He had", writes Godfrey, "previously been Flag Lieutenant and Staff Officer Operations to my predecessor, and I had already made a mental note that I should like him to be my Chief of Staff. When Hall went to London it seemed obvious that Lawrence should take his place at Naval Headquarters with the rank of Commodore 2nd Class. Having travelled extensively in India with my predecessor he knew all the personal complications at India's six ports—Karachi, Bombay, Cochin, Vizagapatam, Calcutta and Chittagong—and at New Delhi, and was thoroughly at home with the heads of the Military Departments at GHQ. An officer of great stamina and initiative and an excellent and loyal Chief of Staff, I never had the slightest anxiety in leaving him in charge when I went on tour. Our happy collaboration developed into firm friendship." Like Braine, Lawrence appreciated the responsibility which Godfrey thrust upon him. He did not always agree with him but was never discouraged from expressing his own views and speaking his mind so that their mutual relations were, as Godfrey says, excellent.

The second officer who joined FOCRIN's staff later on was a young RIN regular, Lieutenant-Commander Tom Sheppard, who, in 1945 succeeded Dixon as Flag Lieutenant, combining this post with that of head of the Signals and Communications Department. "An Irishman with a strong sense of humour and a refreshingly outspoken manner, he would undoubtedly have gone to the top if things had been different. Never outwardly downhearted he was the greatest possible help to me during the difficult months early in 1946." Sheppard, who was serving in Naval Headquarters when Godfrey arrived in India, writes that he immediately 'made himself known to all the naval officers in New Delhi. I recollect him coming into my office (I was a very junior two striper) and sitting down to chat about my job, but more about me. I had never met him before but it so happened that my brother had been his secretary in *Kent*. There was therefore a bond between us however tenuous. Though it was wartime he—and Margaret—were most hospitable to all officers—young and old—and their house at 12 King George's Avenue was a most welcoming one. (Quite different a style from that of his predecessor.) I think this was the form on his many trips to the shore Establishments in India, a genuine attempt to get to know, and be known by, the officers. His commanding presence, and his undoubted intellect did, I believe, militate in some curious way against complete rapport with officers of my seniority—he *was* a formidable person, and somewhat forbidding. I personally could at times have stuck a knife in his back, but for most of the time I believe we got on well—perhaps because I was an outspoken and hot-tempered Irishman! I think people in the RIN must have been aware that Godfrey's influence was strong in Delhi; he was respected by the soldiers, he did meet the government officials who controlled the purse strings, he had presence in government circles. As I have implied, he was not popular—but he was respected. He built up the Naval Staff in New Delhi, and perhaps this did not necessarily endear him to the senior officers in the establishments; there was a lot of jealousy and anti-staff feeling among certain old hands—though I don't think it was the same with ships officers, who I would say felt they did have support from the top. Fitzherbert was popular but nowhere nearly as respected (or feared?) as JHG . . . I believe JHG did far more for India and the RIN.'

Reference has already been made to the Jam Sahib. He was the ruler of Jamnagar, a member of the Imperial War Cabinet and Pacific War Council and a staunch upholder of the British Raj. He was also a faithful and generous friend to the RIN. He had endowed the brand new Torpedo School at Valsura, so one of Godfrey's earliest and most pleasant duties was to pay him a visit and to experience a wonderful introduction to the hospitality and glamour of a well run Indian state. Writing to Margaret at the end of April, Godfrey described the visit as "great fun and the Jam Sahib a wonderful host—a most genial and wise ruler . . . As the Maharajah *is* the State there's no nonsense about getting Finance Department approval for every detail. There's no red tape and nothing much in writing; the ruler is very good to the Navy and most public spirited, practical and helpful. He has 156 cars, a private zoo and a bird sanctuary (instead of a partridge shoot). Meals are terrific and delicious and its very hard to eat moderately as some courses have ten ingredients, all served separately with speed and dexterity. The Maharani is charming and has 1700 saris." Godfrey and the Jam Sahib got on extremely well and this was only the first of many visits. Godfrey was intensely interested in India and its peoples and the Jam Sahib suggested to him that as well as inspecting the RIN's ports and bases and principal recruiting areas he should also visit the more accessible Indian States and tell their rulers, civil servants and business men something about the Navy and India's interest in sea power. In the next three years Godfrey visited twenty-five or so States and must have seen more of India than many British soldiers, civil servants or business men who spent their whole lives there. He obviously enjoyed these tours and the hospitality which he received, but they were all undertaken with the very definite object of drumming up support for and interest in the RIN; Godfrey proved to be a most successful evangelist.

To get to know leading Indian politicians and businessmen was less easy. Contact with Congress leaders was frowned on;

Gandhi and Nehru were in gaol in 1943, but Teddy Srinavasan did introduce his Admiral to Birla, the millionaire businessman, a strong supporter of the Congress movement at whose house Gandhi generally stayed when he was in Delhi. Birla was of great service to the RIN and endowed a pre-training centre for naval mechanics at Pilani in the State of Lharu on the frontiers of Jaipur. He controlled a string of papers and was, Godfrey says, "always ready to print anything I sent him without altering a word. I used to lunch with him occasionally and met the redoubtable Sardar Vallabhai Patel. A barrister-at-law, he was reputed to be very tough, and, as Gandhi's and Nehru's right hand man, became Minister for Home Affairs and liquidated the States when India achieved Independence. But at lunch he showed no signs of toughness and was worried about a rumour that Jinnah was collaborating with the Russians at Lahore—a cock and bull story. Jinnah I only met once, when I paid a courtesy call. I have rarely encountered anyone with less charm. As leader of the Muslim League he had everything to gain and nothing to lose by being on good terms with the Admiral Commanding the Indian Navy which in pre-war years was almost entirely Muslim. Instead he accused me of deliberately favouring Hindoo as against Muslim recruitment. I got the impression of a thoroughly tiresome person, as indeed he proved to be during the 1947 Independence negotiations."

An Indian statesman for whom Godfrey came to have a great admiration was Chakravarti Rajagopalachariar, a close adherent of Gandhi. He was a barrister and had been Prime Minister of Madras from 1937 to 1939 and in 1948 was to succeed Lord Mountbatten as Governor General. "The elder statesman of the Congress movement, mystic, philosopher and author of books on Socrates, Marcus Aurelius, Bhagavadgita and the Upanished and a manual about drink and drug problems in India, he had been many years trying to turn the British out. Now [1945] he found them only too anxious to leave. He said, 'I have only had two years of real responsibility to fit me for the tasks I shall have to undertake so soon when India is independent . . . I am already sixty-six years old . . . a lifetime of criticism and opposition unfits people for the task of governance . . .'. His humility was impressive, he seemed too old for his years, a saintly old man very friendly and kind, a great man in the best sense and very shrewd. I was very anxious to start a Navy League to popularise the Navy and teach India a little about the sea, but was doubtful if the moment was propitious, so I consulted CR. 'Better not . . . yet . . . if you start it the Indian politicians will twist it round and attack you and it will have a bad beginning . . . better leave it to an Indian to start.'

"Having met three people—Rajagopalachariar, Sardar Patel and Birla—who were so close to Gandhi, I feel sorry now that I made no attempt to meet the Mahatma himself. Birla offered to bring about such a meeting, but as neither the Viceroy, Lord Wavell, (unlike Lord Irwin) nor General Auchinleck had made any attempt to contact him when he came out of prison in 1944 I felt it was up to me to follow their example." No doubt Godfrey was right about this, but it is a pity; unlikely as it may seem, Godfrey and Gandhi would probably have got on very well together.

In October 1943, Margaret finally joined her husband. She arrived in Bombay "just as the monsoon broke. It was extra-ordinary to find life going on fairly normally—cocktail parties, evening dresses, but everyone anxious to hear first hand news of London and the Blitz. John had already made many friends amongst the Parsees as well as the Services and the Governor (Lord Colville), so I was welcomed and everything made easy for me . . . FOCRIN's house in Delhi was built by Baker, who had co-operated with Lutyens on many of the official residences. Set in a fair-sized garden with trees and lawns and approached up a wide avenue it was a bungalow with verandah all round and spacious pleasant rooms with an open courtyard in the centre. This pattern had earned them the names of 'Baker's Ovens', as the heat entered the very centre. However, ours had been roofed over by previous tenants and we lunched on the verandah in the winter and dined in the garden in the summer . . . Delhi was crowded with people living in wooden huts in the compound of the Imperial Hotel and also in tents. Those of us with space therefore had Paying Guests filling up the house. We had John's Secretary (Tinniswood, then Braine), Commodore Digby-Beste (to keep an eye on his diet), the Flag Lieutenant, who ran the house for us, the Head of the Womens Royal Indian Naval Service (WRINS) and her small daughter, the additional Indian Flag Lieutenant, 'Tiger' Naha Singh, who slept in a tent in the garden (his Nepalese servant slept across the doorway with a drawn Kukri), while the spare room, which was seldom empty, was occupied by RN officers and others passing through Delhi." A frequent visitor who became an 'adopted daughter' was Tiger's sister, Baiji, who despite her English and Swiss education, had to remain in purdah in Jodhpur but was allowed to go anywhere accompanied by Margaret in Delhi. After the war she lived with the Godfreys in London and Sussex, was assistant to Krishna Menon when he was High Commissioner in London and to Mrs Pandit in Paris and then, on returning to India, secretary to the Maharani Mater of Jodhpur who was elected to the National Assembly. Margaret remarks that this would never have been possible but for "John's whole-hearted support."

Godfrey had always enjoyed entertaining and was an excellent host. "He was anxious", Margaret writes, "that young RIN officers and their wives, coming from all parts of the sub-continent to Delhi, where they might have no friends, should be welcomed at our house so that the often very shy wives might meet each other. We also had dinner parties to meet Indians, civilians, Army and Air Force officers, WRNS and FANNYs. Our excellent Goanese cook could be relied on to produce delicious food . . . he had awaited my arrival before deciding whether to stay; luckily our ideas coincided and we got on well."

For many women the running of such an establishment (even though much of the administration fell to the Flag Lieutenant), would have been a whole-time job, but, despite some reservations on her husband's part, it was not enough for Margaret. After a spell working in the cypher office at Naval Head-quarters, she was persuaded to take over from Lady Hartley, who after many years in India was returning to England, the job of Secretary of the Womens' Voluntary Service (India). Each Province had its own WVS of which the Governor's wife was the President, and whose members were the leading English and Indian women in the area. It was the Secretary's job to co-ordinate their work with the welfare needs of the Army, Navy and Air Force, and it is a striking tribute to Margaret's personality and to the reputation which had preceeded her from ISTD that, knowing neither the country nor the people, she was so quickly chosen for the position. Lady Hartley had used her verandah as an office in the mornings, but Margaret did not think this arrangement could or should be continued and got permission to take over a concrete air-raid shelter, "unused and unneeded, very hot in summer and cold in winter", which she persuaded the WVS President, Lady Wavell to open. A series of conferences in the Viceroy's House of all the Governors' wives brought invitations to visit the different Provinces and travel all over the country. Margaret regarded it as "a unique opportunity to meet the leading Indian ladies, who were doing such splendid work. Lady Wavell was easy to work with and I constantly went to Viceroy's House to confer with her. Although she was most friendly and I never remember her opposing my suggestions, the atmosphere in those days was still formal—I curtseyed on arrival and departure and never referred to her except as 'Her Excellency'. Lunch, to which she kindly invited me when we had not finished our work, was something of a strain. I had a great admiration for Lord Wavell, but, as others have written, he was not easy to talk to. At that time he had so much on his mind with the long drawn out negotiations with Jinnah and Nehru and so many subjects could not be raised, that I felt that I was intruding on his needed relaxation of family lunch . . .

"The variety and colour of the Indian scene has been described often far better than I can do it—the wonders of the Himalayas, the beauty of the Rajputana States, the miracle of the Taj, the endless diversity of races and personalities, the devotion of the ICS officers to their people and provinces, and of the Indian Army officers to their regiments—all these combine to impress those who have lived there with a tremendous feeling for India which transcends the frustrations, the dirt, the poverty, the heat and the insects. I think that I can say that this was true of John and myself. We were very fortunate to be there and experience it in the last years of the British Raj and before Partition; the period when everyone was working towards independence."

CHAPTER THIRTEEN

RIN

AFTER HIS first preliminary tour of inspection of the RIN, Godfrey's immediate preoccupation was to secure help from the Admiralty in the shape of the loan of thirty lieutenant-commanders or commanders to make up for the shortfall of forty officers of this rank caused by the recruitment ban. Anticipating the objections likely to be raised in Whitehall he enlisted the aid of the Viceroy and the Commander-in-Chief, who followed up official letters to the Secretary of State for India with urgent personal telegrams. Godfrey himself wrote to Pound, pointing out the impossibility of running a Service of upwards of 20,000 officers and men with a cadre of permanent officers of lieutenant-commander's rank and above of only 49. The request was received sympathetically but in the end rejected on the grounds that the Royal Navy's own needs rendered its fulfillment impossible.

Godfrey was not prepared to give up and turned for support to Somerville, Commander-in-Chief, Eastern Fleet. Somerville, a totally different character to Godfrey, had not, as we have already noted, been in favour of Godfrey's appointment, but during the course of the next eighteen months the two Admirals collaborated closely and friendly personal relations were quickly established. In a letter of 30 August Godfrey set out the problem with which he was faced and traced the course of the unsuccessful appeal to the Admiralty. He went on to say, "In the meantime we are being overtaken by events. The RIN is being called upon to play an increasingly important part in any impending operations, and instead of receiving the much hoped for and badly needed reinforcements from the RN, is required to lend officers to the EEF for signals, intelligence, security and other extraneous duties, without as yet, any prospect of replacement from the West. I should like to say at this point that the RIN gladly accepts these additional tasks especially as we possess in the officers of the RINVR the only source from which men with certain specialised knowledge can be drawn . . . From a naval point of view the RIN suddenly finds itself in the front row of the stalls and is very ready and anxious to play its part. It can do this better by improving its quality than by increasing its numbers and to do this it *must* receive the support in an active and practical form of the Royal Navy. I feel the moment has arrived when I must invoke your aid on the highest plane to persuade the Admiralty (a) to accompany any new forces that are sent to India by all their essential base and maintenance facilities and personnel, and in other words to regard India as a country whose resources are already too fully stretched; (b) to send at least a few officers to strengthen the more senior ranks of the RIN . . . There should and could be a mutual recognition that although the British sailor can do many things as well and better than the Indian sailor, there are realms of activity in which the Indian and especially the Punjabi Mussulman, is pre-eminent . . . In the more technical spheres of W/T, electrics etc., the Madrassi and the men from Travancore are probably more intelligent than the corresponding recruit in the United Kingdom but they are brittle, and lack, at present, the instinct for leadership which is implicit in the men of the Punjab . . . As an interim measure . . . could three officers of suitable rank in the Eastern Fleet be spared now, and more as and when circumstances permit?"

Somerville replied that he was 'fully alive to the urgent need for officers of the type you mention . . . and quite a year ago I pressed on Fitzherbert the need to ask for such officers and to get them if possible while the going was good. I think that Fitzherbert was reluctant to adopt this suggestion at first, though he certainly became alive to the need . . . later on'. Somerville went on to say that the Eastern Fleet was equally 'at its wits end' to find officers and he could not loan Godfrey even the few he had requested. 'All I can do is to inform the Admiralty I have received this request from you, that I am unable to comply, but that I feel the need to supplement the RIN is so pressing that I hope the question of producing these officers from the United Kingdom may be favourably reconsidered.' Despite this support, little was forthcoming.

The Royal Navy was of course beginning to experience difficulties in providing officers for its own greatly increased requirements. Between 1939 and 1944, when RN personnel reached a peak, the numbers of officers and men grew from just under 120,000 to just under 864,000, a sevenfold expansion. But by 1943 the RIN from a proportionately much smaller base, with no naval tradition behind it, had already expanded twelvefold!

The trouble was that there was little understanding of India's problems or needs in the Admiralty. Lawrence, Godfrey's future Chief of Staff, has recalled how, in 1937, when a Lieutenant-Commander, he attended a meeting at the Admiralty presided over by Admiral Forbes to pick young officers for the executive and engineering branches of the RN and the Indian and Dominion Navies. It was suggested that a candidate, rejected as unsuitable for the RN, might do for the RIN. Lawrence, despite his junior rank, protested that, as India was trying to create a new Service out of nothing, they needed the pick of the recruits not the cast-offs. This point of view had not occurred to Admiral Forbes, but he was so impressed by it that he asked Lawrence to lunch and listened with great interest to what he had to say about India's Navy. Unfortunately the lack of understanding persisted and when, from time to time, RN or RNVR officers could be extracted from the Admiralty too many of them were not really suitable, by age, health or temperament for the testing and trying duties for which they were required.

The Royal Navy also seemed oblivious to India's size and the comparative lack of first class road and rail communications in many areas. Tom Sheppard noted that the British Naval Staff seemed to be 'incapable of grasping the elementary facts of geography. I recall initiating a signal from FOCRIN recommending the establishment of Radar bases at Calcutta, Vizagapatam and Madras for the Bengal escort forces. The Admiralty decreed that spares were always obtainable in Bombay!' Commodore Jefford has referred to 'the rather astonishing but continued lack of knowledge about the exact political status of the Government of India and the Indian Services—particularly the Navy. To some extent this was still going on when I left Pakistan in 1953 (he was the first Commander-in-Chief of the Royal Pakistan Navy). When I went to see the Naval Secretary to ask for my name to be put down as a Commodore of Convoys, he said it couldn't be done as I was earmarked to return to Pakistan as C-in-C of the Navy should war break out within the next three years. He was genuinely surprised when I pointed out that this appointment was in the hands of the Government of Pakistan alone.'

It was not easy, against such a background, for Godfrey to make much progress but he did not give up easily and his official correspondence throughout his three years in India is full of letters trying to explain the Indian situation and the needs of the RIN to the First Sea Lord and the Naval Staff. At least his efforts in 1943 did result in the appointment of two senior RN officers, Commodore W. O. Scrymgeour-Wedder-burn as Commodore, Bay of Bengal, and Commodore G. A. French as Director of Training, a particularly vital post in the light of the enormous influx of completely green officers and ratings. Some other officers were eventually provided by the RN, but in his Memoirs Godfrey says, "Some of the more senior officers sent out by the Admiralty lacked initiative and drive and were unable for other reasons to adapt themselves to the exacting conditions of life in India and to the needs of an expanding Service. These people, so far from being any help to the rapidly growing RIN with its complex racial difficulties, proved to be an added embarrassment. Lacking the basic qualities needed for such work, they demanded status, accom-modation and staff which could ill be spared. They preferred the comparative comfort of Bombay and Calcutta to the arduous touring without which their existence could not be justified. After much reflection I feel that the senior RNR officers, Casey, Dean, Tanner and Blair were much more use to the RIN . . . RNR officers know all about ports and shipping and are more men of the world than their RN contemporaries who have led sheltered lives in a closed Service.

"Neither were some of the RN senior officers at Royal Naval establishments in India any better. Many of them treated Indians with open contempt and rudeness and rode rough-shod over the feelings of people who, with a little consideration and good manners, were quite prepared to give loyal service. At one time there were three such oafs at Bombay, a disgrace to the British Navy and a continuing and admitted source of embarrassment to Admiral Somerville, to Jack Rattray as well as to me. At that particularly difficult time when the walls of the dockyard were plastered with slogans such as 'Quit India' one retired Commander, a contemporary of mine, was going about calling people black bastards—it didn't help. Admirals Somerville and [his successor] Power were conscious of all this, but could do little about it as they, like me, had to accept what the Admiralty sent. The RIN was doing its best to turn Punjabi soldiers into shallow water sailors—landing craft crews—at Mandapam, but when they saw them working off a beach near Bombay two senior RN officers said they'd rather have the worst British landing crews than the best Indian. A year later there had been a reshuffling of the RN and Royal Marine landing crews. The best were needed for the landings in France. Those that we met in Arakan were the dregs, inferior in morale and execution to the Punjabis beside whom they made a poor showing.

"Being wise after the event, I suppose the RIN should have gone all out for Indianisation from the very start, but this ignores the political difficulties that existed in the twenties and thirties and the element of indifference and scepticism regarding all matters appertaining to the Navy at Delhi. Auchinleck was, after all, the first Commander-in-Chief in India who took any interest in the RIN. In London one or two Commanders in Plans Division saw the need for encouraging the naval idea, but were not able to make much headway against the dead weight of opposition in the India Office, whose attitude in those days was one of strong discouragement. It would have been much easier if we could have said [to the Indians], 'We are just here to do all we can to help you create a good Navy by the time you are independent, so make the most of us while you have got us. Benefit by our experience. Suck our brains.' But, instead, the word 'Independence' was tabooed and when it came it came all too suddenly."

At the beginning of December 1943 Godfrey wrote to Sir Andrew Cunningham, who had succeeded Pound as First Sea Lord on the latter's resignation and death six weeks earlier, "When I came out in March I succeeded to a very alive and vigorous little Service, which had passed through a process of very rapid expansion, and was now consolidating in an administrative sense." He recognised the difficulties with which the Admiralty was faced in meeting his requests and expressed his gratitude for Commodores French and Wedderburn but went on to point out the commitments which the RIN had had to meet in developing new bases such as Cochin and Vizagapatam, where RIN personnel now far outnumbered the RN. He also drew attention to the RIN's dependence on its Volunteer Reserve officers. "We have to depend on our RINVR officers for a great many duties which in the UK are performed by regular officers, and one has to realise that the amateur might not stand up to the rigours of real war in the east. For this reason I have asked the Admiralty to replace by RNVR officers twenty or thirty RINVRs that we have lent to the South East Asia Command, returned to their previous employment or earmarked for Burma . . . I have taken your advice and done a good deal of travelling . . . (nearly 20,000 miles) and have seen a great deal of India, Indian ports and Indian high personages. I find a great keeness among Indian statesmen for the future of the Navy, and, as this interest is for the most part non-political, Great Britain could make no better gesture than to help us during this rather critical period of our existence. Really the only criticism I would make would be that we have followed the Canadian model of isolation rather than the New Zealand and Australian model of collaboration and I feel that the period of isolation should end if this small force . . . is to pull its weight during the next two or three years, but of course I realise your difficulties . . ."

Godfrey went on to emphasise the need for any officers coming out to India to be of good health ("Some of our recent experience has not been too happy"), and then commented on the desirable length of the appointment of the Flag Officer Commanding the RIN. "It has been the custom in the past to let the post of FOCRIN run on three and a half, five or six years. This I think was a bad idea, and it would have been far better if it had been limited to say three years in peace time, and not more than two in war time. In each case, I am afraid my three predecessors stayed too long. The health reason . . . applies to all appointments, and from my observation so far I think that everyone suffers from a diminution of energy, go and initiative after his second hot weather season. Moreover the position of a Flag Officer flying his flag 800 miles from the sea is a peculiar one. His contacts with the Royal Navy are confined to the RN officers he meets at Delhi and Bombay, to meetings with the C-in-C EF and very occasional visits to Ceylon. He is bound to get stale and out of date. Lack of *recent* Admiralty experience must also be a great handicap. My task will be to consolidate the training, administration and discipline of the fine force that Fitzherbert has turned over to me. This will take about two years, and *then* I think I should be relieved by a Flag Officer who has plenty of practical experience afloat and a good war record. This will give Indian opinion, and the RIN, a feeling of confidence that the Admiralty and the RN are doing their very best to make the RIN a success and give it the chance it deserves . . . I should really spend at least a quarter of my time in Bombay, and visit all ports every quarter, and this will be my eventual aim when we have got the HQ here completely efficient, and able to set our needs to the Government, follow them up, and to convert them into action . . . What we are aiming for at present, is to make everything as ready as it can possibly be by September 1944."

It is quite clear that after less than nine months in India Godfrey already saw that the RIN was faced with two distinct problems; the short-term one of making the maximum possible contribution to the Imperial war effort (and it should be remembered that at this time very few responsible people in Britain or the United States expected Japan to be defeated by the middle of 1946), and the long-term problem of creating a well-balanced permanent Navy for the future Indian State, whatever that might be. The first objective, which was of course paramount, was not easily reconcilable with the second, nor was the Royal Navy, at this stage of the war, really in a position to give the sympathy and practical help that was essential to either of them.

The arrival of Admiral Lord Louis Mountbatten in India as Supreme Allied Commander South East Asia in September 1943 did nothing to ease matters, because he too needed liaison officers and others with special qualifications from the RIN. Once again Godfrey had to explain his desperate shortage of officers and in fact to press for the return of one single commander, who was urgently needed to take over as Naval Officer-in-Charge, Madras. It required many letters and much lobbying before his return to the RIN could be secured.

The problem of obtaining officers was only equalled by the difficulties of attracting sufficient recruits for the lower deck. The modest pre-war expansion had been achieved by recruiting, for the first time, from the Punjab. This had brought problems because the Petty Officers were, inevitably, still drawn only from the Ratnigiris. However, by 1939, a proper balance was being reached. But, with the enormous expansion demanded immediately on the outbreak of war, emergency measures were called for. The considerable number of small merchant ships commandeered for coastal defence purposes had to be manned somehow. It could only be done by getting as many as possible of their existing lascar crews to sign on as Hostilities Only men, on Merchant Navy rates of pay. These were higher than those for RIN ratings but soon fell behind those obtained by lascars remaining in the Merchant Navy. Moreover the Hostilities Only men were akin to the Ratnigiris, good seamen but of a low standard of education and with few natural martial qualities. Some of them, of course, had to be made Leading Hands and Petty Officers, although ill-suited for these duties, but the majority of regular service Petty Officers were now Punjabis, a reversal of the position in the mid-thirties. The difficulties of different rates of pay and terms of service were realised, but had to be accepted, by the authorities. In an effort to overcome them yet a third class of entry was devised—the Special Service rating. These men were much more akin to the normal continuous service rating, but were entered at the age of eighteen or more instead of as boys and on a five year instead of a ten year engagement. At first this worked well, but quite soon it was apparent that barracks and training facilities were inadequate to cope with the increased numbers, and then, by 1941, the flow of recruits began to dry up. The RIN had not really faced up to the problem of recruiting in direct competition with the Army which, with its long established traditions, was taking the best. This was when recourse had to be had to the south of India. Many of these men were attracted to the Navy only by the fact that it was a job offering far greater pay than they could otherwise have expected, but some did join out of a motive of patriotism and many of them had a far higher standard of literacy and education, and were more fluent in English, than the Punjabis. Such qualifications were essential for the technical ratings in communications, radar, electrics and engineering required for the new ships coming into service. So the lower deck of the RIN very rapidly ceased to be essentially Mussulman. Hindoos and Indian

Christians, not to mention Sikhs, Parsees and many others eventually formed half the total. Unlike the Indian Army, where companies, let alone regiments, of mixed race and creed were rarities, ships, companies and establishments came to be a complete amalgam of races, castes, creeds and colours. To weld such a heterogeneous body of men, very many of whom had never even seen the sea, into a disciplined and efficient fighting force in a matter of months rather than years, to serve an alien government, was a truly Herculean task. Wastage, by discharge and desertion, was high, at least so long as sufficient training establishments and experienced training officers were lacking.

The RIN's problem in this respect was not made any easier by the fact that it had adopted the Royal Navy's Divisional system of man management instead of depending on the Indian Army's well tried method of relying on the Viceroy's Commissioned Indian Officers (VCOs) as a link between the officers and other ranks. The Divisional system was probably the best in the world and worked splendidly in the RIN so long as the Service was small and homogeneous and the officers experienced and fluent in Urdu. "The rapid expansion after 1940", according to Godfrey, "brought into the RINVR a large number of officers, both Indian and British, from the business and mercantile world whose knowledge of India and its peoples was extremely local and whose knowledge of Indian castes and creeds was very sketchy. Auchinleck was always urging me to abolish the Divisional system and adopt the cult of the Viceroy's Commissioned Indian Officer which had been built up through 200-odd years of trial and error in the Indian Army. One cannot bring about a drastic administrative change like this during a war. It was a long-distance project, and I had grave doubts if a scheme that worked with a Ghurka or Punjabi regiment would suit a small ship with Hindoos, Sikhs and Muslims working alongside each other. It was indeed a bold experiment to found a Navy where Muslim, Hindoo, Sikh, Christian and Parsee were all brought together and asked to live at peace with each other in the narrow confines of a small ship's mess deck. Frowned on by the orthodox and dogmatic it was remarkable that it worked at all. That it worked as well as it did for a quarter of a century was due to a small band of devoted British Officers who filled the senior posts in the RIN."

It is really difficult to see how the VCO system could have been successfully introduced into the RIN in peacetime, let alone in the middle of the war.

When Godfrey arrived in India recruitment of RIN ratings was the responsibility of but two officers, based in Bombay. Local recruitment in the Punjab and elsewhere was in the hands of the Army recruiting authorities. They did all they could for the Navy, but naturally their knowledge of naval conditions and terms of service was limited and, with the best will in the world, the Army tended to get the pick of recruits. Godfrey, as usual, determined to see for himself and at the beginning of December set off on an extensive tour of the Punjab to see what could be done to improve the Naval Recruiting Service. This was something that none of his predecessors had undertaken and after an exhausting ten days, in which he visited places as far apart as the Khyber Pass and Patiala and met all sorts of people from Provincial Governors to village headmen and District Commissioners to the fathers of serving RIN ratings, he returned to Delhi full of ideas for improvements in the organisation. In his report to Auchinleck Godfrey remarked that he felt that results had been most valuable, and that "it had certainly opened my eyes to the complexity of the problem and to the urgency of its solution."

Difficulties about pay have already been mentioned. "Sometime during 1944 Sir Mohamed Azizul Huque, Member for Commerce and Industry, had succeeded in getting the pay of lascars on board Indian and British Merchant ships doubled until it equalled the pay of European sailors. Fair enough, but perhaps rather unstatesmanlike, as it ignored the position of lascars recruited into the RIN as 'Hostilities Only' ratings whose pay remained unaltered at its lowly level. The result was two-fold, (a) Hostilities Only ratings tried to leave the Service and join the Mercantile Marine, but were not allowed to do so, and (b) it became impossible to recruit the better type of lascar. The sense of grievance among HO ratings was not without its effect on the rest of the Service and was accentuated by comparisons with the Royal Navy both as regards pay and conditions when RN and RIN ships met. The great disparity of pay between the RIN on the one hand and the Merchant Service, the RN and the Burma and Ceylon Navies on the other was keenly felt. I considered that there was just cause for a

substantial rise in pay for the HO ratings at least. With the
help of the War Department we made out a cast iron case
which was, of course, shot down by the Military Finance
Department. I decided to appeal to the Viceroy, Lord Wavell,
and in due course our petition came before that august body,
the Viceroy's Council, at which all the high-ups including the
Members for War and Supply, Auchinleck and Sir Azizul
Huque, and their Secretaries and, of course, the Finance
Department were present. The Viceroy paid great attention to
all that was said but the wind of politics was blowing fiercely
round him at the time and I had regretfully to conclude that
my appeal had failed and that the Finance Department had
won. Wavell gave no indication of how his mind was working.
Trivedi, who must have known what was going on behind the
scenes, preserved an impenetrable silence. I gained the impression that neither Wavell nor Auchinleck had the feeling of
personal responsibility that they would have experienced had
the HO ratings been part of the Indian Army. Neither did these
two distinguished soldiers, invested with responsibility for a
maritime dilemma, display the interest that one would expect
from a First Lord of the Admiralty or Minister of Defence.
Their silences were impressive. This was the only occasion on
which I invoked the Viceroy's aid. It confirmed my belief that
the political head of a fighting service should be a civilian, not
a soldier or a sailor."

A similar difficulty arose over the request that Chief and
Petty Officers be given the privilege of second-class rail
travel, enjoyed by their opposite numbers in the Royal Navy
and by some non-commissioned officers in the Indian Army.
The proposal was constantly put forward by Naval Headquarters and as regularly turned down by the Military Finance
Department. This refusal was bitterly resented by the Petty
Officers, and, in addition, gave rise to the feeling that Naval
Headquarters were indifferent to their welfare. Although at
first sight a fairly minor matter, it remained a festering sore
which in no way helped to ensure the loyalty and devotion to
the RIN of a body of men which, in any Navy, should be the
backbone of the Service. It was yet another example of the
disadvantages which the RIN had to face in dealing with an
Army orientated bureaucracy.

Despite all these difficulties and despite Godfrey's wish to consolidate and improve quality rather than to continue to expand the Service, the demands on the RIN to man more ships, to provide more facilities, both for itself and the RN, increased month by month as the need to go over to the offensive against the Japanese in Burma, Malaya and the Dutch East Indies was pressed by Whitehall. By the beginning of 1944 it was clear to Godfrey that radical steps would have to be taken to bring the problems of the RIN, current and future, to the attention of the Admiralty and that this could only be accomplished by a visit by himself to Britain and the appointment of a senior RIN officer as liaison officer in Whitehall. Considerable opposition was encountered from the India Office who feared any infringement of its own position as final arbiter of all matters appertaining to India. Commodore French, Godfrey's Training Director, had been back to London on his Department's business. Godfrey reported to Auchinleck that "just as French was leaving the India Office, the Governor General's telegram to the Secretary of State recommending that I should go to England in the spring for a few weeks, reached Mr Bull, the Second Division Clerk who deals with RIN matters. Mr Bull was in some doubt whether he should concur with the Governor General's proposal . . . French naturally replied that it was not for him to comment on a representation coming from India . . . My new Secretary, Paymaster Captain Braine [had also] met Mr Bull at the India Office, and enquired what corresponded to the Admiralty for the Royal Indian Navy. Bull replied 'I am the Admiralty' . . . It seems odd to me that a person of Bull's status should even be asked an opinion on such a matter. His highest contacts at the Admiralty are Second Division Clerks in the Admiralty Secretariat, and it is these who usually inspire the answers which subsequently find their way into the Secretary of State's replies to the Governor General . . . I feel that the best service I can give to the RIN is to encourage and stimulate the interest of the Admiralty and of the Royal Navy in its welfare and development and convince them that the RIN is worth Admiralty support. We have tried the indirect approach via the India Office and it has failed. My proposal is that we should now find a direct link by the Flag Officer Commanding with the various Admiralty Departments, an approach which has been available to and constantly used by Dominion Navies for a quarter of a century. It would be a tragedy if misplaced departmentalism in Whitehall is to deny us this approach . . ."

Thanks to the wholehearted support of Auchinleck, and the Viceroy, the opposition of the India Office was overcome and approval given not only for Godfrey to make a brief visit but for the appointment of Commodore Hall, hitherto FOCRIN's Chief of Staff, as RIN Liaison officer to the Admiralty and Naval Adviser to the India Office. Hall accompanied Godfrey to London at the end of May (1944), and was introduced by him to the heads of most of the Admiralty Departments. In a letter of 9 June Godfrey reported to Auchinleck that "we have found the greatest goodwill everywhere. I think we shall have no difficulty in settling most of the outstanding problems . . . Experience has so far shown that this representation in London has been really essential for a long time and has fully justified the steps you have approved." In a further report a month later he set out under seventeen different headings all the questions which had been discussed and reiterated that the visit had been most valuable, particularly in installing Hall, whose appointment had, in the end, been very much welcomed at the India Office. Hall held the appointment for the rest of the war and did a great deal to dispel the ignorance of and apathy towards India's naval needs which had hitherto prevailed both in the India Office and in the Admiralty. He was succeeded as Chief of Staff by Commodore John Lawrence, previously Captain of the new sloop *Narbada*.

In considering the problems of recruitment for the RIN, there was one source which Godfrey soon realised had hardly been tapped, India's woman power. He not only enjoyed the company of the opposite sex but he did not share the feelings of many of his contemporaries about the role which women could play in a man's world. He was, perhaps mildly by today's standards, a feminist, even though he had considerable reservations about the impact on his own well-being of his wife's activities in the Indian WVS. A month after his arrival in India he had written to Margaret that "The women of India can never be accused of not doing their bit. They provide more than half the unskilled labour for making airfields, roads, barracks and docks. Whole villages and communities take part, the women doing the same work as the men plus cooking, looking after the children and their temporary mat-shed homes.

You see them at it everywhere in their pretty red, blue or purple saris, the babies slung in a blanket hammock nearby." This, however, was of little help to the undermanned Navy. There was, in India, no equivalent to the British Womens Royal Naval Service (WRNS). Godfrey was determined that there should be, and if at first this idea was conceived purely to meet the needs of the Navy, it soon came to have a subsidiary objective, namely to attract young educated Indian women out of purdah and show them just what part they could play in the future development of their country. The formation and the development of the Womens Royal Indian Naval Services (WRINS) was something very close to Godfrey's heart, one of what his Secretary called his 'bees in his bonnet'. To discern the need for a new organisation and to build it up from scratch, against apathy or opposition, was something at which Godfrey excelled, as the history of ISTD at Oxford, amongst other projects, had already demonstrated. The creation of the WRINS, although to his intense disappointment it was disbanded after the war, was not the least of Godfrey's services to India and the RIN.

At the outbreak of war a number of officers' wives and other public-spirited ladies started work as civilians in cypher offices and similar departments for the Army and to a lesser extent the RIN and IAF. After some time they were formed into the Women's Auxiliary Corps (India), (WAC(I)). Although in theory an inter-Service organisation it naturally was organised on army lines and wore army uniform akin to that of the British ATS. Its Director was Lady Carlisle. Mrs M. I. Cooper (now Mrs Skipwith), who became head of the WRINS when they were formed, and who in the early days was working as WAC(I) Recruiting Officer in Bombay and therefore closely in touch with the RIN, has written that 'these khaki-uniformed sub-alterns, sergeants and corporals looked rather incongruous in Naval Offices . . . Undoubtedly the RIN officers were extremely keen that the women who worked for them should wear Naval uniform like themselves and be subject to the same rules and regulations.' There was more to it though than just naval amour propre. Singapore had been a key link in the Imperial Naval communications network. Its loss had thrown an exceptionally heavy burden on the RIN's signal organisation. One means of relieving this pressure was, obviously, to recruit a

considerable number of intelligent, English-speaking girls. The
WRNS in Britain had already shown the extent to which
women could take over men's jobs not only in communications
but in a host of other duties in headquarters, shore establishments and training schools. Godfrey saw that the required
numbers would never be obtained so long as the Navy had no
control at all over recruitment, selection, training, discipline or
amenities. "Deservedly or not, some of the khaki-clad WAC(I)s
had got a bad name and this was exploited by the press. Some
parents were unwilling to let their daughters leave the sheltered
life of an Indian home." In addition the suggestion of forming
a 'Naval Wing', as it was first called, was bitterly contested
by the Army and WAC (I) authorities who could not see the
necessity of forming a separate naval Service and feared that
it could only be done at the Army's expense. In Mrs Cooper's
view 'there is no question that it was John's enthusiasm, and
tremendous driving force which helped us create the WRINS
as a separate entity. He made untiring efforts to overcome the
problems in the way by dealing directly with the C-in-C, Chief
of Staff, War Department, and WAC(I) Directorate. He went
on and on until he wore them down! Finally it was agreed there
should not be a complete break with the WAC(I), as Lady
Carlisle remained the overall Chief of both wings, but we were
allowed to write our own Regulations, wear our own uniform,
adapt our discipline to a modified form of the Naval code and
run our own hostels.' The first step was to get the girls of the
Naval Wing into Naval uniform. Mrs Cooper writes that 'as
two-thirds of the women enrolled were Indian [the proportion
was lower in the much larger Army Wing] two styles of uniform
were developed, one consisting of a white sari with blue border
to suit the graceful Indian girls, and, for the British and
Anglo-Indians, an attractive uniform based on that of the
WRNS . . . It was a great day when gold braid replaced
subaltern' stars and crossed killicks the sergeants' stripes . . . In
spite of the sheltered lives led by most Indian girls prior to
joining up, they proved themselves very adaptable, hard
working and amenable to discipline. Their hostels were run
with the minimum of trouble, although Mohammedans,
Hindoos, Parsees, Pathans, Anglo-Indians and British lived side
by side. The only allowance made for differences in taste were
the meals, two sets being provided. The girls were employed

in some of the most interesting jobs such as cipher, teleprinter and dome teacher operators, and worked in many establishments such as Naval Headquarters, Combined Operations, RIN Tactical Unit, Fleet Mail and Sea Transport, the naval Gunnery School, and most of the RIN training schools.' The Naval Wing, a term disliked both by the 'Naval Wingers' themselves, and even more so by the WAC(I) authorities, numbered 41 officers and 204 ratings at the end of 1943. Two years later there were 242 officers and 746 ratings, by which time 43 per cent of the officers (80 per cent among the juniors) and 77 per cent of the ratings were Indian.

The name 'WRIN' was adopted spontaneously and against official opposition by the girls themselves, who had immediately identified themselves with and given their whole-hearted loyalty to the RIN. Writing to Lady Carlisle in November 1944, Godfrey criticised the name WAC(I) as having no popular appeal to Indians. "It is a deterrent to recruiting and uncomplimentary to Indian national feeling as the significant 'I' is put in brackets at the end." He went on to suggest various alternatives, which did not find favour with her ladyship, and then explained that "since the expression 'Naval Winger' is forbidden the junior members have started calling themselves WRINS . . . I have told senior members to discourage it, but the habit has come to stay whether we recognise it or not." And so it had; WRINS they became, although still in theory, and in a number of rather tiresome administrative ways, part of the WAC(I).

There were innumerable difficulties to be overcome and Godfrey was determined that they should be settled. "A list of 'things to be done' was drawn up by . . . Teddy Srinavasan. Opposite each item 'progress up to date' was recorded. Each week a revised progress report was issued to all concerned to act as a reminder and a goad." Paymaster Captain Braine, who was also heavily involved, recalls that even leave gave no respite from Godfrey's insistent and impatient demands. When two days' march up in the Himalayas on a brief walking tour he was overtaken by a perspiring Government messenger with a request for urgent action from his Chief, with which, of course, he was quite unable to comply.

Although Mrs Cooper is undoubtedly right in her feeling that without Godfrey's persistence and energy the WRINS would never have been created, a great deal of the actual success of the Service, and it was immensely successful, was due to her own personality and influence, and, in Godfrey's words, "to the sense of duty, community and devotion she knew so well how to instil. Her quiet confidence and charm won the hearts of her subordinates, of those with whom she worked or was trying to recruit and of the officials in the Provinces and States without whose help and authority her work would have been difficult if not impossible. Peggy Cooper offered the girls interesting work which only well-educated girls could undertake, well-run and comfortable hostels, which for some reason the Army organisation could not produce, a good welfare service and an attractive uniform. She toured incessantly and so kept in touch with the life in the WRIN depots and hostels in India's six ports and in New Delhi, so nothing had time to go seriously wrong and petty troubles were smoothed out verbally with the minimum of fuss." After her appointment as Deputy Director (Lady Carlisle remained Director) Mrs Cooper moved to Delhi and, when not on tour, she and her little daughter lived with the Godfreys at 12 King George's Avenue.

Godfrey himself was frequently on tour, mostly by air, but occasionally in *Narbada*, or one of the other RIN ships, when they could be spared from operational duties. At ports he went on board all Indian ships in harbour to talk to the officers and crews, and in the shore establishments, of which new ones were being brought into service almost every month, he performed official opening ceremonies and inspected the facilities. Few commanders-in-chief can have done more to try to make himself known to his officers and men and to inform himself of every development within his command. At the conclusion of each tour, and sometimes in the middle of one, he sent detailed reports of all he had found to Auchinleck, who obviously read them with care and interest. These trips, and many others to all parts of the interior of India to stimulate recruiting and arouse Indian awareness of the Navy's needs, involved 35,000 miles travelling in 1943, 41,000 in 1944 and 38,000 in 1945. Over 5000 miles of the total were by car, 8000 by train and 4000 by sea; the remainder by air. It must have been an extremely exhausting schedule. In his Memoirs he asks, "Were some of these journeys really necessary? My job was to supervise the all too rapid growth of a Service which lacked

experienced officers at the top, to exercise benevolent control
of the Sea Transport service, to see the ports did their job
adequately. In addition to these duties I had set myself the
task of trying to bring home to those who ruled India, not only
at the centre but in Provinces and Indian States, the nature of
Sea Power and its importance to the Indian Sub-continent.
Karachi and Chittagong are roughly the same distance apart as
Lisbon and Danzig, and Scotland to the south of Greece
covers the same span as Peshawar to Cape Cormorin. Given
these requirements, the urgency of war, the need of keeping in
touch with the Admiralty, the ineffectiveness of the written
word and the malaise of India, I think, after twenty years, that
my journeyings were needed and that at least half my time
should have been away from Delhi. The difficulty was to resist
the temptation to become static."

Of course, when away from Delhi or Bombay he remained
in constant touch with all the many and varied administrative
and disciplinary problems which continued to plague the
RIN; the creation of a Paymaster Branch and the reorganisation
of accounting procedures: victualling arrangements, as the food
situation in India deteriorated: training of the RIN's growing
anti-submarine escort forces by an RN group under Godfrey's
old friend from the JIS, Captain Baker Creswell: the entirely
unco-operative attitude of the port authorities in Madras: the
devastating explosion of a merchant ship in Bombay which put
half the harbour out of commission for many weeks: sickness
among senior officers, many of whom had had no home leave
for five years: a mutiny in the Landing Craft Wing caused by
the arrogant and ignorant behaviour of a young British officer
transferred to the RIN from the Army; these were typical of
the innumerable matters which had to receive FOCRIN's
personal attention.

By the end of 1944 the RIN comprised 117 vessels, including
seven sloops, a corvette, fourteen fleet minesweepers and
forty-nine coastal craft in addition to the landing craft of the
Landing Craft Wing. The RIN was providing the bulk of the
escorts for convoys in the Bay of Bengal and for trade from the
west coast to the Persian Gulf and the Red Sea. In 1944 and
1945 more and more shore training establishments and depots
were opened; a very modern gunnery school, a radar school
and a boys training establishment at Karachi, a torpedo

school at Jamnagar, a communications school and tactical training unit at Bombay, a mechanical training school at Lonavla were only some of the new developments, one of the results of which was to begin to free the Bombay dockyard, where so much had previously been concentrated, for its proper function. For all these new developments trained staff had somehow to be provided, and each new development called for corresponding changes at Naval Headquarters in Delhi. It would be wearisome to try to describe all of them in detail, but any managing director of a business faced with expansion on this scale, even in peacetime England, let alone in wartime India, will have some understanding of the immense problems involved. The RIN was still tiny in relation to the Royal Navy, but from the seven ships and the small shore establishment at Bombay in 1939 its growth had been an astonishing achievement.

As the number not only of RIN but RN ships in Indian waters increased, the demands on Indian ports, on the Sea Transport organisation and on the dockyards and repair and maintenance facilities increased alarmingly. The reactions of the civilian port authorities varied. In Madras it was, for a time deplorable. 'Business as usual' was the motto and RIN and RN needs were given very low priority, until, after much patient and diplomatic lobbying, the Chairman of the Port Trust was at last persuaded to mitigate his opposition to "anything which interferes in the slightest manner with the cash earnings of the port." Other ports, Calcutta, Bombay and Karachi were much better, but Cochin and Vizagapatam had been developed from minor ports to major bases and needed much attention. The RIN's oldest and principal dockyard, Bombay, was basically the responsibility of the Government of India rather than the RIN and Godfrey was greatly shocked by the conditions of the dockyard workers and the entire lack of any provision for housing and other social services for them. In a letter to Auchinleck at the end of November 1943 he reported, not for the first time, that "the welfare, housing, health, amenities and so on in Bombay Dockyard are very much behind the times . . . We have had several meetings on the subject, and what it boils down to in the first instance is good housing; in fact a housing estate with recreation rooms, playing fields, within five to fifteen miles of the dockyard.

There are plenty of such schemes for us to participate in after the war, but the matter is much too urgent . . . the workers in the dockyard are almost, if not as important as the men who man the ships, and I feel that if they are to give their best, and stand the long hours of work, we cannot do too much for them." Six months later he again reported that "I spent the best part of two forenoons walking around the dockyard and chatting with the workers, who were always most respectful and appreciative, in fact more so than on any previous occasion. I also visited some of their home dwellings which are pretty dreadful. The normal family of six or eight lives and sleeps in a dark room 10' × 10'. The tiny kitchen which adjoins this room is always spotlessly clean and although the surroundings are untidy they can't be described as 'dirty'. Apart from the smells of cooking, there is a surprising absence of stench. The overcrowding is dreadful and, put very briefly, the new housing scheme will provide a family of six with two rooms 10' × 12', a share of a passage and of course a very small kitchen, instead of one room 10' × 10'." Godfrey also managed to get a Maternity Clinic for the workers' wives and families started. He was particularly interested in this clinic and arranged for a lady doctor, Dr S. Gore, to be placed in charge. It was opened in August 1944 and in the first month handled 632 cases (Infants, Toddlers, Adults, Antenatal, and Postnatal); six months later the number of cases treated each month had risen to 2093. Reluctantly, because he intensely disliked anything savouring of personal publicity, Godfrey acceded to the workers' request that it should be named the Godfrey Clinic. He also arranged for the creation of an Institute, selling grain and other commodities, with a canteen, library and sports facilities so that the general conditions could no longer be described, as he had done on his first visit, as "appalling". He rather sadly noted shortly before he left India that the men were demanding overtime for playing hockey on the new playing fields, but in general the reforms for which he had pressed so strongly were greatly appreciated.

Welfare in the RIN itself also needed much attention. Ship and shore based naval canteens had been confined originally to one small canteen at Bombay, run by a private contractor. Others had gradually been established, but the contractor system was open to considerable abuse and in September 1943 steps were taken to form an efficient canteen service within the RIN. By the beginning of 1945 RIN canteen warehouses, with civilian managers and bulk buying facilities, were catering for the needs of all ships and establishments, and worthwhile profits were being made. The owners of the RIN canteens were the ratings themselves and as Godfrey's official report in March 1945 stated, 'The successful creation of an efficient canteen service will ensure the regular provision of funds for practical welfare during the post-war years." This was a very vital need because RIN ratings were not permitted to use the RN NAAFI shops and canteens in India and Ceylon, which came as an unpleasant shock to those Indian ratings who had brought ships out from England where they had naturally had access to such facilities. The basic reason for this decision by the Indian Government was because, if Indian ratings had been permitted to use the NAAFI a similar concession would have had to have been given to the very much more numerous Indian Army and Air Force other ranks, who were on the whole adequately provided for by their own canteens and shops. Unfortunately the accommodation in the modern ships and newer depots of the RIN, let alone their experience of sharing with the RN in Britain and the Mediterranean, had accustomed the Indian ratings to a far higher standard of comfort and welfare than was the case with Indian Army other ranks. Despite the fact that Godfrey arranged for the construction of a really first class Fleet club, the Cornwallis Club at Bombay, and commandeered other buildings in other Indian ports, it was not possible to eliminate the very natural feeling on the part of the RIN men that they were being treated as second class citizens, all the more so as their rates of pay remained well below those not only of the RN but of the Burma and Ceylon RNVRs. All attempts to raise RIN rates of pay came up against the immovable rock of the opposition of the Military Finance Department and the alleged need to maintain exact equality with the Army. Nevertheless with the establishment of Fleet Clubs in all the main ports and a comprehensive Welfare Service and Benevolent Fund to look after families and dependants and to provide additional comforts for the men, the general situation was enormously improved. In January 1945, Sir Feroze Khan Noon, the Defence Member, reporting on a Welfare Tour, stated that he had been 'very much impressed

with the amenities and welfare of RIN establishments, which
. . . were far superior to any in the Indian Army. He was very
pleased to see the good spirit amongst the Officers and Ratings,
and all realised that the RIN were doing everything possible
for the amenities and welfare of their personnel.' This opinion
was reinforced by the Army Director of Quartering in New
Delhi, who remarked that he had no doubt that 'both the RIN
and the IAF (Indian Air Force) place their Indian other ranks
on a much higher plane in all respects than . . . the Indian
Army other rank . . . in fact both these Services in many ways
give the Indian Other Rank equal treatment with the British
Other Rank . . .'

Of course the troubles arising from the ban on RIN ratings
using the NAAFI in India were as nothing compared to those
encountered by crews of ships calling at South African ports on
passage back from the UK. The Indian Government's reaction
was to object strongly to the participation of South African
Navy motor launches in the Arakan campaign and to refuse
to accept South Africans who had joined the British RNVR for
transfer to the RINVR. Godfrey in Delhi and Hall in London
had some difficulty in impressing on the Admiralty the strength
of Indian feelings in this connection, all the more so because
the need for small ships and men for the offensive in Burma
and for operations planned against the Dutch East Indies
continued to increase.

The results of these continual struggles with the Admiralty,
the India Office and the Military Finance Department to
strengthen the administration and fighting efficiency of the
RIN and to improve the discipline and welfare of its personnel,
in fact produced excellent results, but because its ships were,
in the main attached to Royal Navy flotillas and squadrons
and under Royal Naval overall command, the RIN could not
point to any particular battle or campaign which it won on its
own. This did not, however, mean that the part which it
played in the defeat of the German and Japanese U-boats in
the Indian Ocean and in the safe escort of many thousands of
Allied troops to India or in the operations in Burmese coastal
waters, was not an extremely valuable one. Nor could the
Royal Navy have managed without the RIN's shore facilities
and its communications network which stretched from Aden to
Chittagong. It would not be unreasonable to claim that its

contribution to Allied victory at sea was at least as great as that of the Royal Australian Navy and only surpassed by that of the Royal Canadian Navy.

By the beginning of 1944 Somerville's Eastern Fleet had received reinforcements of modern carriers and battleships, and began to undertake raids against Japanese-held ports in Sumatra. Mountbatten was planning for large-scale attacks by sea and land both there and in Burma but his naval and air forces were more than once depleted by the demands first of the Sicily landings and then of the Invasion of Normandy and the South of France. In August 1944 Somerville was relieved as C-in-C by Admiral Sir Bruce Fraser and left to take up the appointment of Head of the British Admiralty Delegation in Washington. In a farewell letter Godfrey wrote that "Sabang was a splendid way to finish off your eventful term of command which started in such poor auspices and which has now improved out of all recognition . . . Looking back on the year and a half I have spent on this job I am very conscious of the help you have been to me on many occasions, and of the knowledge that if I wanted your support it would always be forthcoming . . . I expect you view your next appointment with mixed feelings. At the same time it would be hard to find anybody better equipped than yourself to keep Admiral King [Fleet Admiral Ernie King, the Commander-in-Chief of the US Navy] in order and to guide our future policy in fighting Japan . . ." Godfrey knew Fraser well as he was a near contemporary and had been Controller of the Navy in 1940, but it was not long before he took the major portion of his fleet off to the Pacific to serve under Admiral Nimitz, leaving his second in command, Vice-Admiral A. J. Power, with a still respectable force, as C-in-C, East Indies. In January 1945 Power wrote to Godfrey that 'the RIN Landing Craft Wing are having an exceedingly satisfactory war on the Arakan coast. They have not had a lot of hard fighting, but excellent preliminary work for anything more serious that lies ahead. All reports I hear are most complimentary. Although Akyab was pretty soft, there is some good fighting going on at Myebon, in which *Narbada* and *Jumna* [two RIN sloops] have been of the greatest assistance. Personally I think the RIN should get a very good write up before the monsoon breaks, and I should like to congratulate you in advance.' Two months later Power again praised the RIN's performance: 'There were, as you know, doubts raised by the Army as to whether the RIN was sufficiently well found to carry out the duties which they have done in January. On one occasion in Calcutta at a big meeting I took the opportunity of jumping heavily on a responsible officer who raised doubts to which I refer above.' Mountbatten also wrote to Godfrey to congratulate the RIN and the Landing Craft Wing in particular. The RIN continued to play an active part in the reoccupation of Burma and in the plans for the assault on Malaya and the recapture of Singapore.

In a Navy Day broadcast (first instituted in 1944) on All India Radio on 1 December 1945 Godfrey drew the country's attention to the RIN's achievements. "In January this year our forces began the offensive that led from Akyab to Rangoon and the Royal Indian Navy showed itself admirably suited to fighting in the difficult conditions of the Arakan. The Landing Craft Wing won universal tributes to its skill and courage. India's coastal forces were old enemies of the Japanese on this coast and added to their reputation for daring and enterprise. Our sloops, fresh from sharing in the defeat of the U-boats, supported the army with their guns, penetrating uncharted waterways far inland on the Burma coast. Minesweepers made safe the waters through which our troops and supplies had to pass . . . India's Navy has developed from a Service suited primarily to local defence to one with a sea-going force and proper shore establishments to nourish it . . . Wherever I have gone I have found nothing but enthusiasm for the Naval Service . . . This awakening to the realities of sea power will I feel sure bear fruit in the years ahead of us, and will convince parents that the Navy must be manned by the best of India's youth . . . I ask you to do all in your power to foster the growth of the Royal Indian Navy and to make its vital role in India's defence known throughout the length and breadth of this great land."

CHAPTER FOURTEEN

Mutiny

TOWARDS THE end of 1944 Admiral Harcourt, Naval Secretary to the First Lord, had written to Godfrey to enquire whether he still held the view which he had expressed to Cunningham twelve months previously that FOCRIN's appointment should not exceed two years in wartime. He added that, if he did think so, no indication could be given of when a suitable relief might be found. Godfrey had replied that although he had told Auchinleck exactly the same thing when he became C-in-C, the 'Chief' had felt that two years was rather short. In consequence Godfrey considered that he ought to leave the matter to Auchinleck; he himself would take no further action. There was, moreover, still much to do and he was not anxious to leave at that stage. The expectations of an early end to the war in Europe had been dashed by the failure at Arnhem and it looked as though it would take at least another year to defeat the Japanese. Four months later, however, the situation had changed. Germany's defeat was obviously only days away and the chances of a slightly earlier end to the war in the Far East seemed more promising. Moreover Godfrey himself had reached the top of the Vice-Admirals' list and, not counting Admirals of the Fleet, there were only twelve Flag Officers on the active list senior to him. There was obviously little likelihood of a fresh appointment, and so he was not surprised when, at the end of April 1945, he received a very friendly letter from Harcourt's successor, Admiral Barry, giving him private advance warning that the Board had decided with regret that they could offer him no further employment on the active list commensurate with his rank. He would therefore be placed on the retired list and promoted Admiral when the officer below him on the active list was promoted. In fact this did not happen until the end of September and by then Auchinleck had already expressed a wish that Godfrey should do a full three years whether he was promoted

or not. This meant that he would continue as FOCRIN until
22 March 1946. This was something that he regretted because
although he had been more than ready to stay until the end of
the war, once it was over he had hoped that the task of breaking
down and destroying organisations and activities which had
been built up "carefully, affectionately and not without pain
during the last two and a half years" would fall to his successor.
Auchinleck certainly seems to have been well satisfied with
Godfrey's achievements because it was proposed that Godfrey
should be recommended for a KCIE, but in the end it was
finally decided to wait until he could be made KCSI, the
senior of the two major Indian Orders.

The reduction of the RIN to a peacetime basis could not of
course be sensibly undertaken until its future shape and size had
been decided by the Government of India in consultation with
the Admiralty. There was no question of reverting to the tiny
force of 1939. Thanks to the war, and more particularly to
Godfrey's constant efforts, Indian public opinion was now
much more conscious of the value of sea power and of the need
for a sizeable and well-balanced Navy. The matter could not,
however, be settled in isolation, or indeed settled at all until
India's own future was clearer. Some form of independence
had been envisaged for years but whether as a unified State or
two or even three separate nations, whether within or outside
the British Commonwealth became less and less certain as the
months went by. Moreover the RIN's future was also bound up
with that of the other two Services and with the organisation
and powers of any future Ministry of War or Defence. Planning
therefore had to proceed in something of a vacuum which did
not exactly assist in the process of making definite advance
arrangements for the process of demobilisation.

Despite this, thought had been given in Naval Headquarters
to the post-war Navy as early as the middle of 1943 and
Godfrey had produced a paper for the Commander-in-Chief
outlining plans for the inclusion of cruisers and destroyers in
the future Fleet. He had sent a copy to Somerville, whose
feelings were that the proposals were too ambitious. '. . . It has
always been argued that India is a poor country, with a
regrettably low standard of living, and I am not at all clear
how the very large additional costs of these proposals would be
met except at the expense of the Army. Whilst Indians may

develop into average sailors, if great trouble is taken with them, I have always understood that they can be made above average soldiers without much difficulty . . . To be quite candid, I should find it most difficult if I were in your position to state a convincing case for the development of the Indian Navy on the lines you propose unless "amour propre" is the determining factor.' Godfrey replied that he had to confess that "in putting up these proposals I have been much influenced by the expressed wish of the Chief to include cruisers and destroyers, and by the aspirations of nearly all influential Indians I have met in British India and the Indian States, to carry their Navy a step further to make it something of which the country will be proud." Notwithstanding these initial reservations, plans for the acquisition of up to three cruisers and possibly also a small aircraft carrier in addition to frigates and other smaller craft were pushed ahead and there was much correspondence between Godfrey and Commodore Hall in London on the subject. At the beginning of 1945 Captain Jefford was put in charge of post-war planning at Naval Headquarters and appointed the RIN member of the Joint Services Committee studying the future of India's Defence Forces. It was, of course, not only a question of ships but of dockyards, training facilities and above all skilled officers, petty officers and ratings to man and maintain larger and more complicated warships. In spite of Godfrey's early realisation that the expansion of the RIN had been too rapid and that a period of consolidation was essential, he, like Fitzherbert before him, had been unable to reject entirely demands to take on additional commitments and the strength of the RIN had continued to creep up. By 1945, with the Landing Craft Wing and the WRINS, it was approaching 35,000 officers and men. But the number of regular officers and petty officers had hardly increased at all, and the great majority of the best of the Reserve officers, both British and Indian, would undoubtedly want to return to their civilian occupations as soon as the war was over. How were the trained and experienced officers needed for a substantial peacetime force to be found?

At the beginning of 1944 a decision had been taken to confine cadet entry solely to Indians. Godfrey, basing his opinion not only on the views of his British RIN officers but even more so on several Indians like Teddy Srinivasan, was extremely doubtful of the wisdom of this measure. The Navy had not yet become as popular and respected a service in Indian eyes as the Army or the Indian Civil Service. In a letter to Auchinleck Godfrey stressed that "we must avoid letting in people of the wrong quality by direct entry or emergency measures as the whole future of the Service will depend on the quality of the individual . . . A bad batch of cadets *now* means a bad batch of commanding officers in 1964 . . . The senior cadet entry Indian Officer (the 1931 to 1934 batch) are a fine lot. Keen and highly intelligent men about thirty years old but so far untried in the more responsible posts. Some of them are in command and the next year will show what they are worth . . . There are real jobs to be done and situations to be faced, and a great deal of sea time. Indian officers, unlike their British colleagues, hanker for shore jobs. How it will work out and how they will withstand the drag of the family remains to be seen . . . One of our best Indian Lieutenants thought he was in disgrace when he was appointed to relieve a British officer in command of a corvette, and is still looking regretfully over his shoulder at the staff post he thought he was going to." Godfrey went on to say that such an attitude could only be changed by example, particularly that of mess life in a British wardroom. "Indian Naval officers, if left to themselves, feed in their cabins and go home after official working hours. They think in terms of limited responsibility—one man and one job only—and do not take readily to the idea that in a navy an officer must be ready to turn his hand to anything and that in a ship there's no such thing as overtime . . . For this reason I think that the young Indian officer will need the association of British officers of his own age both ashore and afloat, and will continue to need it until a right sea-minded tradition has been built up . . . It took ten years to convince the Admiralty that an Indian Navy could be officered partly by Indians, but if we go the whole hog, we may lose their support and that would be disastrous." Auchinleck seems to have been rather disappointed by all this, but in a further letter Godfrey remarked that although he had "pointed out the snags, that does not mean that they cannot be overcome. By realising possible Admiralty points of view we may be able to anticipate their reactions, especially as we now have such satisfactory representation in Whitehall . . . You may be sure in any case that I shall do my very best to persuade the Admiralty to see things from our point of view." Godfrey was obviously not against Indianisation. Quite the contrary; but he wanted the process carried out in a way that would be in the best long-term interest of India's Navy.

However, the question became slightly academic when the Admiralty announced that they could not, for some time, take anything like as many Indian cadets as the RIN proposed, and even more so when there was a significant shortfall in the quality and quantity of candidates offering themselves for the open examinations. The only solution seemed to be to obtain as many officers as possible by transfers both of British and Indian Reserve officers to the RIN and the balance, for the time being, by some arrangement for permanent transfer or temporary secondment from the Royal Navy.

In the spring of 1945 Godfrey again paid a short visit to the UK to discuss these and other problems with the Admiralty. On 30 May he wrote to Auchinleck that he had found Plans Division very sympathetic to India's aspirations as regards acquiring cruisers, although the Royal Navy's wartime losses of this class of ship had been heavy and other Dominion Navies were also anxious to obtain such ships. The problem of finding officers was, however, more intractable. India had been thinking in terms of three cruisers, but would be compelled to lower her sights if the difficulty not only of manning the ships but of providing officers with sufficient skill and experience for the technical training schools and other shore establishments, could not be overcome. It was finally decided to offer permanent commissions in the RIN to 66 Indian and 40 British officers of the Indian Naval Reserves (the maximum figure thought likely to be of an acceptable standard out of the estimated number of applicants) and to obtain the balance of some 200 officers by temporary secondment from the Royal Navy. On this basis complete Indianisation would take between ten and fifteen years, but, as Godfrey pointed out to Auchinleck, it was no good ignoring the fact that there were fewer than half a dozen regular Indian officers of lieutenant-commander or commander's rank, let alone any more senior.

Sickness and retirement now began to take an increasing toll of the senior RIN and RN officers on loan. Replacements for a dozen officers of Captain's rank and above had somehow to be found. The Admiralty could not supply them. As Godfrey wrote to Auchinleck in June 1945, shortly before returning from Britain, "On balance we are slightly better off than two years ago, and the removal of very senior officers combined with the added experience of two active war years, has encouraged me to promote in the acting rank and place in responsible jobs, a number of more junior officers, with excellent results . . . I have therefore decided to 'dip down' among Royal Indian Navy senior officers and see if we can't manage without the help of the Royal Navy." Godfrey had already secured the promotion to Rear-Admiral of his second in command, Rattray. This was the first time that an RIN officer had reached this rank and it had of course involved a long battle with the Military Finance Department who only gave way grudgingly and even then continued to insist that the appointment was merely an acting one which would not entitle Rattray to a Rear-Admiral's pension. 'The Military Finance Department at its niggling worst', as Captain Jefford subsequently remarked. However Godfrey did succeed in reshuffling appointments so that he would have a team consisting almost entirely of regular RIN officers in all the key appointments which would see the Service through to the end of the war with Japan and well into the post-war demobilisation period. After submitting a list of names he went on to say ". . . It will be hard to produce, in any Service, a better group and I feel very confident provided they keep well that they will deliver the goods . . . They will have a clear run ahead of them into peace time and this, I hope will facilitate the painful task of demobilisation. There are, of course, many other jobs at present filled by clever and able civilians serving as RINIVR and RINR officers whom it is going to be extremely hard to replace."

Auchinleck replied that he was sure the policy of bringing on the younger RIN officers was sound but enquired whether promising young Indian officers could not be used. Godfrey pointed out that two of the Navy's modern sloops were now commanded by Indian officers as were two of the larger minesweepers. These men, aged at the time thirty-four and thirty-one years, subsequently rose to high positions in the Indian and Pakistani Navies. Godfrey thought highly of them and had taken particular trouble to ensure that they had been given

every help and encouragement from Somerville and Power
when they first assumed their commands and were attached to
the Eastern Fleet or other Royal Navy squadrons.

By the middle of the summer of 1945 it was clear that Japan
was likely to be defeated earlier than anticipated and plans
for demobilisation, for the release of Reserve Officers and RN
officers on loan, and for regular RIN officers to take sixty days
leave were being pushed ahead. But just as the RIN had been
denied time to expand and consolidate in a controlled and
deliberate manner in 1939, so the dropping of the atom bombs
on Hiroshima and Nagasaki and the sudden surrender of the
Japanese on 10 August came before the future size of the Navy
had been settled and the plans for demobilisation finalised.
For a time there was still pressure on the Navy to participate in
operations. Two of the sloops were serving with the British
Pacific Fleet (an indication of the high standard of efficiency
achieved); others and the minesweepers took part in the
reoccupation of Malaya, Singapore and the Dutch East Indies.
The RIN had demonstrated during the past five and a half
years that it was capable of great things and had been keyed
up for a final effort against the Japanese. Inevitably VJ Day
brought a reaction and a sense of anti-climax. Both officers and
ratings were confronted with problems about their personal
future probably more daunting and intractable than those
which presented themselves to most Allied Service men. It was
not only a question of the Navy's size and status but of the sort
of India which Independence, now obviously both inevitable
and imminent, would bring. The Congress Party and the
Muslim League clamoured for the British to 'Quit India'.
What did this mean for the regular British officers who had
been the RIN's backbone? Many of the regular Indian officers
recognised that some continued help from the British was
essential but this would not necessarily be the view taken by
the politicians.

The Reserve officers also had mixed feelings. The majority of
the British, whether recruited in India or the UK wanted to get
back to their civilian jobs and felt frustrated at not being able
to do so if their demobilisation groups were not high enough.
This applied also to some of the Indian officers, but others were
filled with doubts. Never having previously had jobs they were
torn between remaining in a Service in which they had little

interest apart from the pay and throwing themselves on the very uncertain civilian labour market.

As to the long service petty officers and ratings, most of them were anxious to remain in the Service, but they formed only a tiny proportion of the total. It was at first thought that the Hostilities Only men would be easily re-absorbed into the Merchant Navy from whence they had come. Unfortunately the Seamens Union refused to accept them as there were not enough jobs for its own members. The Special Entry ratings, most of them with some pretensions to education and more politically conscious than the Ratnigiris and Punjabis, while not necessarily keen to stay in the Navy, did not relish unemployment ashore and had somehow gained the impression that the Navy would take full responsibility for finding them civil jobs at their Service rates of pay.

Three stages in reduction of personnel were envisaged. An upper limit, required for the immediate post-war tasks; an intermediate figure which would allow a margin of safety depending on the size of the peacetime fleet and give flexibility in planning for leave, sickness, retraining and so on, before the final drop to a figure provisionally fixed at 11,000 which it was hoped might be reached towards the end of 1946. Indian bureaucracy moved slowly and as usual much difficulty was caused by the Military Finance Department. As late as the end of November Godfrey was appealing to Auchinleck for help in obtaining a decision. "I am not at all happy", he wrote, "about the progress that is being made towards the acquisition of our first cruiser . . . Although War Department and especially Trivedi are entirely on our side, Finance are ingenious in discovering new pretexts for delay . . . further delay in making up our mind may jeopardise our chances of getting a cruiser at all as the Admiralty want to decide on the post-war allocation *now* and will not accord priority to a country which seems to be half-hearted (unlike Australia, New Zealand and Canada) . . . I feel that the matter has now become so urgent that your personal intervention on a high plane is needed . . ." The war had been over three months and the Government of India had still not made up its mind about its Navy.

By this time there had been changes in No. 12 King George's Avenue. Margaret had not seen her daughters for nearly two years. Kathleen was serving in the WAAF at Bletchley Park,

Eleanor was studying to become an architect, but Christina, the youngest, was still at school at Down House. In March 1945, with the end of the war clearly in sight and her husband's appointment as FOCRIN drawing to a close, Margaret returned to Britain. She was awarded the Kaiser I Hind medal in the Birthday Honours List for her services to the Indian WVS. Godfrey's Flag Lieutenant, John Dixon, returned to civil life and was succeeded after a short interval by Tom Sheppard in addition to his post as Director of Signals as part of the reshuffle of regular officers already referred to. Peggy Cooper, Deputy Director of the WRINS also left for England. Digby Beste had long since been invalided home, but transient visitors continued to occupy the guest rooms.

Margaret's return to England naturally caused a resumption of her husband's illuminating and interesting letters to her. On 27 July, for example, commenting on the results of the British general election, he wrote, "Odd, how everyone was wrong. Both Tory and Labour HQs expected a Tory overall majority of 40–100. Labour didn't want to get in just yet, at this most difficult time, but I'm glad they have, as otherwise we were bound to have another year or two of Churchill dictatorship. As long as the German war was on one was bound to do what one could to boost Churchill, but it became awkward, whatever he did, always to have to add what 'a great man' he was. We can only do what we can do. There are no supermen who do everything well, and the tragedy of Churchill was that the thing he loved most he did least well i.e. strategy. Early on in the war his decisions were invariably wrong and caused us to lose ships, men etc. unnecessarily and to have the stuff at the wrong place. If you didn't agree with him you were axed e.g. Danks and Tom Phillips. Those who worked with him daily no doubt got inspired by his vitality and wit and there grew up that most dangerous of coteries, a mutual admiration society. Those whom his voice reached over the microphone found their instincts put into glowing words and their determination fortified. To those who were working on the edge of his personal influence he was just an unmitigated pest and bully, interfering without knowledge and throwing spanners into wheels. Politically he was quite unscrupulous and no doubt egged on by that gangster the Beaver destroyed or belittled the reputations of men who tended to outshine him. Cripps, after a most successful mission to Moscow was sent to do a job in India that was bound to fail and could then be relegated to a minor post. Bevin eventually found himself in the wretched position of fighting the union rank and file (not the paid officials) and always there was that evil influence the Beaver (whatever Horder may say about being inside or outside the house). The public of our generation will never know the malignant influence he [Churchill] exerted on the early strategy of the war because he will probably be the first person to write a popular history which, like *The World Crisis*, will show that everything that went well was due to his inspiration and that when things went badly it was someone else's fault. You can do this trick quite easily if you have lots of material to work at and just pick out the bits that suit. No, I'm glad Labour are in . . . Labour will get on with the rehousing and resettlement quicker than the Tories would, I think . . ." It was, as one would have expected from Godfrey, a shrewd but unorthodox judgement, coloured, no doubt, not only by his own experience but also by those of two other men who had been summarily 'banished' to India, Wavell and Auchinleck.

In August Godfrey wrote from Bombay, "The end of the war has come sooner than I expected so we are suddenly precipitated in to all the problems of demobilisation etc. which I was hoping my relief would have to tackle. Fortunately a good deal of preparation has been done and the process of putting machinery into reverse won't be so painful . . ." A few days later he was in Madras after visiting Cochin. "Both here and there my task is to break down activities carefully and painfully built up during the past two and a half years . . . tomorrow and on Saturday I do the same at Vizag and Calcutta. Chittagong has already gone west . . ."

Next month came the notification of his retirement and promotion, and reappointment as FOCRIN. "I suppose they will be thinking about my successor soon . . . Wake Walker's death must have started a landslide of promotions and retirements—the only remaining member of my term of flag rank on the active list is now Bob Burnett . . ." His term had been an exceptional one in the number of flag officers it had produced. Godfrey began to worry about the difficulties which the Admiralty would encounter in finding his successor. He pointed out both to the Admiralty and to the War Department in Delhi that he and Fitzherbert had both found that FOCRIN's allowances, which were based on Indian Army scales, were inadequate and that they compared unfavourably with those that a Vice-Admiral in the Royal Navy could expect in, for example, Malta or Gibraltar. He correctly feared that these conditions would seem unattractive to future candidates for the post and that delays might occur. Just before Christmas Godfrey suggested to the War Department that the India Office should remind the Admiralty that they must find a relief for him quickly. If they had not done so by March he suggested that "Rear-Admiral Rattray should be appointed to take my place. This would be a perfectly satisfactory arrangement and it would be good for the RIN that their most senior officer should, if only temporarily, hold the post of Flag Officer, Commanding . . ."

In November Alanbrooke passed through Delhi and was Auchinleck's principal guest at a dinner party at which Godfrey was also present. Although Godfrey, when he was DNI, had conferred with Alanbrooke almost daily, the CIGS behaved as though they had never previously met and spoke for a quarter of an hour about infantry training. However, three days later Godfrey wrote to Margaret that Alanbrooke had spoken "very appreciatively of the work of NID. Saw him and the Supremo [Mountbatten] off at the airport this morning. Lady Mountbatten asked after you and was very conscious of the splendid work you had done out here . . . Mountbatten is still determined to get back into the Navy as a Captain [he held the acting rank of Admiral at the time], and command his own ship but I warned him that he'd have to be quick, otherwise he'd go over the top and be a Rear-Admiral proper and that all sorts of insidious influences would lead him away from the narrow path that leads to flag rank combined with the confidence of one's subordinates that one is a real admiral and not a knight of the carpet."

In the meantime the problems of demobilisation were beginning to mount up. The reduction to a peacetime basis meant that wartime bases and establishments would have to be closed down and that Bombay would become the centre for demobilisation. Pay and accounts were just being concentrated there and inevitably ships had to be brought back there to await the discharge of their crews to holding depots ashore before they could recommission with long service peacetime crews. Officers were constantly being reposted. In July Rattray had reported that apart from a spate of Court Martials everything was proceeding normally and that he was confident that Bombay would be able to handle the large number of ships and personnel which would be assembling there shortly, but at the end of September Godfrey wrote to Rattray that he was "not quite happy about the speed with which we are demobilising personnel and reducing our bases. It is an imperative necessity to close down Madras, Cochin, Calcutta and Chittagong, but I am told there is no room for any more people in Bombay . . ." Rattray replied that good progress had been made with the Hostilities Only ratings, but that there were considerable difficulties with the ex-army personnel of the Landing Craft Wing due to complexities of their pay. Demobilisation proper was only just starting and lack of accommodation in Bombay was indeed very serious.

There had been over 27,000 ratings in the RIN on VJ Day and it had been hoped to discharge 500 men per week to reach the lower limit for the Service of 11,000 men by June 1946 at the latest. It was difficult to attain this rate of discharge. Godfrey remarks in his Memoirs ". . . the machinery for demobilisation, excellent in itself, worked too slowly . . . An officer or man could not be finally discharged and written off until the last detail of his pay had been settled and agreed and in India, where everything is dilatory and the babu has a rooted dislike to 'closing' a file, this might take months. When the matter seemed to be settled ratings were liable to appeal and this meant further delay. Bombay was full of ratings from ships about to be paid off but with nothing to do but think up grievances. The Navy . . . should now have been reduced to less than ten thousand [men] as quickly as possible. With the means at our disposal and the traditional attitude of the Military Finance department 'as soon as possible' meant at least six months . . ."

This was bad enough in itself but the political climate was now becoming highly charged. The Congress Party activists, led by Pandit Nehru, had embarked on a violently anti-British campaign. Jinnah and the Muslim League were determined to split the subcontinent and create a Pakistan even if this meant fighting both the British and the Congress

Party at the same time. The survivors of the so-called Indian National Army, (the proportionately small number of prisoners of war who had gone over to the Japanese after the defeats in Singapore and Burma) had been brought back and were to be put on trial. The Nationalist press and politicians treated them not as traitors but heroes. Wavell, the Viceroy, had reported to Churchill that there were only two alternatives—either to get tough and stay, or to clear out. Getting tough meant reinforcing the British Army by at least three divisions and holding the country down by force; even getting out might involve blood-shed and plans were made for an opposed evacuation via Bombay. In fact opinion in Britain and war-weariness among British Service men in India and the Far East made any 'tough' policy quite out of the question. There were wide-spread outbreaks of mass insubordination, mutinies in fact though not in name, by the Royal Air Force in India and Malaya. These were followed by similar 'strikes' in the Indian Air Force, and in the Indian Army technical corps. It was not the ideal background for the demobilisation of a Navy which had expanded to twenty times its pre-war size and now had rapidly to be cut back to less than one third of its peak numbers.

Demobilisation in any Service always brings a temporary drop in morale and presents opportunities for malcontents and trouble makers. The RIN unfortunately had no equivalent to the Security side of the Royal Navy's NID, which kept a careful watch on subversive elements and on the general level of morale on the lower deck. Personnel records were inadequate and this combined with the traditionally lenient attitude taken to the not infrequent cases of ill-discipline and insubordination had meant that too many 'bad hats' had been allowed to remain in the Service. Godfrey was well aware of the danger this state of affairs might present and therefore, in August 1945, created a Morale Section at Naval Headquarters and called for regular morale reports from the commanding officers of all ships and naval establishments. These reports should have provided an admirable safety valve, and, without short circuiting senior officers, ought to have kept Headquarters well informed of the morale and state of feeling on the lower deck. However, the accuracy and comprehensiveness of the reports inevitably depended on the personal qualities of the commanding officers, and events were to show that many of them were insufficiently in touch with their men.

By November it had nevertheless become obvious, partly through some of these reports and partly through the receipt of anonymous letters, that all was not well and that discontent was mounting. Two of the worst centres were, as always, HIMS *Talwar*, the Signal School, and HIMS *Shivaji*, the Mechanical Training Establishment. Outbreaks of sabotage and slogan writing were reported from *Talwar*, where, in letters in green paint two feet high, slogans such as 'Quit India', 'Revolt Now', 'Kill the British' and 'Kill the White Bastards' appeared mysteriously on the walls of the buildings. The Commanding Officer considered that although probably only a small minority of the ratings had been involved, it had been carefully planned and well organised. The Signal School was full of men from other Depots and Establishments awaiting demobilisation and there were too few officers to supervise them adequately.

Probably as a result of this incident it was arranged that an experienced Indian Army officer, Lieutenant Colonel Haq Nawaz, should visit all the Establishments in Bombay as a matter of urgency to carry out an independent investigation. On 20 December Godfrey called a meeting of senior officers of the Naval Staff to consider the Colonel's report. It disclosed a very disturbing state of affairs. The minutes of this meeting make interesting reading in the light of events which were to take place only six weeks later.

The first paragraph dealt with politics in the RIN. Haq Nawaz considered that although both Indian officers and ratings were very interested in the forthcoming elections, and in the Indian National Army trials, the question of participation in a revolution to gain political freedom appeared unlikely. Godfrey re-emphasised the necessity for Commanding Officers to report any incidents of slogan writing or ill-discipline immediately.

There was, apparently, some feeling amongst the Indian officers that they were being discriminated against because regular commissions were being offered to only 66 out of 1500 Indian reserve officers while 44 were reserved for the less numerous British officers. In fact only 500 officers, both British and Indian, had applied and a very large proportion

of them were quite unsuitable. Under the heading of Ratings
Grievances came the old question of second-class travel for
Petty Officers, which Godfrey decided to take up yet again on
the highest plane. Other complaints concerned family quarters,
pensions, free education for children of pensioners, and difficulties of getting compensation for loss of kit due to enemy action.
On all these points Godfrey directed that action or further
investigation must be taken very urgently. Two even more
serious points concerned allegations of bad food and 'horrible'
conditions at the main demobilisation centre at Bombay,
including what was alleged to be 'hard manual labour'. The
food situation in India had deteriorated seriously and this and
the great expansion of the RIN had led to the abandonment
of direct purchasing by the Naval Victualling Department in
favour of the Indian Army Service Corps supplying the Navy
in bulk. Haq Nawaz said the quality of the rice issued was very
bad and that far too many meals were being cooked in one
galley. Nor were the officers of the day supervising the issue of
food as they should have done. Godfrey stated emphatically
that these quite justified complaints must be put right immediately and that it was most important that the demobilisation
centre should be efficiently run and well organised; ratings on
return to their homes should take pleasant, not soured memories
of the Navy. Several emergency measures, including the independent purchase of truck loads of rice, were sanctioned.

Colonel Haq Noon also commented that he had observed a
great lack of personal touch between the officers, both British
and Indian, and their ratings, and between the chief and petty
officers and the junior ratings. It was felt that this was due to
lack of interest on the part of officers awaiting release and
communal feeling in the establishments, not the ships, between
the more senior ratings who were Punjabi Mussulmans and the
junior ones who were largely Southern Indians.

Godfrey wound up the meeting by pointing out that they
had in Bombay all the traditional causes of serious trouble on
the lower deck and that it was vital that quick action be taken
to put matters right. In a letter to Rattray, who was of course
in charge on the spot, he wrote "We must get cracking about
this as quickly as possible and no difficulties raised by MES,
or RIASC or anybody else must be allowed to stand in the way
of getting things absolutely right. If you have the least difficulty

refer to me and I will take it up on the highest plane. I attach the greatest importance to the Establishment through which men pass being up to our Naval standard . . ."

On 1 January 1946 Godfrey embarked in the *Narbada* at Vizagapatam for a month's cruise to visit the Andaman, Nicobar and Maldive Islands, Calcutta, Madras, Cochin, Bombay and Karachi. The Commander-in-Chief, Auchinleck, demonstrated his interest in the RIN in a very practical manner by taking passage in *Narbada* from Cochin to Bombay. "He was", Godfrey says, "an ideal guest and enjoyed himself having a good rest . . . He spent a long time on the mess decks and in the offices chatting with the Petty Officers and men and was so impressed by their happiness and with the efficiency and contentment of the ship that he ordered a silver interport trophy (a very expensive one) which, alas, he never presented." Shortly afterwards Godfrey wrote to Auchinleck, "We spoke yesterday of morale reports and you said you would like to see some. Here are two—one of the *Narbada*." The reports have not survived but the Chief replied, 'Very many thanks. Most interesting and encouraging.' At Bombay Godfrey paid farewell visits to the WRIN hostels and "reviewed them on the Signal School parade ground and said a few words, advising them to form old WRIN associations at each port. Mrs Campbell, the First Officer on the West Coast, then rather disconcerted me by replying (usually the Senior Officer has the last word) and calling me their Godfather; they then gave me three cheers, etc. I was deeply touched. As part of the WAC(I) they are to be disbanded and I am fighting a rearguard action to keep something of this fine spirited little corps in being." On 6 February he wrote to Margaret, "I have finished my last inspection and march past, the fifteenth in a week and, I hope, the last I shall ever do. I never want to inspect any more kitchens or drains, or shake any more flabby hands and I really don't see why I ever should. All that remains is to turn over to my relief, about whom there is still no firm information, and, if he does not turn up soon, to hand over to Jack Rattray."

On 15 February Godfrey left for a short tour in Rajputana accompanied by his Secretary, Braine, and his Flag Lieutenant, Sheppard. Four days later on his return journey he learnt that the Navy had mutinied. "As we drew into Udaipur station I noticed an RAF plane on the airfield. This looked a bit ominous and my apprehensions were confirmed when I saw Kirkbride, the Resident, standing on the platform with a sealed envelope in his hand. The letter informed me that a mutiny had broken out in the Signal School and spread to other Establishments in Bombay. There was also communal trouble in the town. The news was not entirely unexpected. Not only had the RIN a tradition of mutiny—there had been nine between March 1942 and April 1945—in addition symptoms of discontent and mass insubordination had been apparent, firstly in the Royal Air Force, then in the Royal Indian Air Force, the Indian Army Signal Corps and in the Indian Electrical and Mechanical Engineers, and lastly in HMIS *Talwar*, the Signal School, in December 1945. I flew to Delhi that afternoon and on to Bombay on 20 February . . . and was glad to find that the Flag Officer, Jack Rattray, had established contact with the instigators of the mutiny (or strike as they preferred to call it). I took it upon myself to turn a blind eye to instructions from the Chief that there should be no parleying and authorised Jack to continue his talks . . ."

Talwar at that time contained not only 700 signal ratings under training but 300 men awaiting drafting or demobilisation. As part of the post-war rearrangements a new Commanding Officer, a regular RIN Commander, had just taken over and had apparently found discipline rather lax. At the beginning of February fresh outbreaks of slogan-writing had taken place and the ringleader, a Leading Telegraphist, whom it was subsequently discovered was a Communist, was arrested. On the 8th the Commanding Officer rebuked the ratings for making catcalls at some WRINs. They subsequently alleged that he had used bad language to them (he was acquitted at a subsequent Court Martial) and on 17 February refused to touch food that was served to them. On the following day they again refused to accept their breakfast and declined to fall in for parade. In accordance with general instructions from the Commander-in-Chief (Auchinleck), Rattray, who perhaps somewhat late in the day had intervened, handled the matter very circumspectly, but the whole establishment was by then in a state of open mutiny and fourteen different complaints, including requests for equal pay with the Royal Navy, better food, better release benefits, and openly political demands for the freeing of the Indian National Army prisoners and the withdrawal of all Indian troops from Indonesia, were put forward. The mutiny now spread rapidly to ships and establishments not only in Bombay (although the WRINS everywhere remained loyal) but to other ports in India and to the Andamans, Hong Kong and Aden.

Somewhat belatedly military guards were posted outside *Talwar* and the Barracks and on the 21st the soldiers were compelled to open fire to prevent the mutineers leaving the barracks and joining the riots and communal disturbances which were now raging in Bombay. The ratings returned the fire. Up to this point the men had claimed that they were merely 'on strike', in the same way as the RAF, RIAF and Indian Army men had done; there had been no casualties; officers had mostly been confined to their quarters but not otherwise molested. But now the situation began to look really ugly and Congress and Muslim League flags were hoisted in place of the White Ensign. Godfrey instructed all officers, both British and Indian, to leave their ships, which they were permitted to do. On Auchinleck's instructions, General Rob Lockhart, GOC Southern Command, had assumed command of the Bombay area, where the situation in the city as well as in the Naval Establishments was getting quite out of hand, and large numbers of troops, artillery and aircraft had been concentrated.

On the afternoon of 21 February Godfrey broadcast the following message to the RIN over All India Radio from Bombay:

"In the present regrettable state of indiscipline in the Service, I have adopted this means of addressing the RIN as being the way in which I can speak to the greatest number of you at one time.

To start with every one of you must realise that the Government of India has no intention of allowing indiscipline to continue, or their actions to be influenced by such indiscipline. It will take the most stringent measures to restore discipline using the vast forces at its disposal if necessary. I ask you to bear this in mind in considering the other things which I have to say to you now.

As regards the requests made by those of you who waited on

the Flag Officer, Bombay, on 19 February, you may be assured
that all reasonable complaints or grievances, if any, will be
fully investigated.

Demobilisation will proceed strictly in accordance with age
and service groups, though you must realise that this will mean
that the Service will lose its trained nucleus of experienced
ratings, especially in the Communications Branch.

The whole question of pay, travelling allowances and family
allowances is now being examined by an inter-Service Committee. This Committee has just been afloat in one of HMI
ships and has visited Establishments in Karachi, Jamnagar
and Bombay.

The situation in Bombay this morning, both afloat and
ashore, is deplorable. A state of open mutiny prevails in which
ratings appear to have completely lost control of their senses.
In order to ensure that ratings confined to barracks did actually
stay there and to avoid a recurrence of the unfortunate incidents
of the day before it was necessary to place small guards of
soldiers on the gates of *Talwar* and Castle Barracks. This
morning ratings from Castle Barracks burst through the guard
which was forced to open fire. The fire was replied to by ratings
inside the Barracks. The only reason for firing in the first place
was to contain ratings within the Barracks and not to coerce or
intimidate them.

I want again to make it quite plain that the Government of
India will never give in to violence. To continue the struggle is
the height of folly when you take into account the overwhelming
forces at the disposal of the Government at this time, and which
will be used to their uttermost even if it means the destruction
of the Navy of which we have been so proud."

This forthright declaration had the desired effect. Although
several of the ships in Bombay, including *Narbada*, had trained
their guns on the town they did not open fire. On the 23rd the
mutiny collapsed. Only in Karachi was it necessary to use force.
There the sloop *Hindustan* refused to comply with an Army
ultimatum; both sides opened fire, but after twenty minutes
and the loss of seven lives, the mutineers surrendered.

In Bombay, on the day following the surrender, Godfrey
went on board *Narbada* and to the Signal School and the Castle
Barracks and addressed the men as follows:

"Now that order has been restored it is your duty to return quietly to work without delay.

No passive resistance to duty will be tolerated.

Normal routine will be resumed.

There will be a full and impartial enquiry into all complaints and grievances, and as I told you on Thursday the whole question of Pay, Travelling allowances and Family allowances is now being investigated by an inter-Service Committee . . .

Many of you have in fact discussed these questions with members of the Committee . . .

You have had the good sense to return to duty and it has therefore been decided to leave most of you on board your ships. It is now up to you to show by your acts that you intend to restore to the Royal Indian Navy the good name it possessed before this unhappy incident took place.

I need hardly say that the restoration of your good name would be a matter very dear to my heart as I have had so much to do with the building up of the Service during the last three years."

The mutiny had lasted three days. It had cost the lives of nine ratings and one officer. It has been suggested that Godfrey 'over-reacted', that he should have followed the example of the RAF and the Indian Army and Air Force authorities, who had rather weakly accepted their men's claims that mass disobedience was merely a 'strike'. It might well have been better for Godfrey personally if he had done so, but whether this would have been in the true long-term interests of the Indian Navy is a very different matter. There can be no such thing as a 'strike' in a fighting Service: disobedience to orders is mutiny, as Lord Mountbatten had told the Air Officer Commanding when confronted with 'strikes' by the RAF in Singapore. Godfrey's firm stand, approved by Auchinleck and made possible by the overpowering force assembled and controlled by General Lockhart, was not only decisive but essential.

A letter to the *Statesman*, signed 'Indian Nationalist', put it all in a nutshell: 'Discipline in the Armed Forces is above everything else. If by chance a breach of discipline is countenanced, then it would be a great disaster for the National Government to come, because the weapon once used would be made precedent even under the national regime. Rightly, therefore

Vallabhbhai Patel advised our boys to surrender . . . Much is
made in our press of Admiral Godfrey's threat "even if it meant
the destruction of the Indian Navy". But he should be clearly
understood. He knows the value of discipline as the first
essential for future nationalist India. He did not want to leave
a bad precedent. Therefore, as *our* Admiral, he issued a definite
warning to the ratings . . . Admiral Godfrey is extremely
sympathetic with India's aspirations for an Indian Navy as
well as with Indians manning the Navy . . . One should study
his speeches and actions . . . He fearlessly did it in the interests
of the Indian Navy, and *not* as a Britisher spitting India's
aspirations [sic]. In the present case, obviously the whole case
of the grievances of the ratings had not reached him. If it had,
the present crisis would have been averted.'

Mutiny, and it was mutiny, let there be no doubt about that,
does not occur casually. Why did the RIN which had overcome
so many difficulties and performed so well during the war,
break apart when peace came, when Independence and a truly
national Navy were just over the horizon? In 1931 Godfrey in
a talk to his officers in *Suffolk* about mutinies in the Royal Navy,
and in particular the then recent affair at Invergordon, had
stated that "Like wars, mutinies have their immediate cause
and their origin. The immediate cause is easy to detect, the
origin is embedded deeply in the history of the previous
generation . . . So although we all hope that *we* shall not get
involved in a mutiny, the fact that there have been at least
seven well-known, and many lesser-known independent affairs,
in the last twenty years should make us ask ourselves 'What shall
I do if one takes place tomorrow?' Do not forget that mutinies
are nearly always unexpected by those officers most immediately
concerned, and that they are all caused by some injustice from
those above in connection with pay, food, leave or leisure."

The origins of the RIN mutiny certainly dated back to an
earlier generation—to the cessation of officer recruitment in the
1920s and to the domination of the Navy by the War Department. The first led to the crippling shortage of middle rank and
senior regular officers in 1939 and the latter to the inability of
the Flag Officer Commanding and his staff to make the
necessary changes and take action in the face of the Finance
Department's insistence on comparability, at every stage, with
the Army. These two grave disadvantages might have been

overcome if the Navy had been given time to grow slowly and steadily. Instead the war resulted in a twentyfold expansion. When Godfrey arrived in India he attempted to call a halt and to consolidate, but the need to win the war was paramount and expansion had to continue. This was the prime cause of the mutiny and for this Godfrey can hardly be held to blame. The immediate causes included a number of legitimate grievances about pay, food, demobilisation, travel allowances, pensions and so on. All of them had been receiving attention but the situation had been aggravated by the famine in India and by the slow process of demobilisation and the need to concentrate ships and men in Bombay. Even so they would not, in themselves, have led to mutiny had it not been for the breakdown of the Divisional system. Whereas the Royal Navy had been able to absorb its Volunteer Reserve officers and imbue them with its own traditions and outlook, the tiny regular RIN had had to pitchfork its volunteers into positions of authority without proper Divisional or disciplinary courses. The enthusiasm and determination of the early volunteers, both British and Indian, overcame this but the quality of some of the later recruits was definitely poor and Colonel Haq Nawaz was undoubtedly correct in his view that far too many officers had lost proper contact with their men. Nor could the Petty Officers fill this gap; they were either Punjabi Mussulmans, unsympathetic to the Hindoos and Christians from southern India, or, if themselves southerners, mainly promoted hastily for technical rather than man management qualities.

Godfrey was not unaware of these weaknesses. One of the most distinguished of the RINVR officers, Commander George Walker, his Judge Advocate, wrote to Godfrey in 1946, 'At my very first interview with you . . . before Fitz had even left, you cross-examined me about the causes of the mutinies which had taken place before that time, and I put the failure of the Divisional system first on the list; all later experience bore this out, but although you pegged away at it almost *ad nauseam*, you were defeated by the apathy of those for whom the old ways were best . . .' Could Godfrey have done more? He most certainly did his best to keep in touch with officers in ships and establishments by constant visits and he gave French, his Director of Training, all possible support. Perhaps he should, after all, have acceded to Auchinleck's wishes and introduced the VCO system although how the change could have been made during the war and whether, in view of the poor quality of some of the RINVR officers, it would have made much difference, it is hard to see.

Walker's remarks suggest that Godfrey did not always receive all the support that he should have done from some of his senior officers. Srinavasan said much the same thing when he wrote, 'Every time you bring up points for discussion in connection with the supply of clothing, rations, and accommodation, etc., the answer from your senior officers has always been that all is well and lovely in the garden. They never appreciate your insistence on the necessity for quick action and in fact appeared at times to resent your endeavours to get things done. I am constrained to say that the senior RIN officers have not had their fingers on the pulse of their ratings.' Secretaries and personal assistants often tend to look at their masters through rose-coloured spectacles, so one should accept Srinavasan's comments with at least a grain of salt. Although many of the RIN regulars were becoming desperately tired after five and a half years of war with no home leave and the incidence of sickness was very high, Godfrey himself had the highest opinion of most of his immediate subordinates. In a report to Auchinleck he referred to "the devoted band of British regular officers who have created the modern RIN and, in turning the Royal Indian Marine into a fighting Service have done a magnificent job." He successfully recommended most of them for decorations. For his second in command, Rattray, he not only secured promotion to Rear-Admiral but a KBE. There was, however, inevitably, the odd disappointed and disgruntled man who failed to play a constructive part in the very difficult post-war situation.

One thing that, with hindsight, does seem surprising is the apparent failure by all concerned to appreciate the extent to which the lower deck had been influenced by the anti-British propaganda of the Congress and Communist Parties and of the Muslim League. In January Nehru had been telling the Indian masses that 'You cannot make a revolution by mere catch-words . . . you can only fight with modern weapons . . . I am glad that recent events have compelled the members of the armed forces to realise that their place is with the rest of their countrymen. It is a pity that Indian soldiers are still forced to

do things which are against India's interests . . .' The Indian
National Army trials and the uncertain way in which they
had been handled, the growing feeling that Independence was
coming and that those who had not demonstrated devotion to
the Nationalist cause would suffer under the new government,
persuaded many of the semi-literate ratings that all India was
on their side. There is also considerable evidence that a
'political' mutiny had been carefully planned and organised.
It is difficult otherwise to explain the rapidity with which the
signal ratings, making full use of naval communications,
managed to persuade men in almost all ships and establishments
not only in India but overseas as well, to make common cause
with them. No one, not Auchinleck himself during his week in
Narbada, nor Haq Nawaz during his specific investigations in
Bombay in December, seems to have fully realised what was
going on. One cannot help being reminded of 1857, when
discipline in the Bengal Native Army had been relaxed and
when in many ways conditions were being improved and when
colonels of regiments maintained stoutly until the last minute
that their men would never mutiny.

As soon as he returned to Delhi Godfrey asked Rattray,
Lawrence, Jefford and some more junior officers like Sheppard
and Srinavasan to give him their entirely frank opinions as to
what had gone wrong. Rattray concluded his long and detailed
report as follows: 'One matter remains to be mentioned. Never
in its history has the Service been blessed with so able an
administrator as its head during the past three years and never
has it had so elaborate or efficient an organisation at Headquarters. It is not on the naval administration that the final
blame must rest but on the system with which it has had to
contend and which has proved too strong for it to overcome.'

There was of course an official enquiry which newspaper
clamour insisted should be held in public. The assessors were
three Indian judges, and Rear-Admiral Patterson, Royal Navy,
and Major General Rees of the Indian Army. The two British
officers were quite unable to mitigate the strongly anti-British
attitude of the Indian members. Godfrey had submitted an
extremely long report, embodying both his own views and
those of his officers and after he had handed over to his relief
offered to remain in India to give evidence in person but this
offer was refused. When the Commission's findings were

completed towards the end of 1946 they were embodied in a typewritten document of 598 pages accompanied by a mass of so-called verbatim evidence. When all these documents were stood on top of each other they made a pile more than three feet high! Vice-Admiral Sir Geoffrey Miles, Godfrey's successor, made a strong plea against the publication of the Report, but it was felt in the end, and probably rightly so, that this would be unwise. In consequence a summary was prepared and issued. It was, considering the circumstances, much more favourable than might have been expected, but nevertheless contained a number of unsupported and ill-considered criticisms of Naval Headquarters, Flag Officer Bombay, and the British officers of the RIN in general. Miles and Philip Mason produced a draft resolution for the Indian Government, which aroused the ire of a number of RIN officers but it had to take account of the prevailing political situation. Miles himself had a number of reservations about the report which he embodied in a private and personal letter to Auchinleck, a copy of which he sent to Godfrey. Amongst other things he remarked, 'Although I have no quarrel with the conclusions arrived at as to the causes of the mutiny . . . the impression I get is that the report does not paint a true picture of life in the RIN. If the full report is read it will be seen that the evidence of a few officers and men are quoted and on their evidence of a particular incident is hung some damning general charge against the RIN . . . there was often little or no attempt to obtain corroborative evidence . . . given by disgruntled or untrustworthy officers and men, who frequently were those who had been dismissed the Service for misbehaving. On the other hand, it was unfortunately the case that there were many loyal and contented ratings who were afraid to come forward . . . on the few occasions when they did, I regret it will be seen that the judges' examination was usually in the nature of trying to ridicule or belittle the importance of the evidence of these witnesses . . .'

Although many of the comments in the Report were slanted and grossly unfair the Commission did state that it was 'in general agreement with Admiral Godfrey in that—

(a) The RIN was asked to take on new commitments and it was bad for the Service to take on so much and to inflate

itself without acquiring the necessary officers and administrative staff.

(b) The chronic shortage of senior officers in the Service was
caused by recruitment being stopped between 1921 and
1928.

(c) The risk of post-war trouble had to be accepted.

(d) The mutiny may be regarded as a 'casualty' arising out of
the vigour with which India carried on the war.'

The Commission went on, 'The RIN expanded very rapidly
during the war from a small nucleus. On the abrupt ending of
the war it was faced with a rapid contraction. The war having
been won the object was lost. Contact between the officers and
men was lost, loyalty disappeared and team spirit vanished.
Men had insufficient work and they were unlikely to be interested in their work when they expected to be out of the Service
soon.'

It was a sad end to Godfrey's forty-three years in the Royal
and Royal Indian Navies, but none of the many people with
personal knowledge of India in 1946 whom the author has
questioned would agree that Godfrey was to blame for the
mutiny. On the contrary examination of the records shows that
he had continuously striven to prevent the very conditions
arising which, in the end, caused the outbreak. The requirements of war had to be given precedence of those of peace, and
given the political climate in India at the time the outbreak
was probably inevitable. It is perhaps worth recording that the
RIN in fact recovered swiftly and that by the time of Godfrey's
death the Navy of the Indian Republic alone was the second
largest in the British Commonwealth, exceeding in size those
of Canada and Australia, and equalling that of the Netherlands. The Navies of India and Pakistan together were as large
as that of West Germany. Their senior officers were men who
had learnt their trade under Godfrey in the RIN.

He sailed for home in the *Mauretania* on 9 May, greatly
heartened by three farewell messages. First Officer Campbell,
Peggy Cooper's successor, had written, 'I should like to tender
the thanks of all WRINS on the West Coast for all you have
done during the last two and a half years, and for all the
encouragement you have shown us. It is difficult to say thank
you adequately but I know that every officer and WRIN

realises that the Service would not have been what it is today without your assistance . . . We have to thank you for our many bodily comforts. For the comfortably equipped messes and Hostels, for the transport to take us to work, and last but not least for the knowledge that we have always had you in the foreground and that we have only to ask and you will give us in abundance. We are all proud of having been attached to the Royal Indian Navy, and are extremely sorry we are so soon going to lose the Flag Officer Commanding, whom no WRIN will ever forget.' Auchinleck wrote, '. . . For my part I would like to tell you how glad I am to have worked with you so long and how greatly I have valued all the help and advice you have given me during this period. I know that you have been up against great difficulties and that you have been subjected to all sorts of pressure from many angles. I can only say that I admire most sincerely the way in which you have dealt with the problems which have confronted you and that I am sorry that our partnership has come to an end. I shall always remember with the greatest pleasure our cruise in the *Narbada* . . .' Rattray sent the following signal with which the Commodore, Bay of Bengal, asked to be associated: 'On relinquishing the appointment of Flag Officer Commanding the Royal Indian Navy, I wish to convey to you the gratitude and admiration of all in my command for all the work you have done to build the Service on a sure foundation. We shall remember that the last three years under your command have been the most eventful in the long history of the Service and that it was under your leadership that the Service took an important share in the Burma Campaign and in the final defeat of Japan. We will not forget that you brought the Service to the threshold of a great future and whilst the recent events coming at the moment of your departure have shocked us all they can only serve to compel us to rededicate ourselves to the task you have set before us. On behalf of all in my command I wish you a safe passage home and many years of happiness in England.'

CHAPTER FIFTEEN

A Very Active Retirement

ALTHOUGH GODFREY had successfully recommended Rattray, the man on the spot, for a KBE, the mutiny ruled out the award of the KCSI with which it had been proposed to reward his own great services to India. Presumably it was felt that it would be politically unwise. One can also imagine that if the First Sea Lord, Cunningham, or any other member of the Board of Admiralty, preoccupied with post-war problems, even thought of righting the injustice done to Godfrey by Pound three and a quarter years earlier by proposing a British honour, such proposals would equally not have been welcomed by Attlee's new Labour government, desperately anxious to solve the Indian crisis in a manner that would keep the sub-continent within the British Commonwealth.

So Godfrey became the only officer of his rank in World War II to receive no official recognition whatsoever for his immense contribution to the Allied victory. Being the man he was he never displayed the slightest resentment or bitterness; perhaps he consoled himself with the old naval adage that 'it was better to have incurred Their Lordships' displeasure than never to have come to Their Lordships' attention at all'. It must, all the same, have been a grievous disappointment and, in a Britain where titles still meant so much to many people, it can have done nothing to help him find paid employment. He tells us that ". . . on my way home in the *Mauretania* I had plenty of time to ponder on my future as a retired Admiral and to make up my mind what the vicissitudes of life, as an elderly person, might have in store for me. I was only fifty-eight years old with no experience of civil life and very little technical knowledge. On my arrival home I had to undergo a rather tiresome operation [for piles]—delayed for the seven war years —followed by convalescence which debarred me from job hunting for two or three months. To be one of the 'unemployed' was a new experience, as throughout my whole career I had never suffered the pangs of half-pay. I had gone from post to post without any gaps and found the experience of having nothing to do vaguely unnerving. Lord Kennet and Admiral Sir Aubrey Smith very kindly made enquiries in the city and in the world of commerce but with negative results; my name was unknown to the public, and having been DNI and FOCRIN was a positive handicap. 'Business' never attracted me greatly and I had no flair for making money, and had soon to reconcile myself to the fact that one had to be very distinguished to get offered a well-paid directorship on the board of a bank or insurance company. Well-meaning friends gave me some bad advice on this subject and I spent much valuable time chasing 'will o'the wisps'. Ian Fleming [by that time Foreign Manager of Kemsley Newspapers] was determined that I should become Naval Correspondent of the *Daily Telegraph* and Ted Merrett that I should take drawing lessons. They both insisted that I should write my memoirs [which he eventually did but not until 1961]. Padre Tubby Clayton, the founder of Toc H and presumably a good judge of such matters, suggested that I should take Holy Orders, but somehow the idea of becoming a curate at the age of nearly sixty did not seem quite right and I should have found difficulty in subscribing to some of the Thirty Nine Articles. Nevertheless the suggestion was made in all seriousness by a dedicated man, with ample knowledge of human nature in all its strange disguises."

One suggestion that Godfrey did pursue actively was that of his friend Douglas Veale, the Registrar of Oxford University, that he should seek an academic career there. Impressed by the voluminous notes which Godfrey had made for his series of lectures at Greenwich on the Revolutionary Wars, Veale had suggested in 1941 that, after the war, he should apply for the post of Chichele Professor of Military History. Godfrey had not forgotten this, but in 1945 had written to Veale from India to say that he really did not feel that he was qualified for this post because "students will not be content with lectures that can tell them only about the past—and many years will elapse before we can get 1939–1945 into its right perspective—they will want to peer into the future and to discuss with discrimination the scientific problems. They will be more interested in the atomic bomb than in the logistics of the Moscow campaign [of 1812] and will demand from their professor the necessary

knowledge and discrimination to guide them in their studies
. . . you need a man of forty who combines the historical sense
with a keen appreciation of the application of science to
war . . ." Veale did not accept this, pointing out that 'the
criticism that has been made about a past holder of the post is
that, although it was a historical chair, the holder of it was
more interested in future wars . . .' He finally persuaded
Godfrey, just before he left India, to apply for the vacancy.
Supported by "most flattering" letters of commendation from
three Admirals, Andrew Cunningham, Howard Kelly and
Charles Little, he was "in due course summoned and came
before that august body, the committee of appointments. The
result was that I got into the 'finals' and Cyril Falls, the well-
known military historian, got the job, but it was a close shave
as the council took two hours to make up their minds. In
calling attention to this episode in my life I feel rather like the
Indian students who put 'failed BA' on their cards. The fact of
having reached this eminence is soothing to one's ego, but I
was never very sure if I really wanted to become part of
Oxford's academic structure and I confess to a slight feeling of
relief when the results were announced." Many people, however, believe that Godfrey would have made an admirable
academic. Like another naval intellectual of an earlier generation, who also never received full recognition from his own
Service, Admiral Sir Herbert Richmond, Godfrey might well
have become a successful Master of a College.

Someone else who tried to help was his father-in-law Donald
Hope, who offered him a non-executive directorship in his firm
Henry Hope & Sons Ltd. Although Henry Hopes had been a
public company for many years it was still very much a family
affair, run in a nineteenth-century patriarchal manner by the
chairman and managing director. Hope liked and respected his
son-in-law, but probably did not intend to do more than
extend, in the traditional manner, a helping hand to a relation.
The fees were small but nonetheless welcome and Godfrey
gratefully accepted. The arrangement was not a success.
Whatever Donald Hope may have thought, Godfrey believed
that he had much to offer this old-established Midlands firm.
Although the company had in fact had a thriving pre-war
export business to China, India, South Africa, South America
and the United States, with a particularly successful subsidiary

company in the latter country, Godfrey felt that its management's outlook was too parochial and its internal structure too autocratic. His father-in-law, on the other hand, who had developed the one hundred and twenty-five-year-old firm until it had become the Rolls Royce of metal window manufacturers, known all over the world for the excellence of its design and the quality of its products, did not relish being told by an ex-naval officer, twenty years his junior, how to run his business. Godfrey was surprised when after some three years his unsolicited but carefully thought out suggestions for improving the organisation and management of the company raised a squall of indignant protest. In the interests of family harmony he was persuaded with some difficulty to resign his directorship.

There had been a suggestion of the Governorship of Western Australia, but that came to nothing in the end and Godfrey confesses that it took him rather a long time to realise that "in seeking a paid job, I was barking up the wrong tree. It also dawned on me that many of the unpaid posts carried with them expensive obligations which only the incumbent could pay for." He was not, however, a man to bury himself in the country and cultivate his garden. He disliked gardening and was not a lover of country sports or even golf. He was therefore all the more delighted when, in 1947, Rear-Admiral Parry, who had succeeded Rushbrooke as DNI, invited him to edit the secret history of the Naval Intelligence Division. Godfrey himself had arranged during the war for Charles Morgan to start this task, but Morgan had never completed it. Godfrey accepted Parry's suggestion with pleasure and, during the next two years, with the help of many of his former staff and with Robin Barratt as an assistant, produced fifty Monographs on every aspect of the work of NID during World War II. He intended the Monographs to be much more than a history and they contained many suggestions for improvements which would be needed in the Division in the event of another war. Godfrey hoped that they would be regularly studied by successive First Sea Lords, members of the Board and DNIs and would in this way help to dispel the ignorance and apathy about Intelligence which had so hampered his work in 1939. For some years they may have served this purpose, particularly when they were in the care of Lt Commander Peter Kemp, the Admiralty Librarian who had served throughout the war in OIC. Later, unfortunately, because they contained references to highly classified information, excessive secrecy took over and they were locked away in a safe and forgotten. When Godfrey started to complete and revise them in the sixties he was neither permitted to take them home nor to work on them in the Admiralty when their custodian was out of the office at lunch! He was by then in his late seventies and found the journey from Sussex to London too tiring for a three hour working day, so the project was not finally completed. Although doubtless now very out of date in some respects, the Monographs certainly still contain precepts and principles as valid as they ever were, but which one fears may be ignored by a generation of officers who have had no personal experience of Intelligence in war.

Still, if writing the Monographs did nothing else, they kept Godfrey in touch with the Navy and the Director of Naval Intelligence. It must be remembered that Roosevelt's theory that he could 'handle Uncle Joe Stalin' (at the expense of the British Empire) had by now given place to the harsh realities of the Berlin Airlift and the Korean War. Attlee, always a realist, had halted the run down of the Armed Forces. Intelligence too was reactivated and swung round to meet a new threat. Typically, Godfrey saw that there was a contribution which he could make. Conscious of the difficulties of finding suitable civilians to meet the needs of a wartime Intelligence Division and anxious not to lose touch with former members of his NID, he invited about a hundred of them, both retired regular officers and civilians, to join an NID dining club, which took the name of 'The 36 Club', from 36 Curzon Street, Blinker Hall's flat in which he had lived as DNI from 1940 to 1943. The current Director and Deputy Director of Naval Intelligence were ex-officio members and so had the opportunity at the Club's dinners or cocktail parties, held four times a year, of meeting some of the old Intelligence hands. Some of them, like Ian Campbell and Ned Denning were still serving officers. Some of the civilians were still at that time young enough to return to their former posts if only, like old Paymaster Captain Thring in 1939, to start the Division off on the right lines. Many more were making names for themselves in journalism, the law, the city, industry, or the academic world, and would be ideal 'recruiting sergeants' if the need should arise. Fortunately it never really came to that, but those of us who occasionally returned to our old haunts for a week's or a fortnight's exercise or war game, certainly found it a great advantage to be known to the DNI or his deputy as a person rather than just a name on an out-of-date list. Apart from this the Club flourished for many years as an enjoyable reunion of old friends, until, inevitably, its ranks began to thin and the trip to London became more difficult financially and physically for the older survivors. Godfrey himself was of course the central figure, and the Club died with him. Ian Fleming came to many of the Club's meetings and obtained not a few ideas for the background to his James Bond romances from chats over drinks with his former colleagues. Bond's 'oo' number, incidentally, was taken from the NID filing system, which used this prefix for its Top Secret dockets.

Godfrey had never been a great 'clubman' and, when DNI, had virtually given up using 'The Senior', the United Services Club just across the Mall from the Admiralty, in order to avoid awkward questions on secret subjects from fellow officers. He later joined and greatly enjoyed the Garrick, where most of the members were actors or lawyers, and also the Athenaeum, where there were certainly more bishops than admirals.

When Godfrey arrived home from India, just in time for Kathleen's wedding to a brilliant young surgeon, John Kinmonth, whom she had met in the RAF, Margaret had sold Braddocks, their house in Sussex, and had bought one in London, in Egerton Terrace, as she was already becoming involved with voluntary work, first with the WVS and then with the Family Welfare Association, The Friends of the Poor, The Family Discussion Bureau, her old school, Wycombe Abbey, and West Heath School in Kent; London also seemed likely to be a better base for John's future activities, whatever they might be. Eleanor, who had qualified as an architect, married another member of her profession, Gordon Michell, in 1947, and the youngest daughter, Christina was married to John Gibb, an ecologist, in 1950.

Writing and editing the Naval Intelligence Monographs was obviously a task of limited duration and Godfrey's other rather peripheral activities were quite insufficient to occupy fully someone still anxious to use his dynamic and creative mind to the full. He was therefore delighted when, early in 1947, as a result of a suggestion by the wife of his Cambridge friend Jim

Passant, he was approached by Mrs Trevelyan, wife of the Master of Trinity, to help with the running of a charity of which she was the Chairman. This was Coram's Fields, the childrens' playground in Islington on the site of the old Foundling Hospital, which had been created by another seaman, Captain Coram, two hundred years earlier to care for illegitimate children. The home itself had been removed to the country and the main buildings demolished in the twenties but the trustees had retained a part of the site and some of the colonade and other buildings as a playground. Bombed and vandalised during the war, it was now in a sorry state. To help to restore the site and its remaining beautiful buildings so as to provide, once more, a pleasant place in which some of London's deprived children could play, was something that immediately appealed to Godfrey and he accepted Janet Trevelyan's invitation to join her Committee with alacrity. He threw himself into the task of arranging for the clearing of the rubble, replacing the boundary fence and restoring the buildings with all his usual energy. Overcoming the reluctance of Mrs Trevelyan, her sister, Mrs Dorothy Ward and the other members of the Committee to spending the capital which they had, with such difficulty, accumulated, he surmounted all the endless difficulties and frustrations of getting planning permission and help which seemed almost insuperable in bomb-battered, post-war London. He used his usual tactics of bullying his influential friends for practical help and cash. Two who were involved were George Walker, his Judge Advocate in India and by then Secretary of Associated Electrical Industries, and Robert Harling, his Contact Registry expert and later member of the famous 30 Assault Unit in NID. Janet Trevelyan, whose health was failing, persuaded Godfrey to take over the chairmanship from her. By the middle of 1948 he had persuaded the Nuffield Foundation, the Goldsmiths Company, London Parochial Charities and many other bodies to provide the necessary financial support, and the work was well on the way to completion.

It was at this time that Nye Bevan was launching his great scheme for a National Health Service. Through the brother of one of the Coram's Fields Committee members, Godfrey was asked to become Chairman of the Management Committee of the newly formed Chelsea Group of Hospitals. He had already been invited to join the council of the King Edward VII Fund for Hospitals and also its distribution committee which had given him some insight into the problems involved. For the next eleven years he was occupied in what was virtually a new career, hospital administration. Present very valid criticisms of the manifold weaknesses of the National Health Service perhaps obscure the enormous tasks with which the founders of the Service were faced in 1948. Many of the difficulties would have been present whatever the system of medical care. Although Britain had not suffered the same degree of devastation as Germany, Russia or Japan, she and Poland had been the only two nations on the Allied side to be engaged from start to finish. All Britain's resources, human and financial, mental and physical, had been devoted to winning the war. Provision for the future had, by deliberate choice, taken second place to the needs of immediate survival. In 1947, with Lease Lend from America withdrawn and the Marshall Plan not yet launched, the national economy was at its lowest ebb. British hospitals were in no better state than the railways, industry, education or housing. Once again, Godfrey was confronted with a task of creating, almost from scratch, and as quickly as possible, an organisation to fulfil a vital need. This was, however, the sort of challenge which he relished and at which he excelled. The post offered was unpaid apart from reimbursement of strictly controlled expenses.

The Chelsea Group of Hospitals included St Stephen's, St Luke's, Princess Beatrice's and the St George's Home for TB patients. Godfrey subsequently wrote that "the Committee over which I had been asked to preside consisted of about fifteen people and formed a representative group of men and women of great good will and with a fair knowledge of Chelsea and its needs, but lacking confidence when it came to replacing a highly centralised London County Council hierarchy of officials with strong central authority at County Hall. It was gradually revealed to us that control of expenditure, even on such essential items as repairs to blitzed buildings was vested in the superior organisation, the South-West Metropolitan Regional Board. The principal hospitals of the [Chelsea] Group, St Stephen's and St Luke's, had been built in the eighteen seventies. Due to neglect during the war they were dilapidated and dirty and moreover had been badly blitzed.

Very little headway had been made with their restoration and patients in undamaged wards looked out on the gaunt and depressing ruins of the two blocks which has been destroyed. The Hospital Management Committee was thus faced with a major problem of rehabilitation which might well prove insoluble due to lack of money and labour. We were not supposed to undertake any structural alterations or rebuilding, not even demolition of ruins, without Regional Board and Ministry of Health approval. Neither of these authorities showed any signs of being forthcoming. However, something had to be done as the buildings were dangerous and parts were developing ominous cracks and showing signs of toppling. The nurses home and recreation room were filthy and lacked modern facilities and equipment. The Management Committee were thus faced with two alternatives: (a) To continue with the policy of laissez-faire with crumbling walls and dirty wards, as for the first six months the Regional Boards were under strict Treasury control which seemed unlikely to relax; (b) To go ahead with demolitions, repairs and redecorations and ignore the Health Act. The Committee chose the second course and I engaged a gang of about thirty carpenters, builders, decorators and plumbers and a working foreman. The more senior hospital officials were horrified at this by-passing of authority. They had been used to referring everything to the London County Council, but they quickly adapted themselves to the new conditions." Surprisingly quickly the old gloomy Victorian buildings were repaired and began to look bright and clean and two twin operating theatres were built, the first in London since the war. The morale of the staff rose by leaps and bounds as their conditions improved and as they realised that they had a Chairman who not only cared but was determined to achieve results even if his methods were distinctly unorthodox.

Once again Godfrey was lucky in his associates (or was it that he brought the best out in them?). The Committee consisted, apart from himself, of four doctors, a social worker and nine lay members, with a Secretary and Assistant Secretary. "I knew little about committee rule", wrote Godfrey, "and to my surprise neither did the rest, so we started off in the healthy condition of having no rules or precedents. One good sign was that they agreed to leave things, between meetings, to the Chairman and the Secretary."

For a time Godfrey had some difficulty with his vice-chairman, a driver on the Underground and a Trades Union Official. He generally opposed Godfrey at committee meetings and tried to sit as far from him as possible and "lob controversial questions across the table. I asked him to sit next to me and in this position he was much more amenable; if he talked too much and too loudly or aggressively I used to kick him gently on the ankle. It took me some time to discover that he was interested in words not deeds and having had his say and wasted a lot of time would support me when it came to a decision. We all liked him; strangely enough he was inclined to take a hard view about patients and staff which, fortunately, was not reflected among the remainder of the Committee.

"I very soon made the discovery that, with notable exceptions, consultant physicians and surgeons seemed to get lost when giving an opinion outside their particular speciality. They were not men of the world. This does not apply to general practitioners. I did my best to avoid the sort of committee meeting where everything is decided in advance, nothing is decided at the meeting or, when everyone is leaving the building, two men get together in a corner and fix what is to be done next.

"A revelation which nearly led to the resignation of the Committee was that negotiations were afoot to carve up St Luke's between the adjacent Royal Cancer Hospital and the Chelsea Hospital for Women, and that the Westminster Teaching Hospital had designs on St Stephen's. This arrangement would have left very little for the Chelsea Management Committee to govern and nowhere for the geriatric patients and the chronic sick to be treated. My Committee encouraged me to protest. I can only assume that the Ministry of Health, who were in a great hurry to get the new act going, had given insufficient thought to the allocation of hospital duties in the south-west and produced a half-baked scheme. Anyhow it was dropped for nearly twenty years."

In 1948 the Godfreys had decided to move out of London. They bought the old school house at Wilmington, a tiny village at the foot of the Downs some six miles from Eastbourne. Margaret, an inspired gardener, created the most beautiful garden, while the house itself, full of character, was charmingly decorated and made extremely comfortable. Although there was a good railway service to London, Godfrey soon found that the extra travelling time, combined with his new appointment to the Chelsea Hospital Group, meant that he must give up his chairmanship of Coram's Fields, situated as they were on the other side of London. He resigned at the end of 1948, very much to the sincere regret of the Committee, although by that time most of the restoration work had been done and the charity re-established on a firm financial basis.

W. Mayne Butcher, who was appointed Secretary of the Chelsea Management Committee shortly after Godfrey's assumption of the chairmanship, and who worked very closely with him, remarks, 'He was a great man, standing head and shoulders above we petty people. I would not have been without the unique experience of working with him for worlds. He was always 'The Admiral', never 'The Chairman'; everyone knew about him from the highest to the most humble. He read deeply and widely, Hansard, the Bar Journal, the Lancet and generally saturated and concentrated his mind between 1948 and 1954 solely and exclusively to the development and improvements of the hospitals in the group. Like all great men he had inexhaustible vigour, tireless energy. "Always keep tablets by your bed, Butcher," he told me, "in case you think of something in the night: it will otherwise have left you by the morning." Not infrequently he would ring me up at home before 8 a.m. or at 8 p.m. or would ask me to dine with him at the Garrick to discuss a problem. Once, when I was departing on holiday, the Admiral said "Always fire a salvo before proceeding on leave, Butcher". He invariably did and everyone was provided with plenty of tasks while he was away . . . Children appeared to take to the Admiral at once. He and I were having tea at the Cheyne hospital and he called in two dirty little urchins who were sneaking past our open door, put them on his knee and fed them with sandwiches and cakes. They loved it and him. He really was a very great man and we tried to get his peacetime work recognised through the usual channels. He discovered this and was very angry—an understatement.'

Probably Godfrey's greatest achievement in his hospital work and certainly the one which gave him the greatest pleasure was the founding of the Centre for Spastic Children at 61 and 62 Cheyne Walk in Chelsea. His attention had first been drawn to the problem by a young physiotherapist, Patsie Phillips (now Mrs Charles Sims), who had been called upon to treat children under five suffering from cerebral palsy. She found herself without much guidance as to the best methods. Godfrey's enthusiasm was at once aroused and, in 1952, with the backing of the Chairman of the South West Regional Hospital Board and of the King Edward VII Fund, he and Sir Zachary Cope FRCS, LRCP, carried out an investigation into the medical provision made for spastic children and the need for a special centre in the South West Region. After discovering the number of children who might need attention and after visiting other centres dealing with spastics, of which the best known at that time were in Ivybridge in Devonshire, in Harborne in Birmingham, and in Edinburgh, they came to the conclusion that although some private clinics were in existence and some hospitals were taking cerebral palsy cases there was a real need for a centre. Neither the National Health Service nor the London County Council would agree to do more than meet the running costs of a centre and then only when it had been established and proved for a full year. Godfrey wrote that "most pioneer projects have been got going by putting the cart before the horse. You must just do what you can when the opportunity offers and hope for the best. The pillage by the Labour Government in 1948 of voluntary (but not teaching) hospital funds struck a cruel blow at voluntary finance, and was followed by the Ministry frowning on appeals or money collections by hospitals. The ban was lifted in 1950 and the formation of associations of 'Friends', with powers to act independently, was evolved to do for hospital things, such as money collection, which they now found it difficult or impossible to do for themselves. At the Cheyne we took full advantage of the newly found freedom to raise voluntary funds for activities which could not be provided by the State. Cheyne finance starting with half-a-crown had by 1967 increased to over £70,000."

The first step, again with the enthusiastic and all important backing of the King Edward VII Fund, was to find suitable premises and engage staff. The best buildings seemed to be The Little Hospital by the River, in Cheyne Walk, occupied at that time by the London County Council as a day nursery. Godfrey, primed as to the needs by Patsie Phillips, displayed all his usual talents and energy in driving the scheme forward; rules and regulations were ignored or brushed on one side,

influential friends enlisted to give financial support and a
devoted Committee of Friends created; very careful investigations were undertaken to establish exactly what was going to
be needed to make the Clinic the best and most advanced of its
kind in the country. Godfrey personally selected the senior
staff; Patsie Phillips, who had been involved in a major way
from the outset, another young physiotherapist, Mary Howard,
and Dr Foley, a neurologist, as Physician in Charge. Visits
were made to other centres and hospitals where spastics were
being treated, and Patsie and Mary sent to Denmark to study
the work being done there by Professor Plumb. These pre-
liminaries took some time and the Centre was not opened until
1955, but in the intervening two years all those concerned had
learnt more and more about how such a project should be run
and the delay in fact ensured that the foundations were
correctly laid.

This is how Mary Howard, now Mrs W. J. Pearce, describes
her reactions to the early days: 'There have been two people
who have really influenced me in my own career and JG [as he
was always referred to by Patsie and Mary, although to everyone else he was 'the Admiral'] was the first of these. He made
his own enthusiasm for the Cheyne project so evident that one
was immediately caught up in the scheme and, once in it, there
was no escape. He was a most ruthless person at that time,
using and exploiting everyone he needed but with such charm
and in so civilised a manner as to completely captivate his
victims. I was fascinated by his wide circle of friends, many of
whom had been with him in Naval Intelligence or connected
with some of the cloak and dagger episodes of that time. He
had numerous parties to which he invited a judicious mixture
of spies and war heroes and heroines and people interested in
the possibilities of the Cheyne project. The more ordinary of
us were flattered and intrigued by the heroes, artists and
intellectuals and they in turn were big enough to show concern
and interest in what we were trying to do. He had endless little
dinners, always ordered in advance and beautifully planned, at
which we discussed the Cheyne project either together with
Patsie or with one special person such as a high ranking doctor,
Minister or educationalist. Usually we went back afterwards
to the flat in Cheyne Walk, whose walls were covered with Roy
le Maistre paintings, and there we would talk about everything

from the Cheyne to philosophy, religion, art, love, and JG's own career. I often crept away at three or four in the morning, exhausted and drained and vowing not to remain involved any longer. Then a day or two later JG would telephone or write with some new scheme or slant on our plans and once again I was drawn back into the net. He was about the most exhausting and emotionally draining person I ever met but he was totally dedicated to the task of setting up the Centre for Spastic Children and that is what he did . . . He picked his first team for the hospital with skill and sensitivity and did not hesitate to pluck out anyone causing discord before damage could be done! (Industrial Tribunals or wrongful dismissal just didn't feature in his way of doing things.) He was constantly around during the first few years and as, [later on,] I gradually assumed the day to day running of the hospital his help and advice to me were invaluable. He gave terrific support at all times and could be terrifyingly angry if one made mistakes. He brought a succession of interesting and famous people to see the Cheyne —Lady Mountbatten, the then Duchess of Kent, the Minister of Health, etc. The hospital never looked like a traditional hospital of that time with cream and green paint. Instead he decorated it with white and dashes of scarlet and gold and black. He hung attractive wallpapers in treatment rooms and rest rooms and collected old prints and photographs of the buildings as they were in the past. He was essentially the moving spirit behind what became a world-renowned research and treatment centre concerned with cerebral palsy in young children. I hope and believe that it gave him as much pleasure and interest as almost anything else he had done in his life and certainly it is a proud memorial to a very great man.'

Anyone who was involved with Godfrey in NID or in India will immediately recognise this description of his techniques, refined and mellowed perhaps but essentially the same, for creating something out of nothing, for launching a project which had fired his enthusiasm and which he was determined should enthuse everyone else he could involve. Someone who saw a good deal of Godfrey at this time was Joan Saunders, widow of Hilary Saunders. Both she and her husband had worked in NID and had of course seen him then at fairly close quarters. She writes that 'I lunched with John every few months and thus heard all the complications that beset the founding of the

Cheyne. Not so much about the financial and business side as the personalities involved. It was obviously a relief to just pour these out and though he was gallant enough to pretend that my advice was valuable it was really just a cathartic effect. I daresay it did help that I was a doctor with two years of neurology behind me. To my mind one of the most remarkable things about NID was that by personality the members of this large organisation fitted so well into their tasks. There were rumbles and grumbles but on the whole it worked smoothly. Of course war brought its own disciplines. Peace did not come so easily at Chelsea. John, as usual, picked a splendid team. They were excellent at their respective jobs, but oh so temperamental. What is certain is that he had mellowed greatly after the war and changed tactics completely. There were no longer the celebrated bursts of rage; he worked everything by conciliation and adroit flattery. And he could say thank you. To give some personal examples: "I try very hard to follow your admirable advice to preserve a serene temper and extreme dignity of motion . . ."; "No one else could do it so well as you, in fact I believe that no one . . . could do it *but* you. Fail me not!" All the women purred. That the Cheyne did a good job I can testify from personal experience. My grandson suffered severe birth injuries (his twin died) in America. Doctors in Washington doubted if he could ever lead any sort of normal life. Back in London he was, by grace and favour, admitted to the Cheyne. He was blissfully happy and within a year was decently normal. He is now at twelve years old participating fully in the life of a Junior House of a Public School.'

The pressures and frustrations of this voluntary peacetime job were, of course, different from those to which Godfrey had been subjected during the war. How far his more equable and patient approach to them was the result of a carefully calculated change in method (and it is unusual for men in their sixties to succeed in altering their natural ways) and how far it was the result of being, to some extent, more his own master, is hard to say. Perhaps, as already indicated, his former tantrums, when not carefully worked up to achieve a particular object, were aggravated by the piles from which he suffered until the operation after the end of the war. Certainly in his DNI days he had something in common with Captain Wilfred Henderson, whose Navigating Officer he had been in *Blanche* in 1913. In

1945 Hillgarth, who had left Madrid to become Chief of British Naval Intelligence, Eastern Theatre, had written to Godfrey to say that 'ever since I first started to serve under you my own interest in this game has been stimulated by the example of energy, enthusiasm and ruthlessness which you taught me. The same spirit remained with me after you departed, but that is entirely due to those years with you. I do not think I have ever said this before, but I may not have another chance.' In a charming letter of thanks Godfrey replied ". . . Ruthlessness is not an endearing quality and looking at the awful mess the Huns made of it and as we know the pathetically poor Intelligence set up they had, I often wonder whether I could not have achieved as good if not better results by more kindly methods . . ." It does, on the whole, seem that Godfrey made a conscious effort to drop Jacky Fisher's three Rs, 'Ruthless, Relentless and Remorseless'. It must have called for considerable will-power.

What was unusual about the Cheyne Spastics Centre was that it was the only predominately medical establishment in the country that tried to cope exclusively with spastic infants up to the age of seven. Godfrey had realised that, if treated early enough and in the right way, the effects of cerebral palsy could be greatly mitigated. Dr Foley carried out careful tests on the young patients by the very latest methods—hearing, sight, speech, movement, brain damage and so on—and meticulous records were kept. The Cheyne was originally a day centre so that children would not be separated from their families and so that the parents could themselves learn how best to look after their children and teach them to overcome their disabilities. This was reinforced later not only by special parents' evenings but by the Home Physiotherapy Service for which a special van was bought by the Friends to enable an experienced therapist to visit the homes of children too young to come to the centre. The parents often found it easier to speak of their difficulties in their home surroundings and the therapist could assess the circumstances and sometimes lend special equipment. By the time the child was old enough to come to the Centre it already knew the therapist and did not find the atmosphere strange and frightening. Initially the children were from age three to six, but later they remained until eight, and the London County Council was prevailed upon to provide teachers so that education could go hand in hand with physical development. Two classrooms were equipped on the ground floor with a veranda opening onto a grass playground. After a time No. 63 was acquired from Professor and Mrs Caplin (Vera Brittain). The badly bombed building was rebuilt and equipped as a hostel for children who lived too far away to make the journey daily and for mothers to stay with infants while Dr Foley was conducting the preliminary tests and detailed examinations before a child could be admitted. All this was paid for by the Friends.

This was very much pioneering work. The Cheyne, under Godfrey's direction, had set out to produce a teaching hospital atmosphere to cope with a handicap about which little was known and for which even reliable statistics had been almost entirely lacking. Eventually it was established that something like 1.5 in every 1000 of the population were affected. By 1962 numbers in the Centre had stabilised at about 28 day patients in two classes, and a number of out patients varying from 20 to 30. The records compiled by Dr Foley of more than 400 children treated since 1955 were to prove quite invaluable for research purposes. Film and sound recording equipment, EEG, EMG, plathismograph and audiometric equipment of the very latest type had all been provided by 'free money' or by the fund-raising efforts of the Friends. Financially it had to be a case of one thing at a time. Thanks principally to the King's Fund and to London Parochial Charities, the Coxen Trust, the Yapp Trust, private donations, 'Mr Pastry's' Fund, and Enid Blyton's charity, not only was the hostel acquired and run but the Centre was equipped within seven years with a Physiotherapy Department, classrooms, staff rooms, an assessment classroom, a filming room, teaching facilities for the deaf, electro-encephalograph, electro-myograph, plathismograph, andrometric apparatus, a lift, a hydrotherapy pool and an ultrasonascope.

It can well be imagined, in spite of the enthusiasm and devotion of the staff and of the Friends, what an enormous amount of time, thought and energy had been demanded of Godfrey himself. In the early years he was fortunate in being able to use a flat in an unoccupied part of the building. This was no anchorite's cell. As with his day cabin in *Repulse*, it was carefully converted and decorated so as to provide a charming and comfortable pied-à-terre for him in London, much to the benefit also of the present Superintendent of the Cheyne who now occupies it. Nevertheless, without it he could not have achieved all that he did. Even so, considering the demands of the Chelsea Hospital Group as a whole, of his commitments to other voluntary work, such as his governorship of Roedean School, the NID Monographs, the 36 Club and an extensive correspondence with naval friends and historians, it was a burden which few men approaching seventy, let alone a retired senior officer who had been subjected to all the strains and pressures of the war, would have so willingly shouldered.

Despite the frustrations and vexations of his hospital work, Godfrey enjoyed life. He had, once again, a really worthwhile job, a service to other people to which he could devote his imaginative and creative energy. He enjoyed also his weekends at Wilmington, entertaining friends, relations and his grandchildren. At least once a year he set off by car to stay with friends all over the country and also made an annual trip by car through France to Menton to stay with Ted Merritt with whom he remained particularly close. He drove well but with the characteristic and quite unfounded expectation that other road users would be as competent as he was, which was sometimes a little unnerving for his passengers. It was in every respect a very full and active life.

It had been Godfrey's intention to resign his chairmanship of the Chelsea Hospital Management Committee on reaching the age of seventy in July 1958, but, acceding to the pleas of his Committee and the staff, he finally agreed to continue for at least a little longer. He was influenced in this decision by the extremely tedious negotiations which were being conducted with the superior body, the South West Regional Hospital Board about a proposal to merge the Kensington and Fulham Hospital Group with the Chelsea Group. Kensington, despite being smaller, demanded equality with Chelsea and the post of Chairman and, more important to Godfrey, that of Secretary were among the issues. Godfrey had a very high regard for Butcher and saw no reason why his future should be put at risk by bureaucratic bumbledom. He was in the end successful in this respect, but the worries of the negotiations, the disagreements with the Chairman of the Regional Board, combined with the effort of living in two places at once, which his London work necessitated, proved too great a strain. He suffered a heart attack and although he recovered fully, it proved to be the beginning of a slow decline in his health. He resigned from the chairmanship in December 1959, to the very great regret of all his colleagues and staff. A rule of the Board prevented him continuing as an ordinary member of the Chelsea Hospital Management Committee, but he did continue as Chairman of the Cheyne Spastics Centre for another five years. When he found that this also was becoming beyond him, a friend from India, Frances Watt, who had been a member of the Friends, took over the chairmanship and Margaret also joined the Committee so that she was able to keep her husband fully informed of the continuing development of a project which, to the end, remained very dear to him. The fifteen years since his return from India had, perhaps to his surprise, been immensely rewarding and successful. The very many expressions of regret, and thanks, which he received from people connected both with the Chelsea Group and the Spastics Centre, make it clear how much they felt was owed to Godfrey and the sense of loss they experienced on learning of his retirement, exactly as had been the case when he left NID at the end of 1942.

Godfrey now started his second period of retirement, but it too was far from inactive. He had always felt that silence was the right policy concerning wartime Naval Intelligence. So many of the tricks of the trade, which he had done much to develop, were secret and were not known or at least not fully understood by Britain's potential enemies. Why hand this priceless information to them on a plate? Moreover he remained firmly opposed to any attempt to publicise his own personal achievements (or to denigrate those of any other of the wartime chiefs). However when, inevitably, leaks began to occur both in Britain and the United States from others with fewer scruples, there was mounting pressure from his friends and former staff, such as Fleming and McLachlan, and from naval historians for some record of his forty-three years service in the Royal Navy to be compiled. He was finally persuaded to write his naval memoirs, although only for private circulation and omitting any material which he thought might still be considered 'sensitive'. He started the task in 1961 and finished the last of the eight typescript volumes in 1966 when he was seventy-eight. They are a fascinating and illuminating record of life in the British Navy at a time when it was still the foremost in the world.

But Godfrey also gradually came to feel that the general public ought to know more about the achievements of his staff in the wartime Intelligence Division. Secrecy was all very well up to a point, but the only revelations were those of British failures, of the Philbys and the other traitors, and of successes by the Americans. It was not a good thing that both the British public and the new generation of politicians and Service chiefs should be allowed to form such a very false impression. He therefore encouraged Donald McLachalan, who resigned the editorship of the *Sunday Telegraph* to undertake the work, to write his much acclaimed book *Room 39*. Godfrey did more; he gave McLachlan an immense amount of help, suggesting contacts, themes and subjects, and commenting on each chapter as it was drafted. This had its disadvantages, because Godfrey steered McLachlan away from controversial subjects and tried to insist that his own achievements should be played down. Nevertheless, Godfrey's help must have been invaluable, and enabled McLachlan to produce an account of Naval Intelligence in action, based on the recollections of many participants who, sadly, are now no longer here to give their views, which remains one of the best books on Intelligence ever written.

Godfrey celebrated his eightieth birthday in 1968 and from then on his physical vigour began to decline. He became less steady on his legs and found staircases difficult to negotiate. He stumbled and fell several times in his garden in Wilmington. He also complained that his memory was less reliable, although those who visited him at that time noticed little evidence of this. In August 1970 Margaret took him for his last holiday in France (Merrett was already dead). A year later he had a really bad fall and cut his head so that nine stitches were needed, but he seemed to make a good recovery. However only two weeks later he fell again and this time fractured his femur. The operation and move to a nursing home proved too much even for his constitution. He died from a heart attack on 29 August 1971, aged eighty-three.

It had been a long life and a full one; a life dedicated to service and duty. Lord Mountbatten considered that he would have reached the highest post in the Royal Navy but for 'a certain inability to get on with his superiors and his colleagues'. Godfrey certainly was not pliant and could not bring himself to tamper with what he considered to be the truth in order to ingratiate himself with his masters, while the fact that he was so consistently right did nothing to endear him to colleagues of lesser mental calibre. But war demands hard men; a softer approach would not, in the time available, have produced the results that were so desperately needed. He did what he had to do without regard to the personal consequences; if these were on occasions to his own disadvantage, he did not complain. In his Memoirs he quotes with approval Mark Twain's aphorism, 'You must do what you think right; it will please some and astonish the rest'. He also wrote, "If I could have my life over again, I would not have chosen anything different". So there were no regrets. If he never received the official honours which his great achievements had so richly merited, his true reward lay in the unbounded admiration and respect which he had inspired in all those who had served with him, whether in the Naval Intelligence Division, in the Royal Indian Navy, in the Chelsea Hospital Group or in the Cheyne Spastic Centre. He had indeed deserved well of the nation.

A SHORT BIBLIOGRAPHY

Although, with the exception of McLachlan, Montagu and myself, only a few of the authors listed below give even a passing reference to Godfrey, I have found their books useful as background information. Obviously, in trying to deal with a period of eighty-three years the list is far from comprehensive.

Babbington-Smith, C., *Evidence in Camera*, Chatto & Windus, 1958.

Barker, R., *Aviator Extraordinary: The Sydney Cotton Story*, Chatto & Windus, 1969.

Beesly, P., *Very Special Intelligence: The Story of the Admiralty's Operational Intelligence Centre*, Hamish Hamilton, 1977.

Bonatz, H., *Die Deutsche Marine-Funkaufklärung*, Wehr und Wissen, 1970.

Clarke, R. W., *The Man who Broke Purple*, Weidenfeld & Nicolson, 1977.

Churchill, W. S., *The Second World War*, Cassell, 1949.

Dilks, D., *The Diaries of Sir Alexander Cadogan*, Cassell, 1971.

Hinsley, F. H., *British Intelligence in the Second World War*, HMSO, 1979.

James, R. R., *Gallipoli*, Batsford, 1965.

James, W., *The Eyes of the Navy*, Methuen, 1955.

Johnson, B., *The Secret War*, BBC Publications, 1978.

Jones, R. V., *Most Secret War*, Hamish Hamilton, 1978.

Kahn, D., *Hitler's Spies: Germany's Military Intelligence in World War II*, Macmillan, 1978.

Leutze, J. R., *Bargaining for Supremacy*, Chapel Hill, 1977.

Lewin, R., *Ultra goes to War*, Hutchinson, 1978.

Marder, A. J., *From the Dreadnought to Scapa Flow*, OUP, 1967.

Marder, A. J., *From the Dardanelles to Oran*, OUP, 1974.

McLachlan, D., *Room 39: A Study of Naval Intelligence in Action*, Weidenfeld & Nicolson, 1968.

Montagu, E., *Beyond Top Secret U*, Peter Davies, 1977.

Plimmer, C. and D., *A Matter of Expediency: The Jettison of Admiral Sir Dudley North*, Quartet, 1978.

Roskill, S. W., *The War at Sea*, HMSO, 1954.

Roskill, S., *Churchill and the Admirals*, Collins, 1977.

Roskill, S., *Naval Policy between the Wars*, Collins, 1968.

Strong, K., *Men of Intelligence*, Cassell, 1970.

Strong, K., *Intelligence at the Top*, Cassell/Giniger, 1968.

INDEX

Hall, Admiral Sir Reginald, 101–2, 103–104, 109, 140, 143, 173, 182, 207, 229
Hall, Commodore J. T. S., RIN, 248, 277, 291
Hallett, Vice Admiral Theodore, 124–5
Haq Nawaz, Lieut Col, 302, 303, 310, 312
Harcourt, Admiral, 289
Harling, Lieut Robert, RNVR, 211, 217, 322
Harris, Marshal of the RAF, Bert, 77–8
Hart, Sir Robert, 8
Harwood, Rear Admiral Sir Henry (Bobbie), 5, 9, 10, 196
Hastings, Commander Eddie, 179, 234, 237
Henderson, Commander, Reggie, 46, 48
Henderson, Capt. Wilfred, 12–13, 16, 330
Hill, Prof. A. V., 174
Hillgarth, Commander Alan, 92, 143–4, 162, 331
Hindustan, 4–5
Hippesley-Cox, Lieut, RNVR, 211
Hitler, Adolf, 85, 97, 116, 117–18, 148, 149, 163, 184, 185–6
Holland, Capt. 'Hooky', 144, 158, 160
Honeysuckle, 28, 29
Hood, 81, 83, 185
Hope, Donald, 61–2, 318, 319
Horlic, Lieut Col James, 56
Howard, Mary (Mrs W. J. Pearce), 328–9
Howe, Ronald, 103
Hugh-Smith, Admiral Sir Aubrey, 103, 117
Hunter-Weston, General, 22, 23
Huque, Sir Mohammed Azizul, 274, 275
Hutton, Colonel Tom, 77, 78

India (*see also* Royal Indian Navy): rumours of Japanese attack, 232–3; Godfrey appointed FOCRIN, 240–1; army, 243, 245, 246, 273, 274, 285, 286; air force, 244, 285, 286; ports, 283–4; post-war uncertainty, 295–6; political unrest, 300–1; mutiny, 304–314
Information Section, 140–2
Inter Service Topographical Department (ISTD), 205–13, 214
Ireland, 136–8

Jam Sahib, 257, 260
James, Sir William, 107–8
Japan: in 1917, 49–50; growing imperialism, 70–2; war with China, 85; attacks Hong Kong, 201; intelligence, 202–4; surrender, 295
Jebb, Gladwyn, 117
Jefford, Commodore J. W., RIN, 258, 267, 291, 294, 312
Johnson, Dr John, 209, 217, 238
Joint Intelligence Committee (JIC), 160–1, 163, 164, 180, 181, 190, 192, 209, 210, 211; purpose, work and composition, 220–7; and Godfrey's dismissal, 230, 231, 232
Joint Intelligence Staff, 222–5, 226
Jones, Sir Roderick, 112, 113
Joubert, Air Marshal Sir Philip, 191
Jutland, Battle of, 67–8, 82, 84, 188

Kell, Col Vernon, 103
Kelly, Admiral Sir Howard, 68, 69, 81
Kelly, Admiral Sir John, 81
Kelly, 155
Kennedy, Joseph, 147, 173, 177, 179
Kent, 68, 69, 73, 74, 259
King, Capt. E. L. S., 76
King George V, 99, 115
Kirk, Capt. Alan, 173, 174, 179, 180, 183
Kitchener, Horatio Herbert, Earl, 19, 20, 28, 33, 37

Lambe, Capt. Charles, 188, 239
Lawrence, Capt. John, RIN, 258–9, 267, 277, 312
Lawrence, T. E., 38, 39–40
Leigh, Capt., USN, 49, 51
Lindemann, Professor, 126
Linlithgow, Lord, 247, 252
Little, Admiral, 78
Lloyd George, David, 47, 59
Lockhart, General Rob, 306, 308
Luard, Trant, 44, 45
Luftwaffe, 114, 160, 163, 180, 185

McLachlan, Donald, xx–xxi, 199, 206, 216, 218–19, 220, 222, 334
McMahon, Sir Henry, 37, 38
Macnamara, Rear Admiral Patrick, 124
Madden, Sir Charles, 61
Majestic, 5, 6
Majorca, 85–6, 92
Manisty, Paymaster Commander, 46, 48